The **Rough Guide** to

Baja California

written and researched by

Jason Clampet

D0954409

ROUGH
GUIDES

NEW YORK · LONDON · DELHI

www.roughguides.com

Contents

Baja California food and drink section following p.64

The ocean and the sea section following p.192

◄◄ Cabo San Lucas marina ◄ Sea kayaks, Isla Espíritu Santo

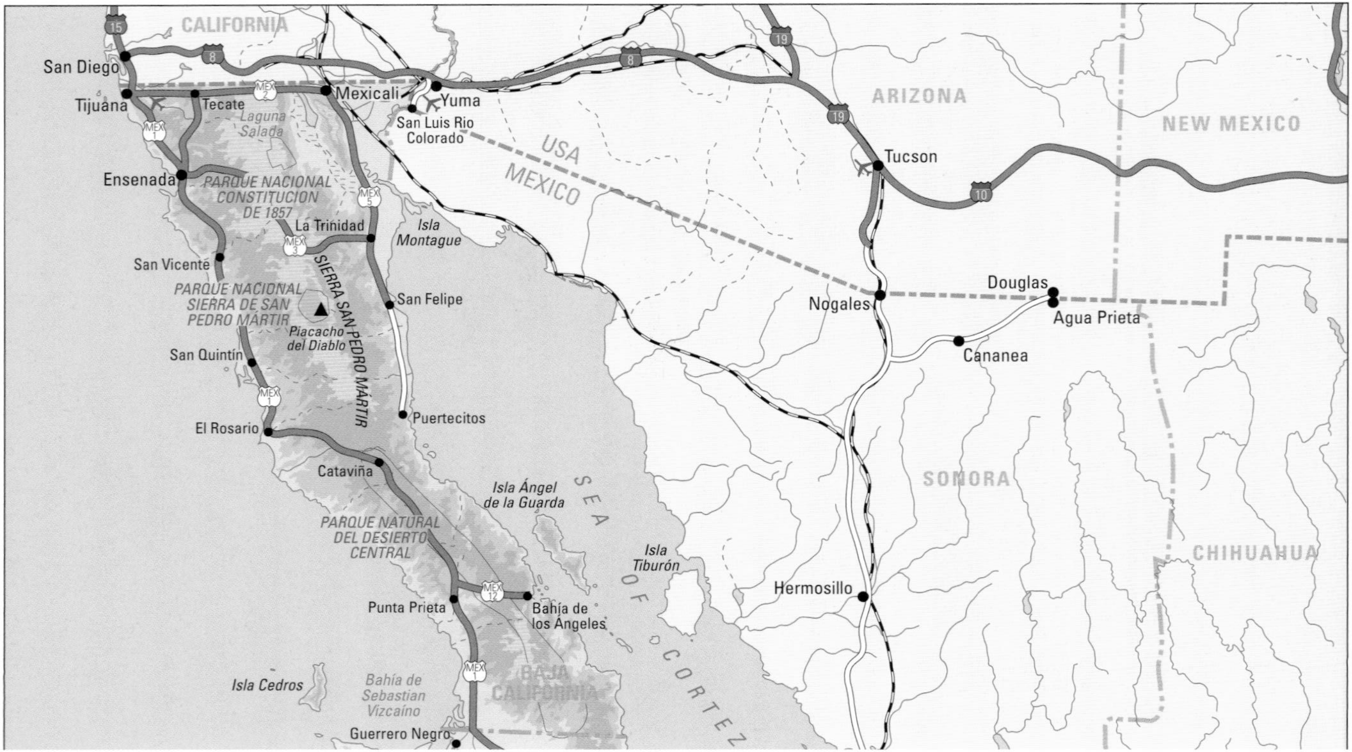
CALIFORNIA
ARIZONA
NEW MEXICO
USA
MEXICO
SONORA
CHIHUAHUA
BAJA CALIFORNIA
SEA OF CORTEZ
San Diego
Tijuana
Tecate
Laguna Salada
Mexicali
Yuma
San Luis Rio Colorado
Tucson
Nogales
Douglas
Agua Prieta
Cananea
Hermosillo
Ensenada
PARQUE NACIONAL CONSTITUCION DE 1857
La Trinidad
Isla Montague
San Vicente
PARQUE NACIONAL SIERRA DE SAN PEDRO MÁRTIR
SIERRA SAN PEDRO MÁRTIR
Piacacho del Diablo
San Felipe
San Quintín
Puertecitos
El Rosario
Cataviña
Isla Ángel de la Guarda
Isla Tiburón
PARQUE NATURAL DEL DESIERTO CENTRAL
Punta Prieta
Bahía de los Ángeles
Isla Cedros
Bahía de Sebastian Vizcaíno
Guerrero Negro
15
8
19
10
MEX 1
MEX 2
MEX 3
MEX 5
MEX 12

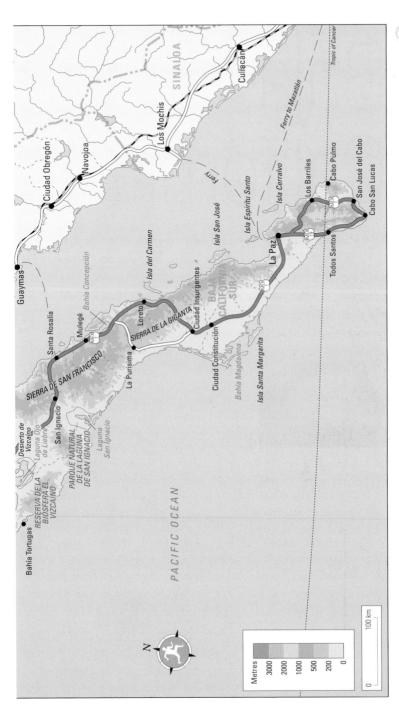

Tropic of Cancer

Ferry to Mazatlán

Ferry

Ferry

SINALOA

Culiacán

Los Mochis

Ciudad Obregón

Navojoa

Guaymas

Santa Rosalia

Mulegé

Bahía Concepción

Isla del Carmen

Loreto

SIERRA DE LA GIGANTA

Ciudad Insurgentes

Isla San José

Isla Espíritu Santo

Isla Cerralvo

Los Barriles

Cabo Pulmo

San José del Cabo

Cabo San Lucas

La Paz

Todos Santos

BAJA CALIFORNIA SUR

Ciudad Constitución

Bahía Magdalena

Isla Santa Margarita

La Purísima

SIERRA DE SAN FRANCISCO

San Ignacio

Desierto de Vizcaíno

Laguna Ojo de Liebre

PARQUE NATURAL DE LA LAGUNA DE SAN IGNACIO

Laguna San Ignacio

RESERVA DE LA BIOSFERA EL VIZCAINO

Bahía Tortugas

PACIFIC OCEAN

N

Metres
3000
2000
1000
500
200
0

100 km
0

Introduction to

Baja California

Seventeenth-century Spanish explorers first thought that the peninsula now called Baja California was an island and, despite over three hundred years of evidence to the contrary, it maintains a palpable air of isolation – from the rest of Mexico and from the other half of its original territory just north of the border with the United States.

Much of that remoteness can be attributed to geographical factors. It lies over 1300 kilometres west of the capital Mexico City, while the sheer distances involved in traversing its length – it's over 1700 kilometres long – does not lend itself to quick exploration. Though the Tijuana border crossing is the most trafficked port of entry in the world, a comparative few of the 130,000 who pass through the city each day venture further into Baja California. Outside of Tijuana, the peninsula is in many ways still in an embryonic stage. Its two states – Baja California in the north and Baja California Sur in the south – weren't designated until the second half of the twentieth century, and the Transpeninsular Highway – the first paved road connecting the north and south – wasn't completed until 1973. Development has proceeded in earnest in the years since, though it has largely been restricted to the areas which are within easy reach of day-trippers from Southern California and to Los Cabos, a prime destination for resort aficionados. For many, what lies in between is both an afterthought and a mystery.

In Baja California, curious and intrepid travellers will find a great deal of opportunity. You'll never need a reservation to eat *ceviche* at a waterfront restaurant in La Paz and there won't be wine snobs judging

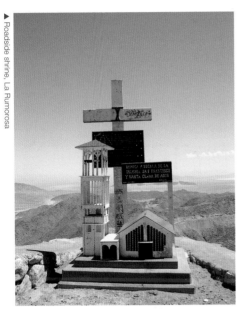

Fact file

• The northern portion of Baja California was granted statehood in 1952 and has its capital in **Mexicali**. The southern half, with its capital in **La Paz**, was the first area settled by the Spanish but was not made a state until 1974. Baja California Sur still has **no official state flag**.

• The state of Baja California was the first Mexican state to elect a **non-PRI governor** and provided the political base for the PAN party **opposition candidate** Vicente Fox's successful run for President of Mexico.

• More land in Los Cabos is owned by foreign residents than Mexican nationals.

• At 10m below sea level, **Laguna Salada** is the lowest point in Mexico.

the bottles you choose at Ensenada's great restaurants. When you arrive on the Sea of Cortez's shores, you'll know that the 600km of waters between Bahía de los Ángeles and Loreto will be yours to explore in blissful solitude. Stretches of the Pacific coast are as untouched now as they were before the arrival of the Transpeninsular Highway, and there are no better places to watch migrating gray whales than in its tranquil lagoons. And you can find a *palapa*-covered café serving fish tacos and cold beer in practically any village.

It's these things and more that make Baja the kind of place to inspire truly devoted fans. Most arrive in light planes or in vehicles capable of heading off across the punishing desert tracks, laden down with fishing and diving gear. Without such means

Curious and intrepid travellers will find a great deal of opportunity

of transport, it's difficult to get to most of the peninsula's attractions – secluded beaches, prehistoric cave paintings in the mountainous interior, excellent fishing, diving and snorkelling, and some of the best kayaking and surfing spots on the planet.

On (and off) the road

Towns in Baja California have a tendency to describe their location as "only six hundred miles south of San Diego" as if a twelve-hour drive is a selling point. Elsewhere that might come off as lunacy, but on a peninsula whose furthest points are separated by over 1600km and linked by one paved road, the Transpeninsular Highway, it makes perfect sense.

Completed in 1973, the **Transpeninsular Highway** stands as one of North America's last great road trips. It's equal parts endurance and beauty, seclusion and camaraderie. What you're driving defines much of the experience: an RVer will encounter some of the peninsula's most long-term visitors; off-roaders will meet locals and visitors who trade tips on fixing flats; sedan drivers will commiserate about that great beach they just can't get to. Part of the thrill comes from the long spaces separating major towns, the narrow segments of highway that snake along precarious cliffsides and the animals and washouts that can block the road. But the biggest draw is the near-constant beauty of the desert, mountain, sea and ocean vistas and their illumination by brilliant blue skies and starry nights.

Before the Transpeninsular, Baja California was best known as the forbidding wilderness of the **Baja 1000** auto race. Motorcycle, buggy and truck drivers started racing through the northwest in 1967 and they still flock to Ensenada every July (for the **Baja 500**) and November with the hope that they'll conquer the all-dirt track. The course isn't easy; it takes racers through the Sierras San Pedro Martír, San Felipe and de Juárez, and the Laguna Salada – only half of the entrants make it across the finish line.

▲ Frontón Jai Alai, Tijuana

The myth of Baja California as a place that's forever set apart from the US and from Mexico is true to an extent, though rapid growth in places is increasingly encroaching upon its sense of isolation. In Tijuana, shantytowns line the western hills in view of shining downtown towers, while in Los Cabos, multi-million dollar condos and US$1500 a night hotel rooms stand within eyeshot of donkey carts and men wearing third-generation pants. Still, the relatively limited infrastructure and the harshness of the environment has meant that most of the peninsula retains a pristine, if dusty, feel.

Where to go

▲ Cabo San Lucas

For many people, **Tijuana** is their first introduction to Baja California. Though it's trumpeted as the most visited city in the world, those trips are often measured in hours, not days, and most of its visitors are back in Southern California by bedtime. In the last twenty years the city has outgrown its reputation for painted donkeys and illicit thrills to become northern Mexico's banking and culinary capital. West of the city, the northwest **Pacific coast** is a low-cost playground for Southern Californians, particularly around the rapidly expanding beach town of **Rosarito**. It's a gorgeous run down the coast to **Ensenada**, a port city where cruise ships fill its harbour and vineyards line the sloping hills around it.

To the northeast, the border towns of **Tecate** and **Mexicali** radiate a sense of normalcy that flies in the face of their transient nature. The former is defined by the brewery of the same name and the latter – the northern state's capital – by a relaxed air and little pandering to tourists. Cotton fields and the dry **Laguna Salada** separate Mexicali from **San Felipe**, a small town on the coast of the **Sea of Cortez** where more people reside in campers with US license plates than in proper homes.

Remote and visually stunning, the central peninsula is Baja California's most passed-over region, despite a wealth of historic and geologic treasures. Vast deserts punctuated by towering cacti spread out from the fishing town of **San Quintín** on the Pacific to the weathered mining town **Santa Rosalía** on the Sea of Cortez. Along this stretch you have access to the sleepy seaside settlement of **Bahía de los Ángeles** and the whale-watching staging points

▲ Misión Nuestra Señora de Loreto Concho, Loreto

at industrial **Guerrero Negro** and colonial **San Ignacio**. From the latter the adventurous can hike deep into the **Sierra San Francisco** to explore some of the continent's oldest and most spectacular **rock art**.

The coastal route along the eastern slopes of the **Sierra de La Giganta** as it falls down to the sea displays Baja California at its most picturesque. The palm-strewn oasis town of **Mulegé** is the traditional starting point for kayakers and divers exploring the nearby **Bahía Concepción**, perhaps the best

9

▲ Sunrise along the Corridor, Los Cabos

kayaking destination on the peninsula. **Loreto**, the first capital of the entire California territory, has survived natural disasters and human abandonment to emerge as a thriving adventure travel destination, without cutting ties to its past.

La Paz marks the beginning of **the Cape**, the object of so much interest from developers and visitors alike. As the capital of the southern state and the cultural centre of the entire peninsula, it's beholden to more than real estate investors, and with its restaurants, street life and beaches, serves as a model for the perfect Baja California city. South of La Paz, the Transpeninsular Highway cuts through the **Sierra La Laguna** and bypasses shuttered mining towns, only briefly touching the Sea of Cortez at the windsurfing mecca of **Los Barriles**. Gung-ho drivers with decent shock absorbers can continue along the **eastern cape** via a coastal route that is as beautiful as it is rugged. Both this dirt road and the highway lead to the resort towns of **San José del Cabo** and onward to **Cabo San Lucas**, sibling cities that are separated by 30km of luxury hotels and united by their scenic appeal. To their north along the Pacific side, **Todos Santos**, with its surfing, swimming and art-centric downtown, stands as an antidote to the excesses of Los Cabos.

Tequila

Tequila doesn't come from Baja California, but if you spend any time in the peninsula's bars, clubs or restaurants you'll quickly realize what an ever-present element of social life it is. Like the lager beer everyone drinks, tequila seems to blend well with the heat – never too heavy and always improved, like beer or a glass of spring water, by a squirt of lime. Tequila comes from blue agave (a type of cactus) plants grown across the Sea of Cortez in Jalisco. Pure tequila is known as 100 percent blue agave, but you're more likely to be drinking *mixto*, a mix of blue agave and cane or other sugars, when you're out at the bar.

You will find some of Mexico's best tequila in high-end restaurants in Los Cabos, La Paz, Ensenada and Tijuana. In such places, you'll forego the lime-and-salt slammer technique in favour of snifters filled with *añejo* blends – which are aged in wood for at least a year – consumed as you would a fine brandy. Never order a top shelf tequila in a margarita; its flavour will be lost in the lime juice.

When to go

Despite the distance between the peninsula's northern and southern extremes, there is little variation in temperature across its length, with only minor fluctuations high in the sierras or immediately around the **Tropic of Cancer**. Crowds are almost never a concern when choosing a time to visit, and Baja Californians don't leave en masse for vacations elsewhere anytime of the year. Rather, **heat** is the primary factor, followed closely by the annual **whale migrations**. For many visitors this opens an extremely wide berth – from early October to late May or even early June – for just about any activity.

Migrating whales ply the Pacific Ocean from **mid-December until late March**. On both sea and land, this is the **mildest time of year** on the peninsula, making outdoor activities like hiking to rock art sites, sea kayaking and cycling the Transpeninsular very appealing. **Spring** is warm, but still manageable for all activities. The heat picks up in **mid-June**, continuing to stay very warm until late **September**. In the **south**, high temperatures are compounded by **hurricane season,** which runs from mid-August to mid-October. In the **northeast** the same period is brutally hot and locals rarely venture out of their homes or offices until after the sun sets. **Prices rise** for the two weeks around Christmas and New Year and this is the only time you will likely have trouble finding a place to stay in the resort areas.

Average temperatures (°F/°C)

	Jan	April	July	Oct
Cabo San Lucas	77/25	84/29	91/33	90/32
San Ignacio	59/15	66/19	80/27	73/23
Tijuana	66/19	70/21	75/24	75/24

things not to miss

It's not possible to see everything that Baja California has to offer in one trip – and we don't suggest you try. What follows is a selective taste of the peninsula's highlights: vibrant towns, azure bays, serene deserts and spectacular drives. They're arranged in five colour-coded categories, which you can browse through to find the very best to see and experience. All highlights have a page reference to take you straight into the guide, where you can find out more.

01 The whales of Laguna San Ignacio Page **186** • Hold your breath as you bob in a tiny fibreglass boat next to a creature the size of a city bus.

03 Reefs of Parque Marino Nacional Cabo Pulmo

Page **251** • Getting anywhere along the eastern cape requires a lot of effort but the largest living coral reef on the continent's west coast is worth it.

02 Mision San Ignacio Kadakaamán

Page **184** • This worn mission rises from a palm-filled valley, adding architectural grandeur to a desert oasis.

05 Charreada

Page **77** • These displays of roping and riding – to a soundtrack of local music – demonstrate that cowboys aren't only from the US.

04 Arts and crafts

Page **129** • Hand-tiled sinks, tin lanterns and skilled leatherwork make shopping in the northwest about more than just getting a good bargain.

06 **The Cantú Grade** Page **95** • With its tight curves and seemingly endless descent through the rocky hills, the route La Rumorosa to Laguna Salada along the Mex 2 toll road is a real stunner.

08 **Going off-road** Page **247** • To see Baja California's best beaches and most striking desert vistas, it's absolutely essential to leave the paved surfaces for dirt tracks and rocky trails.

07 **Sierra de San Francisco rock art** Page **183** • You'll need a guide, strong legs and plenty of water to get close to Baja California's most spectacular and mysterious art.

10 **Ensenada's fish market** Page **144** • Every morning, fishermen haul in the Pacific coast's freshest catch into the market's stalls and pile up the seafood and shellfish on mounds of crushed ice.

09 **Playa del Amor** Page **258** • There's something perversely wonderful about a peaceful beach named for love having an opposite, deadly side known as Divorce Beach.

11 CECUT
Page **74** •
Tijuana's seedy side is nowhere to be found at the region's premier venue for live theatre, dance and performance art.

ACTIVITIES | CONSUME | EVENTS | NATURE | SIGHTS |

12 El Mejor Pan's pastries
Page **91** • This boulangerie and *dulcería* gives multiple reasons for morning diners to skip the *birria* and *chilaquiles* for fresh loaves covered in crystallized sugar and cream-filled pastries coated in fruit frosting.

13 La Bufadora Page **148** • This naturally goofy wonder on Ensenada's south side soaks spectators with a chilly spray after crashing ocean waters rise 60m through a crevice in the rocky coastal point.

14 Camping along Bahía Concepción Page **200** • There's no better place to sample the peninsula's kayaking, snorkelling and camping riches than this twenty-kilometre stretch of coastline along the Sea of Cortez.

15 Santa Rosalía Page **192** • The peninsula's architectural homogeny is lost on Santa Rosalía. Tin roofs, bougainvillea-covered verandas and a prefab iron church speak to the town's divergent origins.

16 The malecón Page **230** • In La Paz and towns along the Sea of Cortez, the coastal walkway replaces the *zócalo* as the centre of urban life.

17 Dolphins at Parque Nacional Bahía de Loreto Page **207** • The peninsula's largest marine park is home to hundreds of species of marine life, though none more playful than its dolphin ambassadors.

18 Boojum Page **170** • All cacti aren't equal. The boojum of the central peninsula twist and turn skyward and wriggle every which way.

19 The Cape Corridor Page **261** • This ever expanding collection of resorts and golf courses where the Sea of Cortez meets the Pacific Ocean is a bubble of luxury and elegance.

Basics

Basics

Getting there

Wherever you're travelling from, you'll most likely get to Baja California through the US, whether through a major international airport such as in Los Angeles or San Diego or via one of the five border crossings that lead directly to the peninsula from the US states of California and Arizona. Planes fly direct from the US to La Paz, Loreto and San Jose del Cabo, while the north of the peninsula is primarily served by San Diego's international airport. While air travel may be the fastest route to these destinations, both states that make up the Baja California peninsula (confusingly called Baja California in the north, and Baja California Sur in the south) are easily accessible by road from both the US and Sonora, Mexico as well as by overnight ferry from the latter and from Sinaloa.

Generally, the most expensive time to fly is **high season**, which in Baja California stretches from mid-November to mid-April. The southern Cape has become a **Christmas** to **New Year's** favourite in recent years, pushing up the prices for the limited flights and hotel rooms there. The tremendous heat from late June to mid-September makes flights **cheap** throughout the peninsula. While the weather during the shoulder seasons between April and June and September and October can be as attractive as during high season, flights at those times are less expensive; plus there's a chance you'll still catch the whale migration during the earliest weeks of spring.

If your flight plans bring you to Baja California via a **stopover** in a **Mexican city**, keep in mind that the first place the plane lands is your point of entry into Mexico; you'll have to collect your bags and go through customs and immigration formalities there, even if you're continuing on via the same plane to other points.

For many destinations in the north and for multi-stop itineraries, a **private car** or a **tour bus** are the best options. The latter only stick to main routes along the highway but provide a high level of comfort and reliability for the few cities that they do service. Your own car offers the greatest flexibility – especially for reaching the out-of-way towns – but the long distances between cities means you should come well prepared with supplies and, preferably, have a second driver in tow. There is **no passenger train** service inside Baja California.

Flights from the US and Canada

The state of Baja California has **airports** in Tijuana and Mexicali that receive limited **flights** from the US and Canada, but it is better served by California's San Diego International Airport, where taxis to the border and car hire are easily available. Baja California Sur's three international airports – at Los Cabos, La Paz and Loreto – have numerous direct flights from major US cities. In addition to direct flights, Mexican airlines offer more frequent service through Hermosillo and Mexico City.

During high season there are daily flights between major markets on both US coasts and Los Cabos. In the low season, US airlines decrease their east coast flights to Los Cabos to twice or thrice weekly. This is also the common year-round frequency from west coast airports to Loreto and La Paz.

Round-trip fare from Los Angeles goes for as little as US$130 to Los Cabos and US$160 to Loreto or La Paz in low season; during high season US$350 is common from the west coast and US$650 and up from east coast markets.

From **Canada**, be prepared to pay around Can$650 from Vancouver and closer to Can$800 from Toronto and Montréal.

For decades **private aircraft** could pop in and out via smaller landing strips, but the Mexican government has curtailed many of these flights and removed port of entry status from some airports in order to fight the drug trade. Some smaller airports do continue to operate legally, and the most up-to-date information on flying craft here can be found from the *Baja Bush Pilots*, 1255 W Baseline Rd, Ste 138, Mesa, AZ (☎602/730-3250, ⓦwww.bajabush.com). The website's message boards provide some of the best (and most colourful) insider information in the region.

Flights from the UK and Ireland

There are no direct flights **from the UK or Ireland** to Baja California; entry will either be through a US airport such as Los Angeles or through Mexico City. The only direct scheduled flights to Mexico City from Britain are with British Airways, on Mon, Wed and Fri from London Heathrow; they head on to Baja California through a separate carrier.

Prices for scheduled return flights from London to Los Cabos with one connecting flight range from £620 low season to £800 or more in high season; through LA expect to pay about £250 less.

Flying from Ireland through London or any European hub will require an additional stop in Mexico City or the US. Return fare from Dublin to Los Angeles is €620; from London £350.

Flights from Australia, New Zealand and South Africa

There are no direct flights to Baja California **from Australia** or **New Zealand**, and most people reach the peninsula by way of Mexico City or US gateway cities such as Los Angeles and San Francisco.

Daily non-stop flights to LA and San Francisco from eastern **Australian** cities cost around Aus$1400, while from Perth they're about Aus$400 more. Figure on another Aus$400 to continue on to Baja California Sur.

From **New Zealand**, most flights are out of Auckland (add about NZ$200–250 for Christchurch and Wellington departures). The best deals are on Air New Zealand, to LA or San Francisco (about NZ$2500) either non-stop or via Honolulu, Fiji, Tonga, or Papeete; or on United Airlines, also non-stop to LA or San Francisco; Air Pacific via Fiji; and Qantas via Sydney (though direct is

cheaper). Via Asia, Singapore Airlines offers the best connecting service to LA and San Francisco, while the best value for the money is on JAL via either a transfer or stopover in Tokyo.

There are no direct flights between **Johannesburg** and Baja California; most people reach the peninsula by way of a connecting flight to a European gateway and then a US west coast city such as Los Angeles.

Driving

There are several border crossings where it's possible to **drive** from the US into Baja California. In California, San Ysidro and Otay Mesa (see box, p.62) serve Tijuana; Hwy 188 South leads to Tecate (see box, p.90); and Calexico (see box, p.99) serves Mexicali. In Arizona, it's possible to cross at Yuma into Los Algodones (see box, p.108).

US, Canadian, British, Irish, Australian, New Zealand and most European driving **licences** are valid in Mexico, but it's a good idea to arm yourself with an International Drivers Permit – available to US citizens for a nominal fee from the American Automobile Association (☎1-800/AAA-HELP, ⓦwww.aaa.com), and to Canadian drivers from the Canadian Automobile Association (☎613/247-0117, ⓦwww.caa.ca). If you run afoul of a Mexican traffic cop for any reason, show that first, and if they abscond with it you at least still have your own, more difficult to replace, licence.

If your car is **leased** you will need a letter from the leaseholder authorizing you to leave the country. This is usually obtained by faxing a copy of a purchased insurance policy (see below) and a cover letter stating your dates of travel. The leaseholder will then provide you with a certified letter in English permitting the trip. Allow at least seven business days for everything to come through. You will not have to show the letter during your visit unless you are in an accident or travel to any other part of Mexico.

US auto **insurance** policies are not valid in Mexico. While it is not illegal to drive in Mexico without an insurance policy, you'll likely spend time in jail if you get in an accident and do not have cover. Take out a

Fly less – stay longer! Travel and climate change

Climate change is a serious threat to the ecosystems that humans rely upon, and air travel is among the fastest-growing contributors to the problem. Rough Guides regard travel, overall, as a global benefit, and feel strongly that the advantages to developing economies are important, as is the opportunity of greater contact and awareness among peoples. But we all have a responsibility to limit our personal impact on global warming, and that means giving thought to how often we fly, and what we can do to redress the harm that our trips create.

Flying and climate change

Pretty much every form of motorized travel generates CO_2 – the main cause of human-induced climate change – but planes also generate climate-warming contrails and cirrus clouds and emit oxides of nitrogen, which create ozone (another greenhouse gas) at flight levels. Furthermore, flying simply allows us to travel much further than we otherwise would do. The figures are frightening: one person taking a return flight between Europe and California produces the equivalent impact of 2.5 tonnes of CO_2 – similar to the yearly output of the average UK car.

Fuel-cell and other less harmful types of plane may emerge eventually. But until then, there are really just two options for concerned travellers: to reduce the amount we travel by air (take fewer trips – stay for longer!), and to make the trips we do take "climate neutral" via a carbon-offset scheme.

Carbon offset schemes

Offset schemes run by ⓦ climatecare.org, ⓦ carbonneutral.com and others allow you to make up for some or all of the greenhouse gases that you are responsible for releasing. To do this, they provide "carbon calculators" for working out the global-warming contribution of a specific flight (or even your entire existence), and then let you contribute an appropriate amount of money to fund offsetting measures. These include rainforest reforestation and initiatives to reduce future energy demand – often run in conjunction with sustainable development schemes.

Rough Guides, together with Lonely Planet and other concerned partners in the travel industry, are supporting a **carbon-offset scheme** run by climatecare.org. Please take the time to view our website and see how you can help to make your trip climate-neutral.

ⓦ **www.roughguides.com/climatechange**

Mexican policy, available from numerous agencies on either side of every border post. Rates depend on the value of the vehicle and what kind of cover you want, but figure on US$18 or so a day for basic liability and limited personal coverage. Long-term policies decrease the daily cost.

To arrange a policy before leaving the US, go through local branches of the Automobile Association or call Instant Mexico Insurance Services (☏ 1-800/345-4701, ⓦ www.mexonline.com/instant1.htm); International Gateways (☏ 1-800/423-2646); Oscar Padilla Mexican Insurance (☏ 1-800/258-8600, ⓦ www.mexicaninsurance.com); or Sanborn's Insurance (☏ 1-800/222-0158, ⓦ www.sanbornsinsurance.com).

To get **discounts** on insurance, it can be worthwhile joining a travel club, such as Discover Baja Travel Club (☏ 1-800/727-BAJA) or Sanborn's Sombrero Club (☏ 1-800/222-0158). These clubs typically also offer discounts on accommodation and free travel advice. Annual dues are US$35–50. For more on general insurance policies, see p.44.

Ferries

For decades the ferries operating out of **Santa Rosalía** and **La Paz** were the only dependable way to access or get supplies to Baja California Sur. Although there are more options today, the ferries remain a scenic and inexpensive way to get to Baja California

Importing your car to Mexico

Other than buying the proper insurance, you do not need to fill out additional paperwork to drive your own car in either state on the Baja peninsula. To drive elsewhere in Mexico, however, you must obtain a **temporary importation permit** (around US$30) from a Banjercito (Mexican Army Bank) at the border. This must be paid for using a major credit card, otherwise you'll be asked for a refundable bond – the amount depends on the make and age of your vehicle, but it will be at least US$400 for a car less than five years old.

In order to get the permit, you'll need to provide:

A valid driver's licence

Passport and tourist permit or other immigration document

Certificate of vehicle ownership or lease contract

Valid registration

Credit card with the same name as owner or leaseholder

Guarantee of return (available online)

If you do not stop at a Banjercito branch when you leave Mexico you will either lose your deposit or have fines added to your credit card. For detailed information and online preprocessing, visit ⓦ www.banjercito.com.mx/site/tramiteitv_ing.jsp.

---

from the rest of Mexico, especially if you're travelling between it and southern Mexico by car. Sinaloa's **Topolobampo**, **Mazatlán** and **Manzanillo** (currently suspended) connect via Baja Ferries to La Paz's port at Pichilingue, 18km north of town (ⓣ612/125-6324). Thrice-weekly service from **Guaymas** connects the Sonoran state with Santa Rosalía's port (ⓣ615/152-1246). If you plan to take your car out of Baja via a ferry you must meet the importation requirements outlined above.

Buses

Greyhound (ⓣ1-800/231-2222, ⓦwww.greyhound.com) provides service from throughout the US and Canada to several stations on the US side of the Tijuana, Mexicali and Los Algodones border crossings, including San Diego, San Ysidro and Calexico in California and Yuma in Arizona.

Airlines, agents and operators

Online booking

ⓦ www.expedia.co.uk (in UK), ⓦ www.expedia.com (in US), ⓦ www.expedia.ca (in Canada)
ⓦ www.lastminute.com (in UK)
ⓦ www.opodo.co.uk (in UK)
ⓦ www.orbitz.com (in US)

ⓦ www.travelocity.co.uk (in UK), ⓦ www.travelocity.com (in US), ⓦ www.travelocity.ca (in Canada), ⓦ www.zuji.com.au (in Australia), ⓦ www.zuji.co.nz (in New Zealand)

Airlines

Aer Lingus UK ⓣ0845/084 4444, Republic of Ireland ⓣ0818/365 000, ⓦwww.aerlingus.com.
Aereo Calafia ⓣ624/143-4302, ⓦaereocalafia.com.mx. Flights between Puerto Vallarta, Las Mochis, Mazatlán and Culiacán and Los Cabos and Loreto.
Aerolitoral ⓣ01-800/800-2376, ⓦwww.aerolitoral.com. LA to La Paz and connection flights through Hermosillo to Loreto.
Aeroméxico US & Canada ⓣ1-800/237-6639 or 713/939-0077, UK ⓣ020/7801 6234, ⓦwww.aeromexico.com.
Air Canada ⓣ1-888/247-2262, ⓦwww.aircanada.ca. Montreal, Toronto and Vancouver to Mexico City.
Air New Zealand Australia ⓣ13 24 76, New Zealand ⓣ0800/737 000, ⓦwww.airnz.com
Alaska Airlines ⓣ1-800/252-7522, ⓦwww.alaska-air.com. LA to Loreto and Los Cabos; Anchorage, Portland, San Diego, San Francisco, Seattle and Spokane to Los Cabos.
America West Airlines/US Airways ⓣ1-800/622-1015, ⓦwww.usairways.com Las Vegas, New York, Phoenix and Sacramento to Los Cabos.
American Airlines ⓣ1-800/433-7300, UK ⓣ0845/7789 789, Republic of Ireland ⓣ01/602 0550, Australia ⓣ1300/650 7347, New Zealand ⓣ0800/887 997, ⓦwww.aa.com.

America West/US Airways UK ☎ 0845/600 3300, Republic of Ireland ☎ 1890/925 065, ⊛ www.usairways.com.
Aviacsa ☎ 1-888/528-4227, ⊛ www.aviacsa.com.mx. Mexico City to Mexicali; Houston to Tijuana.
British Airways US and Canada ☎ 1-800/AIRWAYS, UK ☎ 0870/850 9850, Republic of Ireland ☎ 1890/626 747, Australia ☎ 1300/767 177, New Zealand ☎ 09/966 9777, ⊛ www.ba.com.
Cathay Pacific ☎ 27 11/807-6618, ⊛ www.cathaypacific.com.
Continental Airlines US and Canada ☎ 1-800/523-3273, UK ☎ 0845/607 6760, Ireland ☎ 1890/925-252, Australia ☎ 2/9244-2242, NZ ☎ 9/308-3350, International ☎ 1-800/231-0856, ⊛ www.continental.com.
Delta US and Canada ☎ 1-800/221-1212, UK ☎ 0845/600 0950, Republic of Ireland ☎ 1850/882-031 or 01/407 3165, Australia ☎ 1-300-302-849, New Zealand ☎ 09/379 3370, ⊛ www.delta.com.
Frontier ☎ 1-800/432-1359, ⊛ www.frontierairlines.com. Denver to Los Cabos.
Japan Airlines (JAL) Australia ☎ 02/9272 1111, New Zealand ☎ 09/379 9906, ⊛ www.japanair.com.
KLM UK ☎ 0870/507 4074, ⊛ www.klmuk.com.
Lufthansa US ☎ 1-800/645-3880, Canada ☎ 1-800/563-5954, UK ☎ 0870/837 7747, Republic of Ireland ☎ 01/844 5544, Australia ☎ 1300 655 727, New Zealand ☎ 09/303 1529, ⊛ www.lufthansa.com.
Mexicana US and Canada ☎ 1-800/531-7921, LA to Los Cabos; UK ☎ 020/8492 0000, ⊛ www.mexicana.com.
Northwest Airlines/KLM US ☎ 1-800/225-2525, Australia ☎ 1300/303 747, New Zealand ☎ 09/309 1782, ⊛ www.nwa.com, South Africa ☎ 27 11/881-9696, ⊛ southafricaklm.com.
Qantas Australia ☎ 13 13 13, ⊛ www.qantas.com.au, New Zealand ☎ 0800/0014 0014, ⊛ www.qantas.co.nz.
South African Airways ☎ 0861/359-722, ⊛ www.flysaa.com.
Sun Country Airlines US ☎ 1-800/359-6786, ⊛ suncountry.com. Flights between Minneapolis/St. Paul and Los Cabos.
United Airlines US ☎ 1-800/241-6522, UK ☎ 0845/844 4777, Australia ☎ 13 17 77, ⊛ www.united.com.
US Airways US and Canada ☎ 1-800-428-4322, ⊛ www.usairways.com.
Virgin Atlantic US ☎ 1-800/821-5438, UK ☎ 0870/380 2007, Australia ☎ 1300/727-340, ⊛ www.virgin-atlantic.com.

Agents and operators

Adventure Center ☎ 1-800/228-8747, ⊛ www.adventure-center.com. Specializes in ecologically sound adventure travel. A fifteen-day "Best of Baja & Copper Canyon" trip that includes a five-day Sea of Cortez cruise starts at US$1260.
Adventure World Australia ☎ 02/9956 7766, ⊛ www.adventureworld.com.au, New Zealand ☎ 09/524 5118, ⊛ www.adventureworld.co.nz. Package vacations to Los Cabos resorts.
AeroMexico ☎ 1-800/237-6639, ⊛ www.aeromexicovacations.com. Package tours from US destinations to a luxury resort in Loreto and three classes of service in Los Cabos.
Andiamo Travel ☎ 1-800/661-1325, ⊛ www.andiamo-travel.com. San Diego-based eco-tourism and cultural journey outfitter. Single-day wine country tours and multi-day whale-watching trips departing from San Diego and Ensenada starting at US$500 per person.
Backroads ☎ 510/527-1555, 1-800/462-2848, ⊛ www.backroads.com. Six-day bike, walk and kayak trips near Loreto and Ensenada from US$2900.
Baja Adventure Company ☎ 1-877/560-2252 ⊛ www.bajaecotours.com. Scheduled tours to Laguna San Ignacio (five days from US$1125) as well as custom snorkelling and kayak trips.
Baja Discovery ☎ 1-800/829-2252, ⊛ www.bajadiscovery.com. Camping and hiking specialist that offers group and custom excursions, including cave art and desert hikes. Six-day tours start at US$1495.
Baja Expeditions ☎ 1-800/843-6967, ⊛ www.bajaex.com. Sea kayaking, whale watching, snorkelling and scuba diving, among other tours. Five days' whale watching in February or March costs US$1300.
Baja Wild ☎ 011-52 624/172-6300, ⊛ www.bajawild.com. Surfing, kayak and climbing outfitter with an emphasis on Cabo Pulmo. Multi-sport packages start at US$1500 for seven-day trips.
Black Feather ☎ 705/746-1372, ⊛ www.blackfeather.com. Multi-day kayaking and camping trips in Magdalena Bay, around Isla Espíritu Santo and between Loreto and La Paz, from US$590.
Cathy Matos Mexican Tours UK ☎ 020/8492 0000, ⊛ www.cathymatosmexico.co.uk. Wide variety of tailor-made tours, including whale watching, horseback riding and weddings in Los Cabos.
Cheap Caribbean ☎ 1-800/915-2322, ⊛ www.cheapcaribbean.com. All-inclusive package deals to hotels in Cabo San Lucas and along the *corridor*.
Ecosummer Expeditions ☎ 1-800/465-8884, ⊛ www.ecosummer.com. Up to eight-day sea kayaking and whale watching tours in the Sea of

Cortez and Magdalena Bay from US$1195. Focused on hotel and fishing packages in Baja California Sur.

Future Vacations ℡1-888/788-2545, ⓦ www .futurevacations.com. Vacation packages at Los Cabos-area resorts.

Global Exchange ℡1-800/497-1994 or 415/255-7296, ⓦ www.globalexchange.org. Organization campaigning on international issues which offers "Reality Tours" to increase American travellers' awareness of real life in other countries. Tours change with the political winds, so your favourite tour may only return every few years.

Green Tortoise Adventure Travel ℡415/956-7500 or 1-800/TORTOISE, ⓦ www.greentortoise .com. Converted school buses provide reasonably comfortable transport and sleeping space for up to 35 people; the clientele comes from all over the world, and communal cookouts are the rule. A fifteen-day overland adventure along the peninsula is US$750.

Mag Bay Tours ℡1-800/599-8676, ⓦ www .magbaytours.com. Whale-watching, kayaking, surfing and camping trips in Magdalena Bay and the surrounding islands. Trips don't include kayaks, surfboards or fishing licenses.

Mountain Travel Sobek US ℡1-888/MTSOBEK, UK ℡01494/448901, ⓦ www.mtsobek.com. Outdoor active adventure trips including sea kayaking or whale watching in Baja (7 days for US$1390).

Natural Habitats ℡1/800-543-8917, ⓦ www .nathab.com. Six-day trips to Loreto and Laguna San Ignacio for whale watching, from US$2195.

La Pinta Hotel ℡1-800/800-9632, ⓦ www .lapintahotels.com. Multi-night packages to the chain's six hotels.

Pleasant Holidays–Mexico ℡1-800/742-9244, ⓦ www.pleasantholidays.com. Package flight/hotel deals to Los Cabos.

S&S Tours ℡1-800/499-5685 or 520/458-6365, ⓦ www.ss-tours.com. Whale watching in Bahía Magdalena-seven-day tours range from US$1795.

Searcher Natural History Tours ℡619/226-2403, ⓦ bajawhale.com. These twelve-day tours of Baja California's Pacific coast depart from San Diego and travel to Cabo San Lucas on board a 95-foot US Coast Guard vessel (US$3295).

Smithsonian Journeys ℡1-877/EDU-TOUR, ⓦ www.smithsonianjourneys.org. Eight-day whale-watching cruises from La Paz to Bahía Magdalena starting at US$3490.

Solo Sports Week-long adventure sports trips – surfing, kiteboarding, mountain biking – to the otherwise unoccupied Punta San Carlos. All-inclusive packages start at US$1600.

Suntrips ℡1-800/SUNTRIPS, ⓦ www.suntrips .com. Wholesale travel company offering resort packages to Los Cabos from Denver and Oakland.

Trips Worldwide UK ℡0117/311 440, ⓦ www .tripsworldwide.co.uk. Fly-drive packages from Los Cabos to Loreto from £1450. Also acts as agents for many other recommended tour operators.

Vela Windsurf Resorts ℡1-800/223-5443, ⓦ www.velawindsurf.com. These windsurfing and sport excursions from Los Barilles on the Eastern Cape start at $950 for seven days.

Wild Oceans UK ℡0117/965 8333, ⓦ www .wildwings.co.uk. Naturalist-led tours to observe whales in the Laguna San Ignacio and Sea of Cortez; accommodation on board a comfortable 28m boat. From £2649 for fourteen days, including airfare.

Wilderness Travel ℡1-800/368-2794, ⓦ www .wildernesstravel.com. Eight-day kayaking trips to the Sea of Cortez (US$1550) and nine-day trips to Bahía Magdalena (US$1795).

World Outdoors ℡1-800/488-8483, ⓦ www .theworldoutdoors.com. Days in these week-long active trips around La Paz and the Eastern Cape are divided between snorkelling, sea kayaking, hiking, surfing and, in season, whale watching. From US$1975.

Xplore Offshore ℡1-858/456-1636, ⓦ xploreoffshore.com. Trips from Loreto in a Navy SEAL speed raft around the Sea of Cortez, starting at US$2000 for two weeks.

Getting around

As recently as the 1970s, passage through the vast majority of Baja California was limited to those with their own boat, private aircraft, all-terrain vehicle or a steady mule. Access is easier now, aided both by the completion of the Transpeninsular Highway in 1973 and expanded commercial air service from major US markets. If you want to visit secluded bays, beaches or more than just the major towns, having your own car is almost a necessity to get around Baja California.

It is possible, however, but not necessarily cheaper, to visit even the hard to reach places by a combination of **bus** trips to major towns and hired cars and guides to secluded sites. Intra-peninsular flights are easy if you have your own plane or can hire a bush pilot to do your flying for you. **Commercial flights** between the north and south typically fly though Aeromexico's hub in Hermosillo before returning to the peninsula. **Charter flights** out of Ensenada and Guerrero Negro are common, but travellers' complaints on these routes are even more so, with two- or three-day-long delays the norm.

By car

Distances in Baja California can be huge, paved roads are limited and petrol stations are more sacred than churches, yet **driving** the peninsula remains one of the world's last remaining great road trips. Drivers wishing to **rent cars** are supposed to have held their licences for at least one year (though this is rarely checked); people **under 25 years old** but older than 21 will have to pay higher rates, while those under 21 are generally not allowed to rent cars. Car rental companies (see p.26) will also expect you to have a credit card; if you don't they may let you leave a hefty deposit (at least M$2500), but don't count on it.

In general the **lowest rates** are available by booking in advance through the rental agency's website – M$1500 a week for a subcompact is a fairly standard base rate, although insurance and fuel options double the total cost. Always be sure to get free **unlimited mileage**, and be aware that returning the car in a different city from the one in which you rented it will incur a significant drop-off charge. Also, don't automatically go for the cheapest rate, as there's some difference in the quality of cars from company to company; industry leaders like Hertz and Avis tend to have newer, lower-mileage cars with cheaper add-ons like automatic transmission or GPS systems.

When you rent a car, read the small print carefully for details on **Collision Damage Waiver** (CDW), sometimes called Liability Damage Waiver (LDW). This is not included in the initial rental quote but is well worth considering. It specifically covers the car that you are driving yourself, as you are in any case insured for damage to other vehicles. At M$120–220 a day, it can add substantially to the total cost, but without it you're liable for every scratch to the car – even those that aren't your fault. Mexican rental agencies do not sell insurance that covers punctured tyres or broken windows. Some credit-card companies offer automatic CDW coverage to anyone using their card; read the fine print beforehand in any case.

If you **break down** along the Mex 1D toll road in the north you can summon the highway patrol on one of the emergency phones stationed along the highway. Elsewhere, you can wait for a Green Angel (see p.28); call ☎078 from any phone or rely upon the kindness of strangers.

If you're travelling out of a major town, it is wise to rent a **mobile telephone** from the car rental agency – you often only have to pay a nominal amount until you actually use it, and in larger cities they increasingly come built into the car. Having a phone can be reassuring at least, and a potential lifesaver should something go terribly wrong.

Driving distances

The **driving distances** below are for the major destinations or intersections along the Transpeninsular Highway and other primary paved roads. Times include necessary stops for petrol and army inspections.

Tijuana to Mexicali	1hr 50min	198km
Mexicali to San Felipe	2hr 15min	195km
San Felipe to Ensenada	3hr 10min	245km
Tijuana to Ensenada	55min	109km
Ensenada to San Quintín	3hr	190km
San Quintín to El Rosario	55min	56km
El Rosario to Cataviña	1hr 50min	123km
Cataviña to Parador Punta Prieta	1hr	103km
Parador Punta Prieta to Bahía de los Ángeles	45min	69km
Parador Punta Prieta to Guerrero Negro	1hr 50min	135km
Guerrero Negro to San Ignacio	1hr 30min	146km
San Ignacio to Santa Rosalía	45min	72km
Santa Rosalía to Mulegé	40min	62km
Mulegé to Loreto	1hr 45min	138km
Loreto to Ciudad Insurgentes	1hr 20min	141km
Ciudad Insurgentes to La Paz	2hr 20min	209km
La Paz to Todos Santos	45min	77km
Todos Santos to Cabo San Lucas	55min	77km
Cabo San Lucas to San José del Cabo	25min	32km

Car rental agencies

Alamo US ☎1-800/462-5266, 🌐www.alamo.com.
Apex New Zealand ☎0800/93 95 97 🌐www
.apexrentals.co.nz.
Auto Europe US and Canada ☎1-888/223-5555,
🌐www.autoeurope.com.
Avis US ☎1-800/230-4898, Canada ☎1-
800/272-5871, UK ☎0870/606 0100, Republic of
Ireland ☎021/428 1111, Australia ☎13 63 33 or
02/9353 9000, New Zealand ☎09/526 2847 or
0800/655 111, 🌐www.avis.com.
Budget US ☎1-800/527-0700, Canada ☎1-
800/268-8900, UK ☎08701/565656, Republic of
Ireland ☎09/0662 7711, Australia ☎1300/362
848, New Zealand ☎0800/283-438, 🌐www
.budget.com.
Dollar US ☎1-866/434-2226, 🌐www.dollar.com.
Enterprise Rent-a-Car US ☎1-800/261-7331,
🌐www.enterprise.com.
Europcar US & Canada ☎1-877/940 6900, UK
☎0870/607 5000, Republic of Ireland ☎01/614
2888, Australia ☎1300/131 390, 🌐www.europcar
.com.
Europe by Car US ☎1-800/223-1516, 🌐www
.europebycar.com.

Hertz US ☎1-800/654-3131, Canada ☎1-
800/263-0600, UK ☎020/7026 0077, Republic of
Ireland ☎01/870 5777, Australia ☎08/9921-4052,
New Zealand ☎0800/654 321, 🌐www.hertz.com.
Holiday Autos UK ☎0871/222 3200, Republic
of Ireland ☎01/872 9366, Australia ☎1300/554
432, New Zealand ☎0800/144 040, 🌐www
.holidayautos.co.uk.
National US ☎1-800/CAR-RENT, UK ☎0870/400
4581, Australia ☎02/13 10 45, New Zealand
☎03/366-5574, 🌐www.nationalcar.com.
SIXT Republic of Ireland ☎1850/206 088, 🌐www
.irishcarrentals.ie.
Suncars UK ☎0870/500 5566, Republic of Ireland
☎1850/201-416, 🌐www.suncars.com.
Thrifty US and Canada ☎1-800/847-4389, UK
☎01494/751 600, Republic of Ireland ☎0800/272
8728, Australia ☎1300/367 227, New Zealand
☎0800/737070, 🌐www.thrifty.com.

Fuel

The government oil company, Pemex, has
a monopoly and sells three types of **fuel**:
Premio (93 octane) at M$7 per litre, Magna
Sin (87 octane) at M$6 and Diesel at M$5.

Except in Mexicali, San Felipe and Bahia de Los Ángeles, all stations are full service. Make sure that the attendant clears the amount before beginning to pump your petrol. Los Cabos, in particular, is notorious for the dishonesty of some of its attendants; here it is always necessary to get out of your car and watch every aspect of the fueling process, as well as verbally confirm the amount of money you hand to the attendant. Pemex stations do accept dollars on a M$12 to US$1 exchange rate but don't accept credit cards, traveller's cheques or personal cheques.

Roads and rules

In theory, there are two types of roads in Baja California: **paved** and **unpaved**. The quality of paved roads has increased dramatically under President Vicente Fox's tenure – a generous payback for the peninsula's generally unwavering support for the PAN political party. Unfortunately for anyone planning a day's outing on an unfamiliar track, the vast difference in the types of unpaved roads will make it difficult to determine how long the trip will take or even whether you should undertake it at all.

Baja California driving does require a great deal of care and concentration to avoid hazards produced by: **weather** (washouts and washboarding during rainy season, warping during the summer), **animals** (grazing cows, untethered horses and burros, cartoonishly quick roadrunners, and decomposing assortments of all the above), and **neglect** (cracked roads almost exclusively within city limits).

These conditions are easy to deal with during the day, but at **night** they're terribly dangerous, especially the cattle that wander into the road and are almost impossible to see in time to stop your vehicle. When you do have to travel between cities at night, drive 15–20kph slower than the posted limits and take caution when cresting hills or going around corners.

Obeying the rules of the **road** pretty much ensures you won't be hassled by police any more than if you were driving in your home country. Whether this is due to the integrity or the scarcity of highway patrols is up for debate. Traffic circulates on the right, and the normal speed limit is 40kph (25mph) in built-up areas, 70kph (43mph) in open country, and 90–110kph (68mph) on the Transpeninsular Highway. Driving while talking on a mobile phone is illegal.

Get out of the way of Mexican bus and truck drivers that want to pass (and remember that if you signal left to them on a stretch of open road, it means it's clear to overtake). Every town and village on the road, however tiny, limits the speed of through traffic with a series of *topes* (concrete or metal speed bumps) across the road. Look out for the warning signs and take them seriously; the bumps are often huge. One convention to be aware of is that the first driver to flash their lights at a junction, or where only one vehicle can pass, has the right of way: they're not inviting you to go first.

Any good road map should provide details of the more common symbols used on Mexican road signs. They're also available on the tourism secretary's website ⓦwww.discoverbajacalifornia.com.

In most large towns you'll find extensive one-way systems. Traffic direction is often poorly marked (look for small arrows affixed to lampposts), though this is less of a problem than it sounds: simply note the directions in which the parked cars, if not the moving cars, are facing.

Military checkpoints

Military checkpoints dot the highways throughout both states, primarily to search northbound traffic in an attempt to stop the US-bound flow of illegal drugs. Sometimes you'll be waved through but it's more typical to have to get out of your car and watch as they check the vehicle. Be prepared to tell them where you came from, where you're going and, in some cases, to open your luggage so they can search inside. The soldiers often decorate the exterior of their office with pictures of contraband and their unfortunate owners or their vehicles.

Parking in towns is uncomplicated. Although parallel zones aren't marked clearly, unless the kerb is painted red you're free to join other parked cars.

Tyres suffer particularly badly on burning-hot Mexican roads, and you should carry at least one good spare. Roadside *vulcanizadoras* and *llanteros* can do temporary repairs. While new tyres are expensive, remoulds aren't a good idea on hot roads at high speed. If you have a breakdown, there is a free highway mechanic service known as the **Ángeles Verdes** (Green Angels). As well as patrolling all major routes looking for beleaguered motorists, they can be reached by phone on ☎55/5250-8221. The Ángeles Verdes speak English. Be warned that they travel through central Baja's most isolated areas no more than twice per day.

Should you have a minor accident, try to come to some arrangement with the other party – involving the police will only make matters worse, and Mexican drivers will be just as anxious to avoid doing so. If you witness an accident, you may want to consider the gravity of the situation before getting involved. Witnesses can be locked up along with those directly implicated to prevent them from leaving before the case comes up – so consider if your involvement is necessary to serve justice. In a serious incident, contact your consulate and your Mexican insurance company as soon as possible.

For additional sound advice on driving in Baja California, see the ASIRT report, online at ⓦwww.asirt.org/RoadTravelReports/Mexico.pdf.

It can't be stressed enough that **driving while intoxicated** (DWI) or driving under the influence (DUI) is a very serious offence. You'll be locked up with other inebriates in the nearest jail until you sober up, and your case will be heard by a judge, who can revoke your licence, fine you as much as $1000, or in extreme (or repeat) cases, imprison you for thirty days.

By bus

There are basically two classes of **bus**, first (*primera*) and second (*segunda*), though on major long-distance routes there's often little to differentiate them: First-class vehicles have reserved seats, videos and air-conditioning, though an increasing number of second-class lines have the same comforts. The main differences will be in the number of stops – second-class buses call at more places, and consequently take longer to get where they're going – and the fare, which is about ten percent higher on first-class services. An exception is the well-travelled La Paz–Los Cabos route in the south – one-way tickets are M$120 *segunda* and M$190 *primera*.

On important routes there are also deluxe or Pullman buses, with names like Primera Plus or Turistar Plus and fares around thirty percent higher than those of first-class buses. They have few if any stops, and waitress service and free snacks and drinks over longer distances, comfortable airline-style seating, and air conditioning that works – be sure to keep a sweater handy, as it can get very cold. They may also be emptier, which could mean more space to stretch out and sleep. Almost all Pullman services have computerized reservations and may accept credit cards in payment: these facilities are increasingly common with the larger regular bus lines too.

The *Central Camionera* stations get smaller and smaller as you leave Tijuana, turning into shelters with garbage cans by Cataviña and not amounting to much more until La Paz. There are no ticket sellers or even schedules posted here, so it's essential to get the times in advance or else you'll stand in the sun all day. Weekends, holiday season, school holidays and fiestas can also overload services

---

Hitchhiking

The usual advice given to **hitchhikers** is that they should use common sense; in fact, of course, common sense should tell anyone that hitchhiking in Baja California's unforgiving climate – not to mention the very real dangers posed by people – is a **bad idea**. We do not recommend it under any circumstances.

to certain destinations: again the only real answer is to buy tickets in advance.

Terms to look out for on the timetable, besides *local* and *de paso*, include *vía corta* (by the short route) and *directo* or *expreso* (direct/nonstop – in theory at least). *Salida* is departure, *llegada* arrival. A decent road map will be extremely helpful in working out which buses are going to pass through your destination.

Baja California bus companies

Autotransportes de Baja California (ABC)
℡ 664/621-2424. Service throughout the peninsula.
Estrellas de Baja California ℡ 664/683-5622.
First-class service throughout the peninsula.
Península Ejecutivo ℡ 664/621-3617. First-class service throughout the peninsula.
Suburbaja ℡ 664/688-0082. Service to Mexicali and the northwest coast.
Transportes Aguila ℡ 664/621-2424. Service throughout the peninsula.

By plane

Baja California has a rich tradition of small pilots bouncing between small runways in even smaller cities. *Baja Bush Pilots* (🌐www .bajabush.com) has an online message board that can connect travellers with people flying their direction. Alternately, you can go to fly-in hotels, in places such as Mulegé and *Mike's Sky Ranch* (see p.158). Charter planes charge a per-hour fee per person;

a typical 5hr return flight from Los Cabos starts at US$1000.

Cycling

With the right amount of planning, a cycling tour of parts or the entire length of the peninsula can be fascinating. The one main road linking the entire region makes part of the planning easy – you ride either north or south. The downside is that parts of the route are both narrow and heavily trafficked, there are few places to repair equipment between Los Cabos and Tijuana, and there are very long stretches – up to 300 kilometres – with extremely limited services.

Mex 1D between Playas de Tijuana and Ensenada is the most accessible of the states' rides, and it plays host to a twice-yearly race between Ensenada and Rosarito. Between Ensenada and Mulegé, the road narrows and should only be attempted by seasoned distance riders or groups with support staff.

Buses, often overcrowded, do not routinely have room for cycles, especially if you're getting on in a town without a ticket office. Your best option is to visit the ABC line offices in Tijuana or Los Cabos and enquire about surcharges for extra luggage and booking that space in advance. If you're riding your bike into the country from the US, you must queue with pedestrians at all points of entry along the Mexico–US border.

Accommodation

Baja California hotels may describe themselves as anything from *paradores*, *posadas* and *casas de huéspedes* to plain *hoteles*, all terms that are used more or less interchangeably. In a similar vein, outside of major cities, resorts may actually be motels or even RV parks with a good view. Don't let an accommodation's name create expectations of types of service – that's what the price is for (and it's not always a reliable gauge either).

Finding a room is rarely difficult. In larger towns street signs point to a *zona hoteleria* and in smaller ones they'll be clustered along the Transpeninsular Highway. The only times

you're likely to have big problems finding somewhere to stay are in coastal resorts over the peak Christmas season, at Easter, on Mexican holidays and almost anywhere

Accommodation price codes

Throughout this book, accommodation has been price-coded according to the average cost of the least expensive **double room**. For the few towns that have a genuine high season, it is limited to the weeks between Christmas and New Year: there can be a great deal of fluctuation with room rates, especially in areas like Los Cabos during the holiday and college spring break season, when prices can rise drastically. Many establishments charge more on Friday and Saturday nights, while big-city business hotels often slash their prices on weekends. As the high and low seasons for tourists vary across the region, astute planning can save a lot of money. Watch out also for local events, which can raise rates far above normal. These price codes do not include local tax, which is currently twelve percent, although family-run hotels and B&Bs sometimes roll the tax into the quoted price.

❶ less than M$150   ❹ M$400-600   ❼ M$1000–1400
❷ M$150–250   ❺ M$600-800   ❽ M$1400–2000
❸ M$250–400   ❻ M$800–1000   ❾ more than M$2000

during a local fiesta, when it's well worth trying to reserve ahead.

All rooms should have an official price displayed, though this is not always a guide to quality – a filthy fleapit and a beautifully run converted mansion may charge exactly the same, even if they're right next door to each other. To guarantee quality, the only recourse is seeing your room first – you soon learn to spot which establishments have promise.

A room with one double bed (*cama matrimonial*) is almost always cheaper than a room with two singles (*doble* or *con dos camas*), and most hotels have large "family" rooms with several beds, which are tremendous value for groups. In the big resorts, there are lots of apartments that sleep six or more and include cooking facilities, for yet more savings. A little gentle haggling rarely goes amiss, and many places will have some rooms that cost less, so just ask (*¿Tiene un cuarto más barato?*). At many hotels, the charges can be paid in M$ or US$, but it is important to settle on the US$ rate in advance.

Except for a small minority of establishments in cooler regions or at RV parks, air conditioning (*aire acondicionado*) is usually available, though it's typically noisy.

Campsites

RV owners are partly responsible for the peninsula's popularity, so it's only fitting that they've got some of the best sites for their parks. These parks often include spaces for tent camping, sometimes with *palapa* shelters. There's a large body of books about the subject, but the best and most frequently updated is *Traveller's Guide to Camping Mexico's Baja* (parts online at ⓦwww .rollinghomes.com).

Camping spaces are typically a wooden or palm-frond shack with a hammock slung up inside (or a place to sling your own); they are frequently without electricity, though as a resort gets more popular, they tend to transform into sturdier beach bungalows with modern conveniences and higher prices.

Food and drink

Whatever your preconceptions about Mexican food, if you've never eaten in Mexico, they will almost certainly be wrong – this applies even more so on the peninsula than it does the mainland. Food here bears very little resemblance to the concoctions served in "Mexican" restaurants or fast-food joints in other parts of the world – certainly you won't find *chile con carne* outside the tourist spots. Nor, as a rule, is it especially spicy; indeed, a more common complaint from visitors is that after a while it all seems rather bland.

Basic meals are served at *restaurantes*, but you can get breakfast, snacks and often full meals at cafés too; there are take-out and fast-food places serving *tortas* (sandwiches) and tacos (tortillas folded over with a filling), as well as more international-style food; there are establishments called *jugerías* (look for signs saying "Jugos y Licuados") serving nothing but wonderful juices (*jugos*), *licuados* (fruit blended with water or milk) and fruit salads; and there are street stalls dishing out everything from tacos to orange juice to ready-made crisp vegetable salads sprinkled with chile-salt and lime. The fish taco is the food of choice along the coasts. In the big cities and resorts, of course, there are international restaurants too – pizza, Japanese and Chinese food are ubiquitous.

Breakfast

Breakfast (*desayuno*) on the peninsula can consist simply of coffee (see "Drinking", p.33) and *pan dulce* – sweet rolls and pastries that usually come in a basket; you pay for as many as you eat. More substantial breakfasts consist of eggs in any number of forms (many set breakfasts include *huevos al gusto*: eggs any way you like them), and at fruit-juice places you can have a simple *licuado* (see "Drinking", p.33) fortified with raw egg (*blanquillo*). Freshly squeezed orange juice (*jugo de naranja*) is always available from street stalls in the early morning. Chicken and pork make regular appearances; the former in *chilaquiles* – where yesterday's tortillas are fried and placed atop a layer of torn chicken and peppers and *queso* – and the latter as *chorizo* mixed into eggs.

If you go out to the clubs on a weekend night, chances are come morning on Saturday and Sunday you'll do as locals do and dip into a steaming pot of *menudo*, a spicy tripe stew.

Mid-morning snacks

Snack meals mostly consist of some variation on the taco/enchilada theme (stalls selling them are called *taquerías*), but tortas – sandwich rolls heavily filled with meat or cheese or both, garnished with avocado and chile and toasted on request – are also wonderful, and you'll see take-out torta stands everywhere. Failing that, you can of course always make your own snacks with bread or tortillas, along with fillings such as avocado or cheese, from shops or markets.

Lunch

You can of course eat a full meal in a restaurant at any time of day, but you'd do well to adopt the local habit of taking your main meal at **lunchtime**, since this is when *comidas corridas* (set meals, varied daily) are served, from around 1pm to 4pm: in more expensive places the same thing may be known as the *menú del día* or *menú turístico*. Price is one good reason: you'll usually get three or four courses for M$70 or less (sometimes half that price in fact), which can't be bad.

One reason to stay out of the restaurants, though, is to experience the open-air cafés, street and market food in larger towns like Tijuana, Ensenada, La Paz, Todos Santos and San José. Unless they're located next to a nightclub, these spots shut down around 5pm and take their roasted and barbecued meats, fish tacos, *cockteles*, *ceviche* and tortas with them. When there is seating at these places, it tends to be on plastic chairs arranged on dirt floors and, in the spots worth stopping at, an awning or *palapa* roof for shade.

Dinner

Dinner is typically eaten after 8pm and, for part of the week, combines eating and drinking activities into one long event. Dinners at places that cater to tourists open around 6pm and can be multi-course, *queso*-covered affairs, but locals tend to stick to smaller portions of vegetable dishes like *ensalada nopales*, grilled meats or fish. The peninsula's restaurants are sleepy in the early part of the week, while locals focus on work. They come alive again at the end of the week – near payday – when dinners become longer and serve as the beginning of a longer night of consorting with friends and family.

What to eat

The basic Mexican diet is essentially one of corn (*maíz*) and its products, supplemented by beans and chiles. These three things appear in an almost infinite variety of guises. Some dishes are spicy (*picante*), but on the whole you add your own seasoning from the bowls of home-made chile sauce on the table – these are often surprisingly mild, but they can be fiery and should always be approached with caution.

There are at least a hundred different types of **chile**, fresh or dried, in colours ranging from pale green to almost black, and all sorts of different sizes (large, mild ones are often stuffed with meat or cheese and rice to make *chiles rellenos*). Each has a distinct flavour and by no means all are hot (which is why we don't use the English term "chilli" for them), although the most common, *chiles jalapeños*, small and either green or red, certainly are. You'll always find a salsa on the table when you eat, and in any decent restaurant it will be home-made and served in the pestle it was pounded in; no two are quite alike.

Chile is also the basic ingredient of more complex cooked sauces, notably **mole**, traditionally served with chicken, but also

sometimes with enchiladas (rolled, filled tortillas). Half of the fifty or so ingredients in this extraordinary mixture are different types of chile, but the most notable ingredient is chocolate. Another speciality to look out for is *chiles en nogada*, a bizarre combination of stuffed green peppers covered in a white sauce made of walnuts and cream cheese or sour cream, topped with red pomegranate: the colours reflect the national flag and it's served especially in September around Independence Day, which is also when the walnuts are fresh.

Beans (*frijoles*), an invariable accompaniment to egg dishes – and with almost everything else too – are of the pinto or kidney variety and are almost always served *refritos*: boiled up, mashed and refried (though actually it is the first time they're fried). They're even better if you can get them whole in some kind of country-style soup or stew, often with pork or bacon, as in *frijoles charros*.

Corn, in some form or another, features in virtually everything. In its natural state it is known as *elote* and you can find it roasted on the cob at street stalls or in soups and stews such as *pozole* (with meat). Far more often, though, it is ground into flour for tortillas, flat maize pancakes of which you will get a stack to accompany your meal in any cheap Mexican restaurant (in more expensive or touristy places you'll get bread rolls known as *bolillos*). Tortillas can also be made of wheat flour (*de harina*), which you'll encounter when servers ask if you'd like *maíz* or *harina* tortillas.

Tortillas form the basis of many specifically Mexican dishes, often described as *antojitos* (appetizers, light courses) on menus. Simplest of these are tacos, typically two warm small tortillas filled with almost anything, from fried fish to roast beef or pork. With cheese, either alone or in addition to other fillings, they are called *quesadillas*. Enchiladas are rolled, filled tortillas covered in chile sauce and baked; enchiladas *suizas* are filled with chicken and have sour cream over them. Tostadas are flat tortillas toasted crisp and piled with ingredients – usually meat, salad vegetables and cheese (smaller bite-size versions are known as *sopes*). Tortillas torn up and cooked together with chicken and beans are called *chilaquiles*: this is a traditional way of using up leftovers for breakfast.

Seafood is almost always fresh and delicious, especially the aforementioned fish taco, a culinary joy that combines tempura-fried filets with lime juice, light mayo and cabbage and should be devoured in any coastal city (but avoided during the hotter months in Tijuana, Mexicali and any inland stretch of Mex 1). Shrimp or other seafood cocktails (*coctél/campechana de camarón* or *pulpo*) are the appetizers of choice, as is any version of *ceviche*, fish marinated in and cooked by lime juice and served cold with crispy tortilla. Fresh clams and Pacific lobster are served almost year-round as well. Fishermen around Ensenada haul in tuna that will become the main ingredient in excellent *carpaccio* (thinly sliced raw tuna typically served in olive oil) served in the area's better restaurants. Baja California's ranching and farming legacy has given it the edge on the rest of Mexico when it comes to good beef, pork and game. Argentine-style grill-ups are popular and include multiple cuts of beef alongside warm beans and fresh tortillas.

Eggs feature on every menu as the most basic of meals, and at some time you must try the classic Mexican combinations of *huevos rancheros* (fried eggs on a tortilla with red salsa) or *huevos a la mexicana* (scrambled with onion, tomato and chile).

The **ice cream**, more like Italian *gelato* than the heavy-cream US varieties, can also be fabulous and comes in a huge range of flavours. US-style ice cream is available at the many Thrifty parlours that dot the townscapes.

Vegetarians will have a difficult time unless they ignore the fact that their vegetables and fruit will share the kitchen with lard and other animal products they'd rather not know about, while vegans should cook their own meals.

Drinking

Soft drinks (*refrescos*) – including Coke, Pepsi, Squirt, and Mexican brands such as apple-flavoured Sidral (which are usually extremely sweet) – are on sale everywhere. Far more tempting are the real **fruit juices** and *licuados* sold at shops and stalls displaying the "Jugos y Licuados" sign and known as *jugerías* or *licuaderías*. **Jugos** (juices) can be squeezed from anything that will go through the extractor. *Naranja* (orange) and *zanahoria* (carrot) are the staples, but you should also experiment with some of the more obscure tropical fruits, most of which are much better than they sound. *Licuados* are made of fruit mixed with water (*licuado de agua* or simply *agua de* …) or milk (*licuado de leche*) in a blender, usually with sugar added, and are always fantastic. *Limonada* (fresh lemonade) is also sold in many of these places, as are **aguas frescas** – flavoured cold drinks, of which the most common are *horchata* (rice milk flavoured with cinnamon) and *agua de arroz* (like an iced rice pudding drink and absolutely delicious), *agua de jamaica* (hibiscus) or *de tamarindo* (tamarind). These are also often served in restaurants or sold in the streets from great glass jars. Make sure that any water and ice used is purified – street stalls are especially suspect in this regard. Juices and *licuados* are also sold at many ice-cream parlours – *neverías* or *paleterías*. In the larger cities you will find chain cafes and small shops for **coffee** and **tea**; they'll also be empty by 10am or as soon as the sun burns off the morning chill. **Espresso-based** drinks are hard to come by outside of the northern and southern extremes of the peninsula, locals preferring instead American-style drip coffee.

Baja California's year-round heat and pace of life has fostered a drinking culture centred on **cerveza clara**, a lager-style brew best served in ice-cooled bottles. In the north, most people drink the local Tecate while in the south it's Pacifico. Corona and Modelo are available everywhere, the first a favourite among tourists, the latter among the budget-conscious.

You'll normally be drinking in bars, but if you don't feel comfortable – this applies to women, in particular – you can also get takeout beer from most shops, supermarkets and, cheapest of all, *agencias*, which are normally agents for just one brand – like the prevalent "Modelo-rama" storefronts. When buying from any of these places, it is normal to pay a deposit of about 30–40 percent of the purchase price: keep your receipt and return your bottles to the same store.

Wine (*vino*; *tinto* is red, *blanco* is white) is seen primarily in the northwest around Ensenada and in Los Cabos around the resorts (where it's much more expensive and has a high percentage of bottles that are either corked or damaged from temperature fluctuations). L.A. Cetto and Domecq are the largest producers, although it's well worth your time to seek out bottles by Monte Xanic and Casa Piedra.

Tequila, distilled from the agave cactus-like plant and produced mainly in the state of Jalisco, is of course the most famous of Mexican spirits, usually served straight with lime and salt on the side. Lick the salt and bite into the lime, then take a swig of tequila (or the other way round – there's no correct etiquette). If you're drinking it straight, the best stuff is aged (*añejo* or *reposado*) for smoothness; try Sauza Hornitos, which is powerful, or Commemorativo, which is unexpectedly gentle on the throat.

Good tequila is the key ingredient in the **margarita**, a close second behind beer as the official drink of the peninsula. A good bartender will make it from three parts tequila, two parts fresh lime juice and one part triple sec, and serve it over ice in a salt-rimmed glass. The frozen margarita is typically only served in tourist hotels and bars. In Los Cabos, bartenders will replace the triple sec with *damiana*, a local liqueur rumoured to be an aphrodisiac (which, like any other liqueur, becomes so after four or five servings).

When drinking other spirits, you should always ask for *nacional*, as anything imported is fabulously expensive. Rum (*ron*), gin (*ginebra*) and vodka are made in Mexico, as are some very palatable brandies (brandy or *coñac* – try San Marcos or Presidente). Sangrita is a non-alcoholic mixture of tomato and fruit juices with chile, often drunk as a mixer with tequila.

Relaxed drinking environs can be found in hotel bars, tourist areas or any place that describes itself as a "ladies' bar". Traditional **cantinas** are for serious and excessive drinking, have a thoroughly threatening, macho atmosphere, and usually bar women; more often than not, there's a sign above the door prohibiting entry to "women, members of the armed forces, and anyone in uniform". Big-city cantinas are to some extent more liberal, but in small and traditional places they remain exclusively male preserves, full of drunken bonhomie that can suddenly sour into threats and fighting.

The media

Baja California's media deviates from the Mexican norm by having a number of fiercely independent media outlets and heavy doses of international concern running through its pages and newscasts. Papers are still lurid scandal sheets, brimming with violent crime depicted in full colour, but they frequently pull the tales from the other side of the border and from around the world. Tijuana, Mexicali and La Paz have their own papers – dailies and weeklies in both Spanish and English.

Newspapers

You get a good sense of the power of the press in any town by how quickly you're besieged at a stop sign or red light by a vendor hawking **newspapers**. In Tijuana – where journalists face very real danger if they speak out – the bravest of voices appear in the weekly *Zeta* (Ⓦwww .zetatijuana.com). The paper's credibility rests on the dedication of its current leader

Jesús Blanornelas and on the reputations of former editors and publishers Héctor Félix Miranda, Luis Elizaldi and Francisco Franco, each of whom was murdered by Tijuana drug cartels and local political leaders who didn't like their coverage. Tijuana's daily, *Frontera* (ⓦwww.frontera.info) doesn't take as many chances but still provides decent local and national information.

Perhaps because of the danger of being a member of the press in Tijuana, some of the more challenging pieces come out across the border in the English-language *San Diego Union-Tribune* (ⓦwww.signonsandiego.com). The paper's coverage of the trans-border area is so consistent it's often criticized by some of its readers who wonder whether San Diego is part of Mexico. You can pick up copies at hotels in Tijuana and Mexicali.

The north is also served by two dailies in Mexicali; *La Crónica* (ⓦwww.lacronica.com), which has extensive and sober coverage of state and national politics, and *La Voz de la Frontera* (ⓦwww.lavozdelafrontera.com.mx), which adds a lurid tint to the same subjects. On the northwest coast, Ensenada is home to the dailies *El Cachania* and *Ensenada* (ⓦwww.ensenada.net), and Rosarito has the twice-weekly *Ecos de Rosarito* (ⓦwww.ecosderosarito.com), a good source for Spanish-language updates on local property battles and public safety issues.

As you move south from the border, the papers are more concerned with issues on both sides of the Sea of Cortez and tend to downplay border issues. La Paz's *Sudcalifornia Hoy* (ⓦwww.sudcaliforniahoy.com) and *La Voz de Sudcalifornia* (ⓦwww.lavozdesudcalifornia.com) are the main voices of Baja California Sur.

The peninsula supports two twice-weekly English-language newspapers, the *Gringo Gazette* (ⓦwww.gringogazette.com), with northern and southern versions, and *Baja Times* (ⓦwww.bajatimes.com), concerned primarily with the north. The first is curmudgeonly and mainly concerned with the interests of old-school gringo property owners. The *Times* shares many of the same concerns but presents them in a light-hearted fashion. Both provide good event listings and info about new sights and lodgings for tourists.

TV and radio

Like newspapers, television reflects the trans-border culture of the region. Mexican **TV** runs US shows dubbed into Spanish alongside *telenovelas* – soap operas that dominate the screens from 6pm to 10pm and pull in audiences of millions on both sides of the border. Plot lines are like national news, while *telenovela* stars become major celebrities in both Mexico and southern California. In the northern state, people are as likely to get their news from San Diego and Yuma-based channels as they are from their Mexican counterparts.

Cable and satellite are now widespread, especially since traditional broadcast signals are such a hassle in the mountainous and remote region. Even quite downmarket hotels offer numerous channels in both English and Spanish.

If you have a short-wave **radio**, you can pick up the BBC World Service (ⓦwww.bbcworldservice.com), which is broadcast on various frequencies depending on the time of day. The main ones are 5975KHz, 6195KHz, 11,675KHz, 11,835KHz and 15,390KHz. The Voice of America (ⓦwww.voa.gov) broadcasts 24-hours on a number of frequencies including 5995KHz, 6130KHz, 7405KHz, 9455KHz, 9775KHz, 11,695KHz and 13,790KHz.

Festivals and holidays

Stumbling upon a fiesta in Baja California may prove to be the highlight of your travels. Everywhere, from the remotest village to the most sophisticated city suburb, will take at least one day off annually to devote to partying. Usually it's the local saint's day, but many fiestas have pre-Christian origins and any excuse – from harvest celebrations to the coming of the rains – will do. Baja's two states are now experiencing a series of 100–150-year anniversaries, which are routinely honoured in two-week or month-long festivals that shut down city streets in the evenings.

Traditional dances and music form an essential part of almost every **fiesta**, and most include a procession behind some revered holy image or a more celebratory secular parade with fireworks. The only rule is that no two will be quite the same. The most famous, spectacular or curious fiestas are listed below, but there are many others, and certain times of the year are party time almost everywhere.

Carnaval, the week before Lent, is celebrated throughout the Roman Catholic world, and is at its most exuberant in Latin America. It is the last week of taking one's pleasures before the forty-day abstinence of Lent, which lasts until Easter. Like Easter, its date is not fixed, but it generally falls in February or early March. Carnaval is celebrated with costumes, parades, eating and dancing, and works its way up to a climax on the last day, Mardi Gras or Fat Tuesday.

The country's biggest holiday, however, is **Semana Santa** (Holy Week) beginning on Palm Sunday and continuing until the following Sunday, Easter Day. Still a deeply religious festival in Mexico, it celebrates the resurrection of Christ, and has also become an occasion to venerate the Virgin Mary, with processions bearing her image a hallmark of the celebrations. During Semana Santa, expect transport to be totally disrupted as virtually the whole country is on the move, visiting family and returning from the big city to their village of origin: you will definitely need to plan ahead if travelling then. Many places close for the whole of Holy Week, and certainly from Thursday to Sunday.

Secular Independence Day (Sept 16) is in some ways more solemn than the religious festivals with their exuberant fervour. While Easter and Carnaval are popular festivals, this one is more official, marking the historic day in 1810 when Manuel Hidalgo issued the Grito (Cry of Independence) from his parish church in Dolores, now Dolores Hidalgo, Guanajuato, which is still the centre of commemoration. You'll also find the day marked in the capital with mass recitation of the Grito in the primary public space, followed by fireworks, music and dancing.

The **Day of the Dead** is All Saints' or All Souls' Day and its eve (Nov 1 & 2), when offerings are made to ancestors' souls, frequently with picnics and all-night vigils at their graves. People build shrines in their homes to honour their departed relatives, but it's the cemeteries to head for if you want to see the really spectacular stuff. Sweetmeats and papier-mâché statues of dressed-up skeletons give the whole proceedings a rather gothic air.

Christmas is a major holiday, and again a time when all work ceases, yearly bonuses are paid, people are on the move and transport is booked solid for weeks ahead. Gringo influence is heavy nowadays, with Santa Claus and Christmas trees, but the Mexican festival remains distinct in many ways, with a much stronger religious element (virtually every home has a nativity crib). New Year is still largely an occasion to spend with family, the actual hour being celebrated with the eating of grapes. Presents are traditionally given on Twelfth Night or Epiphany (Jan 6), which is when the three Magi of the Bible arrived bearing gifts – though things are shifting into line with Yankee custom, and more and more people are exchanging gifts on December 25.

Outdoor activities and sports

The travellers who can lay claim to being the earliest champions of the peninsula are outdoor adventurers and naturalists and with good reason. As inhospitable as Baja California can be, its vast size, never-ending coastline, diverse landscapes and rich natural resources make it a ready proving ground for any athlete or explorer. You'll find excellent opportunities for whale watching, surfing, scuba diving, deep-sea fishing, snorkelling, kayaking, golf, tennis and horseback riding – available to both the self-sufficient and those who stay within the confines of the upscale resorts. The best deals are typically available by booking ahead through one of the tour operators listed on pp.23–24.

Diving and snorkelling

The Sea of Cortez is one of the planet's premier destinations for **diving** and **snorkelling**. Its oft-tranquil waters provide an excellent introduction for novices and its more challenging dive sites include rare natural wonders that are unmatched anywhere else in the world. Along the Pacific as well there are good opportunities, particularly around Ensenada's islands and the coast near La Bufadora, but it's not until you travel south along the Sea of Cortez from the central coast to the Cape that you'll appreciate the peninsula's possibilities. Paramount among these are the marine parks in Loreto and Cabo Pulmo, which offer beguiling underwater seascapes and brightly coloured aquatic life. Local dive operators have a range of equipment and services available, including certification at a number of levels.

Whale watching

From December until late March, the Pacific coast is witness to migrating whales on their way to and from mating and spawning sites. Each year this annual journey plays an ever-increasing role in the peninsula's tourism industry and with good reason – taking a delicate *panga* boat out in a pristine bay to see a gray whale up close is a quintessential Baja experience. **Whale watchers** descend in droves to see the cetaceans in prime spots like Laguna Ojo de Liebre and Bahía Magdalena.

Surfing

The northwest Pacific coast, the Eastern Cape and the beaches near Todos Santos are becoming something of a centre for **surfing**. They have absolutely no facilities to cater to the casual boarder – a surfer's must-haves include a four-wheel drive vehicle, rope for rappelling, first-aid kit, all provisions and anything else you need to surf in the middle of nowhere – but plenty of Californian surfers follow the weather south here over the winter. The state's tourism offices publish leaflets on participatory sports, and can also advise on such things as licences and seasons.

Kayaking

The Sea of Cortez is one of the easiest places to learn how to **sea kayak**, and it also provides more seasoned paddlers with the chance to travel long distances with relatively few impediments. Bahía de los Ángeles is the northernmost spot that has consistently good conditions, but the better sites begin near Mulegé's estuary and continue another 400 kilometres or so to the Cape. The Pacific is too rough in many places to kayak, but you're protected from the waves in Bahía Magdalena in the south and Laguna San Ignacio in the middle – just look out for whales.

Outdoor tour specialists arrange week-long excursions between Mulegé and Loreto and La Paz and the eastern cape, as well as bike-kayak trips from La Paz to Bahía Magdalena.

Sport fishing

Sport fishing has always been hugely popular in the north near Ensenada and around La Paz and Los Cabos; the rich Sea of Cortez housing the "world's aquarium" as Jacques Coustou dubbed it in the 1960s. In the days before the Transpeninsular Highway, legendary US tough guys Ernest Hemingway, John Wayne and Bing Crosby would fly down for a week of relaxation and the closest man could get to actually shooting fish in a barrel. In the last two decades the federal government has placed more restrictions on the hook-based pastime, but it's done little to dampen the enthusiasm or the bookings. You can see how strong the market is, as well as how down-market it has travelled, by counting how many times you're harassed by boat owners while taking a simple walk alongside Los Cabos' marina.

Hiking

Hiking to and from cave paintings and dilapidated religious ruins is the easiest option: with less gear to haul or rent, planning can be your sole focus, which it better be if you're going to survive out there. In recent years, companies have developed maps for GPS navigation devices that some hikers (and cyclists) find useful. If you're unfamiliar with an area you should at least get preliminary trail information from a local guide, if not hire one outright. There are more guides around the national parks in the north, the majority of them based in Ensenada and San Felipe.

Cycling

Both **mountain biking** and **road cycling** are popular in the northwest – the former around the parks and wine country, the latter along the toll road coastal route. As you move further south, it's absolutely essential to have all your repair equipment with you; finding parts is difficult. Even more essential is a supply of water and food that will last you between towns. Cyclists traversing the Transpeninsular Highway between El Rosario and Santa Rosalía should have shelters and cooking equipment. Between Ensenada and Cataviña the roads are especially narrow and curvy, leaving little room for traffic in both lanes, not to mention cyclists. As well, cyclists are somewhat of a rare sight throughout much of the peninsula, and drivers tend not to anticipate their presence.

Golf

A round of golf on one of the courses lining the corridor of Los Cabos will likely be among the best a person has ever played – as well as one of the most expensive, with green fees starting around US$160. The Cape has a wealth of greens designed by the likes of heavy-hitters such as Tom Weiskopf, Jack Nicklaus and Robert Trent Jones II. To enjoy the most exclusive ones, like Palmilla, Querencia or El Dorado, you'll need to stay at a specific resort or, in the case of the latter, be a member or guest of a member.

The rest of the peninsula is rather free of greens and bunkers. Loreto has an 18-hole course along the Sea of Cortez and there are three courses in the northwest, all within a 45-minute drive of Tijuana. Prices here are a fraction of Los Cabos but the courses are not nearly as challenging.

Spectator sports

Mexico's chief spectator sport is **soccer** (*fútbol*), but in Baja California watching it is restricted to the TV. **Baseball** (*béisbol*) is the dominant sport, drawing crowds to major and minor league matches in the north and to secondary school games throughout the rest of the peninsula. The peninsula's best team is Mexicali's Águilas, as well as its youth league, which produced 2005's little league national champions.

Mexican **rodeos** (*charreadas*), mainly seen around Tijuana, Mexicali and the northwest, are as spectacular for their style and costume as they are for the events. Bullfights are an obsession in the north, primarily in Tijuana – which has two bullrings – and Mexicali. When the rings aren't being used for *mano-a-cow* matches, they're used for light and middleweight boxing matches that are typically the last step to big debuts in a Las Vegas or Atlantic City venue.

Another popular bloodsport, usually at village level, is cockfighting, still legal in Mexico and mainly attended for the opportunity to bet on the outcome. Squeamish tourists who like the sound of saying they went to a bull- or cockfight can attend 'bloodless' ones in a Los Cabos stadium that conveniently uses English as the *lingua franca*.

Masked wrestling (*lucha libre*) is very popular in Mexico, too, with the participants, Batman-like, out of the game for good should their mask be removed and their secret identity revealed. Nor does the resemblance to comic-book superheroes end in the ring: certain masked wrestlers have become popular social campaigners out of the ring, always ready to turn up just in the nick of time to rescue the beleaguered poor from eviction by avaricious landlords, or persecution by corrupt politicians. For more on wrestling, see p.105.

Shopping

Outside of the northwest and around La Paz, shopping on the peninsula mainly amounts to bargain hunting. Baja California has a strong tradition of craftsmanship, but it is not rich with the indigenous-inspired arts that are so prominent in other parts of Mexico.

Southern Californians descend upon Tijuana, Rosarito and Ensenada to buy up leather goods along with duty-free handmade furniture and ceramic tiles for a third to a half of what they'd pay in the US; and they're increasingly coming to Ensenada to buy wine (and regularly skirt the 1L limit on imports). The most popular purchase by far is **prescription drugs**: pharmacies are as prominent as craft stores along the shopping streets of Tijuana. US pharmaceutical companies frown upon these purchases, but when done at a reputable pharmacy and with a prescription they are completely legitimate within certain limits (see box, p.85). Crafts from other parts of Mexico – like Michoacán, Oaxaca, Chiapas and the Yucatán – are available in most markets and storefronts in Ensenada hawk Taxco-wrought silver.

FONART shops, which you'll come across in major centres throughout the peninsula, are run by a government agency devoted to the promotion and preservation of crafts – their wares are always excellent, if expensive, and the shops should be visited to get an idea of what is potentially available. Where no such store exists, you can get a similar idea by looking at the best of the tourist shops.

It is illegal to buy or sell antiquities, and even more criminal to try taking them out of the country (moreover, many items sold as valuable antiquities are little more than worthless fakes) – best to just look.

For bargain hunters, the **mercado** (market) is the place to head. In Tijuana, Rosarito, Guerrero Negro, Ciudad Constitución and La Paz the markets are open every day; in others, you'll find them only one or two days out of the week. By and large, mercados are mainly dedicated to food and everyday necessities, but most have a section devoted to crafts, and in larger towns you may find a separate crafts bazaar.

Bargaining and haggling are very much a matter of personal style, highly dependent on your command of Spanish, aggressiveness and, to some extent, on experience. The old tricks (never show the least sign of interest, let alone enthusiasm; walking away will always cut the price dramatically) do still hold true; but most important is to know what you want, its approximate value, and how much you are prepared to pay. Never start to haggle for something you definitely don't intend to buy – it'll end in bad feelings on both sides. In shops there's little chance of significantly altering the official price unless you're buying in bulk, and even in markets most food and simple household goods have a set price.

Unless you're completely hopeless at bargaining, prices will always be lower in the market than in shops, but shops do have a couple of advantages. First, they exercise a degree of quality control, whereas any old junk can be sold in the market; and second, many established shops will be able to ship purchases home for you, which saves an enormous amount of the frustrating bureaucracy you'll encounter if you attempt to do it yourself. On the other hand, shipping can be prohibitively expensive and on large objects can easily cost more than the value of the purchase.

Travel essentials

Costs

Accommodation is likely to be your biggest single expense in Baja California, and it will typically be more expensive than other parts of Mexico. Few hotel, motel or B&B rooms cost under M$300 a night; you're likely to pay more than M$550 for anything halfway decent in a major town. Owing to few competitors and the scarcity of resources, rates in rural areas are not much cheaper. In the Cape, it may well be difficult to find a double for less than M$800 a night (see box, below). There are no officially recognized Hostelling International hostels in Baja California, but there are numerous RV campgrounds that have either sheltered campsites or small huts available for M$150 or less a night.

As for **food**, M$120 a day on a diet of tacos and self-catered items from the grocery stores is possible, while for around M$180 a day you'll be able to afford *huevos*

rancheros for breakfast, a *torta* or two tacos for lunch and a margarita-accompanied dinner at a basic, Spanish-language only restaurant or café.

The rates for **getting around** Baja California, especially on buses, are inexpensive considering the quality of service; the trip from Tijuana to Los Cabos is about M$1000. If you plan to drive your own car or rent one, figure on paying around M$6 per litre of petrol (see p.26) and budgeting around M$185 a day for the cost of Mexican car insurance. Car rental (see "Getting around," p.25) will save you the exorbitant cost of **taxis** in the Cape area but excessive fees for tyre and windshield repair may keep you from exploring the more enticing dirt roads.

Although the entire peninsula is a duty-free zone, a **sales tax** of twelve percent is added to virtually everything you buy in stores and will not be included as part of the marked price. There are also separate tax laws for **wine** (25 percent) and a mandatory 15

Los Cabos costs

In **Los Cabos** you can easily drop more on dinner than you ever would on a lesser meal in Tokyo, Los Angeles or London – meals at gourmet restaurants easily run to M$1200 per person (the mark-up on wine alone is especially exorbitant). Scarcity of resources was once the reason for the area's **high costs**, but prices here are far higher than the simple rules of supply and demand warrant. If you pre-book a hotel, eat at sand-floor restaurants and avoid the usurious taxis, you can get by on M$1500 a day; staying and eating at a nice resort along the corridor can easily run you M$5000 a day – before the bar tab (read more about the Cape in Chapter 7, p.240).

percent **gratuity** at some high-end hotels in Los Cabos.

Crime and personal safety

Despite popular tales of corrupt cops and *bandidos* preying on tourists, you are unlikely to run into trouble in Baja California unless you engage in illegal or reckless behaviour. The peninsula is predominantly rural and shares similar natural dangers and pleasantly carefree habits with rural places the world over.

In Tijuana, Rosarito and Los Cabos **petty theft** and **pickpockets** are your biggest worry; don't wave money around, try not to look too obviously affluent, don't leave cash or cameras in hotel rooms and be sure to deposit your valuables in your hotel's safe if it has one (make a note of what you've deposited and ask the hotelier to sign it if you're worried). Crowds, especially on public city transport, are obvious hot spots: thieves tend to work in groups and target tourists. Distracting your attention, especially by pretending to look for something (always be suspicious of anyone who appears to be searching for something near you), or having one or two people pin you while another goes through your pockets, are common ploys, and can be done faster and more easily than you might imagine.

When using ATM machines, use those in shopping malls or enclosed premises, and only in daylight when there are plenty of people around. In **Tijuana**'s *La Revo* and *Zona Norte* neighborhoods robbery and sexual assault on tourists by cab drivers are enough of a problem to warrant warnings by the US State Department. At night the beaches at Rosarito and Playas Tijuana are also potentially dangerous.

Drugs, while widely available in Tijuana and Rosarito, are never a casual matter; if you buy or use drugs here you have a very real chance of living out (or dying) a horror that even the most patronizing TV special or government-sponsored message would think too melodramatic to promote. In Tijuana dealers settle scores with vats of acid and paramilitary hit squads staffed by turncoats from US-trained anti-drug squads.

Drivers are likely to encounter problems if they leave anything visible in their car on a public street; the vehicle itself is less likely to be stolen than broken into for the valuables inside. To avoid the worst, always park legally and either take your valuables with you or store them out of sight.

Disabled travellers

Baja California is not well equipped for **people with disabilities**. At the top end of the market, though, it shouldn't be too difficult to find accommodation and tour operators who can cater for your particular needs. It is essential, however, to check beforehand with tour companies, hotels and airlines that they can accommodate you specifically. Then repeat, making sure not to leave out any question too obvious.

If you stick to up-market tourist hotels, you should certainly be able to find places that are wheelchair-friendly and used to having disabled guests. US chains are very good for this, with Choice, Days Inn, Holiday Inn, Leading Hotels of the World, Marriott, Radisson, Ramada, Sheraton and Westin claiming to have the necessary facilities for at least some disabilities in most of their hotels. Always check in advance, however, that the hotel of your choice can cater for your particular needs. If you have a **service animal** you may encounter problems at small hotels and restaurants, as they are treated as any other animal may be.

You'll find that your **own car** is the best way to get around. Baja California airports use stairs rather than ramps for embarking and disembarking and staff are often clumsy and untrained with their help. Buses rarely cater for disabled people, and certainly not for wheelchairs. When travelling on a lower budget or getting off the beaten track you'll find few facilities. Ramps are few and far between and when they are present they are hopelessly steep and generally pointless. Pavement, in general, is not in a good state.

Electricity

Mexico **electricity** operates on the same voltage as the US and Canada: 110v/60c. Cell phones, laptops and chargers for digital cameras from these countries will work fine without an adapter; as anywhere, though, a surge protector is recommended for items of great value. Outlets in kitchens and bathrooms are typically three-pronged and two-pronged everywhere else. UK and European electronics that run on 220v and Australian devices on 240v will need a two-prong adaptor and converter to operate in Mexico.

Entry requirements

Citizens of the EU, US, Canada, Australia and New Zealand can enter Mexico with just a **passport** and may stay in the country for up to sixty days. South African visitors must fill out a visa application and apply in person at an embassy or consulate.

Most visitors must obtain a **tourist card** for US$20, which is included in your ticket if arriving by air. **US visitors** accustomed to travelling to Mexico with only their birth certificate or driver's licence must obtain a US passport in order to return to the US by air or sea after December 31, 2006; crossings at land borders will require passports one year later. English-language details about non-tourist travel and other types of visas are available at the New York City Mexican Consulate's website ⓦ www.consulmexny .org/eng/visas_fmt.htm.

Mexican embassies and consulates abroad

Australia

Brisbane 9 Broadmoor Street, Kenmore Hills, Qld ⓣ 07/3374 3969, ⓕ 3374-0366
Canberra 14 Perth Ave, Yarralumla, ACT 2600 ⓣ 02/6273 3963, ⓕ 6273 1190
Darwin 3163/1 Export Drive, Darwin Business Park, East Arm, NT ⓣ 08/8947 0588, ⓕ 8947 0769
Melbourne 1038A Dandenong Road, Carnegie, Vic ⓣ 03/9571 1866, ⓕ 9563 6220
National embassy website: ⓦ www.embassyof mexicoinaustralia.org

Canada

Montréal 2055 rue Peel, Bur 1000, QC H3A 1V4 ⓣ 514/288-2502, ⓦ www.consulmex.qc.ca
Ottawa 45 O'Connor, Ste 1000, ON K1P 1A4 ⓣ 613/233-8988, ⓕ 235-9123
Toronto 99 Bay St, Ste 4440, ON M5L 1E9 ⓣ 416/368-2875, ⓦ www.consulmex.com
Vancouver 710-1177 W Hastings St, BC V6E 2K3, ⓣ 604/684-3547, ⓦ www.consulmexvan.com

National embassy website: ⓦ www .embamexcan.com

Ireland

Dublin 43 Ailesbury Rd, Ballsbridge, 4 ⓣ 01/260 0699, ⓦ www.sre.gob.mx/irlanda

New Zealand

Wellington 111-115 Customhouse Quay, Piso 8, ⓣ 04/472-0555, ⓔ mexico@xtra.co.nz

South Africa

Pretoria 3rd Fl, One Hatfield Square, 1101 Burnett Street, Hatfield, 0001, 12/362-2822, ⓕ 12/362-1380, ⓔ embamexza@mweb.co.za

UK

London 16 St George St, Hanover Sq, W1S 1LX, ⓣ 020/7499 8586, ⓕ 020/7495 4035
National consulate website: ⓦ www .mexicanconsulate.org.uk
National embassy website: ⓦ www.embamex .co.uk

United States

Washington, DC 1911 Pennsylvania Ave NW 20006, ⓣ 202/728-1600, ⓕ 202/728-1698
There are forty-six Mexican consulates throughout the US; a complete list is available at the embassy website below by clicking "Consular Services".
National embassy website: ⓦ www .embassyofmexico.org/

Embassies and consulates in Baja California

Canada Av German Gedovius 10411, Zona Río, Tijuana ⓣ 664/684-0461
UK Blvd Salinas 11150, Fracc Aviación, Tijuana ⓣ 664/681-5320
United States Tapachula 96, Col Hipódromo, Tijuana ⓣ 664/622-7400; State Department Emergency Center ⓣ US202/647-5225; Blvd Marina Local C-4, Plaza Nautica, Cabo San Lucas ⓣ 624/143-3566, ⓕ 624/143-6750

Tourist cards

A **tourist card** isn't necessary if you stay within the border–San Felipe–Ensenada rectangle for 72 hours or less. Every other visitor needs a tourist card (or **FMT**–folleto de migración turística). You can get tourist cards at all border crossings by pulling over into the "to declare" lane and telling the officer you need an FMT. Airline and cruise-ship travel will include the cost of the FMT in the price of the ticket. If you're entering by land your card is good for up to six months.

Don't lose the tourist card stub that is given back to you after immigration inspection. You are legally required to carry it at all times, and if you have to show your papers, it's more important than your passport. If you are flying or travelling by ship it must be handed in on leaving the country.

Should you lose your tourist card, or need to have it renewed, head for the nearest immigration department office (Departamento de Migración); there are downtown branches in the biggest cities. In the case of renewal, it's far simpler to cross the border for a day and get a new one on re-entry than to apply for an extension; if you do apply to the immigration department, it's wise to do so a couple of weeks in advance, though you may be told to come back nearer the actual expiry date. Whatever else you may be told, branches of SECTUR (the tourist office) cannot renew expired tourist cards or replace lost ones – they will only make sympathetic noises and direct you to the nearest immigration office.

Gay and lesbian travellers

In the right places, Baja California can be a very enjoyable destination for **gay and lesbian travellers**. The region, especially the smaller, high-end resorts around Los Cabos, possesses some firm favourites on the gay North American travel circuit, and gay-friendly accommodation can also be found in La Paz, Loreto and the northwest coast. However, elsewhere – particularly in rural areas – you will find conservative attitudes toward gay couples are very much the norm. Though the more exclusive resorts of Los Cabos readily cater to southern California's gay community, even there romantic behaviour between same-sex partners is looked down upon by both locals and other tourists in public places like Médano Beach or San Jose del Cabo's central square. Be cautious, then, with open displays of affection.

Health

No inoculations are required for Baja California and most travellers get by without any problems. When they do have trouble, it's typically not much more serious than a dose of Montezuma's Revenge (caused by the bacteria in Mexican food, which are different from those found in other Western diets). Drink plenty of fluids (bottled water is widely available) and get enough sleep and rest, as it's easy to become run-down if you're on the move a lot, especially in a hot climate.

The lack of **sanitation** in Mexico is exaggerated, and it's not worth being obsessive about it or you'll never enjoy yourself. Even so, a degree of caution is wise – don't try anything too exotic in the first few days before your body has had a chance to adjust to local microbes, and never eat food that looks like it has been on display for a while or not freshly cooked.

For comprehensive coverage of the health problems encountered by travellers worldwide, consult the *Rough Guide to Travel Health* by Dr Nick Jones.

If you have severe **diarrhoea**, and whenever young children have it, add oral rehydration salts – *suero oral* (brand names: Dioralyte, Electrosol, Rehidrat). If you can't get these, dissolve half a teaspoon of salt and three of sugar in a litre of water. Avoid greasy food, heavy spices, caffeine and most fruit and dairy products; some say bananas, papayas, guavas and prickly pears (*tunas*) are a help, while plain yogurt or a broth made from yeast extract (such as Marmite or Vegemite, if you happen to have some with you) can be easily absorbed by your body when you have diarrhoea. Drugs like Lomotil or Imodium plug you up – and thus undermine the body's efforts to rid itself of infection – but they can be a temporary stop-gap if you have to travel. If symptoms persist for more than three days, or if you have a fever or blood in your stool, seek medical advice.

Medical resources for travellers

US and Canada

CDC ⓦwww.cdc.gov/travel. Official US government travel health site.
International Society for Travel Medicine ⓦwww.istm.org. Has a full list of travel health clinics.
Canadian Society for International Health ⓦwww.csih.org. Extensive list of travel health centres.

What about the water?

In a hot climate and at high altitudes, it's essential to increase **water** intake to prevent dehydration. Most travellers, and most Mexicans if they can, stay off the tap water, although a lot of the time it is in fact drinkable, and in practice impossible to avoid completely: ice made with it, unasked for, may appear in drinks, utensils are washed in it, and so on.

Most restaurants and *licuaderías* use **purified water** (*agua purificada*), but always check; most hotels have a supply and will often provide bottles of water in your room. Bottled water (generally purified with ozone or ultraviolet) is widely available, but stick with known brands, and always check that the seal on the bottle is intact since refilling empties with tap water for resale is common (carbonated water is generally a safer bet in that respect).

There are various methods of **treating water** while you are travelling, whether your source is from a tap or a river or stream. Boiling it for a minimum of five minutes is the time-honoured method, but it is not always practical, will not remove unpleasant tastes, and is a lot less effective at higher altitudes – including much of central Mexico, where you have to boil it for much longer.

Chemical sterilization, using either chlorine or iodine tablets or a tincture of iodine liquid, is more convenient, but leaves a nasty aftertaste (which can to some extent be masked with lemon or lime juice). Chlorine kills bacteria but, unlike iodine, is not effective against amoebic dysentery and giardiasis. Pregnant women or people with thyroid problems should consult their doctor before using iodine sterilizing tablets or iodine-based purifiers. Too many iodine tablets can cause gastrointestinal discomfort themselves. Inexpensive iodine removal filters are available and are recommended if treated water is being used continuously for more than a month or is being given to babies.

Purification, involving both filtration and sterilization, gives the most complete treatment. Portable water purifiers range in size from units weighing as little as 60g, which can be slipped into a pocket, up to 800g for carrying in a backpack. For those planning to spend time in remote areas where clean water is not available, some of the best water purifiers on the market are made in Britain by Pre-Mac. For suppliers worldwide contact Pre-Mac International Ltd, Unit 5, Morewood Close, Sevenoaks, Kent TN13 2HU ☎01732/460333, ⊛www.pre-mac.com.

Australia, New Zealand and South Africa

Travellers' medical and Vaccination Centre ⊛www.tmvc.com.au, ☎1300/658 844. Lists travel clinics in Australia, New Zealand and South Africa.

UK and Ireland

British Airways Travel Clinics ☎012776/685-040 or ⊛www.britishairways.com/travel/healthclinintro/public/en_gb for nearest clinic.
Hospital for Tropical Diseases Travel Clinic ☎020/7387-5000 or ☎0845/155-5000, ⊛www.thehtd.org.
MASTA (Medical Advisory Service for Travellers Abroad) ⊛www.masta.org or ☎0113/238-7575 for the nearest clinic.
Travel Medicine Services ☎028/9031 5220.
Tropical Medical Bureau ☎1850/487 674, ⊛www.tmb.ie.

Insurance

Getting health **insurance** in advance of a trip to Baja California is highly recommended. Even though hospitals on the peninsula are more highly regarded than those in any other Mexican state, there aren't many of them between the northern border towns and La Paz, and Medavac transport is pricey. A typical travel insurance policy usually provides cover for the loss of baggage, tickets, and – up to a certain limit – cash or cheques, as well as cancellation or curtailment of your journey. Most policies exclude so-called **high-risk activities**, such as mountain biking, surfing and rockclimbing, unless an extra premium is paid; be sure to check on this before you buy. If you do take medical cover, ascertain whether benefits will be paid as treatment proceeds or only after you return home, and whether there is a 24hr medical emergency number.

Rough Guides has teamed up with Columbus Direct to offer you **travel insurance** that can be tailored to suit your needs. Products include a low-cost **backpacker** option for long stays; a **short break** option for city getaways; a typical **holiday package** option; and others. There are also annual **multi-trip** policies for those who travel regularly. Different sports and activities (trekking, skiing, etc) can be usually be covered if required.

See our website (ⓦwww.roughguides insurance.com) for eligibility and purchasing options. Alternatively, UK residents should call ☎0870/033-9988; US citizens should call ☎1-800/749-4922; Australians should call ☎1-300/669 999. All other nationalities should call ☎+44 870/890 2843.

The Internet

The Internet is booming in Baja California, and Internet cafés are easy to find in most cities and towns. Depending on where you are, Internet access can cost anything from M$5 to M$20 an hour. Los Cabos cafés are most expensive (around M$70 an hour) but the city also has a handful of coffee shops that have WiFi connections for the price of a cup of coffee. Internet businesses are typically open from 10am until 10pm.

Hotels were slow to wire their buildings for high-speed LAN bandwagon, leaving past travellers to contend with dial-up ports and access numbers. Hotels, motels and B&Bs are now more likely to have WiFi capability that you can use with your own laptop either for a fee (typically M$120 a day) or for free. When booking a hotel that advertises WiFi, ask if all rooms have it or if it's only accessible in public spaces or in newer rooms. Most hotels have a desktop terminal in the lobby that guests can use for free to check email or surf the web for limited periods of time.

Living in Baja California

Living in Baja California without income earned in Mexico is something plenty of foreigners on the northwest coast and in San Felipe and Los Cabos do quite easily. Anyone who signs a contract to lease a parcel of land, rent a house on a long-term

basis, or purchase property needs an FM-3 Visa. This is renewable every year for five years. The requirements aren't too stringent: proof of income of US$1000 per person or $1500 per couple, a letter saying you'd like to be a resident, a utility bill in Mexico, a copy of your tourist card, photos, some application forms and fees of M$1055 per person. If you're going to reside in Mexico full-time, you don't do anything different except check the box for FM-2 (permanent resident) instead of FM-3 (temporary).

There's virtually no chance of finding **temporary work** in Mexico unless you have some very specialized skill and have arranged the position beforehand; work permits are almost impossible to get hold of. The few foreigners who manage to find work on their own do so mostly in language schools or in businesses that cater to gringo ex-pats, like real estate. It may be possible, though not legal, to earn money as a private English tutor by simply advertising in a local newspaper or on notice boards at a university.

Study and work programmes

The best way to extend your time in Mexico is on a study programme or volunteer project. **AFS Intercultural Programs** is a global UN-recognized organization that runs summer programmes to foster international understanding. For further information, call (US) ☎1-800/AFS-INFO, (Canada) ☎1-800/361-7248 or 514/288-3282, (UK) ☎0113/242 6136, (Australia) ☎1300/131736 or ☎02/9215-0077, (NZ) ☎0800/600 300 or 04/494 6020, international enquiries ☎+1-212/807-8686, ⓦwww.afs.org.

From the US and Canada

American Institute for Foreign Study ☎1-866/906-2437, ⓦwww.aifs.com. Language study and cultural immersion, as well as au pair and Camp America programs.
AmeriSpan ☎1-800/879-6640 or 215/751-1100, ⓦwww.amerispan.com. Selects language schools throughout Latin America, including Mexico, to match the needs and requirements of students, and provides advice and support.
BUNAC USA (British Universities North America Club) ☎1-800/GO-BUNAC, ⓦwww.bunac.org. Offers students the chance to work in Australia, New Zealand, Ireland or Britain.

Council on International Educational Exchange (CIEE) ☏ 1-800/40-STUDY or ☏ 1/207-533-7600, ⓦ www.ciee.org. Leading NGO offering study programs and volunteer projects around the world.

Earthwatch Institute ☏ 1-800/776-0188 or 978/461-0081, ⓦ www.earthwatch.org. International non-profit that does research projects in over 50 countries all over the world.

From the UK and Ireland

BTCV (British Trust for Conservation Volunteers) ☏ 01302/572 244, ⓦ www.btcv.org.uk. One of the largest environmental charities in Britain, with a programme of national and international working holidays (as a paying volunteer).

BUNAC (British Universities North America Club) ☏ 020/7251 3472, ⓦ www.bunac.co.uk. Organizes working holidays in the US and other destinations for students.

Camp America Camp America ☏ 020/7581 7373, ⓦ www.campamerica.co.uk.

Council Exchange ☏ 020/8939-9057, ⓦ www .councilexchanges.org.uk. International study and work programmes for students and recent graduates.

Earthwatch Institute ☏ 01865/318 838, ⓦ www .uk.earthwatch.org. Long-established international charity with environmental and archeological research projects worldwide.

Mail

Mexican postal services (*correos*) are reasonably efficient. Airmail to Tijuana, La Paz and San Jose del Cabo should arrive within a few days, but it may take a couple of weeks to get anywhere else. **Post offices** (generally Mon–Fri 9am–3pm, Sat 9am–1pm) usually offer a poste restante/general delivery service: letters should be addressed to Lista de Correos at the Correo Central (main post office) of any town; all mail that arrives for the Lista is put on a list updated daily and displayed in the post office, but is held for only two weeks. You may get around that by sending it to "Poste Restante" instead of "Lista de Correos" and having letter-writers put "Favor de retener hasta la llegada" (please hold until arrival) on the envelope; letters addressed thus will not appear on the Lista. Use only two names on the envelope and capitalize and underline your surname to prevent incorrect filing. To collect, you need your passport or some other official ID with a photograph. There is no fee.

American Express (ⓦ www.americanexpress .com/travel) also operates an efficient mail collection service, but they only offer services in Ensenada, La Paz, San Jose del Cabo and Tijuana. If you don't carry their card or cheques, you have to pay a fee to collect your mail, although they don't always ask.

Mailing letters out of Baja California is easy enough, if slow. Anything sent abroad by air should have an airmail (*por avión*) stamp on it or it is liable to go surface. Letters should take around a week to North America, two to Europe or Australasia, but can take much longer (postcards in particular are likely to be slow). Anything at all important should be taken to the post office and preferably registered rather than dropped in a mailbox.

Sending packages out of the country is drowned in bureaucracy and expensive. Regulations about the thickness of brown paper wrapping and the amount of string used can occupy hours, but most importantly, any package must be checked by customs. Take your package (unsealed) to any post office and they'll set you on your way. Stores will send your purchases home for you but will charge you heftily for their inconvenience (and will usually recommend you take your item on the plane instead).

In the peninsula's major cities you also have the option of using DHL, UPS and Federal Express for shipping. Visits to their offices are less fraught with waiting and paperwork but you will pay slightly more for the convenience. You will, however, have greater assurance that your package will arrive.

Maps

A good, Baja-centric **map** is essential for any Transpeninsular journey. General Mexico maps do not have enough detail to help you on the road, and are often too out of date to provide you with the most useful information. One of the best options is the rip- and water-proof *The Rough Guide to Baja California Map* (1:650,000). Produced in conjunction with the World Mapping Project, the map clearly displays the peninsula's roads, contours and physical features.

Baja Almanac out of Las Vegas, NV publishes detailed topographic maps in two versions: a fold-out one (US$5.95) and a 200+ page almanac (US$24.95) with detailed information on even the most remote areas. Esparza Editores has a fold-out of the entire peninsula (US$9.95; 1:800,000), as well as city maps of Ensenada, La Paz and Los Cabos. They're available widely at Sanborn's department stores and bookshops in Mexico. Local, free maps are available at tourism offices. They're exclusively devoted to local businesses and do not provide helpful information outside of the tourist areas.

More detailed, large-scale maps – for hiking or climbing – are harder to come by. The most detailed, easily available area maps are produced by International Travel Map Productions, whose 1:1,000,000 Travellers' Reference Map series includes Baja California. INEGI, the Mexican government mapmakers, also produce very good topographic maps on various scales. They have offices in Mexicali and La Paz, but unfortunately stocks can run rather low, so don't count on being able to purchase the ones that you want.

Money

Mexico's unit of **currency** is the peso, or *moneda nacional*, denoted in listings at businesses as N$; for clarity in this guide any amount in pesos will be preceded by M$. At the time of writing the exchange rate was around M$19 to the pound sterling, M$13 to the euro and M$10 to the US dollar.

Mexican currency comes in **bills** of M$20, M$50, M$100, M$200, M$500 and M$1,000. The smaller currency is physically smaller and each denomination is a different colour. Peso coins begin with M$10 and include M$5 and M$1.

Cash and an **ATM** or **debit card** are the best way to carry and obtain money while in Baja California, for both American and foreign visitors. US dollars are used throughout the peninsula and are the preferred currency in Los Cabos and the border–Ensenada–San Felipe rectangle. For simplicity's sake, and to avoid nasty looks from cashiers, don't carry denominations higher than US$20 bills. When you're travelling between Ensenada and La Paz it's essential to have at least M$2,000 on you to cover the cost of gas and hotels – no Pemex takes credit and large towns are hundreds of miles apart.

Any ATM or debit card issued in the US should work in all *cajero permanentes* (**ATMs**); travellers from elsewhere should make sure their card is part of the Cirrus or Plus network. ATMs from multiple branches can be found in Tijuana, Tecate, Mexicali, San Felipe, Ensenada, San Quintín, Guerrero Negro, Loreto, Ciudad Insurgentes, La Paz, Todos Santos and the Los Cabos area. Many are open 24 hours. The ATMs charge a fee of M$5–10, in addition to any fee your own bank may add.

It's a good idea to carry a **credit card** or two in case of emergency; MasterCard and Visa are accepted more places than American Express, but all are accepted at most restaurants, large stores and hotels.

If you'd rather not carry around a lot of cash, you might want to supplement your dollars with **travellers' cheques**, which offer the security of knowing that lost or stolen checks will be replaced. In theory travellers' cheques can be used the same as cash in virtually all shops, restaurants and hotels, but central Baja towns without banks are very **reluctant** to accept them because of the difficulty of cashing them (which typically involves travel on their part or mailing the checks to a relative in another city). Most businesses and banks will not levy fees to cash a travellers' cheque but those in the middle of nowhere may, just to offset the inconvenience.

Banks and exchange

Banks are generally open from 9am until 5pm Monday to Thursday, and 9am to 6pm on Friday, sometimes with a break around 1pm in the smaller towns. **Foreign wire transfers** must transpire before 1pm, which means lining up before noon to ensure success. ATMs are usually accessible 24 hours a day. Most major banks change foreign travellers' checks and currency as well. **Exchange bureaus**, found at airports, tend to charge less commission than banks: Thomas Cook and American Express are the biggest names.

Public holidays

The main **public holidays**, when virtually everything will be closed, are listed below. In addition, many places close on January 6 (Twelfth Night/Reyes).

Jan 1 New Year's Day
Feb 5 Anniversary of the Constitution
Mar 21 Benito Juárez Day
Late March/April (varies) Good Friday
May 1 Labor Day
May 5 Battle of Puebla
Sept 1 Presidential address to the nation
Sept 16 Independence Day
Oct 12 Día de la Raza/Columbus Day
Nov 1 & 2 All Saints/Day of the Dead
Nov 20 Anniversary of the Revolution
Dec 12 Virgin of Guadalupe
Dec 24–26 Christmas

Opening hours and public holidays

The **siesta**, though, is still around, and many places will close for a couple of hours in the early afternoon, usually from 1pm to 3pm or 2pm to 4pm. The strictness of this is very much dependent on the climate and time of year; where it's hot – especially on the Sea of Cortez side south from Santa Rosalía – everything may close for up to four hours in the middle of the day, and then reopen until 8pm or 9pm.

Museums and galleries tend to open from about 9am or 10am to 5pm or 6pm. Many have reduced entry fees – or are free – on Sunday, and most are closed on Monday. Some museums may close for lunch, but archeological sites are open right through the day

Phones

Local phone calls in Baja California are cheap, and some hotels outside of Los Cabos will let you call locally for free. Coin-operated public phones, rapidly disappearing, also charge very little for local calls. In the north they accept US quarters. Many newer public phones accept credit cards, but these are loosely regulated and should be avoided unless there are no other options available. Internal and external long-distance calls are best made with a Ladatel phonecard at a Telmex phone booth. These are available from telephone offices and bodegas near phones that use them (especially in bus and train stations, airports and major resorts). Card calls run M$5 per minute to the US or Canada, M$20 to the British Isles or Europe, M$25 to Australia or New Zealand.

The cheapest way to make an international call is via the Internet, a service available at most of the peninsula's Internet cafes. This can cost as little as M$0.1 a minute to anywhere in the world. If you're travelling with your own laptop an even cheaper option is to open a VOIP account with a provider such as Skype. Calls using VOIP can sometimes be free and will always be cheaper than any other method. You'll find that many hoteliers offer Internet access as part of the room charge and that a number of restaurants, cafés and bars will allow you to log on for the price of a cup of coffee or no more than M$10 per hour.

More expensive are *casetas de teléfono*, phone offices where someone will make the connection for you. These are well-marked by blue and white signs at the entry to settlements in the central portion of the peninsula. Some are simply shops or bars with public phones, indicated by a phone sign outside, in which you may only be allowed to make local calls. Specialist phone and fax places display a blue-and-white *Larga Distancia* (long-distance) sign. You're connected by an operator who presents you with a bill afterwards – once connected, the cost can usually be seen clicking up on a meter.

Dialing codes

To call collect or person-to-person, dial ☎92 for interstate calls within Mexico, ☎96 for the US and Canada, ☎99 for the rest of the world.

Calling from long-distance public phones
Mexico interstate ☎01 + area code + number
US and Canada ☎001 + area code + number
UK ☎00 44 + area code (minus initial zero) + number
Ireland ☎00 353 + area code (minus initial zero) + number
Australia ☎00 61 + area code (minus initial zero) + number
New Zealand ☎00 64 + area code (minus initial zero) + number
South Africa ☎00 27 + area code (minus initial zero) + number

Calling Mexico from abroad
From US and Canada ☎011 52 + area code + number
From UK, Ireland and New Zealand ☎00 52 + area code + number
From Australia ☎0011 52 + area code + number
From South Africa ☎090 52 + area code + number

If you want to use your **mobile phone** in Mexico, you'll need to check with your phone provider whether it will work there and how the calls are charged. Most plans require international activation prior to departure. There are two GSM providers in Baja California, Telcel and Movistar, and both have roaming agreements with most foreign providers. You'll find consistent coverage on the northwest coast between the border and El Rosario, and throughout the north including Mexicali and San Felipe. Unfortunately there is no coverage in the Desierto Central or much of the south until you get to Ciudad Constitución.

Senior travellers

Baja California, like the rest of Mexico, is not an area that offers any special difficulties to **senior travellers**. In fact, as the cost of real estate and health care has increased in the US, the peninsula has become a destination for older travellers on extended stays as well as retirees looking for a second home. In some communities along the Sea of Cortez – San Felipe foremost amongst these – senior travellers outnumber all other visitors.

But the same considerations apply here as to anywhere else in the world. If choosing a package tour, consider one run by an organization such as Saga, Vantage or Elderhostel, which is specifically designed for over-50s.

If travelling independently, don't choose too punishing a schedule. Remember that in

many parts of Baja California, high altitude and desert heat can tire you out a lot faster than you might otherwise expect, and especially in such conditions it is wise to take it easy. If you plan on doing a lot of sightseeing, consider setting aside a few days when you have absolutely nothing specific to do. As far as comfort is concerned, first-class buses are generally pretty pleasant, with plenty of legroom. Second-class buses can be rather more boneshaking, and you won't want to take them for too long a journey if you can avoid it.

Most of the hotels we recommend in this book should more than meet your needs, and in general even relatively low-budget hotels are clean and comfortable. Remember that senior citizens are often entitled to discounts, especially when visiting tourist sights, but also on occasion for accommodation and transport, something which it's always worth asking about.

Time

The state of Baja California operates on Pacific Standard and Pacific Daylight Time (GMT-8); Baja California Sur on Mountain Standard and Mountain Daylight Time (GMT-7). The dividing line is the 28th parallel, which is the border between the two states. The state of Baja California changes standard and daylight times in April and October.

Tourist information

Both states maintain their own tourist boards and websites. Baja California's bilingual efforts, both in the materials collected in its city offices and online (🌐 www.discoverbajacalifornia.com) are much more consistent than the south's, which seems to be plagued by underfunding (🌐 www.bcs.gob.mx).

The state tourism offices themselves are helpful affairs, as are the offices run by the cities' own visitors bureaus. You can expect to find bilingual brochures and thematic itineraries about local or regional features. In the smaller towns, offices will be able to point you towards local guides and speciality outfitters. They're also sometimes adjacent to or shared with spaces run by the Instituto Nacional de Antropología e Historia (a complete list of sites in English is available at 🌐 www.inah.gob.mx/inah_ing/cein/htme/cein02.html). Information about city office addresses and hours of operation are located along with other city-specific information in each chapter.

The information put out directly by the national government tends to be too general to be of much use. The Secretaría de Turismo (SECTUR) oversees the general efforts of national tourist promotion by providing information through INFOTUR (☎ 01-800/903-9200, US ☎ 1-800/482-9832) and the Mexican Tourism Board (US ☎ 1-800/446-3942, ✉ contact@visitmexico.com; Europe ☎ 00-800/1111-2266, ✉ visitemexico@over-marketing.com).

Tourist offices and government sites

Australian Department of Foreign Affairs
🌐 www.dfat.gov.au, 🌐 www.smartraveller.gov.au.
British Foreign & Commonwealth Office
🌐 www.fco.gov.uk.
Canadian Department of Foreign Affairs
🌐 www.dfait-maeci.gc.ca.
Irish Department of Foreign Affairs 🌐 www.foreignaffairs.gov.ie.
New Zealand Ministry of Foreign Affairs
🌐 www.mft.govt.nz.
US State Department 🌐 www.travel.state.gov.

Travelling with children

The peninsula's popularity as a driving destination makes one element of **travelling with children** – lugging around their stuff – much easier. The accessibility to US roads means that travelling with younger kids is very common – you will find that most Mexicans dote on children and they can often help to break the ice with strangers.

The main concern when considering travelling to Baja California with your children is their extra vulnerability – especially in a climate that can be harsh. Even more than their parents, they need protecting from the sun, unsafe drinking water, heat and unfamiliar food. Remember too that diarrhoea can be dangerous for younger children: rehydration salts are vital if your child goes down with it. Make sure too, if possible, that your child is aware of the dangers of rabies and other animal-borne illnesses; keep children away from all animals and consider a rabies shot.

Unless the establishment clearly states otherwise, children are generally warmly welcomed at restaurants and hotels. You shouldn't, though, rely upon either to provide high chairs or cribs. Breast-feeding in public is not common and you may be asked to remove yourself from the room if you engage in it.

For **entertainment**, there are children's museums and mini-theme parks in Tijuana and Mexicali, but the real attraction for kids is the breadth of **recreational activities** available. If the children are old enough, the same whale watching, kayaking, hiking and snorkelling trips that appeal to parents are open to children. That said, what might be the most fun outing on the peninsula for kids is **camping**, and there are few places more enjoyable to set up a tent or park an RV than along Baja's coast, particularly the Sea of Cortez.

Guide

Guide

1

Tijuana and around

CHAPTER 1 # Highlights

✳ **CECUT** Tijuana's cultural centre is home to the world-renowned Orquesta de Baja California and its daring music director, Angel Romero. See p.74

✳ **Mercado Miguel Hidalgo** Whether you're looking for a quick snack or preparing for a fiesta, you'll find it at Tijuana's central market. See p.75

✳ **Hipódromo Caliente** Make a wager on the greyhounds and watch the day's races in style from the track's *Turf Club*. See p.76

✳ **Caesar's Sports Bar & Grill** The birthplace of the Caesar Salad is one of the few places on La Revo that doesn't leave a bad taste. See p.80

✳ **Tecate Brewery** Take a tour of the brewery followed by a tall cold one on the outdoor patio. See p.89

△ Sombreros, Tijuana

Tijuana and around

For a city that's not only northern Mexico's financial, business and cultural centre, but also one of the busiest tourist destinations in the world, Tijuana doesn't try awfully hard to make a good first impression. It looks dusty, dangerous and crass at first glance because, in many ways, it is. Decades of catering to its northern neighbour's vices and poor civic planning have taken their toll, and Tijuana's relative youth – it wasn't officially founded until 1889 – and prosperity are belied by cracked roads, endless graffiti and an air of indifference.

But if you can get past the grit and the tourist pandering near the border, you'll discover a place much smarter than it looks. It is among the wealthiest cities in the Mexican republic, buoyed by the region's duty-free status and its legion of **maquiladora** assembly plants – where raw or semi-assembled materials are brought across the border duty-free, assembled by cheap labour, and exported with duty levied only on the added value. This promise of work has increased Tijuana's population – now numbering one and a half million – by 50 percent in just the last ten years. Enterprising newcomers have breathed life into the city's restaurant industry and used cultural institutions like Centro Cultural Tijuana (CECUT) as a breeding ground for homegrown artistic and cultural movements. Downtown, beyond the areas where most tourists venture, the modern concrete and glass buildings wouldn't look out of place in Southern California.

As gleaming and sophisticated as some parts are, to most travellers Tijuana will always be the definitive border town. Cheap prescription drugs, drinks and *tchotkes* are readily available, and an almost round-the-clock trolley can take US visitors back home, sans sins, in under an hour. The main commercial drag **Avenida Revolución**, or **La Revo**, caters exclusively to the hordes of day-trippers who make up the majority of the 40 million people passing through California's San Ysidro border crossing every year. La Revo and its surrounding streets brim with hundreds of tacky souvenir stands, cut-rate medical and dental offices, cut-rate auto-repair shops, and countless bars and restaurants – pricey by Mexican standards but cheaper than anything found north of the border. The prostitution and sex shows that made La Revo notorious have moved a few blocks to the north, although the tourist drag still has its share of insalubrious gentlemen's bars. And, as ever, Tijuana thrives on **gambling**. At the off-track-betting parlours throughout the city you can place money on just about anything that moves – especially greyhounds – and monitor progress on banks of closed circuit TVs.

The fact that impressions of Tijuana are often formed solely along the well-worn track to and from La Revo is not entirely a result of a singular focus, however. Visitors on foot, who make up the vast majority of the tourist influx, oftentimes do get shaken down by both police and cabbies when they veer off

TIJUANA & AROUND

N

PACIFIC OCEAN

Islas los Coronado

0   5 km

San Diego

San Diego Bay

San Diego

75

5

885

Tijuana

905

San Ysidro

Otay Mesa

Upper Otay Lake

Lower Otay Lake

CALIFORNIA

USA
MEXICO

94

Canyon City

Mexicali

Tecate

Tecate

Presa el Carrizo

Colonia Hindú

Valle las Palmas

BAJA CALIFORNIA

El Alamo Bonito

El Florido

Valle Bonito

Presa Rodríguez

Aeropuerto Internacional de Tijuana

Tijuana

Playas de Tijuana

La Joya

San Antonio del Mar

Rancho del Mar

Santa Mónica Sur

Libertador

Independencia

Rosarito

Ensenada

The illegal drug trade

Whatever strides Tijuana is making, there's no getting around its most insidious problem – the **illegal drug trade** and the sway it holds at virtually every level of the city's social and municipal structure. Business owners pay to avoid trouble, and politicians, the press and even the clergy openly collaborate with known associates of narco traffickers. In many ways it's difficult to blame them. Enforcement of drug laws is horribly lax and retribution is brutal – bodies are dissolved in acid, priests are killed execution-style and dinner parties are disrupted by kidnappings that end not with a ransom but a mutilated corpse. And there's really nowhere to turn for help: the police are both target and collaborator and, either way, they're outgunned.

As pervasive as the illegal drug trade is, visitors are rarely, if ever, caught up in the turf battles. The overwhelming majority of the victims belong to a cartel or are part of a group that openly opposes their ways.

Avenida Revolución – especially after drinking. Public transportation is confusing, and the city's fractured layout makes exploration daunting. That said, if you are able to break away, the payoff is hugely rewarding. A US$4 cab ride from the border can take you to any of the great nightclubs and restaurants around **Zona Río**. Much maligned for their land grabs during construction in the 1970s, city leaders were attempting to improve the city's image and fortunes by shifting the focus from La Revo to a tree-lined cultural and commercial district on the east side of town. Free of painted donkeys and other gimmicks, Zona Río offers the best glimpse of Tijuana's other life – one that has more in common with San Diego than the adult-themed carnival atmosphere of La Revo.

The blue waters of the Pacific give **Playas de Tijuana**, the city's westernmost district, or *delegación*, a character distinct from its landlocked neighbours. Tucked between the ocean and a line of rolling hills, Playas is a rectangle of relative calm. There is little for visitors to do besides walk the beach or, in season, visit the colosseum-like Bullring by the Sea. Residents, however, relish the seclusion and the sea breezes.

Tecate, a comparatively sleepy enclave 30km to the east of Tijuana, is a markedly more down-to-earth border town. Life for its fifty thousand or so residents still resolves around its central square, and to a lesser extent, the baseball diamond. The large Tecate brewery at the centre of town, a constant source of pride and jobs as it churns out bottles of the peninsula's most popular lager, is one of the few reasons people linger before moving south into the Valle de Guadalupe or east through Mexicali and on to mainland Mexico. And although Tijuana's factories and office parks are stretching ever eastward, the flow of traffic through Tecate's border crossing is still but a tiny fraction of its neighbour's.

Tijuana

TIJUANA, one of Mexico's most rapidly expanding cities, exhibits more than its fair share of growing pains. Makeshift semi-permanent shelters and cookie-cutter middle-class residential developments blanket the rolling hills. Despite the influx of so many coming here to live or visit, signs of wealth and civic pride are not easy to come by. What indications do exist – the sights of Zona Río and upper-class homes in the Hipódromo neighbourhood – are relatively new.

The city's defining feature is its 75-kilometre long secured border with the US, an imposing melange of walls, fences, trip wires and earthen dams that begins in the waters off Playas de Tijuana, runs eastward along the city's northern limits, across the Río Tijuana and off towards Tecate. Built in 1994 as the backbone of the US's "Operation Gatekeeper" (see box, p.60), its defenders and detractors agree that its presence has brought stability to both sides of the border, even if it has pushed problems to other parts of each country. While a vast nature preserve lines the US side and border guards patrol dirt roads on bicycles and trucks, development on the Mexican side abuts the border for most of its length, much of which has become a popular medium for delivering political and artistic statements.

Tijuana's seven *delegaciones* spread southward from the border, but most visitors won't venture outside the first of these, **Zona Centro**, which is easily accessed via a pedestrian street from the parking lots on both sides of the border crossing. Radiating south from the San Ysidro gate, this *delegación* contains **La Revo** and the downmarket shopping and drinking district that feeds off the Avenida, the **Zona Río** business and dining area, and the consulates and stadiums of **Hipódromo**. La Revo's classy double is Zona Río's main drag, **Paseo de los Héroes**, a grand six-lane street spotted with hotels and restaurants that would make Baron Haussmann proud.

The remaining six *delegaciones*, moving roughly west to east, are Playas de Tijuana, San Antonio, La Mesa, Otay, La Presa and La Presa Rural. Playas has a healthy mix of business, residential and leisure; San Antonio, La Presa and Otay are largely devoted to industry; while the others are largely residential or, in the specific case of La Presa Rural, virtually uninhabited. Unless you're particularly adventurous, you're only likely to pass through these areas if you're moving east towards Tecate or south on to Rosarito and the rest of Baja California.

Almost without exception, you can regain your bearings by looking up for the **bandera monumental**. This enormous Mexican flag – 46 by 26m – sits atop a hill about three blocks south of where Avenida Revolución turns into Boulevard Agua Caliente.

Some history

Tijuana's name can be attributed to either the word "Tiguan" which the Kumiai – the area's original inhabitants – gave to the nearby river, or to an expansive nineteenth-century ranch set in the area and named for its owner, Tía Juana (Aunt Jane). The **US–Mexican War** and the Mexican Cession of 1848 led to a new international border being established across the ranch's valley, with Mexico retaining Baja California but losing Alta California. Over the following decades the ranch took on the feel of a border town, albeit an ill-defined one. During these formative years, Tijuana's population ebbed and flowed in rhythm with regional mineral strikes and land and water claims, and it was not until 1889 that the town was officially founded. While most of the peninsula's trading and principal economic ventures were based in southern towns like Loreto and La Paz, Tijuana remained a sleepy town along the banks of Río Tijuana.

The first harbinger of Tijuana's imminent transformation came in the form of a government decree that legalized **gambling** here in 1908. It wasn't until after a rebel takeover in May 1911, however, that the industry really got its legs. When 220 insurrectionists and mercenaries took over the town, their leader

Caryl Ap Rhys Pryce, a peripatetic Welshman in his mid-thirties, expanded gambling concessions in order to raise more cash for the rebel cause. The rebellion was stamped out by July, but it kick-started a link between vice industries and Tijuana's leadership that endures to this day.

More than anything, though, Tijuana's most spectacular period of upheaval and debauchery was spurned by moral reform movements in the US. Mounting pressure from progressive groups led to a crackdown on gaming, prostitution and drinking in California in 1913 and the nationwide institution of **Prohibition** in 1920. The effect this had on Tijuana was profound, if predictable: while California and the rest of the US may have been dry, anyone with a car or train ticket and a hankering for a drink simply crossed the border into Mexico. Drinking wasn't the only thing that attracted the foreign visitors. Gambling was already accepted in Tijuana, but it went big-time in 1916 when US financiers opened the city's first horse track, the Lower California Jockey Club. The track was directly linked to San Diego by rail, effectively opening the city to US tourism on a grand scale. In a few short years, the town changed from a relative dusty backwater into an ancestor to Las Vegas, attracting a mainly foreign and wealthy clientele with casinos and a red light district whose legendarily depraved floorshows appealed to baser instincts.

In the early years there was a high-class sheen to some of the proceedings: casinos like the faux Moorish palace and the one-time health spa Agua Caliente catered to Hollywood celebrities and, for a brief period, turned Tijuana into a mini Monte Carlo. Mexicans throughout the country came to the city for their sliver of the economic pie, and in a decade the population doubled. This influx raised unemployment throughout the region and led to the first ring of shantytowns around the city. When US states began repealing Prohibition laws in 1933, the Agua Caliente Casino adjusted by expanding the hotel, adding more lavish amenities and raising the stakes at its gaming tables, trying to deliver a level of sophisticated gaming the US couldn't match. But the lustre faded abruptly when **President Lázaro Cárdenas** outlawed gambling in 1935; in one day eliminating 5000 jobs and the main reason Southern California's smart set visited. Without the lure of gambling or banned booze, the border town that had thrived on sating the desires of its northern neighbour found itself scrambling for a purpose. The expansion of **Naval Station San Diego** in the decade leading up to World War II solved the quandary, not necessarily in a good way. Restaurants, bars and stores near the border began offering shore-leave thrills and filling the sailors' need for cheap products. Tijuana's reputation as a hotbed of red-light shenanigans and cut-rate pharmaceuticals took hold.

With little work to be had around Tijuana and the promise of a better life just to the north, Tijuana became the primary staging ground for illegal immigration into Southern California. And instead of alleviating troubles, the birth of the *maquiladora* program (see box, p.73) in 1965 didn't reduce local unemployment; it simply attracted the unemployed from other parts of Mexico. The frenetic atmosphere and an often desperate populace proved to be an especially fertile breeding ground for drug smuggling, which the Arellano Félix drug cartel dominated in the 1980s. Each year **smuggling methods** grow wilier while the US Border Patrol tries to keep pace with higher walls, more floodlights, increased staffing and tougher document control at border checkpoints.

Operation Gatekeeper (see box, p.60) and the North American Free Trade Agreement (NAFTA) both came into effect in 1994. The former changed the physical layout of the city, the latter the number of factories and jobs in Tijuana and along the border. NAFTA-related growth has exacerbated existing problems related to housing, water quality and population; half of all new

Operation Gatekeeper

In 1994 the US administration launched **Operation Gatekeeper**, a multi-million dollar initiative intended to stem the tide of illegal immigrants across the California–Mexico border by temporarily augmenting the US–Mexico border south of San Diego. Prior to Gatekeeper, US officials estimated that a quarter of all **illegal immigrants** entering the US did so through a five-mile stretch of land north of Tijuana. From the beginning, the most visible, and controversial, component of the plan was the construction of a fence running from the Pacific Ocean 47 miles eastward to Tecate. The Immigration and Naturalization Service erected light towers, installed underground sensors, purchased helicopters, and increased the Border Patrol's size by 140%.

The number of illegal entries in the Tijuana–San Diego corridor dropped dramatically, and property values on the northern side increased. **Deaths** of would-be border crossers increased too, as people determined to cross into the US have resorted to crossing through Tecate's hills nearby and Arizona deserts further east. Although parts of Texas and Arizona have enacted monitoring plans similar to Gatekeeper and have seen dramatic drops in the number of interdictions, they've also seen a dramatic increase in fatalities. Estimates by groups opposed to Gatekeeper – such as Amnesty International and the American Civil Liberties Union – estimate that during its first decade three thousand people died of dehydration, hypothermia, and other causes in their attempts to cross the border.

Supporters of Gatekeeper are pushing to turn what was originally planned to be a temporary solution into a permanent one, and they're relying on scare tactics that warn of a Mexican-born 9/11 plot to gain adherents. Opponents on both sides of the border, however, point out that the real issue is **US labour practices** that punish illegal workers yet allow the companies that employ them to operate without interference.

residents end up in squatter communities that lack clean water or a sewer system. And although it's not a problem entirely of its own making, the city's growth is draining to a trickle the water resources it shares with the San Diego metropolitan area.

As disparate as the two cities are, they've always been deeply of a piece, and they continue to share an increasing interdependence with one another – and Tijuana isn't always in second place. A third of San Diegans and almost half of Tijuana residents have family on the opposite side of the border, while over thirty thousand Mexicans cross the border legally each day to work in Southern California.

Arrival

With the exception of the sometimes agonizing northbound wait for cars at the border, Tijuana is designed to get you in and out quickly and efficiently. Choose from parking lots on either side of the border, parking garages and lots at prominent locations and hotels, tour bus services, three different types of taxis, or even charter vans from the location of your choice in Southern California. Streets are well marked – at times half a block in advance – and blue signs on lampposts identify the distance to prominent locations. It's also served by two airports: its own just east of downtown and San Diego's on the US side of the border.

By car

Entering Mexico by car at either of California's two Tijuana border crossings – San Ysidro or Otay Mesa – is a simple affair that may not even require you to bring your car to a complete stop (see box p.62). Once across the San Ysidro border, the road splits off into a series of right exits, starting with Carretera Internacional which leads west to Playas de Tijuana and the scenic toll road (the latter alternately referred to as Ensenada Cuota 1D and Carretera Escénica Tijuana–Ensenada), Calle 3a which heads downtown, Paseo de los Héroes into Zona Río and Via Rápida Poniente toward Tecate. From the Otay crossing, follow signs to the airport, and stick to the main road, which changes names from Camino al Aeropuerto to Boullevard Cuauhtémoc and finally to 16 de Septiembre once it reaches downtown Tijuana in the Zona Río.

△ San Ysidro border crossing

By foot

Day-trippers coming from the San Diego area often park at Border Station Parking, 4570 Camino de la Plaza (US☎619/428-6200; US$7) in San Ysidro and use the **pedestrian route** and **walking bridge** to reach downtown Tijuana. **San Diego Trolley** passengers access the same route by walking directly west from the trolley's own station and over the highway.

Crossing the border

If you have the right documentation, passing through either Tijuana **border crossing** is normally a breeze, though, depending on the day and hour, you may have to wait in a very long line before returning to the States. Drivers should pause at the crossing and look to the adjacent signal box for either a green light (cleared to go) or red light (move right for inspection). Walkers have their version of this, too – a signal box with a button that generates a random red or green light. The red light typically means you'll need to show the immigration officer your passport or papers and explain where you're headed; sometimes it results in an inspection and more thorough examination, but this is rare. It's also possible to cross the border by shuttle bus, though it usually costs more and sometimes takes longer than walking over and picking up transport the other side (see below).

Because of its proximity to the Tijuana airport and nearby factories, trucks use the **Otay Mesa** crossing. While US-bound waits at this crossing seldom stretch past an hour, it's a twenty-five minute drive from downtown Tijuana and about as long from Otay on I-805 to reach central San Diego. Both San Ysidro and Otay Mesa crossings are open 24 hours.

Crossing into Mexico

If you plan to move on past Tijuana, Ensenada and San Felipe, or stay beyond 72 hours, be sure to purchase your **tourist card** and get it stamped at *migración*; recent upgrades to the San Ysidro crossing have made this relatively painless. If you're walking, pop into the first office on your left at the border, tell them you need your tourist card and walk another 50 metres to pay your US$20 or M$210 at the Banamex. Return to the office to pick up your validated form. If you're driving, stay in the right lanes and go through the "Items to Declare" lanes, tell the inspectors you need your card, and park in the adjacent lot. You'll use the same office the walkers do, which is the northernmost one in the border plaza.

If you're taking your **car** beyond Baja you'll need to fill out provisional importation forms at the nearby Banjercito branch (for details see Basics: Getting there, p.20). This will require a US$400–800 deposit (depending on the age of your car) by cash or credit card.

After crossing into Mexico on foot, it's only a **short walk downtown** – through the Viva Tijuana shopping mall, over the footbridge, and along Calle 1a to Revolución. Alternatively you can catch a bus headed downtown (look for those marked "Centro" or "Revolución") or to the bus station (blue-and-white buses marked "Buena Vista/Central Camionera") from the public bus and taxi terminal right by the entrance to Viva Tijuana. There are also fixed-fare yellow taxis that stop between Calle 2a and Calle 3a on Madero and can take you to the Central Camionera for about M$50 after bargaining. Caliente's main off-track-betting parlor on Revolución offers a free van ride from the tourist information office, just next to the taxi stand. Mexicoach also operates a **shuttle service** between the border and Revolución, to Rosarito (M$50), Hipódromo's Plaza El Toreo (M$25) and the Bullring by the Sea (M$50).

By bus

Tijuana's **long-distance bus station**, Central Camionera La Mesa (☎664/621-2982), is at Lázaro Cárdenas 15751, just north of Canal Alamar and the river and 8km east of the city centre. To reach downtown, board the blue-and-white local bus marked "Centro" which runs to the centre via Calle 2a. Despite the 30-minute-long trip, the M$6 bus saves you a bundle compared to the M$120 taxi ride. A smaller station – a parking lot actually – just south of the river at Lázaro Cárdenas 900 handles buses arriving from throughout northern Baja (☎664/621-2399).

The three **downtown bus stations** are all within walking distance of one another on La Revo and are near the border. Anyone travelling via Mexicoach arrives at **Terminal Turístico** at Avenida Revolución at Calle 6 (☎664/685-1470). Buses from Rosarito and Tecate drop you at the **Central Vieja** at the corner of Calle 1 and Madero. Buses from Ensenada and a small number of other cities in the peninsula's northwest arrive at **Central de Autobuses de la Línea**, adjacent to Plaza Viva Tijuana.

By plane

Aeropuerto Internacional de Tijuana, Camino al Aeropuerto, at Carretera Internacional (☎664/683-2418, 683-2118) 8km east of town, is simple for travellers to negotiate: there's only one terminal, and all services are contained in the kiosks that line its walls. **Shuttles** to downtown and further afield are at the east end of the terminal; the trip to La Revo is M$60. City **buses** (M$6 or US$.55) pick up passengers in front of the terminal; their destinations are posted near the door or written in soap on the front left-hand side of the windshield. For a **taxi** to the city centre, exit to the north and look for a kiosk marked taxi where you can pre-pay for a fixed rate (around M$200) or cross Camino al Aeropuerto and haggle for a cheaper fare (M$120–150) on its far side, right next to the border fence. Car rental firms are in the main terminal as well, with Budget, Avis, Alamo, Thrifty, Hertz and National represented. The **information booth** located at the base of the stairs near the centre of the terminal gives out brochures from the state tourism board and has listings of larger hotels.

Going under the border

Stymied by increased border patrols and more sophisticated searches at points of entry, smugglers have taken to **digging under the border** to funnel their goods or people between Mexico and the US. In one recent case a tunnel led from a ground-floor apartment near the San Ysidro border crossing to a storm drain in a parking lot on the San Diego side. Smugglers simply backed up a truck to the drain and used a trapdoor in the cargo hold to connect unseen with the tunnel. In Tecate, a 366m-long tunnel lined with tracks, electricity and a ventilation system led from a house to another on the US side of the border. The most sophisticated tunnel discovered so far was found in February 2006 near the Otay Mesa crossing by Mexican police and a US inter-agency tunnel taskforce. Smugglers, most likely tied to the Tijuana cartels, dug a 1.5m-high, 1m-wide reinforced passageway 18m deep. The tunnel, which also had electricity, a ventilation system and a water pump, connected two warehouses over 1km away from one another.

Border officials assume there's been minimal use of the tunnels for illegal human crossings – construction is far too expensive to be used to traffic people. When the Tecate and San Ysidro ones were discovered, 270 kilograms of marijuana were found in the first one and 1300 in the second.

City transport

Tijuana has a bewildering array of options for moving about the city. There are at least five standards of taxi service (some with meters, some communal), a handful of tourist-centric shuttles as well as public buses. Still, **walking** is often the best method of getting around. Tijuana's main attractions are a short distance from the border as well as from each other. Walking to other parts of the city centre is safe but not always rewarding; a stroll from La Revo to Mercado Miguel Hidalgo and then CECUT will take only fifteen minutes, but getting to the bullring or stops further along Boulevard Agua Caliente is a dusty, sweaty trek that's best skipped in favour of a ride.

Driving

Rental cars are available at the airport, but unless you've brought and insured your own car, you're best off relying on taxis during your stay to avoid added insurance costs, parking fees and road hazards, not to mention concerns about **driving** an unfamiliar vehicle through fast-moving, unforgiving city streets. If, however, your own car gets dinged, there's comfort in knowing that Tijuana is one of the most able towns in the world for bodywork.

If you have an accident, call the tourist helpline at ☎078. They can dispatch a Green Angel for auto assistance or police and rescue services for more serious incidents.

Taxis and city buses

Of Tijuana's three types of **taxis**, the red-striped, white **taxi libre** cars are the best choice for anyone worried about their Spanish skills or getting ripped off; libre taxis have meters, and drivers must use them. Spotting them near the border crossing and La Revo is easy, but you'll have to wade through less salubrious and more aggressive taxis to hail one; it's worth asking your restaurant or hotel to call one for you. The 1970s-era station wagons packed with up to a dozen passengers are **route taxis** that run set routes like city buses (for about M$7), but are more reliable. Each route has a different colour scheme to

---

Downtown street names

Downtown numbered city streets running at right angles to Avenida Revolución go by **secondary names** that often appear without reference to their numerical designations. An additional shorthand is used, too, simply calling them C 1a or C 3a instead of Calle 1a or Calle 3a.

Numerical designation	Secondary name
C 1a	Artículo 123
C 2a	Benito Juárez
C 3a	Carrillo Puerto
C 4a	Díaz Miron
C 5a	Emiliano Zapata
C 6a	Flores Magón
C 7a	Galeana
C 8a	Hidalgo
C 9a	Zaragoza
C 10a	Sarabia
C 11a	P.E. Calles

Baja California
food and drink

In this hot, desert climate, you'll find Mexican food at its most basic. But don't let the simplicity fool you; Baja's cuisine is some of the best you'll find in the country. Grilled meats and fish take the place of heavy staples like rice and beans and a simple squirt of lime juice replaces complex sauces like mole. The emergence of the wine industry in the north has garnered interest from the outside world, even though you're more likely to find locals sipping on a cold beer than a chilled Chardonnay.

What's on the menu

By sea and by land

The peninsula's pervasive heat dictates that ingredients be fresh and local; just-caught seafood and both free-range and farm-raised beef, lamb and poultry fill the menus. Avocados, peppers and tomatoes are available year round, but by and large, vegetarian dishes are a luxury indulged in only by foreign visitors.

Though the swankiest resorts in Los Cabos will sometimes serve exotic fish from other parts of the globe, Baja's enviable location between the Sea of Cortez and the Pacific Ocean ensures that just about any seafood you'd hope to eat can be found off its shores. The bounty of the ocean is on full display at the Ensenada fish market – the only one in either state – where merchants sell giant abalone, 25cm-long shrimp, dorado and big-eye tuna caught only hours earlier. In other coastal towns it is possible to walk to the shore in the late afternoon and purchase a fresh catch from local fishermen landing their *panga* boats, while at sport-fishing havens along the central coast and the eastern cape, anglers bring the day's catch back to their resort for the kitchen to cook. The peninsula's reverence for the sea, however, is most evident in the small town of Puerto Nuevo, which consists entirely of restaurants selling succulent fried or grilled Pacific lobster, an oversized cousin to the langoustine.

Preparation and presentation of fish is never fussy. If it's grilled, there will be a side of clarified butter and a pinch of sea salt. Raw fish is as common in Baja as it is in Tokyo: at high-end restaurants in Ensenada and Tijuana you'll find tuna *carpaccio* drizzled with olive oil and flecked with fresh basil; in La Paz, you can indulge in lime-soaked sea bass *ceviche* for less money than a Big Mac, and in Los Cabos it's easier to find good sushi than a decent burrito. Equally popular are seafood staples like octopus, clams and shrimp, which are roughly chopped and mixed with fresh herbs and tomatoes to make *cocteles* appetizers.

Anyone who has travelled down the Transpeninsular Highway is aware of the prevalence of cattle, lamb and goats on the peninsula. Local meat can be broiled, stewed, or fried, though grilled is the preferred method. Ubiquitous *carne asada* – grilled beef marinated in lime juice – is served sliced inside warm tortillas as tacos and fresh rolls as tortas, or simply as steaks.

You'll also find a broad selection of down-market yet delicious variations of meat, like dry-roasted beef or Lebanese-inspired marinated pork on a spit, from street vendors and market stalls.

Whereas garlic adds zest to many dishes on the Mexican mainland, cilantro, or coriander, is the dominant flavour on the peninsula. It shows up in multiple forms: raw, chopped and sprinkled onto a *carnita* taco (often with raw onion, too); dried, ground and rubbed into a cut of beef; and whole leaf like decorative parsley. Avocados are grown around Mulegé,

Fisherman with a fresh catch

Todos Santos and El Rosario, but they make it onto menus across the peninsula, served as either a salad topped with sea salt, cilantro and *queso fresco*, in a freshly mashed side of guacamole or sliced to accompany a grilled steak. The tomatoes and peppers of San Quintín are fat, red and earthy, tasting of the soil rather than hydroponic artificialities.

Ceviche

Beating the heat

Like the cuisine, what's on tap and in coolers is largely a reaction to the heat of the peninsula. Perhaps it's no surprise then that a Baja Californian cantina invented the margarita – which, in the hands of the right bartender, is capable of being as elegant and smooth as 007's martini. In the southern state, margaritas are made with Damiana, a Triple Sec-like liqueur made from the leaves and stems of the local damiana bush giving the drink a more mellow, less fruity taste than the norm. Cold, lager-style beers like the locally produced Tecate and Pacifico from

The fish taco

The **fish taco** was most likely the product of an Ensenada fish market merchant inspired by the tempura cooking methods of Japanese fishermen who began plying the peninsula's waters during the late nineteenth century. People in Baja California and the rest of Mexico had been stuffing fish into tortillas for hundreds of years, but the combination of a lightly battered fish like red snapper and the now-standard suite of shredded cabbage, vinegar-marinated onions, radishes, hot sauce, light mayo and a squirt of lime was a revelation. Almost overnight, Ensenada became known as the birthplace of *tacos de pescado*, and the fish market is now the site of dozens of merchants who claim they were the first.

Music and drinks

across the Sea of Cortez are the drink of choice for just about anyone who isn't lifting a margarita or tequila to their lips. The latter is best sampled in larger towns where bartenders create tasting menus of small-batch tequilas made from local agave plants, served with lime and salt, or maybe a chaser of sangrita – a thick mix of ground chile, grenadine and tomato and orange juices.

The wines coming out of the Guadalupe and Santo Tomás valleys are produced largely for export to other parts of Mexico and for visitors to bring surreptitiously into California, and are rarely consumed in any significant quantity outside of the northwest. Over one hundred years since the first vines were planted, vintners continue to experiment, which is why Cabernet Sauvignon is grown down the dirt road from Swiss Chasselas and across a dry riverbed from Italian Nebbiolos. Still, smaller operations in the Valle de Guadalupe, like Mogor Badán and Monte Xanic churn out some lovely bottles that are best enjoyed locally, where restrictive Mexican taxes don't drive up the cost as high as they do outside of the country.

The peninsula is also, however, the creator of clamato – an unholy combination of clam and tomato juices whose popularity is inexplicably enduring.

Just a squirt of lime

It's virtually impossible to sit down at a table or visit a street-side food cart, and not be presented with fresh **limes**. Mexican **limes**, like the West Indian and Key limes, are smaller, rounder and juicier than the large, oval Persian or Tahiti limes that

dominate the aisles of many foreign supermarkets. They're also more acidic, which is why trying to replicate the taste with their larger cousins will fall flat without the addition of some lemon juice. For margaritas, limes are sliced in half and pressed using a hand-squeezed juicer that matches their small shape and blocks out the numerous seeds. At restaurants and food stalls, limes are sliced into shield-like slivers that you can squeeze between your thumb and forefinger. They're present in most dishes – particularly marinated steak, baked chicken and ceviche – and a multitude of drinks.

differentiate it from the others; for instance, the brown and beige *rutas* along Calle 3a run to CECUT. To hail any of them, stand on a main street headed where you want to go and flag one down.

Border taxis are yellow and lay in wait in front of the border tourist information office and around La Revo. If you do use one, be sure to haggle and set the price in advance. Somewhat unreliable, **city buses** have destinations printed on the front and loading side of the vehicle and fares are a flat M$6. Buses only run from 7am to 9 or 10pm.

Information

Two of Tijuana's four very helpful **tourist offices** are right at the border – one for pedestrians (Mon–Thurs 9am–5pm, Fri & Sat 8am–5pm, Sun 8am–3pm; ☎664/683-4987) and the other for drivers (Mon–Thurs 8am–5pm, Fri & Sat 8am–7pm, Sun 8am–3pm; ☎664/683-1405); either is well worth a visit to pick up a free map and some leaflets. The main tourist office is in the centre of downtown at Avenida Revolución between Calle 3a and Calle 4a (Mon–Thurs 10am–4pm, Fri–Sun 10am–7pm; ☎664/685-2210). There is also an outpost at the airport near luggage carousel E (daily 8am–3pm; ☎664/683-8244).

Accommodation

Since a sizeable proportion of Tijuana's visitors leave before nightfall, the city offers fewer types of **accommodation** than one would expect. Many that do stay for any period linger only long enough to engage in vices or move quickly across the border, and there is no shortage of inexpensive options that cater to them. Therefore a number of the low-end offerings should be avoided for safety reasons: none of the budget places along Calle 1a heading west from Revolución or north of Calle 1a (Zona Norte) is recommended – particularly not for lone women.

La Revo

Accommodation south of Calle 1a in the **La Revo** district is geared for tourists and, while rather dated or seedy in some cases, is a safe bet for cheap beds in the heart of the tequila and dancing scene.

Arreola Av Revolución 1080 ☎664/685-9081. A basic, clean budget motel with hot showers, and a step up from other bottom-rung options. Cash only. ❶

Catalina C 5 2059 at Madero ☎664/685-9748. Old but modernized hotel with clean, spacious en-suite rooms. ❷

Lafayette Av Revolución 325 ☎664/685-3940. A spartan hotel well placed and well run, although street noise seeps in. Good prices for singles and better rates for groups that book blocks in advance. ❷–❸

Nelson Av Revolución 721 at C 1a ☎664/685-4302. Smack dab at the top of La Revo, this stucco palace can't be beat for location, but the street noise can be relentless at times. Nelson is one of La Revo's oldest hotels, so although the rooms have cable TV, they're otherwise quite dated and worn. ❹

Plaza de Oro Av Miguel Martínez 539 ☎664/685-3776. Comfortable, modern 36-room motel with cable TV but little character. ❸

San Nicolas Av Madero 768 at C 1a ☎664/688-0418. Slightly noisy gay-friendly hotel adjacent to

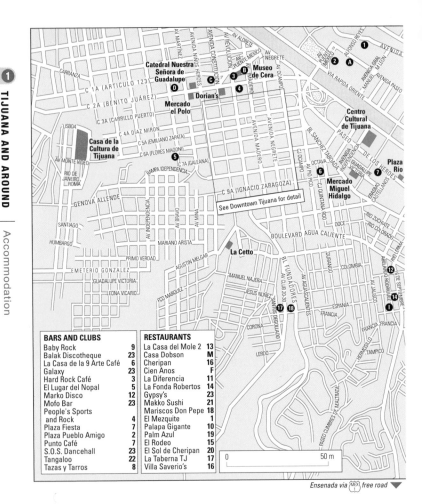

BARS AND CLUBS		RESTAURANTS	
Baby Rock	9	La Casa del Mole 2	13
Balak Discotheque	23	Casa Dobson	M
La Casa de la 9 Arte Café	6	Cheripan	16
Galaxy	23	Cien Anos	F
Hard Rock Café	3	La Diferencia	11
El Lugar del Nopal	5	La Fonda Robertos	14
Marko Disco	12	Gypsy's	23
Mofo Bar	23	Makko Sushi	21
People's Sports		Mariscos Don Pepe	18
and Rock	4	El Mezquite	1
Plaza Fiesta	7	Palapa Gigante	10
Plaza Pueblo Amigo	2	Palm Azul	19
Punto Café	7	El Rodeo	15
S.O.S. Dancehall	23	El Sol de Cheripan	20
Tangaloo	22	La Taberna TJ	17
Tazas y Tarros	8	Villa Saverio's	16

Ensenada via (MEX 1) free road ▼

the Central Vieja bus station. Rooms are tiny and plain, but always clean. ❸–❹

La Villa de Zaragoza Av Madero 1480 at C 7 ☎664/685-1832, ⓦwww.hotellavilla.biz. This conveniently located US-style motel/hotel complex

sits just to the east of the Jai Alai Frontón Palace. Choose from remodelled or older rooms, some with kitchenettes. A security guard watches over the parking lot. ❹–❺

Zona Río

Proximity to Tijuana's best restaurants, attractions, shopping and nightlife comes with a hefty tag in **Zona Río** – prices here rarely dip beneath M$900 for a double. But the higher rates get you a pool and secure parking, as well as an easy walk to the clubs in Plaza Fiesta and Plaza Río, the restaurants along Boulevard Taboada, and attractions like CECUT and Mercado Hidalgo.

Camino Real Paseo de los Héroes 10305 ☎664/633-4000, ⓦcaminoreal.com/tijuana. The

Real's exterior walls are practically electric with colour, and the interior decoration – wood panelling,

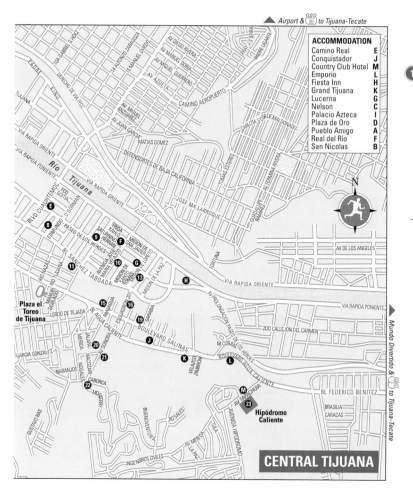

ACCOMMODATION

Camino Real	E
Conquistador	J
Country Club Hotel	M
Emporio	L
Fiesta Inn	H
Grand Tijuana	K
Lucerna	G
Nelson	C
Palacio Azteca	I
Plaza de Oro	D
Pueblo Amigo	A
Real del Río	F
San Nicolas	B

CENTRAL TIJUANA

bold colour schemes – has more character than most chains. The 263 rooms are decked out with cable TV and bottled water. Live music and cocktails pull locals into the lobby bar, but there's also a tequila-centric cantina and a Mexican restaurant on-site. ⑦–⑧

Fiesta Inn Paseo de los Héroes 18818 ☎664/636-0000, ⓦwww.fiestainn.com. Set near the original site of the Agua Caliente, the *Fiesta Inn* has a faux Moorish exterior that evokes the grandeur of the former spa and casino. Thermal waters fill the outdoor hot tub at *Fiesta*, and there's a spa with a full suite of treatments, too. Rooms with cable TV, dataports for dialup and coffee makers. ⑤–⑥

Lucerna Paseo de los Héroes 10902 ☎664/633-3900, ⓦwww.hotel-lucerna .com.mx/tijuana/index.html. The six-storey main

building and three annexes surround an outdoor pool with a mini waterfall. The best rooms, along with two restaurants and a bar, face this court-yard area. Every room has satellite TV, a balcony, coffee maker, a/c and purified water, as well as wireless Internet access for about M$120 per day. ⑦

Pueblo Amigo Via Oriente 9211 ☎800/026-6386, ⓦwww.sdro.com/pueblo. Adjacent to the plaza of the same name, this neglected 108-room busi-ness-style hotel owned by the Caliente gambling family no longer carries the panache it once did; visitors come for its proximity to the border, not the dated, poorly-maintained rooms. ⑦

Real del Río Av Jose María Velazco 1409 ☎664/634-3100, US 800/026-6677,

Ⓦ www.realdelrio.com. *Río*'s next-door placement to the restaurant *Cien Años* is the only feature that distinguishes this rather bland business hotel from its competitors. Guests in any of the 105 rooms have cable TV, in-room safe, room service and the use of a business centre. Ⓖ

Hipódromo

Hipódromo's proximity to the Campestre golf club and consulates makes its hotels popular with business travellers – who may also be drawn by the thrills of the Hipódromo Caliente racetrack.

Conquistador Blvd Agua Caliente 10750 ⓣ 664/681-7955, Ⓦ www.hotelconquistador-tij .com. The two-storey white stucco and red tile roof, heavy wood furniture and tapestries may evoke a colonial era Tijuana never really had, but they give it character otherwise absent from the neighbourhood. Rooms open to the parking lot or the pool. Ⓖ

Country Club Hotel Blvd Agua Caliente and Tapachula 1 ⓣ 664/681-7733, Ⓦ www .bajainn.com. The best deal beyond the Zona Centro looks like its interiors were flash-frozen during the Rat Pack days and just recently thawed. Standard rooms are small yet appointed with TVs, desks and full baths, and – along with a good in-house restaurant and bar – look out onto the pool and golf course or across the street to the dog track. Ⓓ–Ⓖ

Emporio Blvd Agua Caliente 11553 ⓣ 664/622-6600, Ⓦ www.hotelsempoRío.com. *Emporio* is the four-star spot of choice for visitors who find the nearby *Grand* too Trump-like. The 210 taste-fully decorated rooms have the usual amenities you would expect from a hotel in this class, but the hip sushi bar and swank palm-lined pool and patio are a pleasant change of pace in town. Ⓖ–Ⓗ

Grand Tijuana Blvd Agua Caliente 4500 ⓣ Mex 664/681-700, US 800/472-6385, Ⓕ 664/681-7016. Twin 23-storey towers – only one of which houses guest rooms – and lots of marble and shiny surfaces signal Tijuana's brashest hotel. On clear days top-floor rooms have excellent views of the city, Pacific and San Diego. Rooms have all standard business traveller amenities; there's also a pool and secure parking. Ⓖ–Ⓗ

Palacio Azteca Blvd Cuauhtemoc Sur 213, Col. Davila ⓣ 664/681-8100, Ⓦ www.hotelpalacioazteca .com. This newly opened 200-room hotel has a pool, large computer centre, restaurant, and rooms that overlook the city or pool. There's also a free airport shuttle. Ⓖ

Playas de Tijuana

Since **Playas** is predominantly residential, accommodation is limited (although you can arrange long-term condo rentals before arriving through online book-ing services). There are beachfront hotels near the bullring, but they're not recommended and, overall, the beach neighbourhood is the least attractive, hotel-wise, in the city.

Century Beach Resort Km 25 Mex 1D ⓣ 664/631-3250, US 888/709-9985, Ⓦ www .centurybeachresort.com. The first big resort along the coastal route is a Moorish-style gated commu-nity at the south end of Playas de Tijuana. Many of the 100 hotel rooms have private patios. and views of the ocean. Ⓓ–Ⓖ

Hacienda del Mar Paseo Playas 116 ⓣ 664/630-8603, US 888/675-2927, Ⓦ www .ventanarosahotels.com. A spruced-up, pastel toned motel with a secure parking lot, heated pool and weekly rates. Ⓓ

Playas Coronado Colina 101 ⓣ 664/680-2833. This two-storey hotel is too far from the beach to make an honest claim to *Playa*, but it is close to shopping and the movie theatre. Basic rooms with views of a parking lot. Ⓓ

Real del Mar Km 19.5 Mex 1D ⓣ 664/631-3670, US 800/803-6038; Ⓦ www.realdelmar.com .mx. An all-suite, resort-style hotel in Marriott's *Residence Inn* chain. The hotel looks down on the ocean from hills southwest of the city. Most of the guests who come here are looking for an out-of-town location for business meetings, aided by the excellent restaurant and the 18-hole, par 72 golf course. Ⓖ–Ⓗ

San Ysidro and San Diego hotels

If you're planning to stay on the US side of the border and make forays into Tijuana and Northern Baja, there are several options to consider; some of the better choices are listed below.

HI-San Diego, Downtown 521 Market St, San Diego CA ☎619/525-1531, ⓦwww .sandiegohostels.org/downtown.htm. The closest hostel to the peninsula hosts day-trips to Tijuana. Dorm-style lodging for singles, private rooms for up to four people and 24-hour check-in. ❷–❸

Motel 6 160 East Calle Primera, San Ysidro CA ☎619/690-6663, ⓦwww.motel6 .com. This inexpensive old-school motel only a mile from the border has an outdoor pool and parking. ❸

Seacoast Inn 800 Seacoast Dr, Imperial Beach, CA ☎619/424-5183, ⓦwww .theseacoastinn.com. Enjoy views of Playas de Tijuana from the San Diego side at this three-storey motel. Rooms are well-maintained, if dated, and have views of the ocean and private beach. Suites with kitchenettes are also available. ❻

Travelodge Inn 643 E San Ysidro Blvd, San Ysidro CA ☎619/428-2800, ⓦwww .Travelodge.com. Basic but clean chain hotel with free breakfast and parking; the border crossing is only a block away. ❺

The City

Tijuana's surprisingly expansive radial layout begins right at the San Ysidro crossing, from which the city's most famous temptations are just a walk away. **Avenida Revolución**, Tijuana's main commercial thoroughfare, strikes southward from the border, passing under the enormous **El Arco Monumental** along the way before reaching its namesake district, hedonistic **La Revo**. On the parallel Avenida Constitución, one block west, the **Zona Centro** takes on a different flavour and caters almost exclusively to residents. The half-dozen *colonias* here consist primarily of small shops and residential blocks, and are punctuated by **Catedral Nuestra Señora de Guadalupe**, the city's most inspired ecclesiastical edifice, and the hillside **Casa de la Cultura de Tijuana**.

Vía Poniente runs at a southeast slant from the border along the banks of Río Tijuana and into the **Zona Río**, the main financial district and an upscale, modern alternative to La Revo – even though one of its real treasures is the dated, old-world **Mercado Miguel Hidalgo**. Four large bronze monuments lend a grandiose air to the district's main artery, **Paseo de los Héroes**, and Tijuana's only real destination for a breezy stroll. The mammoth, earth-toned sphere that fronts **Centro Cultural Tijuana**, or **CECUT** as it's commonly referred, far and away the region's most important cultural institution and performance space, sticks out amidst the area's otherwise placid collection of hotels and shopping areas.

Just to the south, **Hipódromo**, the neighbourhood surrounding the **Hipódromo Caliente** racetrack along a long stretch of Boulevard Agua Caliente, could be defined as the city's main sporting district; though the included fields of play – a bullring and a dog track – are not exactly home to legitimate sports.

Retaining an identity distinct from the rest of the city's districts, **Playas de Tijuana** can thank its stretch of the Pacific for its leisurely and sun-soaked appeal. While the bullring area is overrun on match days, for the rest of the year a stroll along the waterfront is the more popular diversion.

Pedestrian foot bridge & San Ysidro border crossing

DOWNTOWN TIJUANA

N

BARS & CLUBS
Cave	4
El Foro	11
Multikulti	6
Las Pulgas	5
Salón de Baile	2
Voodoo House	12

C 3A (BENITO JUÁREZ)

C 4A (DÍAZ MIRON)

C 5A (EMILIANO ZAPATA)

C 6A (FLORES MAGONI)

C 7A (GALEANA)

Frontón
Jai Alai

C 8A (HIDALGO)

ACCOMMODATION
Arreola	B
Catalina	C
Lafayette	A
La Villa de Zaragoza	D

C 9A (ZARAGOZA)

0   50 m

RESTAURANTS
Caesar's Sports Bar & Grill	1
Chiki Jai	7
La Costa	8
D'Tony	9
Tia Juana Tilly's	10
Tortas Ricardo's	3
Vittorio's	13

AVENIDA CONSTITUCIÓN
AVENIDA REVOLUCIÓN
AVENIDA NIÑOS HEROES
AVENIDA MADERO
AVENIDA NEGRETE
AVENIDA OCAMPO

La Revo

A brash stretch of margarita shacks, nightclubs, leather shops and pharmacies, **La Revo** holds a place in the first-time visitor's imagination that far surpasses its Avenida Revolución's length. The pedestrian route – which eventually becomes Calle 1a – leads to La Revo from the border and cuts diagonally through a continuous phalanx of merchants, through Plaza Viva Tijuana (See Shopping, p.84), over the typically dry concrete river bed, through the Mercado de Artesanías, and to the base of **El Arco Monumental** on La Revo. This 50 metre-high arch, with a sign suspended by cables which helpfully spells out the city name, is the by-product of Tijuana's submission to the bad-ideas-related-to-celebrating-the-millennium competition that every city with more ambition than smarts erected to commemorate the year 2000.

A turn to the right here leads downhill – literally and figuratively – to the red-light **Zona Norte** district, which is best avoided. Instead, follow the rest of the crowd to the left and begin the eight-block long gauntlet of strip-club operators, leather dealers, trained animals, and guacamole makers. The lights aren't too bright, but it is quite noisy, what with the dance music pounding from clubs to sellers imploring you to buy something. The most appropriate starting point for a crass stretch like this is the **Museo de Cera**, Calle 1a 8281, at Avenida Madero (daily 10am–6pm; M$15; ☎664/688-2478), a wax museum so cheesy it makes Madame Tussaud's look like the British Museum. It's not without its charms, of course; Frida Kahlo and Emiliano Zapata share space with Marilyn Monroe, John F. Kennedy and six-dozen more icons of the twentieth century.

Many of La Revo's shops sell the same stuff – from handmade leather goods to shirts that proclaim how drunk you got – so don't jump into purchases immediately. The action comes to a conclusion at **Frontón Jai Alai**, Avenida Revolución, at Calle 7a. Built in 1947 to showcase the fast-moving Basque game Jai Alai, the Frontón burned down ten years later but was quickly rebuilt

△ La Revo

Shopping in La Revo

One reason for La Revo's totemic status is that it's home to a frenetic **shopping** and consuming experience that's alien to many of its visitors. Every single establishment has at least two people pacing the sidewalk in front of and calling out to passers-by. These men promise that if you'll only step inside you'll most certainly find the best price on hats, pills, beers, lap dances, paintings on velvet – the technique is the same no matter the product. To shop successfully, look at the price, chop it in half and begin to bargain politely. With the possible exception of pharmaceuticals, there's nothing here anyone absolutely needs – well, maybe a drink after two blocks – so don't get too caught up in the action.

by a community that had become ardent fans of (and bettors on) the game. Interest eventually waned, however, and it stopped hosting matches in 1995. The building, which seats 2100 spectators, is now used for concerts and special events (tickets are typically available at Ⓦticketmovil.com.mx). A betting parlour on the south side is still open.

Zona Centro

Avenida Revolución is at the centre of the **Zona Centro** area, but it may as well be blocks away. **Avenidas Constitución** and **Niños Héroes** pack a cross-section of Tijuana's population and a wide range of goods that can be browsed and purchased without the incessant hectoring commonplace along Avenida Revolución. Speciality shops selling boots, stationery or *piñatas* share space with street vendors and larger merchants, such as **Dorian's** department store, Calle 2a 1735 (Ⓣ664/688-0888).

The activity spills westward along Calle 2a in the direction of **Catedral Nuestra Señora de Guadalupe** at Niños Héroes, something of a religious showpiece in a city not exactly known for its sacred architecture (Mon–Fri hourly services 7am–9am, Sat 4pm, Sun 7am–9pm; Ⓣ664/685-3620). Building started in the 1920s and finished with the towers in the 1930s and, while it's an impressive sight, its appeal can't quite match that of its neighbour across Calle 2a, the **Mercado el Popo**, between Niños and Constitución. Merchants inside this covered market sell fresh fruit and vegetables, artisanal cheese and candy, meat and religious objects in a beguiling swap meet-like atmosphere (daily 7am–6pm).

Though out of the way, the two-storey brick and stone **Casa de la Cultura de Tijuana**, C Lisboa 5 (free; Ⓣ664/687-2604), is well worth visiting if only to pick up flyers and periodicals that will direct you to events you'd otherwise miss out on. It can be reached on foot via a staircase at the end of Calle 4a – be careful, the bottom steps are rubble – or by hailing a blue-route taxi on Calle 3a between Niños and Miguel Martinez. If you use a taxi to get up here, take the time to walk towards the staircase for a view of the city below; on a clear day you can take in the city eastward to Otay Mesa. The Casa's schedule of events – primarily geared toward locals – includes lectures, readings and regular classes. There are also movie screenings and art exhibits, the latter an attempt to pick up some slack for **Galeria de Arte de la Ciudad** until it reopens in late 2006 in the old City Hall on Calle 2a and Avenida Constitución. The in-house **Café Literario** (Mon–Sat 1–8pm) has evolved into a screening room and artist hangout that stays open late for special events.

L.A. Cetto, the largest bottler in the wine-producing Valle de Guadalupe (see Chapter 3), has an outpost a good fifteen-minute walk south at

NAFTA and the maquiladora debate

NAFTA (North American Free Trade Agreement), or **TLC** (El Tratado de Libre Comercio) in Mexico, went into effect on January 1, 1994, and created the largest free-trade area in the world. The comprehensive agreement sought to improve virtually all aspects of trade between its three partners – Mexico, the US and Canada – with many trade duties immediately cut and the rest to be phased out by 2009. Ever since, however, the benefit of NAFTA has been widely disputed and remains a contentious subject among the three countries involved.

At the epicentre of this debate sits Mexico's blossoming *maquiladora* program, with the dramatic population increase and the host of environmental and humanitarian problems it has brought to Mexico's borderlands. *Maquiladora*, from the Spanish *maquilar* (to perform a task for another), today refers to a Mexican corporation, entirely or predominantly owned by foreigners, which assembles products for export to the US or another foreign country. Sometimes referred to as "production sharing" or "the global assembly line", the program was touted as a win-win situation for all – foreign businesses could reduce overheads and enjoy larger profits, giving Mexicans more labour opportunities and less reason to cross the border, and thus earning Mexico the foreign exchange while retaining its citizens.

With the passage of NAFTA, scores of US companies rushed to Mexican border towns to capitalize on cheaper labour and less stringent environmental laws, as well as to outsource more of their raw materials and, in most cases, only pay customs duties on any non-US portion of their products. The *maquiladora* plants that subsequently sprang up now employ a quarter of a million people in northern Baja; after petroleum and tourism the *maquiladora* program is the third most important source of foreign exchange.

But the picture is not entirely rosy. In the richest-ever manifestation of US financial spillover (except, perhaps, the drug industry), Mexican migrants now crowd the border towns in search of employment, and the area lacks the necessary infrastructure to sustain such numbers. Moreover, numerous environmental studies assert that *maquiladoras* have dumped everything from raw sewage to toxic metals into the local land. Toxins at dumpsites have poisoned children and defunct *maquiladoras* have left behind drums of hazardous waste in their abandoned factories. Lab samples from waterways in several borderlands, too, have revealed abnormal deposits of industrial chemicals, petroleum and various industrial solvents. In 1995 the Mexican Federal Attorney for Environmental Protection declared that a shocking 25 percent of hazardous and toxic wastes produced by the *maquiladora* industry had not been accounted for. What's more, *maquiladora* worker abuses have also entered the picture, and employees have come forth with horrific tales of unjust working conditions and treatment. Fortunately, third-party coalitions have sprung up to improve the working and living conditions of workers in the industry along the border and forced the governments to take note.

While Mexican policy-makers originally proclaimed the *maquiladora* industry as the necessary, temporary evil to aid Mexico's troubled economy, it now seems part of the backbone of the country's long-term economic strategy. And though Mexico has perhaps the strongest anti-NAFTA following of the three countries involved, pro-NAFTA devotees are equally abundant, especially in the north, where new fortunes can and have been made. Unfortunately for this new wealthy management class Mexico is losing business at an alarming rate to other parts of the world with even lower-cost labour, especially China and Southeast Asia. The proposed FTAA (Free Trade Area of the Americas) would also give Mexico more labour competition for the North American market from smaller, impoverished Latin American nations. NAFTA and regional free trade remain hotly contested issues, but for the time being are here to stay.

Avenida Cañón Jonson 2108 (Mon–Sat 10am–5pm; tour is free, with tasting M$20; ℡664/638-3641). Since the tour consists of some oak barrels and the company store, the best time to come is during an organized wine tasting or for one of Cetto's quarterly festivals or monthly concerts (event information at ℡664/638-5848; ⓦcettowine.com.

Zona Río

From the San Ysidro crossing the less-travelled Vía Poniente leads to the south-east along the Río Tijuana towards **Zona Río**. The district's backbone, Paseo de los Héroes, is Tijuana's grandest boulevard and should be the first priority for visitors, especially those turned off by La Revo. Its tree-lined stretch contains the city's finest institutions, which frame a rich snapshot of Tijuana's restaurant, shopping and nightlife scenes.

CECUT

The prestigious ✈ **Centro Cultural Tijuana**, or **CECUT**, Paseo de los Héroes, at Avenida Independencia (daily 10am–7pm; M$20; ℡664/687-9635; ⓦwww .cecut.gob.mx), opened in 1982 as the first – and last – in a proposed network of regional cultural centres backed by the Mexican government; the rest of the plan was scrapped due to monetary issues. The centre houses a major perform-ance space, recital halls, a lobby for temporary visual art exhibits, an Omnimax movie theatre, an arts library, a garden, a bookstore and the Museo de las Californias. In addition to attracting performing groups, CECUT has ties with regional schools and universities and has its own drama school, the Centro de Artes Escénicas del Noroeste.

CECUT gets its nickname "La Bola" from the giant, brown stone **globe** that fronts the complex. Architects Pedro Ramírez Vázquez and Manuel Rosen Morrison – who also did Mexico City's Aztec Stadium and Anthropological Museum – wanted the gigantic ball to represent the earth breaking out of its shell. Inside this sphere, the **Cine Omnimax** (Tues–Fri 1–9pm, Sat & Sun 11am–9pm; M$50 for screening and entrance to exhibits) operates as a plan-etarium and movie theatre. Hourly multimedia shows are screened daily on its giant movie screen; the programme changes by season and sometimes features English-language films. The plaza around the globe plays host to the city's yearly jazz and autumn festivals.

Behind La Bola, the north wing of the main building houses the **Sala de Espectáculos**, a 1000-seat theatre home to the Orquesta de Baja California and numerous local theatre, dance and music companies. Touring international arts organizations stop here as well (frequently favouring it over San Diego) and Spanish-language versions of popular Broadway and international shows (*The Graduate* played recently) are often staged. Tickets are available at the main box office and are often discounted the day of performance.

Baja's history isn't as exciting to recount as that of mainland Mexico – too much geology and not nearly enough blood, gold and political intrigue. It's surprising, then, that the **Museo de las Californias** in the east wing manages to pull together a coherent and compelling narrative from such a short modern record and across geographically disparate parts of the peninsula. The museum's permanent exhibit begins in the pre-Columbian period and continues through Baja's history using dioramas, scale models, original artefacts, touch-screen monitors and reproductions. There's no glossing over the bad bits – models of missions, primary documents and captions tell the story of the religious orders that wrought devastation on the indigenous people. The photographs and newspaper clippings near the end of the exhibit are devoted to stories of the revolutionaries that raised hell along the border in the early twentieth century, most notably the Magonistas (see box, p.98), followers of the rebel Ricardo Flores Magón who were led by Caryl Ap Rhys Pryce, a Welsh soldier of fortune. The open space beneath the museum's permanent collection is used for travelling visual and decorative art exhibits.

Adjacent to the museum's entrance is a bookstore selling art, history and fiction titles, including a sizable section devoted to Tijuana authors and border issues. Just outside, the 6000-square-metres square **Jardín Caracol** nearly doubles CECUT's space. Half-hour long, Spanish-language tours of the garden (daily noon, 1, 3, 4 & 5pm) weave through the collection of cacti, flowering plants and reproductions of pre-Columbian sculpture from throughout Mexico.

Along the Paseo

Four large monuments punctuate **Paseo de los Héroes** from Avenida Independencia to Avenida Abelardo Rodriguez, each providing a historical snapshot. Near the Paseo's northern end, **Monumento a la Raza**, at Avenida Independencia, rises aggressively before tapering up to a not-so ominous, erect clothespin; its jagged edges are meant to complement the smooth curves of the adjacent CECUT ball. On the next block, a three-storey high statue of the defeated Aztec leader **Cuauhtémoc** watches over the intersection with the street that bears his name. A bronze statue of a lean **President Abraham Lincoln** stands at Avenido Diego Rivera, the broken shackles falling from his wrists symbolizing his role as emancipator; his presence on a Mexican street is also testament to his opposition to the US-Mexican war. Mexican hero **General Ignacio Zaragoza** straddles a horse at Avenida Rodriguez. His victory over the French gave the country its most popular holiday, Cinco de Mayo.

Founded in 1955, **Mercado Miguel Hidalgo**, Avenida Independencia at Guadalupe Victoria (daily 7am–7pm), is the city's largest outdoor market. Early fears that it would be swept up in the demolitions that preceded the creation of Zona Río in the early 1960s were never realized, and the market has become one of the neighbourhood's most popular destinations. You can buy a little of everything at the colourful stalls that line its perimeter: fruits and vegetables, seafood, desserts, *piñatas*, toys and clothing are some of the more common goods on display. Some of the stalls double as restaurants, but if you can't find anything to your liking, there are a number of bakeries and fish taco joints along the nearby streets Guadalupe Victoria and Avenida Mina. The Mercado is within walking distance of more upscale shopping at Plaza Río and Plaza del Zapato (see Shopping, p.84).

The updated family-friendly **Mundo Divertido** theme park, Rápida Poniente 15035 (Mon–Fri noon–8.30pm; Sat & Sun 11am–9:30pm; free, purchase tickets for rides; ⓣ664/701-7043, ⓦwww.mundodivertido.com.mx), reopened in an expanded location in the fall of 2005. It employs small carnival rides, mini-golf courses, a go-kart track and countless video games to provide entertainment. It's a popular place for picnics and birthday parties, and if you haven't brought your own food you can choose from taco vendors inside the food court.

Hipódromo

At Avenida Revolución's southern tip near Calle 11a, the avenue becomes Boulevard Agua Caliente as it makes a sharp turn east toward the bullring, Hipódromo Caliente, and the surrounding **Hipódromo** district. The demolished **Agua Caliente Casino** was once the heart of Tijuana's tourism industry,

The Hank Rhon family

Hipódromo Caliente and the entire Caliente gaming company are owned by **Jorge Hank Rhon**, the youngest son of former Mexico City mayor Carlos Hank Gonzales and brother of billionaire financier Carlos Hank Rhon. Until his death in 2001, Gonzales was one of the most powerful men within the PRI, Mexico's dominant political party. Hank Gonzales the elder is as widely known for being the brains behind disgraced president Carlos Salinas as he is for using his four decades as a public servant to build a billion-dollar empire ("A politician who is poor is a poor politician," Gonzales is famous for saying). When he died, each son's portion of the inheritance was half a billion dollars.

Since taking over the racetrack from a group of Sicilian-American investors through a series of questionable deals and court orders in the early 1980s, Jorge Rhon has turned it into Tijuana's seat of gaming. His Caliente betting company controls the gaming industry in Mexico and parts of Latin America and Europe. With at least 18 children, three wives and a private zoo filled with illegal exotic animals, Rhon is quite the colourful figure.

The operations of "Grupo Hank" are often scrutinized by US law enforcement agencies, but allegations haven't stuck and indictments have never been issued. Jorge's Baja California business partners aren't always far removed from the Arellano-Felix drug cartel and his brother Carlos' banking activities have been penalized by the US Securities and Exchange Commission. They have powerful friends on both sides of the border: it took lobbying by former US Senator Warren Rudman to stifle a study for the US FBI and Drug Enforcement Agency called "Operation White Tiger" (named so because of Jorge's exotic animal fetish) that referred to the family as "a significant criminal threat to the United States".

The most persistent allegation that's dogged Jorge is that he was involved in the 1988 assassination of *Zeta* journalist and one-time friend Héctor Félix Miranda. Two employees of the racetrack were convicted of the murder after one of the killers was linked to a payment of US$10,000 from the track the day of the killing. The case is still officially open.

In 2004, Jorge Hank Rhon turned to politics and became the PRI candidate for mayor of Tijuana. After beating out his PAN opponent by only five thousand votes, he became the first PRI mayor in Tijuana in five terms. A voter interviewed by the *San Diego Union-Tribune* expressed hope in the candidate, pointing out that because of Jorge's vast fortune "He won't need to steal."

with its own train station, airport and bungalows surrounding pools and canals. The only reminder of this almost-grand past is the 40-metre high minaret that stands at the northwestern edge of this neighbourhood. The area now takes its name from the racetrack at the foot of the Agua Caliente hills, **Hipódromo Caliente** at Tapachula 12027 (races Mon–Fri 7.45pm; Sat & Sun 2pm & 7.45pm; grandstand seating free, box seating M$110; ☎664/633-7300). Erected in 1929, the grandstand and complex were initially home to horse racing (Seabiscuit won the Caliente Handicap in 1938) and, in the smaller in-field track, dog racing. It now only features greyhound racing and off-track betting: horse races were eliminated in 1992 after a labour dispute between the track and jockeys. Once a year, in the departed jockeys' honour, track owner, amateur zoologist, millionaire and current mayor Jorge Hank Rhon (see box, above) dips into his personal primate collection and presents a race of greyhounds with costumed monkeys strapped atop their backs.

If you want to watch the races from the racetrack's gentlemanly *Turf Club* bar (no phone; reserved ticket to races allows access, only open during race days.), you must wear a jacket and be a man (or bring one along) – women must be escorted.

Plaza El Toreo de Tijuana, Avenida Santa María 221 (May–Oct, Sun 4pm; box office ☎664/664-1510; ⓦ www.bullfights.org) doesn't have the grand backdrop of the Pacific Ocean for its bullfights like the Bullring by the Sea, but its placement downtown makes it a prime site for outdoor concerts, rallies and other non-blood sport events, in addition to the seasonal fights. There's a box office open one hour before events, but you may also purchase tickets at a booth on Avenida Revolución and Calle 2a in front of the *Hotel Lafayette* or as part of package tours with Mexicoach at its office on the same street.

Playas de Tijuana

Cut off from the rest of Tijuana by a hill packed with shelters built out of concrete blocks, plywood and discarded metal scraps, **Playas** has developed a separate identity that's a little sleepier and a little richer. For years its singular attraction has been the **Bullring by the Sea**, but as the city continues to decrease the amount of waste it dumps into the Pacific, more and more residents are finding it a better alternative to Tijuana's landlocked neighbourhoods. New homes are sprouting up on tiny lots near the beach, and developers are busy clearing entire blocks for new complexes.

On each Sunday from May to September, sixteen thousand fans – and half a dozen unfortunate cattle – file into the red and white concrete **Plaza Monumental**, also known as the Bullring by the Sea (Sun 4pm; ☎664/680-1808), to watch celebrity matadors wave capes and dodge horns. A Sunday here is the social equivalent of a football match and orchestra performance – as classy an affair as a real blood sport can be. Fans picnic in the park north of the ring and merchants set up shop for a day's worth of auxiliary activities. Cheap seats in the sun start at M$100 and box seats surpass M$1000 for special matches.

The more family-friendly **Charreada** at El Cortijo San Jose, Avenida del Agua 777 (Sunday afternoons; ☎664/630-9714) has roughly the same May–September season as the bullfights. This rodeo and fair is a hodgepodge of performing cowboys, animal trainers and musicians. Families come and go throughout the afternoon, turning the events into a large neighbourhood social.

△ Playas de Tijuana and the Bullring by the Sea

The **beach** is just west of the bullring behind a string of small hotels, restaurants and bars; it becomes cleaner the further south you go. On the northern end near the bullring, a six-metre-high ramshackle border fence cuts one hundred metres into the water. Just steps away, though, a concrete staircase leads down to the beach and a boardwalk popular with joggers, walkers and in-line skaters that runs towards the southern end of town. The water is too cold for swimming except in summer, but wet-suited surfers brave the chill year round. Near the southern end of the boardwalk, along the last stretch of Paseo Ensenada, an open-air **street market** (Mon–Sat 7–11am) begins at Avenida Llama and ends a block before the road turns to dirt. Stalls line both sides of the street, and merchants sell fruit and vegetables along with clothing and household goods. The neighbourhood's main shopping area is directly adjacent to the turnoff from Mex 1D and includes a Calimax, Sanborn's and Star Cinema theatre.

Bullfighting

Soccer and wrestling may be more popular, but there is no event more quintessentially Mexican than the **bullfight**. Rooted in Spanish machismo and imbued with multiple layers of symbolism and interpretation, it transcends a mere battle of man against animal. Many visitors arrive in Mexico revolted by the very idea of what may appear to be a one-sided slaughter of a noble beast, and there are certainly elements of cruelty in the proceedings. But spend an hour watching one on TV and you may well find yourself hooked; and if nothing else, it is worth attending a *corrida de toros* to see this integral part of the Mexican experience. It is a sport that transcends class barriers, something that is evident on Sunday afternoons when men and women from all walks of Mexican society file into the stadium – though some admittedly end up in plush *sombra* (shade) seats while the masses occupy concrete *sol* (sun) terraces.

Each *corrida* lasts around two hours and involves six bulls, all from one ranch, with each of three matadors taking two bulls. Typically there will be two Mexican matadors and one from Spain, which still produces the best performers: Enrique Ponce and Julián Lopez (always referred to as "El Juli") are currently the two top Spanish names, and if you see them billed you should definitely try to get along.

Each fight is divided into three *suertes* (acts) or *tercios* (thirds), each announced by a trumpet blast. During the first *tercio* several *toreros* with large capes tire the bull in preparation for the *picadores* who, from their mounts atop heavily padded and blindfolded horses, attempt to force a lance between the bull's shoulder blades to further weaken him. The *toreros* then return for the second *tercio*, in which one of their number (and sometimes the matador himself) will try to stab six metal-tipped spikes (known as *bandilleras*) into the bull in as clean and elegant a manner as possible.

Exhausted and frustrated, but by no means docile, the bull is now considered ready for the third and final *tercio*, the *suerte de muleta*. The matador continues to tire the bull while pulling off as many graceful and daring moves as possible. By now the crowd will have sensed the bravery and finesse of the matador and the spirit of the bull he is up against, and shouts of "Olé!" will reverberate around the stadium with every pass. Eventually the matador will entice the bull to challenge him head-on, standing there with its hooves together. As it charges he will thrust his sword between its shoulder blades and, if the stroke is well executed, the bull will crumple to the sand. However barbaric you might think it is, no one likes to see the bull suffer and even the finest performance will garner the matador little praise without a clean kill.

Successful matadors may be awarded one of the bull's ears, rarely two, and perhaps two or three times a season the tail as well. An especially courageous bull may be spared and put out to stud, a cause for much celebration, although this is an increasingly rare spectacle. Many believe the quality of fighting bulls has declined of late, and in recent years the sports pages have been full of discussion on the matter.

Getting to Playas

There are three different *ruta* taxis that head west **to Playas**, all costing about M$7, but the most direct is route number 1 from the cream and white taxis at Calle 3a and Miguel Martínez. Blue and white number 1 or 2 buses that read "Playas" travel along Calle 3a (look for kerbs with "Playas" stencilled in black or red paint) and will take you from downtown to the shore in twenty minutes for M$4. Shared taxis from the city centre will cost M$10 – confirm the rate in advance. During bullfight season (May–Sept) private shuttle services like Mexicoach deliver people from the San Diego Trolley stop or the Tijuana Bus Terminal to the bullring for the price of the fight ticket and a M$70–100 surcharge. If you're driving from Tijuana, just follow any sign that reads "Playas" or "Mex 1D" and you'll be dumped off near the bullring. Avenida Playas de Tijuana and Paseo Ensenada are the main north-south drags and eventually connect at their northern and southern ends.

Islas los Coronado

Four tranquil islands make up the **Islas los Coronado** that sit roughly 14km west off the coast of Tijuana. Their inhabitants include pelicans, sea lions and seals but, with the exception of a small naval garrison on the southernmost island, no humans. To see the islands up close you'll need to have your own boat or join a fishing or dive trip departing from San Diego; two-day trips run on average US$350. Operators include H&M Landing (US☎619/222-1144; ⒺＨhmmail@hmlanding.com), Fisherman's Landing (US☎619/221-8500; Ⓔinfo@fishermanslanding.com) and Point Loma Sportfishing (US☎619/223-1627; Ⓦwww.pointlomasportfishing.com).

Eating

The best by-product of Tijuana's population boom is its **vibrant restaurant scene**. Diners can sample regional specialities from throughout the country as well as indulge in successful Mexican variations on international cuisine. The city claims one culinary invention – the first Caesar salad was made at the hotel of the same name on Avenida Revolución – as well as the clam juice and tomato drink Clamato – definitely an acquired taste.

La Revo's restaurants are dressed up Tex-Mex style, almost all of them with the requisite party atmosphere. While cheap, they aren't indicative of what the rest of the city has to offer. **Zona Río** has the best selection of restaurants, with several sandwiched between Paseo de los Héroes and Boulevard Sánchez Taboada. The options along Boulevard Agua Caliente and Avenida Tapachula cater to the city's middle and upper classes.

US chain restaurants, such as *McDonald's* and *TGI Friday*, are ubiquitous around La Revo and the pedestrian walkway. The local *taquería* chain *Tijuana JR's* is a safe bet, as is a local variant of *Starbucks*, *D'Volada*, which operates about two dozen outposts throughout Tijuana selling coffee and pastries.

Menu prices in La Revo are listed in both dollars and pesos, and predominantly in pesos throughout the rest of the city (the final bill, though, typically lists both dollars and pesos). Credit cards are not always accepted, so bring cash. If you are paying with credit, always write the appropriate currency name after the amount to avoid confusion with the shared $ symbol; a good rule to follow throughout the peninsula.

La Revo

Persistent waiters at every restaurant along **La Revo** will attempt to pull you inside for a meal. There are a few hidden gems amidst the dross, and you shouldn't hesitate to stop in for happy-hour specials on drinks and salsa and chips.

 Caesar's Sports Bar & Grill Av Revolución 1071 ☎664/638-4562. Caesar Cardini first whipped up his eponymous salad here in 1924, and it is still prepared tableside with raw egg and garlic, Parmesan cheese, anchovies and hearts of Romaine (M$70) in an elaborate ceremony. The long, narrow space is predominantly a sports bar, albeit one that accents its many televisions with high ceilings, dark-wood wall panels and leather booths.

Chiki Jai Av Revolución 1388 ☎664/685-4955. A resident of the strip since 1947, this restaurant has outlived the game it was named after. The Spanish menu includes seafood dishes like *bacalao* (dried salt cod; M$120) and homemade sausage specialties (M$50–70).

La Costa C 7a 8131 ☎664/685-8494. You can get one of the city's finest multi-course fish dinners here (M$600 per person), or come for lunch and enjoy oysters or grilled fish at more reasonable prices (M$80–150). Breakfast served as well.

D'Tony Av Madero 2421 ☎664/685-5077. Romantic, upscale Argentine restaurant with one of the better steaks (M$110) in town and a wide selection of South American wines. Tango music is piped in all day long. Closed Sundays.

 Mariscos Don Pepe Blvd Fundadores 688 ☎664/684-9086. Some would argue that the decor could use updating, but that might subtract from the inventive formula that helps *Don Pepe* churn out some of the most dependable, fresh and affordable seafood in town; including a *ceviche* starter that takes the place of the standard salsa and chips and jumbo shrimp wrapped in bacon.

La Taberna TJ Blvd Fundadores 2951 ☎664/638-8662, ⊛www.tjbeer.com. The dishes here – a Continental, American and Mexican hodge-podge of pub-quality fare – are secondary to the small-batch lager beers produced by the city's only microbrewery. Closed Sundays.

Tia Juana Tilly's Av Revolución 1420 ☎664/685-6024. This popular Tex-Mex restaurant, linked to the Fronton Jai Alai, has terrace seating along a quiet stretch of La Revo. Bow-tied waiters serve up main courses such as steaks, chicken and seafood (M$80–140).

Tortas Ricardo's Av Madero at C 7a. A massive range of Mexican dishes served in American diner surroundings; hearty pork sandwiches (M$40) and *huevos rancheros* (M$50) are popular with late-night and early-morning crowds. Breakfast served.

Vittorío's Av Revolución 1687. Red and white checked tablecloths and the scent of garlic set the stage for Italian basics like spaghetti (M$90) and small pizzas (M$70).

Zona Río

In addition to the restaurants described below, there are a number of inexpensive eateries inside Mercado Miguel Hidalgo and Plazas Fiesta and Pueblo Amigo, both of which are also good bets if you're going clubbing afterwards.

Los Angulo Paseo de los Héroes 4449 ☎664/634-6027. Although it's massive, the 50-foot-high pitched *palapa* roof creates enough atmosphere for almost any type of outing. Dine on grilled, baked, stuffed or fried shrimp (M$100) and seafood dishes (M$70–120) with four hundred of your closest friends.

La Casa del Mole Poblano 2 Paseo de los Héroes 10501 ☎664/634-6920. Dark chocolate and hot chillies flavour the Oaxacan sauce this restaurant uses to coat chicken legs and breasts (M$60) and other meat dishes. A nice atmosphere for a bargain spot, with waterfalls, plants and, on weekends, roving musicians.

Cheripan Av Escuadrón 201 3151 ☎664/622-9730, ⊛www.cheripan.com. New location and slightly spiced-up version of the Hipodrómo Argentine grill (see p.82). The menu contains steak dishes (M$150) and pastas (M$120) and also includes an extensive wine list and the city's best chips, coated in parsley and garlic (M$30).

 Cien Anos Av José Maria Velazco 1407, ☎664/634-3039. This spot-of-the-moment has drawn notice for its use and adaptation of Aztec recipes. Gourmands swear by the corn fungus and marrow dishes (M$150–250); tamer items such as honey-roasted duck or chicken *mole* are available for the less intrepid.

△ Prepping the salad at Caesar's

La Diferencia Blvd Sánchez Taboada 10611-A ☎664/634-7078. Along with neighbour *Cien Anos*, *Diferencia* has a more daring menu than most places in Tijuana, with satisfying takes on pre-Columbian meals. Unfamiliar dishes like beef tongue strips and chillies, the Aztec delicacy crepes Cuitlacoche (an edible corn fungus), or cow brain tacos (M$150–220) are made more appealing within a romantic setting replete with a courtyard and fountain.

Gypsy's Paseo del Centenario 9211, inside Plaza Pueblo Amigo ☎664/683-6006. This Spanish restaurant and bar is fronted by a mural of Salvador Dali and opens out to a pedestrian mall. The tapas menu (M$20–50 per dish) is the perfect accompaniment to pitchers of sangria and the well-made margaritas. Open late.

El Mezquite Av Padre Kino 9970 ☎664/973-1242, ⊛restaurantbarelmezquite.com. Large portions and its proximity to the border make this budget Mexican restaurant especially attractive to day-trippers. The menu (about M$80 per person) includes lamb, beef, fish and, on weekends, goat.

Palapa Gigante Paseo de los Héroes 4449 ⏰ 664/634-6027, ⓦ www.lapalapagigante.com .mx. The restaurant's name gives a good indication of the interior, where you can order just about any kind of Mexican dish. Their most inspired work – grilled shrimp, *ceviche* and whole grilled fish – comes straight from the sea.

Villa Saverio's C Escuadrón 201 3151 ⏰ 664/686-6442. Even though it's one of the fanciest places in town (it's best to bring a jacket), the high-end Mediterranean cuisine and variations on Baja basics won't break your budget; appetizers start at M$70 and entrees top out at M$200.

Hipódromo

Street food isn't Tijuana's strong point, but Boulevard Agua Caliente in **Hipódromo** has two long-standing stalls you shouldn't miss: *El Güero*, on the south side of the boulevard, just across from a Chevy dealership, sells M$5 tacos; the other is a nameless *torta* stand (ask about the old "Wash Mobile Tortas") just north of *Motel Olvera* on Calle Jalisco, which serves a grilled steak sandwich with avocado, onions, grilled peppers and hot sauce (M$30).

Casa Dobson Tapachula 1, inside *Hotel Country Club* ⏰ 664/686-2218. This Mexican outpost of a San Diego stalwart recreates favourites like mussels bisque (M$70) with the added draw of a view over the golf greens of Club Campestre. The restaurant's bar is a popular destination for post-racetrack cocktails.

La Fonda Robertos Av Cuauhtémoc 2800 ⏰ 664/686-4687. The fountain in the middle of the room is a conventional touch for such an odd Pueblan restaurant. Old-school dishes lean on Aztec recipes like *huazontle* (twigs covered in pork and cheese – M$50), to create a menu Montezuma would approve of, while a superb chilli verde sauce covers more readily recognizable dishes like enchiladas. Closed Mondays.

Makko Sushi Av Sonora 3240-6 ⏰ 664/686-2133. One of the best of the city's many sushi restaurants offers excellent views over the golf course. Sushi rolls (M$40) are joined on the menu by a wide range of Japanese meat dishes.

Palm Azul Blvd Salinas 11154 ⏰ 664/6229773. If you missed or enjoyed the recreations in CECUT, you can dine surrounded by replicas of Baja's mysterious cave paintings, or on the large patio surrounding an open fireplace. Besides the atmosphere, the raw bar is the main draw, as are the daily seafood-centric specials like black sea bass (M$170–200). Closed Sundays.

El Rodeo Blvd Salinas 1647 ⏰ 664/686-5640. For a cowboy-themed restaurant, *Rodeo* has a lot in common with Korean barbecue. The signature *parrilla* grill (M$300 for two), is cooked tableside over charcoal and accompanied by a host of small plates that include pickled vegetables and cheese, beans, warm tortillas and potatoes.

El Sol de Cheripan Av Sonora 3240 ⏰ 664/971-0099. Original outpost of Argentine grill famous for its succulent steaks (M$130), chops and extensive wine list.

Playas de Tijuana

With the exception of *San Roman*, the beach's restaurants don't take chances like those in the city, catering instead to diners looking for something straightforward after a day in the water.

Club Boomerang Paseo Playas 330 ⏰ 664/630-9998. Sports bar and club along the beach that serves basic Mexican dishes before the sun goes down, then gets loud with either DJs or a game on TV.

Mariscos Tito's Paseo Isla Coronado 1107 ⏰ 664/630-0306. Playas' largest restaurant is famous for its Mexican breakfast buffet during the week and enormous brunch on Sundays.

Rincón San Roman Km 19.5 Mex 1D, inside *Real del Mar* (see p.68) ⏰ 664/631-2242,

ⓦ www.rinconsanroman.com. Much-lauded chef Martin San Roman takes local seafood traditions and employs his French techniques to produce *nuevo* Continental dishes like penne with shrimp in Pernod (M$180) or scampi with chili sauce (M$200). The romantic dining room has views of the Islas los Coronado.

Yoghurt Place C Cantera 360 ⏰ 664/680-2006. Located incongruously next door to the bullring, this organic vegetarian café serves tempeh stir fries and soy-stuffed burritos. Breakfast and lunch only.

Nightlife

The rowdiest action in Tijuana is along **La Revo**, where numerous nightclubs pump out rock music and hip-hop. English is the lingua franca, dollars are the currency of choice, and the playlist is solidly American Top 40. More traditional Mexican bars, as well as those featuring "exotic dancers," cluster around Calle 1a and Avenida Constitución and on Avenida Revolución at Calle 6a. Locals, visitors in the know, and those who've outgrown beer bongs shun La Revo in favour of clubs and bars clustered around the shopping areas of **Zona Río**, where the beats are louder, the clubs larger and the scene doesn't slow down until morning.

Movies, the theatre and performing arts sometimes share space with one another as well as with bars, lounges and cafes. The best way to discover smaller events is by picking up the free Spanish-language weekly *De Noche y De Día la Guía*, which covers current cinema, concerts and DJ events, as well as listings for clubs, cafés and restaurants. New editions are published on Thursdays and can be found at most *Café D'Volada* outposts and other locations around town. The competing weekly *Bitácora* is available at many of the same places beginning Wednesdays as well as online at Ⓦwww.bitacoracultural.com. Get tickets for bigger events through Ticketmovil (Ⓣ664/681-7084; Ⓦticketmovil.com.mx).

La Revo

With competition fierce, cover charges are rare and drinks are often offered two for the price of one; taking a walk along either side of Avenida Revolución is the best way to discern which joint is the most happening on any given night. Do, however, expect to pay a cover from M$50–100 at music clubs.

Cave Av Revolución 1137. Ground-level disco populated with just-turned-18 San Diegans behaving in ways they couldn't legally at home.

El Foro Av Revolución at C 7a, inside Frontón Jai Alai. Downtown's biggest indoor concert venue typically charges M$100 for performances. What you'll hear depends on the promoter; Mexican folk music one night, death metal the next.

Hard Rock Café Av Revolución 520 Ⓣ664/685-0206. The Tijuana outpost of the international chain hosts bands until 2am every weekend. The menu – burgers and the like – is served until 10pm.

People's Sports and Rock Av Revolución 786 at C 2a. There's a harder edge to the music here at one of La Revo's more established rock clubs. Be prepared for the bar staff's attempts to pour tequila down your throat in an effort to loosen the purse strings.

Las Pulgas Av Revolución 1127 Ⓣ664/688-1368. The evening never really ends at this modern Latin disco – doors open at 10am and don't close until 5am.

Salón de Baile C 6a, between Avenidas Revolución and Madero. Don't be put off by the lurid paintings, this is the real thing: a traditional dance hall with an almost Caribbean feel playing salsa, *cumbia* and *norteño*. Easy enough to spot – look for the big red star.

Voodoo House C 8a 530. A small cover charge will get you into this rock club to see both local and touring acts from both sides of the border.

Zona Centro

The streets around La Revo house smaller cafés that typically serve as meeting places for people in the city's creative industry. The hours at these spots can be erratic, so call ahead to make sure they're open before heading out.

La Casa de la 9 Arte Café C 9a at Quintana Roo Ⓣ664/688-0113. Musicians and artists show off their work at this bustling café and exhibition space. Live jazz and bossa nova keeps the doors open until 1am on weekends.

El Lugar del Nopal Callejón 5 de Mayo 1328 Ⓣ664/685-1264, Ⓦwww.lugardelnopal.com. Tijuana's creative class turns up in this café-cum-performance space for exhibits, screenings and live music. Open Fri & Sat only.

Multikulti Av Constitución 13131 ⓔ info@multikulti.org.mx. The gutted, open-air Bujazán Cinema is now used to host small concerts, underground arts festivals and DJ events.

Zona Río and around

The **Zona Río** is the city's premier destination for nightlife. At dusk many of the district's cafés turn their lights low and let DJs take over, while varied clubs offering mechanical bull rides and sophisticated ambiance draw those who have long since graduated from La Revo.

Baby Rock C Diego Rivera 1482 ☎ 664/634-2404. The exterior and fake boulders says Flintstones but the inside is all lasers and techno beats. Cover starts around M$100; for an extra M$50 they'll park your car.

Balak Discotheque Via Oriente 9211, inside Plaza Pueblo Amigo ☎ 664/683-6244, ⓦ www .balakdisco.com. Tijuana's largest club doesn't skimp on anything, whether it's the sound system (it reportedly cost over US$1 million), its guests (Ricky Martin in his heyday) or the light system (blinding). The cover is typically a steep M$150–200 but free before 11pm.

Galaxy Via Oriente 9211, inside Plaza Pueblo Amigo. Dance club with regular appearances by respected touring DJs and local superstars like Nortec Collective.

Marko Disco Governador Balarezo 2000. Old-school nightclub from the 1970s – with columns, mirrored walls and disco balls – is still a popular venue for travelling DJs and local talent.

Mofo Bar Callejón Alfonso Reyes 9351, inside Plaza Pueblo Amigo ☎ 664/683-5427. Foreign films are screened on slow nights but weekends belong to house music spun by live DJs.

El Perro Azul Paseo de los Héroes, inside Plaza Fiesta. Arty, bohemian place with live acoustic music, exhibitions and a mixed, friendly clientele. Open until 2am.

Plaza Fiesta Paseo de los Héroes 1001. Can't decide where to go? Locals often head here without a specific place in mind, preferring to wander between the bars and clubs until they find a scene that appeals to them. Standouts include *El Callejón* (☎ 664/687-4953), *La Cantina* (☎ 664/684-0705), *Monastario* (☎ 664/634-1729) and *Sótano Suizo* (☎ 664/684-8834). Most spots are quiet before 11pm.

Plaza Pueblo Amigo Via Oriente 9211. Same idea as Plaza Fiesta, but with larger clubs. *Galaxy* and *Balak* (both above) get more attention, but *Papparazi* (☎ 664/607-3441), *La Casa de la Trova* (☎ 664/638-4900) and the techno meets mechanical bull-riding palace *Rodeo Santa Fe* (☎ 664/682-4967) are quite popular, too.

Punto Café Paseo de los Héroes 1001, inside Plaza Fiesta ☎ 664/634-1240. This trendy, low-key café with outside seating and magazines to flick through has an incredible range of coffees. A great staging ground for forays into Plaza Fiesta, *Punto* ditches the coffee-shop sheen around 11pm when the DJs begin playing house and lounge beats.

S.O.S. Dancehall Blvd Agua Caliente 12027. Performance space inside the Caliente racetrack that is as likely to be used for a teenage girl's *quinceñara* party as it is a club night. Look for listings in magazines, above, or flyers at *El Lugar del Nopal* (see p.83).

Tangaloo Av Monterrey 3215 ☎ 664/681-8091. Giant, laser-light filled club in an otherwise sleepy area between the Zona Río and Hipódromo. The 1000+ capacity space hosts some all-ages events amongst its roster of touring DJs and live acts.

Tazas y Tarros Edmundo O'Gorman 2345 ☎ 664/634-6621. This low-key café doubles as a destination for touring DJs and is a favourite haunt of electronica fans.

Shopping

More than a third of Tijuana's visitors come just to **shop**. Many of them will make their purchases from the shops that populate Avenida Revolución and the open-air pedestrian malls on either side of Río Tijuana, **Plaza Viva Tijuana** and the **Mercado de Artisanías**. These areas swell with a mix of duty-free goods and stalls selling souvenirs, fake and genuine designer clothing and jewellery. Of the shops along La Revo, the craft marketplace **Tolan**, between Calle 7a and Calle 8a (☎664/688-3637) has the widest selection of Mexican crafts and sells them in a haggle-free environment. You can find more upscale artisan goods, along with food, inside **Sanborn's**, Avenida Revolución at Calle 8a (☎664/688-1462). Still, you will almost always find better-quality products at stores one block to the west along **Avenida Constitución**, the **Mercado del Popo** on Calle 2a, and next door at **Dorian's** department store, Calle 2a 1735 (☎664/688-0888).

Plaza Río, next to CECUT at Paseo de los Héroes 9698, is the city's largest mall (☎664/684-0402), with a typical array of restaurants and outdoor spaces to sit and ponder your next purchase. Just across the street, there are bargains to be found at **Mercado Miguel Hidalgo** (see p.75) and the nearby **Plaza del Zapato**, but you'll need to pay cash and have a familiarity with Spanish to get the best deals. The Mercado specializes in perishable and non-perishable food, as well as *piñatas* and toys, leather goods, and kitchenware. Across Avenida Independencia, Plaza del Zapato only sells shoes and foot-related goods; you can purchase name-brand trainers and dress shoes for half what you'd pay north of the border.

Adventurous travellers will find the best bargains at markets in the La Mesa and San Antonio *delegaciones*. **Swapmeet Lázaro Cárdenas**, Calzada Lázaro Cárdenas 785 (Thurs–Mon), can be reached through an opening in the middle of the 5y10 shopping centre and directly across from a mini-bus station. You can find practically anything in this maze of covered stalls: bootleg CDs and DVDs, wedding dresses, Nike sneakers, toys, hair extensions and home appliances; there's a similar swap meet at **Plaza Fundadores** at the intersection of Boulevard Fundadores and Rosas Magallón on the northern edge of San Antonio.

Prescription drugs

Rising health-care costs in the United States have driven a broad spectrum of the populace to seek cheaper medicines and services in Canada and Mexico. About a quarter of a million US visitors a month come to Tijuana to purchase **prescription drugs** at discounts up to seventy percent what they'd pay at home. The US Food and Drug Administration speaks of this trade in terms that evoke the end of the world, but when done above-board at legitimate pharmacies, it's considered completely safe.

If you're going to purchase prescription drugs and play by the book, there are two sets of rules you're going to need to abide by: those of Mexico and those of the country you're heading back to. For everything to be above-board, buyers must obtain a prescription – with seal and serial number – from a Mexican doctor. You're free to pass through San Ysidro or Otay Mesa without a prescription if you have fifty or fewer doses. With a prescription you can carry through ninety days' worth of your medicine. These amounts can vary at the airport and other crossings, so check with your consulate ahead of time.

Playing by the rules is complicated by the fact that so many people aren't. A number of pharmacies will sell you what you want without a prescription. At the shopping centre just across the Otay Mesa border visitors can easily purchase steroids, pain-killers and medicine usually reserved for animals and cross back into the US. Keep in mind that if you're caught, it doesn't matter whether you're carrying legitimate heart medicine or a bushel of horse tranquillizers – pleading ignorance won't help. According to the US consulate in Tijuana, about two hundred Americans are currently serving jail terms in Tijuana for prescription drug-related offences.

Sports

The one sport, besides bullfighting, that Tijuanese are passionate about is baseball. The **Tijuana Potros** are in the northern conference of the *Liga Mexican de Beisbol* and play on the outskirts of Otay at the new 12,000-seat ⚾**Estadio de Calimax**, Río Euphrates s/n (March–July; tickets start at US$1; ☎664/660-9863, ⓦwww .potrosdetijuana.com).

Real del Mar (see p.68) and **Club Campestre**, Boulevard Agua Caliente 11311 (Mon–Fri US$30, Sat & Sun US$40; ☎664/681-7863), in the foothills of Agua Caliente are the city's only **golf courses**.

Listings

Airlines Aeromexico/Aerolitoral, Plaza Río ☎664/683-8444, 684-9268, ⓦwww.aeromexico .com; Aviacsa/Aeroexo, Plaza Guadalupe, Suite 6 Blvd Sánchez Taboada ☎664/622-5086, 622-5024, ⓦwww.aviacsa.com; Aerocalifornia, Plaza Río, ☎664/684-2100, 684-2876, ⓕ664/634-1716, Mon–Fri 8am–8pm; Mexicana, Diego Rivera 1511 ☎664/634-6545, 634-6566, 634-6593, ⓦwww.mexicana.com.mx, Mon–Fri 9am–6:45pm, Sat 9am–2pm; Aerolíneas Azteca, Paseo de los Héroes 10051 ☎664/633-9226, 634-7286, ⓦwww.aerolineasazteca.com, Mon–Fri 9am–7pm, Sat 9am–2pm.

American Express There's an office in Viajes Carrousel travel agency (Mon–Fri 9am–6pm, Sat 9am–noon) way out on Blvd Sánchez Taboada at Clemente Orozco, but their rates are poor.

Banks US dollars are accepted almost everywhere in Tijuana, but you do get a slightly better return on pesos. If you're visiting no further south than Ensenada there's really no reason to change your currency – you'll lose in the exchange rate whatever savings you'd get buying in shops. If you do change it's really no problem, with *casas de cambio* on virtually every corner. Most offer good rates – almost identical to those north of the border – though few of them accept travellers' cheques, and if they do, they charge a heavy commission. For cheques you're better off with a bank, most of which are on Constitución, a block over from Revolución. ATMs along both of these blocks dispense both dollars and pesos.

Books Sanborn's department store, at Revolución and C 8a, has books and magazines, some from across the border.

Consulates Australia/Canada, Germán Gedovius 10411-101 ☎664/684-0461; Germany, Cantera 400-305, Playas de Tijuana ☎664/680-2512; UK, Blvd Salinas 1500 ☎664/686-5320; US, Tapachula 96 ☎664/622-7400, ⓦwww.usembassy-mexico .gov/tijuana/Tijuana.htm.

Hospital Paseo de los Héroes 2507 ☎664/634-7002, 7001-3434.

Internet access The best Internet cafés are branches of SpaceBooth.com; one is at Revolución between C 2a and C 3a; the other at C 11a near C Pio Pico. Both have good prices (M$20 per hr) and serve coffee, drinks and snacks.

Left luggage Bags can be left at the Central Camionera (daily 6am–10.30pm), in lockers over the border in the Greyhound station (24hr), or next door at Pro-Pack (Mon–Sat 9am–6pm).

Police If you become a victim of crime, a rip-off or simply want to make a complaint, pick up any phone and dial 078.

Post office Negrete and C 11a (Mon–Fri 8am–4pm, Sat & Sun 9.30am–1pm), though to send international mail you're better off crossing the border.

Telephones The post office (see above) has large *distancia* phones, as does the Terminal Turístico, but you're better off crossing the border to make long-distance calls. Buy Telmex phone cards in any corner store to make local calls.

Moving on from Tijuana

Mexicoach, Revolución and Calle 7a (☎664/685-1470, US☎619/428-9517), runs **shuttles** to San Ysidro (M$25). Once on the **US side** at San Ysidro there's excellent local transport into downtown San Diego – buses (US$2.25) and

Early March
Mozart Festival CECUT's Mozart Festival (🌐 www.mozartbinacional.org) is a week-end devoted to interpreting Mozart's music.

Early April
Expoartesanal A four-day outdoor gathering of arts and crafts at CECUT's plaza (🌐 www.expoartesanal.com).

Late April
International Dance Festival A week-long affair hosted by CECUT that draws individual and group performers from the US, Latin America, East Asia and Europe.

First Sunday in May
Start of the bullfight season The kick-off to Tijuana's bullfight season begins with matches at the downtown's Plaza El Toreo de Tijuana and the Bullring by the Sea in Playas de Tijuana (🌐 www.bullfights.org).

First weekend in June
Feria del Libro The city's book fair takes place in front of the Frontón Jai Alai and L.A. Cetto winery has its own Feria de la Paella y el Vino, consisting of wine tastings, paella cook-offs and live entertainment.

First Sunday in July
Romeria Tecate's summer festival is a week-long party with *charredos*, carnival floats and music.

Last week of August
Tijuana City Fair Rides, contests and exhibitors crowd Parque Morelos, Boulevard Insurgentes 16000, for this four-week event that ends in late September.

September 16th
Independence Day Tijuana and Tecate celebrate Mexican Independence Day with horse and motor races, mariachi, dancing, gambling and fireworks.

Second weekend in October
Tequila Festival Avenida Revolución hosts the annual Tequila Festival.

November
Nov 1 Día de Todos los Santos (All Saints' Day)
Nov 2 Día de los Muertos (All Souls' Day)

December
12 Día de la Virgen de Guadalupe in **Tecate** celebrates the climax of ten days of activities with a procession and a lively fiesta. **Tijuana**'s cathedral hosts its own celebration.

trams (the San Diego Trolley begins no later than 4.45am and runs until 1am, with a Sunday morning special at 2am. Trolleys leave every half hour and take 45 minutes to reach downtown; US$2.50, US☎619/231-8549) run every few minutes—and there are plenty of alternatives if you're heading farther north. Vans and minibuses, as well as Greyhound and other services, run almost constantly to Los Angeles; the Greyhound terminal is right across the border.

Buses operated by Peninsula Ejecutivo, Autotransportes de la Baja California (ABC) and Transportes Norte de Sonora depart from **Central Camionera La Mesa** (see p.63) and link Tijuana with all Mexican destinations, with numerous departures at all hours to the west coast and hourly buses down Baja. Tijuana to Cabo San Lucas (24hr trip) will cost you M$900, whereas a ticket to Mexico City (36–48hr) will cost you at least M$1000. Some operators offer large discounts for students, so bring an ID. Buses to Ensenada (every half hour 7am–9:30pm) leave from **Central de Autobuses de la Línea**, and buses to Rosarito (hourly 8am–8pm) leave from La Revo's **Central Vieja**. For US destinations you can pick up Greyhound buses (roughly hourly 6am–6pm) from the Central Camionera; they go on to pick up from the Central Vieja station then cross the border, stopping at San Ysidro. Slightly more expensive, Transportes Intercalifornias run nine times daily from the airport, Camionera Central, the centre of town and both sides of the border to Los Angeles.

Though they vary greatly depending on demand, **flights** to the rest of Mexico, and particularly to the capital (16 daily; 3hr), can be surprisingly cheap from Tijuana, sometimes the same price as a first-class bus. Flights to other destinations are less competitive, such as Guadalajara, Acapulco, La Paz, as there are fewer flights and they can charge more. The airport is reached on buses marked "Aeropuerto" from Madero and Calle 2a. Viajes La Mesa, at Madero and Calle 1a (T6/688-1511), can help with bookings, but it pays to shop around for the best prices.

If you're **driving east** toward Tecate or Mexicali, follow **Via Rápida Poniente** along the south side of the river and follow signs for the toll road Mex 2D Cuota. To **head south**, follow **Carretera Internacional** as it shadows the border. This links up with **Paseo Playas de Tijuana** and **Mex 1D** (Carretera Escénica Tijuana-Ensenada), the scenic toll road running along the Pacific coast to Rosarito and beyond. **Mex 1** (Carretera a Ensenada), a second, free road south, is accessed from Paseo Héroes and Boulevard Taboada by following **16 de Septiembre** southward. The toll road Mex 1D has the better views, but the short stretch of Mex 1 free road between **Puerto Nuevo** and **Playa la Misión** is equally stunning during its hill-hugging run.

Tecate

Some 30 minutes due east of Tijuana, **TECATE**'s a border town that's the polar opposite of its sprawling, frenetic neighbour. Although the town's most famous export is the lager beer that bears its name, its mood and tenor have more in common with the wellness resort *Rancho La Puerta* on its western edge – mellow yet proud.

The town sits at the southeastern base of the almost 1220-metre high Mount Cuhama (or Kuchumaa) that's off-limits to anyone but Native Americans with clearance from the US side. If entering the town from the California border or from Tijuana via Mex 2 or Mex 2D to the west, you won't notice you're over two thousand feet above sea level until you leave town tumbling south into the Valle de Guadalupe or east towards Mexicali. And move on is what you're likely to do; as pleasant as it is, there's not much to keep you here beyond a cross-border pit stop, the brewery or campgrounds on the outskirts of town.

The Town

All roads into Tecate lead to **Parque Miguel Hidalgo**, on Avenida Benito Juárez between Calle Lázaro Cárdenas and Calle Ortiz Rubio, the central square

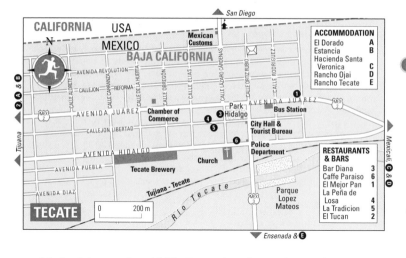

and hub of the town's social life. Even when there isn't an official citywide festival – one seems to take place every weekend – the park is full of merchants, balloon salesmen, travelling performers, strolling families and cruising teens, with musicians filling the gazebo on weekend nights.

The Cervecería Cuauhtémoc-Moctezuma, more commonly referred to as **Tecate Brewery**, Avenida Hidalgo, at Calle de la Huerta (Free tours Sat 10am; ☎665/654-9478) is the town's biggest draw. During the week, its shaded Jardín Tecate, Callejón Libertad 1 (Tues–Sat 10am–5pm; ☎665/654-3453) is a popular place for lunch and afternoon gatherings. On weekends, organized trips from US and Mexican cities pull in for a tour and tasting. The tour moves through different parts of the brewery based on the current manufacturing schedule, and headphones provide a running narration of the life of beer in such great detail that, if the unlimited free beer at the end of the tour didn't mess with your head, would give you all you need to know to run a brewery. To the east of the brewery and park are the town's sprawling sport and culture grounds around the **Estadio Manuel Ceseña** baseball park and **Casa de la Cultura**. The complex also contains soccer and youth soccer stadiums; a museum; gymnasium, tennis and basketball courts; and a building for lectures, arts classes and workshops.

Practicalities

The main **tourist office** (Mon–Fri 9am–7pm, Sat 9am–3pm, Sun 10am–2pm; ☎665/654-1095) and the **police station** are next to one another on the south side of Parque Hidalgo. Fondo Mixto de Turístico de Tecate, immediately to the right after crossing the border south, provides information on hiking, horseback riding and camping. **Banks**, including an HSBC branch, line the western border of Parque Hidalgo.

Bus service within Tecate is spotty and, since the fleet is a mismatch of discarded school buses from the north, is identifiable only to the disciplined eye. The long-distance inter-city bus station is at Avenida Juárez and Calle Rodriguez, just two blocks east of Parque Miguel Hidalgo. Return tickets can be purchased for travel throughout Baja. Getting to California requires going through Tijuana's Central Camionera.

Crossing the border at Tecate

The same **border crossing** rules as at San Ysidro and Otay Mesa apply at Tecate, but you can take comfort in the fact that you won't wait nearly as long. From the US, the path through an old set of gates is generally a quick and painless affair, and chances are you'll be in the middle of Parque Miguel Hidalgo before you know it. If you've taken a taxi from the US they'll drop you here, where you're within walking distance to almost all the city's attractions. The US-bound return funnels travellers along a new stretch of road to the east of the southbound crossing. As it's relatively new, the signage to reach it isn't entirely in synch – from Parque Miguel Hidalgo, drive east on Avenida Benito Juárez as it becomes Carretera Libre Mexicali and get in the left lane once you've passed the large roundabout. Turn left onto the concrete road at the sign reading "Border" and proceed. A new duty-free shop sits on the south side of the street halfway along this road. This new crossing replaces a previous one that required you to weave in and out of residential streets and play a guessing game as to where the line began.

The only remaining **train access** is via the Pacific Southwest Railway Museum outside of San Diego, 31123-1/2 Highway 94, Campo, CA (US☎619/465-7776, 478-9937, ⊛www.sdrm.org). Monthly excursions (US$40) from Campo aboard refurbished cars deliver passengers to Tecate's restored rail station, followed by a tour of the brewery and the town before boarding the train and heading back.

The **motels** along Mex 2 and 3 attest to the fact that Tecate's primarily a resting point for travellers coming from the US or those who've pushed passed Mexicali on the overland route from Sonora and the rest of Mexico. The ones along Avenida Benito Juárez are well-situated if you're travelling east–west or want to stay near downtown. *Estancia,* Av Benito Juárez 1450 (☎665/521-3066, ⊛www .estanciainn.com, ⓔinfo@estanciainn.com; ❺), is the final option on the road toward Tijuana. The large, clean rooms face a secure parking lot and have cable TV, a/c and Internet access and continental breakfast is included. Closer to the centre of town, *El Dorado,* Esteban Cantú 160 (☎665/654-1333, ⓔeldorado@yahoo .com.mx; ❺) is a simple courtyard motel with a pool and the restaurant *El Tucán,* a popular breakfast spot. Towards Ensenada, the *Rancho Tecate Resort & Country Club,* Km 10.5 Mex 3 (☎665/654-0011; ❺) rooms guests in the clubhouse or more modest *Posada Inn.* The restaurant fills up for Sunday brunch, but the three-hole golf course never seems busy.

Both campgrounds are along the road to Mexicali. ⅍ *Hacienda Santa Veronica,* Km 35 Mex 2, then follow signs south at El Hongo (☎665/655-2195, 665/653-4705; ❺), is a combination RV campground and resort motel. Ride horseback or hike on site, as well as swim, play tennis, or race off-road vehicles. At *Rancho Ojai - KOA Kampground,* Km 20 Mex 2 (☎665/655-3014, ⊛www .tecatekoa.com, ⓔrojai@telnor.net; ❶–❻ depending on type of camping) guests ride horses or bicycles, jump in the pool or just relax at this working ranch 20km east of Tecate. There are separate tent, cabin and car camping areas.

Most of the town's inexpensive **restaurants** and **bars** are located along Avenida Benito Juárez. Locals have favourites, but there is little difference between Juárez's half-dozen open-air *taquerías*: red and white are the

Tecate's area code is 665.

Rancho la Puerta

Rancho la Puerta, Tecate's most famous non-alcoholic destination, attracts over 7000 visitors a year. Founded by naturalist and philosopher Edmond Szekely as a short-term refuge from unhealthy living, the pioneering ranch (US☎800/443-7565, ⓦwww.ranchopuerta.com, US$3000 per week) welcomed its first guests in 1940 to week-long camping at the foot of Mount Cuchama. Over the years the tents became cabins, then eventually *casitas*, and the per-week fee went from $17.50 to around US$3000.

Private vehicles and shuttle buses from the San Diego airport arrive and depart every Saturday. The clientele – most of which are women – spend the week swimming, playing tennis, taking arts, wellness and fitness classes, doing yoga and taking sunrise hikes near the mountain. The ranch has been recognized as having one of the best chefs at any North American spa, and a significant portion of the food served is grown on a large organic farm just west of the Tecate border crossing, while the surplus harvest from the ranch's garden is taken to Tijuana hospitals.

dominant colours, and tacos run about M$8. When the wind is blowing right, the smell of grilling meat is overpowered by that of baking pastries and breads at the 24-hour *El Mejor Pan*, Av Juárez 331, where the coffee is free and the doughnuts, cinnamon rolls, flan and other sweets are made around the clock. *Bar Diana*, C Cárdenas 35 (☎665/654-0515), is one of the town's oldest bars, but to get a drink on the square you'll need to order from *Caffe Paraíso* on the southwest corner at Lázaro Cárdenas 20. Just to the east of the square along Callejón Libertad are two of Tecate's finer dining spots, *La Tradición Restaurante & Bar*, Callejón Libertad 200 (☎665/ 654-8040) and *La Peña de Losa*, Callejón Libertad 201 (☎665/655-7648); both have traditional Mexican menus.

Libertad is at right angles to Cárdenas and Tecate's main drag of shops. A bookstore with some English-language titles and periodicals, Librería España, sits at Lázaro Cárdenas 54.

Moving on from Tecate

If your onward plans include anything but Tijuana, you need to stop and **fuel up** before departing. There's a Pemex with diesel on the north side of Avenida Juárez on the way toward Tijuana. Two smaller filling stations are nearby on the south side of the street, between Calle Elias and Avenida Alorete. If you're beginning an extended trip into Baja, this is a good place to get into the habit of filling up your tank whenever you see a petrol station.

For travellers moving on to California, the border crossing on the north side of town offers a very short wait and a scenic 45-minute drive along US highways 188 and 94 before arriving in San Diego.

Three of Baja's primary highways cut through Tecate: Mex 3 starts here before winding its way through the Valle de Guadalupe to Ensenada. The free road Mex 2 and the tollway Mex 2D run Tijuana–Tecate–Mexicali; Avenida Benito Juárez turns into Mex 2 once it's outside the city limits. To access the toll road, look for signs on major streets reading "Carretera Cuota Tijuana–Mexicali 2-D." Mex 2 libre to Mexicali ends 75km to the east at the La Rumorosa crossing, requiring a toll of M$25 to get across the mountains.

2

The Northeast

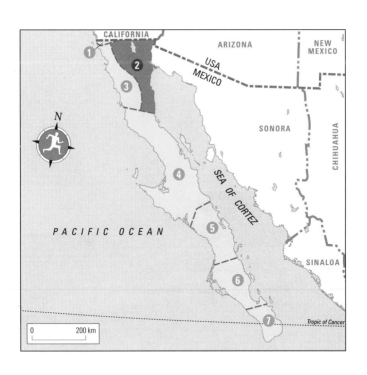

CHAPTER 2 # Highlights

✻ **Cantú Grade** Mex 2 highway's dramatic 25km descent
is most striking at sunset. See
p.97

✻ **El Nido de los Águilas**
Churros and a Tecate beer
are the perfect complements
to a game at Mexicali's
new major league baseball
stadium. See p.104

✻ **Sol del Niño** Bring a child
to this hands-on museum,

or just behave like one. See
p.105

✻ **Playa San Felipe** An urban
beach with blue-green waters
in one direction, fish tacos
and margaritas in the other.
See p.111

✻ **El Vallecito cave paintings**
The most accessible collection of prehistoric art on the
peninsula. See p.115

△ Playa San Felipe, San Felipe

The Northeast

The drive east from Tijuana to Mexicali is worthwhile for the views alone: as the mountains suddenly drop away to reveal a ribbon-like highway seemingly tossed into the rocks, a huge salt lake and hundreds of kilometres of desert spread out across the horizon. This is the only place in Baja California touched by Sonora's stark Desierto de Altar, and it's a startling change from the landscape that precedes it in the west.

It's hard to match the drama of a vertigo-inducing highway, so it's no surprise that **Mexicali** is a bit of a letdown. It may be the stronghold of the National Action Party (PAN) – the only political party ever to upset the once-dominant PRI – but you'll have to look hard to find anything too reactionary. The sedate city is worth a visit, though, if only to dispel the notion that all Mexican border towns thrive on sex, drugs, smuggling, corruption and drink.

South of Mexicali lies the vast, arid plain of the **Laguna Salada**, the lowest point in the country. The lagoon's western shores are bordered by verdant, spring-fed canyons that give way to the formidable **Sierra de Juárez** mountains. In the heart of the range is the **Parque Nacional Constitución de 1857**, a remote and arresting park that is one of the peninsula's great escapes. Mex 5 skirts the eastern edge of the lagoon before turning southeast along the **Sea of Cortez**. Even at this point, where the silty mouth of the Río Colorado dirties the sea's northern reaches, the sea projects an azure serenity that is its hallmark before it merges with the Pacific Ocean 1400 kilometres to the south.

The peninsula's northernmost settlement on the Sea of Cortez is shrimp-obsessed **San Felipe**, the majority of whose population is made up of seasonal US expatriates who have set up semi-permanent homes along the unregulated white sand coast.

Mexicali and San Felipe share the 686 area code. Calls from other parts of Mexico require 01 before the area code; only the last seven digits are needed in town.

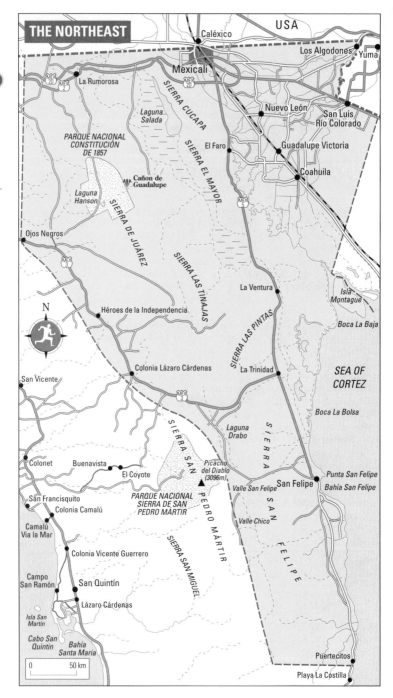

THE NORTHEAST

USA

Caléxico

Los Algodones Yuma

Mexicali

La Rumorosa

SIERRA CUCAPA

Nuevo León

San Luis
Río Colorado

Laguna
Salada

El Faro

Guadalupe Victoria

PARQUE NACIONAL
CONSTITUCIÓN
DE 1857

SIERRA EL MAYOR

Coahuila

Cañon de
Guadalupe

Laguna
Hanson

SIERRA DE JUÁREZ

Ojos Negros

SIERRA LAS TINAJAS

La Ventura

Isla
Montague

Héroes de la Independencia

SIERRA LAS PINTAS

Boca La Baja

San Vicente

Colonia Lázaro Cárdenas

La Trinidad

SEA OF
CORTEZ

Boca La Bolsa

Colonet

Buenavista

El Coyote

Laguna
Drabo

SIERRA SAN

Picacho
del Diablo
(3096m)

Punta San Felipe

San Francisquito

PARQUE NACIONAL
SIERRA DE SAN
PEDRO MÁRTIR

Valle San Felipe

San Felipe

Bahía San Felipe

Colonia Camalú

Camalú
Vía la Mar

Valle Chico

PEDRO MÁRTIR

SIERRA SAN FELIPE

Colonia Vicente Guerrero

SIERRA SAN MIGUEL

Campo
San Ramón

San Quintín

Lázaro Cárdenas

Isla San
Martín

Cabo San
Quintín

Bahía
Santa Maria

Puertecitos

Playa La Costilla

0   50 km

N

96

The Cantú Grade

The land around Mex 2 between Tecate and Mexicali is relatively fertile and, going eastward, climbs deceptively and gently into the small town of La Rumorosa, where the free (Mex 2) and toll (Mex 2D) versions of the highway merge. If you're driving with the windows down you will soon sense something's changed. The air becomes incredibly dry, then the breezes heat up considerably before the land falls away dizzily to the burnt plain and the highway splits into two distant ribbons each forging their separate paths up and down the rocky hills. This 25km stretch – known as the **Cantú Grade** – teeters between crags seemingly scraped bare by the ferocity of the sun, which only makes driving it all the more white-knuckle and thrill-inducing. The danger in negotiating it is evident in the piles of twisted metal that can be spotted down below. If you're heading east along it in the late afternoon, be sure to pull cautiously into one of the half-dozen scenic stops and watch the hills below take on the purple and gold hues of the setting sun before they pass into darkness.

Mexicali and around

The capital of Baja California, **MEXICALI** is a large, wealthy city, one of northern Mexico's most important business centres and a vital road and rail junction for goods crossing into the States. Despite the desert heat – it's unbearably hot in summer, though winter nights can drop below freezing – it's an agriculture power, thanks largely to its location within the southern reaches of California's Imperial Valley and at the heart of the fertile Río Colorado delta. To meet the increasing needs of migrants looking for work in the *maquiladora* industry (see box, p.73), the city is increasingly turning over the delta's once valuable farmland to housing and factory sprawl. Even with the rapid growth in some sectors, the city retains a very neat and tidy core; the well-manicured main avenues are fronted with large hotels and shopping areas, while the rest of the streets showcase a collection of one- and two-storey homes and buildings dating primarily from the 1950s.

Mexicali shares more similarities in terms of commerce and lifestyle with the nearby Mexican state of Sonora or the US state of Arizona than with Ensenada or San Felipe. Mexicali's tourist infrastructure – or lack thereof – caters entirely to businessmen, so you're not going to find resort-style offerings. Instead, you'll see its residents, especially the large middle class, making use of the malls, cultural centres, museums and parks rather than tourists. If you stick to where they go, and have a good handle on Spanish, you can keep busy here for a day or two without feeling the need to move on to someplace more traditionally "Baja."

Some history

Pre-Columbian Yumano tribes once farmed the Río Colorado delta to grow vegetables like squash and corn and used medicinal herbs both cultivated in small plots and culled from the desert. Small, rustic communities of the surviving Cucapá descendants can be found along the Mex 5 highway to San Felipe; the tribe's ancestors were decimated by diseases carried by the missionaries who moved into the peninsula from Sonora in the early nineteenth century.

Modern Mexicali began in 1904 when the Colorado River Land Company purchased vast amounts of the river delta on both sides of the border. Wary of Mexican labour, the CRLC relied on Chinese workers to build the irrigation systems; it not being terribly difficult to reassign them from laying railroad tracks to digging irrigation canals. Although mortality rates were high – a portion of the Desierto de San Felipe is still known as El Chinero for the 160 labourers who died while being forced to cross it – some Chinese set up businesses near the border. In Mexicali's first five years it grew five-fold, and quickly became a regional power. Baja California's governor Esteban Cantú moved the capital to here from Ensenada in 1915 to personally capitalize on this newfound sway and skim greedily from the gambling and vice trades.

The CRLC failed to fulfil its promise to settle more Mexican farmers in the region, so by the 1920s the area's largest ethnic group was the Chinese. This first generation of Mexicali residents quickly grew to control a broad range of legitimate commercial interests and an equal breadth of the city's growing vice

The Magonista revolution

Even though the Treaty of Guadalupe Hidalgo of 1848 split Alta and Baja California between the US and Mexico, constant cultural and commercial interchange in the region has kept it largely of a piece. For the first fifty years following partition, Mexicans in the transborder area were often outnumbered by US and English-born residents (as in Ensenada) or Chinese (in Mexicali). This international flavour as well as Baja California's remoteness from the rest of the country made the northern part of the peninsula a hotbed for intrigue and constant whisperings about filibusters from the US or independent-minded revolutionaries.

The last significant threat to territorial integrity came from **Ricardo Flores Magón** and the handful of quasi-anarchists and socialists that ran the **Partido Liberal Mexicano** party from Los Angeles. After planning a series of failed insurrections in 1906–08 carried out with ally Francisco Madero, and some jail time in the US, Magón set about planning more striking revolutionary activity in northern Baja California.

PLM forces – a ragtag mix of Mexican nationals, southern Californians and soldiers for hire – took Mexicali on January 29, 1911. Their control of the city was much more restrained than their later administration of Tijuana, but they were still resented for extorting local farmers to generate a needed influx of cash to buttress the PLM's hold on the area and to finance its dreams of expansion.

The PLM's troops were led by the Welshman **General Caryl Ap Rhys Price**, who soon after his ascent to power decided to move on Tijuana from Mexicali. The taking of Tijuana on May 9, 1911 turned out to be the end of the PLM's military ambitions, a major factor being that their antagonist President Porfirio Díaz was already conceding to revolutionary movement, but the one led by Madero instead of the PLM.

Although the US looked down upon the revolutionaries and kept arms from freely flowing across the border, they did nothing to impede the PLM's activities; Price travelled without hindrance between Mexicali, Tijuana and Los Angeles, the PLM operated freely out of LA, and San Diego residents took the train to watch battles in Tijuana (and looted the city following the defeat of Mexican Federal troops).

After Tijuana's capture that May, the PLM couldn't decide what to do next. Price left command after arguing that Madero's revolt had already won and becoming convinced that Magón and the PLM preferred publishing their revolutionary newspaper *Regeneración* to actually expanding the front to Ensenada and creating a new country. Federal troops took back Mexicali on June 17 and five days later forced the Tijuana Magonistas across the border and into the hands of the US military, which temporarily imprisoned them in a San Ysidro base.

industries – mainly gambling, prostitution, opium dens and heroin distribution – that US Prohibition had made especially profitable. Locals and visitors from the Imperial Valley flocked to the city to gamble and drink; at one time it was home to the world's longest bar – its length owed to the fact that it had to make room for both men and women.

Mexicali's bureaucratic class helped it stay steady after the end of Prohibition, the ban on gambling and the US depression. It wasn't all good news: thousands of *braceros* (Latin American migratory farm workers) displaced by the Depression flooded the city and quickly grew to resent the well-off Chinese community. The backlash resulted in violent, bloody anti-Asian sentiment and a rapid drop in the Chinese population.

After World War II the city shook off the last shackles of the CRLC and began to differentiate itself from Tijuana by focusing on attracting educational institutions – it's home to the Universidad Autónoma de Baja California (UABC) and CETYS Universidad among other post-secondary schools – and trade with the rest of Mexico. In recent years it has grown by serving the energy and health care sectors of the US. Two large power plants on the west side send 75 percent of their juice north, while upon completion a pipeline from Ensenada will deliver liquid natural gas through Mexicali to the Imperial Valley and Arizona. In addition to a large collection of doctors, nearby Los Algodones has one of the highest dentist-teeth ratios in the world – all the better to residents of the American Southwest who can no longer afford care in the US; some even rely on cross-border health insurance that encourages and pays for the use of the Mexican health care system.

Arrival, information and getting around

US Hwy 111 crosses the border at Calexico, California at which point it becomes Boulevard Adolfo López Mateos and leads into Mexicali. It's a straightforward **drive** (see box below) as is entry along the well-maintained highways from Tecate, San Felipe and Sonora. Even though signs will direct you to the *centro*, the centre is more a collection of orderly parts than a cohesive whole. Instead Mexicali sprawls out from the border along Boulevard Mateos, which cuts a wide swath southeast before turning into the Sonora-bound stretch of Mex 2. Mex 5 north from San Felipe becomes Boulevard Benito Juárez, the city's main north-south artery. Mex 2 from Tijuana enters the city from the southwest; proceed to the centre using either Boulevard Lázaro Cárdenas, the southern border of the city, or by driving north on Heroico Colegio Militar.

Buses from Mexico arrive at the Central Camionera, Boulevard Anahuac at Calzada Independencia (☎686/557-2410). Buses from California and Arizona arrive at the Greyhound station in Calexico, 123 First St (US ☎760/357-1895;

Crossing the border at Mexicali

The city has two **border crossings**: a large 10-lane affair feeding into Boulevard Mateos 24 hours a day and a second, smaller crossing to the east that's open 6am to 10pm. Except at morning and evening rush hours, the downtown border is usually relatively quiet, with straightforward procedures. Remember to visit *migración* if you're travelling farther into Mexico.

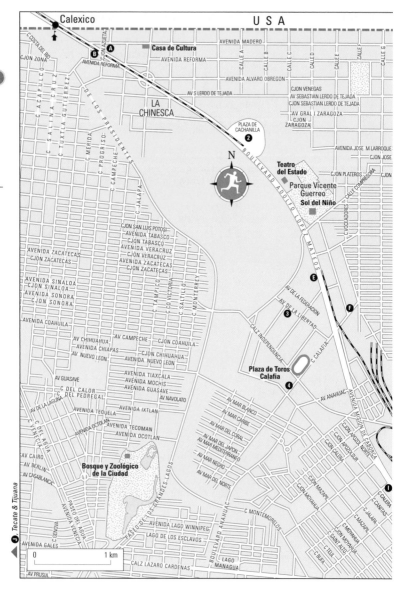

Mon–Sun 5:30am–11:30pm); travellers are then shuttled across the border via waiting taxis arranged by the bus company.

Aeropuerto Internacional de Mexicali, Km 23.5 Mesa de Andrade (☎686/552-2148, ⊛aeropuertosgap.com.mx) lies 20km east of the city along a two-lane road branching off from the Mexicali–Los Algodones highway. It primarily services government officials flying in from Mexico City or business

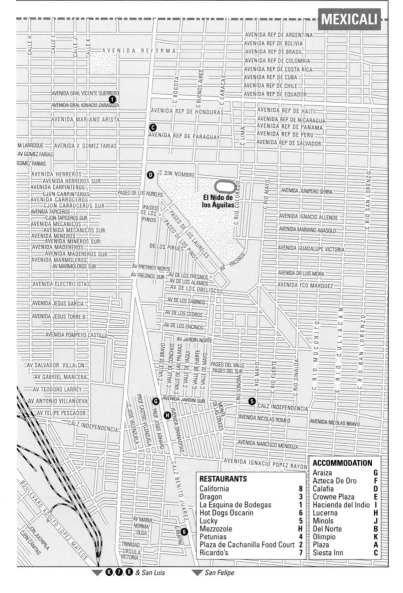

MEXICALI

RESTAURANTS	
California	8
Dragon	3
La Esquina de Bodegas	1
Hot Dogs Oscarin	6
Lucky	5
Mezzozole	H
Petunias	4
Plaza de Cachanilla Food Court	2
Ricardo's	7

ACCOMMODATION	
Araiza	G
Azteca De Oro	F
Calafia	D
Crowne Plaza	E
Hacienda del Indio	I
Lucerna	H
Minols	J
Del Norte	B
Olimpio	K
Plaza	A
Siesta Inn	C

people seeking deals with the state government or local factories. Budget, Hertz and Alamo have car rental desks on the east side of the building. Buy tickets for shared taxis that leave every 15 minutes from an enclosed booth near the departures gate; fares into Mexicali range from M\$250–400 depending on the zone.

There is a **tourist information** booth (daily 8am–7pm) opposite the vehicle entrance at the border, but it's not always open in the late summer, especially in the afternoon. The more helpful **main office** (Mon–Fri 8am–5pm; ☎686/557-3276) is off Mateos at Avenida Camelias in the Centro Cívico, the city's new municipal headquarters.

Mexicali is not a city best explored on foot. With the exception of a cluster of shops and pharmacies near the border, Mexicali's streets exist to connect cars between far-flung shopping centres, office plazas and residential neighbourhoods – none of them very interesting to travellers. The **city bus system** is a collection of private bus companies operating their own lines. There are no signs along the routes, and it is necessary to flag one down if you'd like it to stop. The standard fare is M$6. **Taxis** are clustered around the border area, Centro Cívico and in front of the hotels on Boulevard Benito Juárez.

Accommodation

Although not as expensive as Tijuana, Mexicali's **hotels** and **motels** charge higher rates than any other city in the state. You do tend to get more for the money, however: high-speed Internet access (via wireless or LAN) is cropping up everywhere, and the intense heat means that even the smallest motels have air conditioning and a pool. The city's cheapest beds are near the border, but they're suspect even on a good day; if proximity to the border is what you're after, the Centro Cívico area is the nearest cluster of safe motels and hotels. Business people and Mexican families favour the *zona hotelera* – the stretch of Benito Juárez between Justo Serra and the UABC. A string of motels in the M$250 range line Avenida San Luis along the *maquiladora* zone in *colonias* southeast of town. Although small and lacking extras like restaurants or pools, they're tidy, safe and well-situated if you're moving on to San Felipe. The only time you definitely need to book ahead is during the yearly Fiestas del Sol (see p.105) from late September until mid-October.

Centro Cívico and west

Azteca De Oro C de la Industria 600 ☎686/557-2185, ⓦ www.hotelaztecadeoro.com/. If the train station ever reopens, this will be your closest option; in the meantime, *Azteca* banks on its proximity to Sanborn's department store and restaurant. Amenities, which include satellite TV and a/c, are better and the public spaces more appealing than others in the price range. ❹

Crowne Plaza Blvd López Mateos, at Av de los Héroes 201 ☎686/557-3600, ⓦ crowneplaza.com. The city's most expensive hotel and clearly not its best; its proximity to the Centro Cívico is its greatest asset. Standard business hotel with features such as concierge, business centre, Internet access, fitness centre, underground parking and a pool complement the otherwise unremarkable rooms. ❼

Hacienda del Indio C Fresnillo 101, at Blvd López Mateos ☎686/557-2277, US ☎866/218-0546, ⓦ hotelelindio.com. The palm-lined motor court and cast-iron railings add character to this two-star motel not far from the Centro Cívico.

Rooms come standard with TV, a/c and phone. The front desk can expertly arrange guided tours to El Vallecito (see p.115) and Cañón de Guadalupe (see p.116). ❹

Minols Km 1.5 Mex 2 Mexicali–Tijuana ☎686/555-9200, ⓕ686/555-9334. This small motel on the city's outskirts is quiet enough for being on the highway. Rooms are clustered around the courtyard, which closes at night for security purposes – possibly to keep the cows grazing nearby from wandering in. Rooms are small and clean, and some even have Jacuzzi baths. ❷

Del Norte Av Madero 205 ☎686/552-8101, US ☎888/227-8504, ⓦ hoteldelnorte.com.mx. *Del Norte* is the one border hotel worth staying at. Its location just south of the border makes it the most pedestrian-friendly of hotels; you can walk to all the nearby restaurants and shops and use the adjacent taxi stand to get everywhere else. Rooms are clean, plus there's free coffee and an inexpensive breakfast buffet. ❹

Staying in Calexico

There's hardly a reason to stay on the US side of the border unless you're looking for familiarity; you can get a much better room for the same amount of money on the Mexican side. The **rooms** you'll find in **Calexico** are standard two-star chain hotel fare. *Best Western John Jay Inn*, 1km from the border at 2421 Scaroni Rd (US☎760/768-0442, ⓦbestwestern.com; ⑤), has a pool, exercise room and a parking lot that accommodates RVs. Nearby is the 73-room *Holiday Inn Express*, at 2501 Scaroni Rd (US☎760/768-6048, ⓦichotelsgroup.com; ⑤) with a pool and free parking.

Zona hotelera and east

Araiza Blvd Benito Juárez 2220 ☎686/564-1100, ⓦaraizahoteles.com. Although it's relatively new, the *Araiza* looks dated with its blandly patterned bedspreads and heavy furniture. Still, the service is superb and the pool and sleek lobby bar temporarily distract you from the fact you're in a brutally hot desert. ⑥
Calafia Av Justo Sierra 1495 ☎686/568-3311, ⓦaraizahoteles.com. Popular with groups, this spread-out hotel complex has a pool, mediocre restaurant and clean, albeit plain, rooms – some of which can pick up the wireless Internet signal. ④–⑤

🏃 *Lucerna* Blvd Benito Juárez 2151 ☎686/566-4700, ⓦhoteleslucerna.com. Though parts of it are identical to hotels of the same name in Tijuana and elsewhere, *Lucerna*'s two pools and well-shaded public areas speak to Mexicali's particular needs. Large bungalows in the courtyard are good for families, and the cheap rooms in the tower have balconies, satellite TV, coffee makers and wireless Internet access. ⑤

Olimpio Km 11.5 Mex 2 Mexicali–San Luis ☎686/561-6825, ⑤686/561-6835. Its proximity to industrial parks and the highway makes *Olimpio* well-suited for budget travellers or low-level *maquiladora* middle managers going to or coming from Sonora. The clean rooms have a/c and surround a less-than-photogenic gravel motor court. There's no restaurant on site and it's not walking distance to any restaurants or bars, but you can make San Felipe in time for breakfast if you're moving south. ②
Plaza Av Madero 366 ☎686/552-9757, ⑤686/554-0915. Centrally located budget motel has room service and a hair and nail salon. Rooms feature TV, bar, safe and a/c. ④
Siesta Inn Calz Justo Sierra 899 ☎686/568-2001, ⓦhotelsiestainn.com. This two-storey business-oriented motor inn is smaller than its peers yet packs significantly more charm. There's a central pool and fountain, a decent enough restaurant and Internet access in all the rooms. ④

The City

On the north side of town, the streets around **Avenida Madero** from Calle E to Justo Sierra boast a handful of city galleries and regional museums. **Boulevard López Mateos** between Madero and Lázaro Cárdenas is the closest the city gets to having a centre; in the vicinity you'll find the **Sol del Niño** children's museum, bullring, shopping centres and **Parque Vicente Guerrero**, the peninsula's largest urban park. The **Centro Cívico**, while a dominating presence, holds no interest to the traveller, either historically or architecturally. If you need a government contract, you'll come here; otherwise the 1970s–era compound is only useful as an orienting landmark.

Avenida Madero

Once you get past the blighted areas in the old Primera Sección neighbourhood, directly to the southeast of the border, the city's most established section looks well-manicured yet oddly evocative of US suburbia circa 1970. **Avenida**

Madero is the main street through this area, and most places of interest are on it and the surrounding streets.

Instituto de Cultura de Baja California

The **Instituto de Cultura de Baja California** (ICBC) administers the state's cultural programs from its offices at Av Alvaro Obregón 1209. Public events are held on the first-floor **Galería de la Ciudad** (Mon–Fri 9am–3pm, 5–8pm, Sat 9am–1pm), which showcases a surprisingly diverse roster of locally curated works and touring exhibits. As one of the few places in Baja California to see contemporary art – or any kind of art for that matter – openings are well attended and their merits debated by the small yet cosmopolitan art community.

Museo Regional de la UABC and the Casa de Cultura

The small **Museo Regional de la UABC**, Avenida Reforma and Calle L (☎686/552-5715, closed Monday; M$12), does more with its space than many larger institutions. It displays new shows monthly, and is as likely to follow a regional photography exhibit with a geology study or works by local sculptors; each exhibit manages to cram a wealth of information (often in English and Spanish) in limited space. The neighbourhood draw – where touring regional and national performing arts groups make regular visits – is just to the east at the white stone **Casa de Cultura**, Avenida Madero at Calle Jose María Morelos (☎686/552-9630). It's no CECUT (see p.74), but when baseball isn't in season this is one of the few public places where locals gather.

El Nido de los Águilas

If it's fall, there are few better ways to end a day in Mexicali than with a baseball game at the nearby 16,500-seat **El Nido de los Águilas**, Calle Rio Colorado and Calzada Cuauhtémoc (☎686/567-0010, ⊛aguilasdemexicali.com.mx; season Sept–Dec; tickets M$5-40). The home team Águilas, Baja California's only major league team, play in the Liga Mexicana del Pacífico. The climate has taken its toll on the field, but the stands are packed with fans for every evening game. The concessions are inexpensive – an ice-cold beer and three tacos cost about M$40 – and the atmosphere is so friendly it's almost unsettling.

Boulevard López Mateos

The rest of Mexicali's sights are either on **Boulevard López Mateos** or on intersecting streets as the avenue cuts a swath southeast from the border.

La Chinesca

Two cities on the peninsula make claims to having a Chinatown, and while La Paz's isn't really worth mentioning, Mexicali's is, if only for its history. Nowadays, **La Chinesca** is unfortunately a shadow of its former glory; there are now more Chinese restaurants outside of La Chinesca than in. What remains is centred around Avenida Zuazua and Calle Morelos, but it's only a fraction of what it was during the first half of the last century when Mexicali's Chinese community outnumbered ethnic Mexicans by more than ten to one. The current iteration consists of a worn gold and green pagoda, a few dozen shops, cafes and restaurants and a smattering of red lanterns on the streets. Mexicali residents will tell you that the tunnels and subterranean warehouses so essential to the city's Prohibition-era underground economy are still in full swing – though you have to be Chinese Mexican to access them.

Plaza de Cachanilla

There is some border area shopping that appeals to Calexico day-trippers, but the locals shop a dozen blocks down Mateos at the region's largest mall, **Plaza de Cachanilla**, between Avenida Tejada and Calle Compresora. The Mexican department store Coppel anchors one end, a multiplex fills the other and in between there are electronics, leather goods, clothing and CD stores, as well as a large food court.

The neighbourhood around the mall comes alive during the massive **Fiestas del Sol**, a three-week long street festival held every year from late September to early October (Ⓦfiestasdelsol.com.mx). The city celebrates the end of the harvest season with carnival rides, bands and DJs from all over Mexico, and some of the best street food you'll ever sink your teeth into.

Parque Vicente Guerrero, Teatro del Estado and Sol del Niño

A statue of a three-storey high, sword-wielding horseman looms threateningly at Mateos' intersection with Avenida Alfonso Esquer Sández, looking on to the expansive **Parque Vicente Guerrero**, which is home to the city children's museum and the state theatre. The **Teatro del Estado**, Boulevard López Mateos at Milton Castellanos (Ⓣ686/554-6419, Ⓦbajacalifornia.gob.mx/icbc) is the primary venue for the resident Ballet Folklórico Ehécatl, international touring groups like the Bolshoi Ballet and other prominent dance companies and national orchestras. It and CECUT in Tijuana (see p.74) are the two major cultural venues in the state, and it's a rare evening when an event isn't taking place here.

The theatre may have pedigree, but Mexicali's most enjoyable cultural outing can be had next door at the **Sol del Niño** interactive children's museum, Boulevard López Mateos at Avenida Alfonso Esquer Sández (Ⓣ686/554-9595, Ⓦsol.org.mx, Tues–Thurs 9am–5pm, Fri 9am–8pm, Sat & Sun 10am–8pm; M$44, children M$38). Although it's designed to engage children's minds, adult visitors are likely to get just as much out of the hands-on exhibits. With the exception of the educational films, everything is interactive, from the human gyroscope to indoor mountain climbing and miniature tornados generated inside glass boxes and illustrated with steam.

Plaza de Toros Calafia

The bland-looking **Plaza de Toros Calafia**, Calzada Independencia at Calle Calafia (Ⓣ686/557-1417; bullfight season Sept–May; M$50–250) seats eleven thousand spectators for bloodsports – both the requisite bull against man battles as well as boxing. During the off-season, the ring is used to host wrestling spectacles and rock concerts.

Bosque y Zoológico de la Ciudad

The kid-friendly **Bosque y Zoológico de la Ciudad** on Calle Alvarado (Ⓣ655/558-6376, Ⓔbosquecd@telnor.net; Tues–Sun 9am–4pm, summer until 6pm; free admission to park grounds but zoo and water activities require tickets) just west of Río Nuevo is a fifteen-minute walk from Boulevard Mateos. The zoo's reptile collection largely consists of local species – campers headed into the mountains should swing by as a reminder to shake out their sleeping bags – but the most popular attraction, with kids at least, is the lion pit. The park also contains a small archeological museum, a pond for fishing, a water park and shaded picnic areas and sports courts.

Eating and drinking

Eating out in Mexicali is, for the most part, a dull prospect. Menus tend to be rather straightforward, and the only clear culinary advantage to the century of cultural blending that's taken place here is being able to order a well-made margarita to drink with your orange beef or salt and pepper shrimp.

Independencia east of Benito Juárez has a large concentration of local favourites such as *Lucky Chinese* and the kebab cart directly across the street. Juárez itself has both moderately expensive standbys in the *zona hotelera* and equally dependable budget selections near the UABC. In this area you'll also find the city's biggest dance **clubs** – often housing more than one under one roof. Across town, a number of rock venues around the Centro Cívico give that otherwise staid location a real pulse after dark. Unless noted, restaurants are open for lunch and dinner and clubs are open Thursday through Sunday.

Restaurants

California Km 7.5 Carretera a San Luis Río Colorado. Its proximity to Costco doesn't do much for its atmosphere, but a white stone exterior, plate glass windows and pendant lamps make up for any geographical slights. The menu is a mix of pasta and burgers at moderate prices (dinner runs M$150 per person).

Dragon Av Libertad 990, at Centro Cívico. Mexicali's grandest Chinese restaurant looks like a 16th-centural imperial pagoda outside and a tricked-out dining hall inside. The Peking duck (M$120) is their signature dish. Dinner only.

La Esquina de Bodegas Av Zaragoza at C L ☎686/554-8919. White stucco walls, glass front and stained, wood accents give this outpost of Bodegas de Santo Tomás (see p.155) an exclusive on cool in city. Wines are served by the glass (M$50) and can be paired with the pan-Mediterranean menu (starting at M$100). Dinner only.

Hot Dogs Oscarin Blvd Benito Juárez at Normal. Dead by day and sleepy in the early evening, after 9pm it comes alive with the smell of sizzling franks: the double-length outdoor grill dishes out loaded hot dogs (from M$20) to walk-up or dine-in customers.

Lucky Av Independencia and C Mayo. This is one of the more popular small Chinese joints in town, but the bright lights, TVs and dining-hall interior detract from the well-executed Cantonese-centric menu (main courses M$60).

Mezzozole Blvd Benito Juárez 2151, inside *Hotel Lucerna* ☎686/564-7000. The low-lit dining room with views of the illuminated pool beyond the windows makes for one of the only romantic dinner settings in town. Excellent service, typified by the Caesar salad made tableside (M$80), adds a level of sophistication to the standard interpretations of Tuscan dishes. Dinner only.

Petunias Plaza Cholula 1091. Centro Cívico lunchtime café serving sandwiches (M$30) and fresh-squeezed juices to office workers. Breakfast and lunch only.

Plaza de Cachanilla Food Court Mateos s/n, between Av Larroque and Calle Compresora. Although similar in concept to US mall dining, the *Plaza* has local vendors instead of global chains, and sells fast-food versions of Mexicali Chinese food, fat *tortas*, and non-mall staples like *birria* (a sort of barbecued goat or lamb stew) and *menudo* (a stew of tripe, hominy and peppers). Lunch from any of the counters shouldn't cost more than M$55.

Ricardo's Calz Venustiano Carranza 2054 ☎686/592-5332. The excellent *tortas*, such as the *carne asada* with avocado (M$45) are served all day long and a popular diner-style breakfast pulls in regulars in the morning.

Bars and clubs

Academia Del Hospital and Avenida de los Pioneros. Centro Cívico's mega-club draws a combination of hip hop and club music fans and turns them into sweaty masses with the help of a high-end lighting and sound system. After 10pm there's a cover charge of at least M$50.

Cucapá Brewing Company Justo Sierra 190 ☎686/568-4205. Named after a near-extinct indigenous people, this brewery's poor taste fortunately does not extend to its suite of homemade libations – pilsner, dark lager, hefeweizen, pale ale and barley wine – all of which are excellent, and there's serviceable Tex-Mex-style pub food. Dinner only.

Dune Club and Billiards Calz Justo Sierra 1500 ☎686/566-3115, ⊛clubdune.com. The perfect nighttime destination for someone who can't decide on boogieing, shooting pool or downing a Tiki-inspired cocktail with a few thousand other patrons. It's within staggering distance of the city's better hotels.

Little Rock Café Av Libertad at Centro Cívico. Downtown's best music club specializes in bottled beer and rock en Español acts.

Rincón Panchito Blvd Benito Juárez 1990. On weekend nights locals pack the two-storey night-club with their sweaty, dancing bodies and their bilingual pickup lines. Cover varies depending on how badly the doormen want you to come inside.

Ritmo Mexicano Blvd Benito Juárez 3450 ☎686/561-6123. Both bands and DJs play this theatre-sized venue on the far south side of town; take the phone number of a taxi company along with your ID.

La Tabla Calz Justo Sierra at Av República de Brazil. Local and regional DJs inspired by the Tijuana-based Nortec Collective fill this small joint with UABC students and the neighbourhood's arty regulars.

Listings

Airlines Aeromexico, Pasaje Alamos 1008-D ☎686/557-2551; Aviacsa, Av Zaragoza, at Calle I ☎686/554-3219; Mexicana, Av Alvaro Obregón 1170 ☎686/553-5401.

Banks and exchange Banamex, Blvd López Mateos, at Av de los Héroes ☎686/557-4601; Bancomer, Madero 800 ☎686/554-9201; HSBC Blvd López Mateos, at Centro Cívico ☎686/557-2801.

Car rental Alamo, Blvd Benito Juárez 1004 ☎686/553-4109, Ⓔalamomxl@telnor.net; Optima, Justo Sierra 901 ☎686/568-1589; Budget, Blvd Benito Juárez 1050 ☎686/568-2400, Ⓔbudgetmxli@hotmail.com; Dollar Blvd Benito Juárez 1340 ☎686/566-2991, Ⓔmexicali @dollar-rentacar.com.mx; Hertz, Blvd Benito Juárez 1014, ☎686/582-5222, Ⓔhertzmexicali@hotmail .com.

Cinemas There are five multiplex theatres in the city. Online showtimes and locations can be found at Ⓦcinepolis.com.mx and Ⓦcinemark .com.mx.

Hospital MexicoAmericano Siglo XXI, Av Reforma 1000, at Calle B ☎686/552-2300.

Immigration Mexicali downtown border crossing ☎686/552-9050.

Internet access Internet cafés tend to launch and close quickly thereafter, but you can always find a cluster of cafés around the southern campus of UABC on Blvd Benito Juárez. Expect to pay M$10–20 per hour.

Newspapers and books The Spanish-language *La Crónica* (Ⓦlacronica.com) and *La Voz de la Frontera* (Ⓦlavozdelafrontera.com.mx) are published locally and daily. *Librería Universitad* across from the southern campus of UABC stocks English-language books.

Phones Payphones in the city centre accept phone cards, pesos and US quarters.

Police Spanish language ☎066, English ☎078; highway patrol ☎686/554-2909.

Post office The main branch is on Madero east of Mateos ☎686/563-8839; Mon–Fri 8am–7pm, Sat 9am–1pm.

Public pool Centro de Desarrollo Humano Integral, at Lázaro Cárdenas and San Luis Rio, daily 7am–8pm; Centro Deportivo Juventud 2000, at Calzadas Anahuac and Laguna Xochimilco, ☎686/559-2053.

Taxis Taxis stand at Av Madero and Blvd López Mateos. Eco Taxi ☎686/562-8262; Taxibaja ☎686/554-7272; Taxi Jets ☎686/556-0131; Taxi Red ☎686/552-1010 or 554-9088.

Moving on from Mexicali

The roads toward mainland Mexico and southwestern Arizona – the four-lane Mex 2 Mexicali–San Luis to **San Luis Río Colorado** in **Sonora**, and the two-lane BCN 8, which leads to the border crossing at **Los Algodones** – run relatively parallel. Boulevards Lázaro Cárdenas and López Mateos merge southwest of town and become Mex 2 Mexicali–San Luis. The majority of this stretch of highway was resurfaced in 2005, making the trip east into central Mexico fast and smooth. If the car you're driving is registered outside of Mexico, you'll need to make the US$400–800 deposit and fill out the proper paperwork at the Sonora state border (see Basics, p.22). San Luis Río

(see Basics, p.22)

Crossing the border at Los Algodones and San Luis Río Colorado

The two-lane **border crossing** on the north side of **Los Algodones** is a tiny affair that's open daily from 6am to 10pm. The border is currently being expanded to account for Los Algodones' recent growth, so some of these directions may change.

Southbound traffic makes an immediate right onto Calle Alamo, which will feed you onto Avenida A westbound. If you need to stop for your tourist card, pull over just past the customs declaration area and fill out the paperwork in the customs house. Travellers moving on to Mexicali or San Felipe should follow Avenida A to Calle 6a and turn left for BCN 8.

US-bound traffic is currently a bit of a mess. Calle Saratoga, the main road leading to the border, is undergoing extensive repair and expansion and the detour is confusing. Better off to drive along Avenida A to Calle Alamo, turn right to join the arriving cross-border traffic and make a U-turn at the tail end of US-bound traffic. Once across you'll be on Route 188 in the small town of Andrade, just a few kilometers south of US Interstate 8.

When Mex 2 Mexicali–San Luis crosses the Río Colorado it leaves Baja California and enters the state of Sonora. The city of **San Luis Río Colorado** sits on the Sonoran side of the border, just south of the US state of Arizona. There's a 24-hour, six-lane border crossing here but be wary of using it if you entered Mexico through Baja California; the peninsula's unique car importation rules (see Basics, p.22) mean you could be hassled by a meticulous border patrol agent.

Colorado is a small oasis of a town with a large cultivated valley watered by the Río Colorado. It's essential to fill up on petrol here before heading deeper into the Desierto de Altar – the next Pemex station is 350km away. For Los Algodones and the BCN 8 rural route, follow the eastbound Calzada Aviación out of Mexicali towards the airport until the road divides. If you're taking this route, be sure to fill up at the Pemex station on Calle 2 and Santa Isabel and watch for the frequent air funnels moving dust and twigs across the road and fields like mini-tornados. There aren't many services along the road, but there is lodging at *El Moro*, Blvd Aeropuerto 3598 (☎686/565-6070; ❷), a bright white Moorish-themed affair with a pool and clean rooms with TV, phone and a/c; one room has its own private pool.

Traffic bound for Tijuana leaves town on Lázaro Cárdenas and traverses Mex 2D through the **Laguna Salada** to **La Rumorosa**, where the highway splits into toll and free roads to both Tecate (M$40) and Tijuana (M$60). San Felipe visitors should take Benito Juárez south and follow signs for Mex 5. **Buses** leave the Central Camionera throughout the day for regional destinations like San Felipe and Ensenada, but long-haul journeys typically depart early in the morning. Over fifty buses a day make the long journey south (twenty of these to Mexico City), and there's at least one local service an hour to Tijuana.

Los Algodones

BCN 8 enters **LOS ALGODONES** from the southwest and becomes Calle 6a, the town's western border. Follow eastbound Avenida B to the intersecting Calles 5a–1a. Avenida A is the closest street to the border, with avenidas up to E making up the rest of the central grid. There's not much to the town, other than some places providing inexpensive medical care and prescriptions. The sporadically staffed tourist office on Calle 2a at Avenida A (Mon–Fri 9am–noon, 2–4pm; ☎658/517-7775) has information about travel to Mexicali and San Felipe.

All of the town's better eating options surround the packed-dirt town square at Avenida B and Calle 4a. Red steel-framed awnings shelter food stands selling tacos of tripe, *carne asada* and roast pork; across the street at the outdoor *Taquería Mal Verde* two fat *tacos pernil* and a bottle of Coke go for M$27. The nearby dim and dusty *Hotel Central*, Avenida B at Calle 5a (☎658/517-7930; ❷) is one of the few lodging options.

South along the Sea of Cortez

Mexicali's stifling heat will leave you longing for cool breezes and cooler waters, but you'll have to traverse 200km on Mex 5 through the southern half of the routinely dry Laguna Salada before you reach **San Felipe**, the first permanent settlement heading **south along the Sea of Cortez**. The sea appears as a sliver of blue at Km 100, shortly followed by entrances to beachfront RV communities and nascent housing developments.

For all practical purposes the road ends just over eighty kilometres farther on at **Puertecitos** – sooner for those unfortunate travellers who lose their exhaust or puncture a tyre on the horrendous road.

San Felipe

The trailer parks that line the highway north of seaside **SAN FELIPE** are a paradise for those travelling in RVs. If that means you – and even if it doesn't – it's hard to turn your nose down at the prospect of camping here: a relatively unspoiled beach to yourself for very little money, the clear and calm waters of the Sea of Cortez and, perhaps best of all – nobody will hassle you. The majority of these dozen or so communities are beyond walking distance to the heart of relaxed San Felipe, and its downtown beach, cafés and clubs that front the malecón.

San Felipe first came to the attention of fishermen who, in the early 1950s, took advantage of the new tarmac road – built to serve the American radar station to the south on what is now called Punta Radar – to haul in vast schools of tortuava, a species fished squarely onto the endangered list. Fishermen spread the word, but they were quickly overrun by landlocked US citizens looking for cheap beachfront property. These newer residents tend to be decent stewards of the area, but you can still find some of them tearing through the sand on dune buggies and balloon-tyred ATVs. San Felipe's swimming tops most places on the Pacific coast – at least at high tide – and if you are confined to the peninsula's north, it's an ideal place to rent a catamaran or just relax for a day or so.

Arrival and information

Buses from Mexicali, Tijuana and Ensenada pull in at the station, Avenida Mar Caribe and Calle Manzanillo (ⓣ686/577-1516; daily 5am–11pm), a short walk from the waterfront. Charter and private **flights** arrive at the international airport (ⓣ686/577-1368) 10km south of town. Real estate agents promise impending deals with international carriers flying out of Arizona and California, but for now there's nothing. The only **car rental** agency in town is Thrifty, Av Mar de Cortez 75-B (ⓣ686/577-1277, ⓦthriftysanfelipe.com).

The **tourist office**, C Manzanillo 300 (Mon–Fri 8am–7pm, Sat 9am–3pm & Sun 10am–1pm; ⓣ686/577-1155, ⓔturismosf@yahoo.com.mx), hands out town maps and a smattering of brochures. Internet y Papelería JC, C Chetumal and Mar de Coral, has a few **Internet** terminals for M$15 an hour. The BBVA/Bancomer, Av Mar de Caribe 165, is the only **bank** in town and has the lone ATM for hundreds of kilometres; the **money exchange**, C Chetumal 101 (ⓣ686/577-2525), has its own monopoly, too. The **post office** is on Mar Blanco just off Chetumal.

Accommodation

The **hotels** in San Felipe are not particularly cheap – and you don't get much for your peso either. Prices during the weekend jump by at least M$200 per night. Anytime of the week, parties larger than two will get a much better deal by renting an apartment from a part-time resident through an online service – ⓦsanfeliperentals.com, ⓦsanfelipe.tv and ⓦsanfelipe.com.mx are a few of the more comprehensive outfits.

The three-storey *La Hacienda de la Langosta Roja*, C Chetumal 125 (ⓣ686/577-1608, US ⓣ800/967-0005 ⓦsanfelipelodging.com; ⓿), is the cleanest downtown hotel and has rooms overlooking both the sea and its popular restaurant. *Posada del Sol*, Av Mar de Cortéz 238 (ⓣ 686/566-9804, ⓦposadadelsolbaja.com; ❸), has the cheapest rooms on the waterfront. While not posh, they're clean and come with refrigerators, satellite TV and a/c. At the south end of the malecón, the *Riviera*, Mar Báltico and C Manzanillo (ⓣ686/577-1185, ⓦgeocities.com/rivieraservicios; ❺), is a family-friendly hotel with a pool and grills. Next door, the pink stucco *El Capitán*, Mar de Cortez 298 (ⓣ686/577-1303; ❻), is close to the water and has pool, TVs and a/c. *San Felipe Marina* is south of town on the road to Puertecitos, Km 4.5 Carretera San Felipe–Aeropuerto (ⓣ686/577-0820, ⓦsanfelipemarina.net; ❼). With indoor and outdoor pools and beachfront waiter service, it's more luxurious than San Felipe's central hotels.

RV parks dominate the shores for the 20km leading into town and, while **camping** here is possible and quite relaxing, some of these communities can be quite cocoon-like, with residents tending to only eat at the onsite restaurant. If you want to go to a bar or restaurant in town, you're rather cut off – especially if you came by bus. One exception to the parks' prevailing insularity is *Pete's Camp*, Km 177.5 Mex 5 Mexicali–San Felipe (US ⓣ909/676-4224, ⓦpetescamp .com; ❶). This longstanding RV community has its own restaurant and bar (with happy hour) that's popular with non-residents and saves the best part of the beach for campers. In town, there is a cluster of parks to the northeast of the

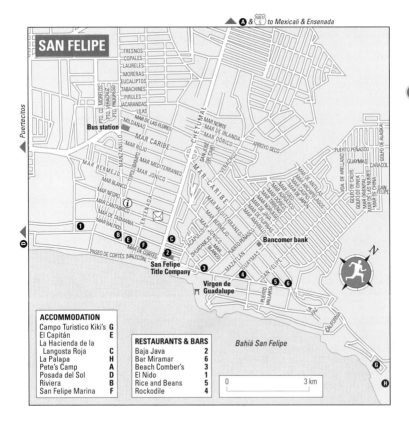

to Mexicali & Ensenada

SAN FELIPE

Bus station

Bancomer bank

San Felipe
Title Company

Virgen de
Guadalupe

Bahiá San Felipe

ACCOMMODATION	
Campo Turistico Kiki's	G
El Capitán	E
La Hacienda de la	
Langosta Roja	C
La Palapa	H
Pete's Camp	A
Posada del Sol	D
Riviera	B
San Felipe Marina	F

RESTAURANTS & BARS	
Baja Java	2
Bar Miramar	6
Beach Comber's	3
El Nido	1
Rice and Beans	5
Rockodile	4

0   3 km

malecón that includes the beachfront *Campo Turístico Kiki's*, Golfo de California
703 (☎686/577-2021; showers and toilets; ❶) and *La Palapa*, California at C
La Paz (no phone; ❶).

The Town

A set of double arches signals the end of Mex 5 and the beginning of the beach-
bound Calle Chetumal. Halfway to the water, a turn south on Avenida Mar de
Caribe leads to the small marina 4km south of town and the dirt road to points
farther south. Chetumal ends at **Avenida Mar de Cortez**, the beachfront
malecón that's the centre of San Felipe's social life and the urban ribbon dividing the town from its beach, **Playa San Felipe**. The town and all its neighbourhoods rest beneath the hilltop shrine to the Virgen de Guadalupe that rises from
Punta el Machorro, its rocks jutting into the **Bahía San Felipe**. The bay itself is
protected from drilling and any manner of large-scale fishing, but the town has
nothing to guard itself from the snowbirds and spring breakers that migrate to
the area during temperate months (Nov–April) and university holidays.

With the exception of retiring to one of the nearby coastal RV parks, there
isn't much to do here except claim your spot on the beach and then **fish**, **drink
beer** and **eat shrimp** – not a bad prospect, true – or pay upwards of M$300 an
hour to hire an ATV or dirt bike from the vendors who will approach along the

malecón. Sport-fishing trips are best booked before arrival (see Basics, p.38). If not, shorter trips can be arranged through downtown hotels and speciality shops on the north end of Mar de Cortez. If you want to **swim** at Playa San Felipe you can change in the public restrooms and showers at both its north and south ends (have some change to tip the attendant). The beaches at the RV parks are cleaner and wider, but the crowds there are mainly restricted to residents.

San Felipe's non-sea related claim to fame is the **San Felipe Title Company** bookstore, Chetumal and Mar de Cortez (℡686/577-0471, ⑩blueroadrunner .com/sfbooks/default.htm). Retirees and novel- or guidebook-starved travellers pick up new and used books or come for readings by visiting authors and local scribes.

Eating and drinking

San Felipe's speciality is, not surprisingly, **seafood**, with several **restaurants** and numerous stands selling shellfish cocktails along the waterfront. *Langosta Roja*, C Chetumal 125, has the fanciest surroundings, but the food doesn't stand out from the rest of what's on offer on the waterfront, which caters better to the town's down-tempo atmosphere. The steakhouse chain *El Nido* offers a beefy alternative on Av Mar de Cortez 348 (℡686/577-1028) and *Baja Java*, Calle Chetumal and Mar de Cortez (⑩blueroadrunner.com/bajajava/default.htm) has house-blend coffee and the only bagels around.

Along the malecón, the line between restaurant and **bar** shifts with the current and time of day. *Rice and Beans* (℡686/577-1770) begins the day serving US-style breakfasts and ends with margaritas. Bar hopping is easy enough on the stretch between Chetumal and Mar de Caribe (but don't walk between them with any alcoholic drink), which is lined with several clubs and restaurants. *Rockodile* (℡686/577-1453, ⑩4rockodile.com, noon–3am) is the rowdiest of the bunch, with room for a couple of thousand and a Spring Break atmosphere year-round; *Beach Comber*'s (℡686/577-1670) has a similar vibe. The 50-year-old *Bar Miramar* (℡686/577-1192, Wed–Mon 11am–2am) is the granddaddy of the strip, and manages to keep up with pool tables, karaoke and skilled bartenders.

South to Puertecitos

If the road through the cactus desert south of here to Mex 1 ever gets improved to the point where it can be negotiated by low-clearance vehicles, this could become an interesting alternative route to southern Baja, but for the moment the ramshackle hamlet of **PUERTECITOS**, 85km south, is as far as ordinary cars can get – and even then with difficulty. The pavement disappears 40km beyond San Felipe and after that all but the hardiest of vehicles should drive no faster than 20 km/hr and never at night. Unless you're visiting friends, once you arrive in Puertecitos you'll wonder why you braved the roads; it's a fishing village in only the most unromantic sense. There's a Pemex station if you're in need of petrol, but you'll likely purchase your fuel from a man selling it from a plastic container rather than the routinely inoperable pumps. Camping along the coast is a well-accepted practice, but the most scenic spot with potable water is back towards San Felipe at *Punta Estrella Beach Club*, Km 13 Carretera San Felipe–Puertecitos (☎686/565-2784, ✉puntaestrella@mexico.com; ❶); from a tent beneath the beachfront palapas, the beach and sea appear to go on forever.

Parque Nacional Constitución de 1857

Although it's hundreds of kilometres in the opposite direction, Mex 3 La Trinidad–Ensenada is the most reliable way to travel south from San Felipe. The route cuts through a gap between the Sierra de Juárez and the Sierra de San Pedro Martír and offers several tempting off-road excursions, though none more so than **PARQUE NACIONAL CONSTITUCIÓN DE 1857**. If you have a four-wheel drive or a car with clearance above 50cm you'll be able to quickly appreciate this imposing park. Set inside the Sierra de Juárez, its twelve thousand acres are filled with streams, evergreens stands, the **Laguna Hanson** mountain lake, **Cañón de Guadalupe**'s hot springs and, sometimes, a layer of snow. The difficulty of getting in and out of the mountains – as well as valid concerns about obtaining basics like food and shelter – dissuades many visitors, but with a little bit of planning and the right guide, even the most novice of outdoorsmen can experience at least a portion of the park.

△ The Sierra de Juárez

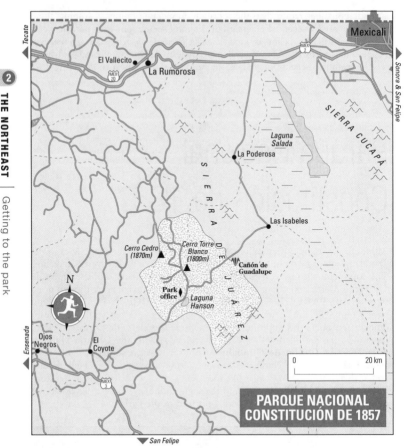

Tecate

Mexicali

Sonora & San Felipe

El Vallecito

La Rumorosa

SIERRA CUCAPÁ

Laguna Salada

La Poderosa

SIERRA DE JUÁREZ

Las Isabeles

Cerro Cedro (1870m)

Cerro Torre Blanco (1800m)

Cañón de Guadalupe

N

Park office

Laguna Hanson

Ensenada

Ojos Negros

El Coyote

0   20 km

**PARQUE NACIONAL
CONSTITUCIÓN DE 1857**

San Felipe

Getting to the park

When pulp detective novelist and tireless Baja California promoter Erle Stanley Gardner visited the area in the 1950s he had the advantage of custom-built helicopters and off-road vehicles and could enter the sierras from anywhere he pleased. If you're not a millionaire gentleman explorer you're limited to two entrances and, if the weather's right, three. The first two, from **Mex 3** and **Mex 2** via La Rumorosa, will bring you to **Laguna Hanson**, the centre of the park and its highest points. The third option skirts around the shores of **Laguna Salada** and bring you to the park's eastern edges and the springs and waterfalls of **Cañón de Guadalupe**. This option brings you to the sierra's foothills and offers no access to the lake and interior camping areas.

From Mex 3

The easiest way to approach the park is by taking the km 55 exit on Mex 3 Ensenada–La Trinidad. **Ojos Negros**, fifteen minutes west of this exit, is the

The cave paintings of El Vallecito

The peninsula has a rich trove of pre-Columbian art, much of which is accessible only with a professional guide and two days' worth of hiking in the mountains of Baja California Sur. The few exceptions to the rule include the six sites that make up **El Vallecito** west of La Rumorosa. Although easily accessible, the work here doesn't compare in scope or subject – appearing more as independent drawings rather than compositions – to those further south, and has more in common with art in the US Southwest than Baja California Sur. Of the eighteen paintings here, the one standout is a small drawing of a devil-like figure that does a neat trick once a year. At winter solstice (between Dec 21 and 22), the light entering the cave strikes the eyes of "El Diablito", illuminating the red pigment and giving the figure an eerie glow.

To get to the site, exit Mex 2 Tecate–Mexicali along a dirt road that runs north between kms 72 and 73. Drive north 4km and pull into the parking lot across from *Rancho Santa María del Oro* and follow the short path by foot. Open Wed–Sun 8am–5pm.

only settlement in the area where you can gather supplies. Once you stock up, skip the Ojos Negros rural road and drive 17km east along Mex 3 to km 55 and a dirt turnoff for **Laguna Hanson** that's well-marked – if you're looking. As always on the state's rural roads, stick with the well-trod one to prevent ending up somewhere unexpected. The lake is sometimes called Laguna Benito Juárez; follow these signs too.

From Mex 2 via La Rumorosa

From the hill town of **La Rumorosa** – where you should buy supplies sufficient for your visit to the park – exit Mex 2 at km 72 and drive 61km down the dirt road. This is a rough way to enter the park, and from February to late March may be impassable.

From Laguna Salada

The sierras are bordered to the east by the typically arid **Laguna Salada**. If it's dry, you're in luck and can turn off the Mex 2 Tecate–Mexicali at km 28 (there's a sign on both sides of the road) and take the dirt and sand roads to the

The Laguna Salada

Though there's usually barely a trace of moisture in it, the **Laguna Salada** becomes the peninsula's largest inland body of water after a downpour or an extended rainy season. From north to south it spans over 200km and east to west it covers 90km. The lake bed crosses landmarks and highways starting in the north with Mex 2 between the Sierra de Juárez and Sierra de los Cucapás, then southeastward across Mex 5 and finally into the Río Colorado delta and the Sea of Cortez. February sometimes brings rain, and rare seabirds with it, but it's more common than not for the lake to go years as a cracked, bleached expanse. Its flat surface is a favourite of off-road enthusiasts who tear across the parched earth with reckless abandon. The only thing with the potential to slow them down is the glare reflecting from the salt deposits in the soil. The effect can be blinding at noon, but is otherworldly on clear nights when the moon is full. For one surreal night in 2003, the lake became an enormous moonlit venue for Luciano Pavarotti's self-proclaimed swan-song to Latin America – perhaps the only space large enough to accommodate one of the opera world's largest egos.

lush **Cañon de Guadalupe**. Once you've left Mex 2, follow the tracks 44km directly south along the western bank of the lake. Halfway down the road passes the tiny settlement of La Poderosa. Although there are no markings, you should turn right along the first well-worn road you see. If you're skittish, drive until you hit Las Isabeles, a second tiny settlement and retrace your path to the first turn on your left. The canyon and its hot springs are only 10km to the south-west (see Practicalities for more details).

The Park

Parque Nacional Constitución de 1857 is overwhelmingly untamed wilderness; the more popular sites like Laguna Hanson and Cañón de Guadalupe may not have a ranger on duty when you arrive or at any time during your stay, and once you go to one portion of the park, it's often a very long drive hundreds of kilometres out of your way to see another part. The services that do exist are at privately owned inns and campsites, and these places are your best source for information on hiking, swimming or mountain biking in the area.

Though there may not be a wilderness centre to greet your arrival, you will at least be welcomed with stunning mountain scenery and silence – unless some of your fellow campers have brought their off-road vehicles along with them. If their motors don't scare off the animals, you might see deer, rabbits, coyotes, cougars and an ornithologist's notebook full of birds, including hawks, woodpeckers and quail. There are working ranches inside and around the park, so you're likely to run into their cattle and other livestock, too.

The one established hiking trail is a 10km circuit around **Laguna Hanson**, which lies at an elevation of 1600 metres. As you approach the lake from either Mex 2 or Mex 3 you'll cross older roads and trails that once connected the sierra's now-abandoned mining villages. These are well-suited to mountain bikers and experienced hikers and, like the Laguna Hanson hiking trail, can be found by looking for well-trodden paths leading out from the parking lot on the lake's southwest corner.

Practicalities

Even though **buses** between Mexicali and Tecate stop in La Rumorosa and the one plying the San Felipe–Ensenada route can dump you at the entrance to Laguna Hanson, unless you're a seasoned survivalist, tackling the park without your own means of transport is not recommended. There are **no banks** in between the coasts, and the first **Pemex** station between the Mex 3 southern entrance and San Felipe is after 140km at Colonia Lázaro Cárdenas. For **road conditions**, call the Delegación de El Real del Castillo (☎646/153-3033, Spanish only).

Group excursions can be arranged in advance through agencies in Mexicali. Baja Terra (☎686/564-9370, ✉bajaterra@telnor.net) conducts eco-tours and standard camping visits, while Edge Biking (☎686/552-9016, ✉edgebiking@hotmail.com) organizes mountain biking excursions. Academics with archeology, history and anthropology credentials can arrange custom trips to undisclosed cave painting sites through the Instituto Nacional de Antropología e Historia (☎686/552-3591, ⓦinah.gob.mx).

The effort involved in getting to the **Cañón de Guadalupe** is amply rewarded by the serene *Guadalupe Canyon Hot Springs*, which can only be reached by following directions through Laguna Salada and looking for the "Campo 1" sign (US☎714/673-2670, ⊛guadalupe-canyon .com; ❸). Hot tubs outside each campsite are fed by the canyon's thermal waters, and organized tours from the campsite hike further into the canyon to the waterfalls and cave art sites. You can go hiking or horseback riding in the park by spending a few nights on its outskirts at *Rancho Club Hacienda*, Km 72 Mex 2 Tijuana–Mexicali (☎686/575-0095, ⊛rchacienda .com; ❷–❸). The self-contained ranch with campgrounds and cabins has sports courts, an open-air restaurant and guided trips into the hills.

On the south side of the park, *Rancho Góngora* Km 55.2 Mex 3 (☎646/172-2101; ❷) has six-person cabins, tent camping, a pool and showers. The adjacent *Rancho Pino Colorado* Km 55.2 Mex 3 (☎646/176-2161; ❷) doesn't have a pool but rents two cabins that each fit up to fifteen. Laguna Hanson's **campgrounds** are in a marked area on the southwest side of the lake alongside the main road, with pit toilets and no showers (if a ranger is on duty he may collect a fee of M$40 per person, but it isn't likely).

Travel details

Buses

Mexicali to: Tijuana (through Tecate) 10 daily, 3 hours; Ensenada connecting bus through Tijuana; San Felipe 5 daily, 2 ½ hours.
San Felipe to: Tijuana (through Ensenada) 4 daily, 5 ½ hours; Mexicali 5 daily, 2 ½ hours.

Flights

From Mexicali there are flights to Mexico City, Hermosillo and Monterrey via AeroCaribe, Aeromexico and Mexicana.

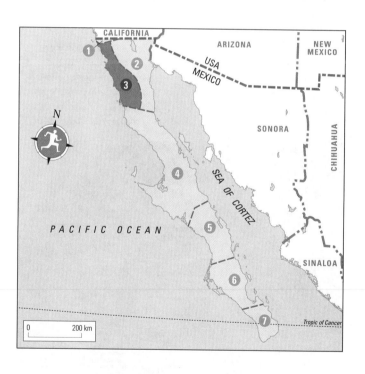

3

The Northwest

CHAPTER 3 # Highlights

✻ **Puerto Nuevo** A small village built upon grilled lobster can't be a bad thing, no matter how crowded it gets. See p.132

✻ **La Misión** Step back into the Baja of the 1970s at *La Fonda* and relax on the best beaches south of Rosarito. See p.135

✻ **Salsipuedes** Seasoned surfers brave steep roads to surf this secluded stretch. See p.136

✻ **Mercado Negro** Morning is the time to trawl Ensenada's stellar fish market for the day's best catches. See p.144

✻ **Hussong's Cantina** There's a convincing case that the margarita – the quintessential Baja cocktail – was invented here. See p.147

✻ **Valle de Guadalupe** Take a wine tour of one of the valley's numerous bodegas and see an unexpected size of a land dominated by beer and margaritas. See p.149

△ Wine barrels, Valle de Guadalupe

The Northwest

Baja California's most populous and geographically diverse region, the **northwest** provides a beguiling introduction to the peninsula's undeniable appeal. From just south of the US border to the northern reaches of the Desierto Central, the region offers breathtaking Pacific vistas along the epic Transpeninsular Highway (Mex 1), the wine-producing valleys of Guadalupe and Santo Tomás, the sometimes snow-capped peaks inside Parque Nacional Sierra de San Pedro Mártir, and the dormant volcanoes along Bahía San Quintín.

In the north, **Rosarito** has evolved from a one-hotel settlement that catered to royalty and Hollywood stars to a boomtown struggling to balance the needs of weekend party animals and masses of *maquiladora* workers. In sharp contrast is steady **Ensenada** which, like La Paz in the south, is one of the peninsula's few cities with a healthy mix of industry and tourism; the port is home to both cruise ships and their throngs of passengers and a giant fishing fleet that hauls in net after net of the coast's best seafood. The 100km between the two cities contain small **coastal settlements** that aren't much more than one-hotel or one-campground communities frequented by fiercely loyal repeat visitors. The most charming of these, like **Calafia** and **La Fonda**, ramble along shorelines and cliffs and wow with simpler pleasures – fireplaces, private patios, non-uniform rooms – and forego frills such as telephones, cable TV and credit-card readers. With few exceptions each place has an on-site bar and restaurant with hours and live entertainment options that vary by season.

Playa la Misión, the coast's only easily accessible beach outside of Rosarito, signals the end of one of the more developed stretches on the peninsula. Soon after, Mex 1D rises high above the water and the only people determined enough to enter the Pacific are local fishermen or wetsuited surfers who negotiate the hills at **Salsipuedes** or brave rocks at **Playa San Miguel** to catch the perfect wave.

Though the coast is never too far away, the rural townships inland from the highway maintain a character all their own, focused as they are on farming and ranching. While it's possible to get a sense of this from Mex 1, it's worth taking time to get more of a feel for the northwest's agronomic roots, and there are few better ways to do this than on a tour of the nascent wine-producing **Valle de Guadalupe**, which lies between Ensenada and Tecate. The land to the east of the highway from Ensenada to San Quintín that isn't farmed is protected as part of the massive **Parque Nacional Sierra de San Pedro Mártir**. Like Parque Nacional Constitución de 1857 to the north, the park appeals more to the experienced outdoor adventurer than

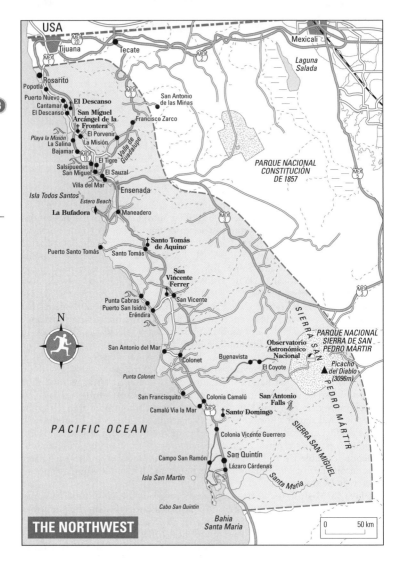

USA

Tijuana Tecate Mexicali

MEX 2D MEX 2

Laguna Salada

MEX 1

Rosarito
Popotlá
Puerto Nuevo **El Descanso**
Cantamar
El Descanso **San Miguel
Arcángel de la
Frontera** Francisco Zarco

San Antonio
de las Minas

MEX 3

El Porvenir
Playa la Misión
La Salina La Misión
Bajamar El Tigre
Salsipuedes
San Miguel El Sauzal
Villa del Mar Ensenada

Valle de Guadalupe

*PARQUE NACIONAL
CONSTITUCIÓN
DE 1857*

MEX 5

Isla Todos Santos
Estero Beach
La Bufadora Maneadero

MEX 1D

Puerto Santo Tomás Santo Tomás

† **Santo Tomás
de Aquino**

MEX 3

**San
Vincente
Ferrer**

Punta Cabras
Puerto San Isidro San Vicente
Eréndira

N

San Antonio del Mar

Colonet Buenavista

Punta Colonet

*Observatorio
Astronómico
Nacional* *PARQUE NACIONAL
SIERRA DE SAN
PEDRO MÁRTIR*

El Coyote

SIERRA SAN PEDRO MÁRTIR

▲ Picacho
del Diablo
(3096m)

San Francisquito Colonia Camalú **San Antonio
Falls**

Camalú Via la Mar MEX 1 † **Santo Domingo**

PACIFIC OCEAN

Colonia Vicente Guerrero

SIERRA SAN MIGUEL

Campo San Ramón **San Quintín**

Isla San Martin ○ Lázaro Cárdenas

Santa Maria

Cabo San Quintín

*Bahia
Santa Maria*

THE NORTHWEST

0 50 km

the casual visitor, particularly with the peninsula's highest point, Picacho del Diablo. Occupying an enviable position to the southwest near gorgeous Pacific beaches and some of the best fishing spots along the peninsula, **San Quintín** is not much more than a glorified truck stop, with little to offer in the way of charm or distraction. It does, however, provide a clear transition from the peninsula's comparatively crowded, industrialized north to its sparsely populated central and southern segments.

Rosarito

Baja California's original border town, **ROSARITO** began life as not much more than a few cattle ranches. From 1788 until the treaty that ended the Mexican War in 1848, a line running from its valley to end of the Río Colorado delta in the east divided Baja from Alta California. For the century and a half following California's post-war split, it lived in Tijuana's shadow and under control of its city hall as the suburb of Playas de Rosarito. It broke away in 1995, becoming the self-sustaining Rosarito, which has allowed the town to keep for itself the ever-growing chunk of taxes and revenue generated by a booming tourist trade. In the years since, it has doubled in size by heavily promoting its enormous beach – still known as Playas de Rosarito – to weekending Southern Californians, and by luring a share of *maquiladora* business from Tijuana.

Rosarito's tourist industry owes much to the men and women of Naval Station San Diego and US university students that flock here on weekends, especially during spring break every March and April. These hordes eschew the traditional lay-out-on-the-beach-and-go-for-a-swim vacation in favour of all-night parties at oceanfront clubs, engaging in the type of unregulated hedonism encouraged by tequila bars, quarter beers, yard-long margaritas, foam-filled dance floors and cages of dancing girls. Visitors party at mega clubs, play beach volleyball, ride ATVs and horses along the shore and, if the margaritas haven't completely incapacitated them, use the town as a base to explore surf spots and lobster restaurants to the south.

Outside of weekend rush, Rosarito carries on, juggling the typical tug and pull of a boomtown struggling with industrial and tourist expansion. Its proximity to California – and the comforting fact to many that it's not Tijuana – has made it the centre of real estate expansion along the coast; American expats have set up trailer homes and permanent ones in small communities to the north and south. These gringo newcomers, who began rolling in en masse around the same time Rosarito separated from Tijuana, feel a sense of ownership that can't be entirely tied to white entitlement: many of them came before the town's population boom,

Buying a piece of the northwest coast

There's a simple reason most of Baja's earliest US emigrants came with wheels on their homes: land titles for foreigners were once a tricky business. For years it was illegal for non-Mexicans to own land within 50km of the ocean or 100km from the border. In 1971 the Mexican government passed a law that allows foreigners to purchase land right on the coast – if they do so through a bank trust.

Since the 1970s and the recent rise in reputable title insurance firms, real estate transactions have become more transparent and fairly dependable. This security, hand in hand with a flush US real estate market in the early 2000s, fuelled the current construction spurt along the **northwest coast** and has helped revive long-dormant projects.

But while the growth of title insurance businesses has eased many buyers' concerns, neither the state nor the national government regulates real estate agents. Agents do not have to disclose known problems, as they do in other countries, and they may be on the payroll or even a financial backer in particular developments. Self-regulating groups such as *Asociación Mexicana de Profesionales Inmobiliarios* (@ampimexico.com) offer the greatest assurance that you're dealing with someone on the up and up.

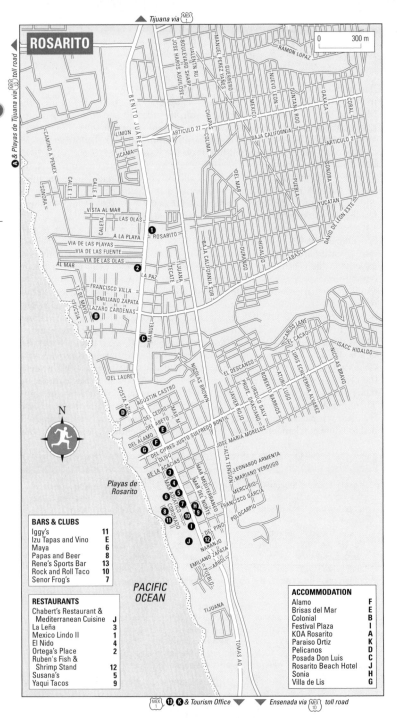

ROSARITO

Tijuana via MEX 1

& Playas de Tijuana via MEX 1D toll road

& Playas de Tijuana via toll road

0   300 m

RAMON LOPAZ

BENITO JUAREZ

BOULEVARD SHARP
JOSE HAROS AGUILOSE
VALENTIN RU
MANUEL PEREZ YANES
GUERRERO
NUEVO LEON
FONTANA ROD
OAXACA
CORAL

MANUEL
CHIAPAS
COLIMA
MEXICO
BAJA CALIFORNIA
ARTICULO 27

CAMINO A PEMEX
LIMON
JICAMA
ARTICULO 27

DAVID DE LEON ESTE
YUCATAN
SONORA
PUEBLA
HIDALGO
DEL MAR

CALLE 1
CALLE 2
SONORA

VISTA AL MAR
CALETA
LAS OLAS
A LA PLAYA
● 1 ROSARITO
BAJA CALIFORNIA SUR
DURANGO
TABASCO

VIA DE LAS PLAYAS
VIA DE LAS FUENTE
VIA DE LAS OLAS
AL MAR
● 2
LA PAZ
TIJUANA
TECATE

16 DE MAYO
FUCSIA
FRANCISCO VILLA
EMILIANO ZAPATA
LAZARO CARDENAS
● B

● C
MANUEL

DEL LAURET
CARLOS LANE
EL CACAO
ISACC HIDALGO
NICOLAS BRAVO

EL DESCANSO
ATURO LUGO
URSULO GALV
ROBERTO BARRIOS
PROFE. GRACIANO
JAVIER ROJO
LUIS ECHETERIA ALVAREZ

COSTA AZ
● D
AGUSTIN CASTRO
DEL CEDRO
MAR M
NICOLAS BROWN
JUSTO SULFREDO BONTIL
LEONARDO ARMENTA
MARIANO VERDUGO
FRANCISCO GARCIA
MERCURIO
POLOCARPIO

DEL ABETO
● E
DEL ALAMO
● F
DEL CIPRES
OLIVO
● G
DE LA ACACIAS
JOSE MARIA MORELOS
ALTA TENSION

● 3
● 4
● 5
MAR MEDITERRANEO
MAR DEL NORTE
MAR CORONADO
● H
Playas de
Rosarito
● 6
● 7
● 8
● 10
● 9
● 11
● I
DEL PINO
● 12
NARANJO
EMILIANO ZAPATA
PUEBLO
ARBOL
● J

PACIFIC
OCEAN
TIJUANA
TOMAS AQ

BARS & CLUBS
Iggy's   11
Izu Tapas and Vino   E
Maya   6
Papas and Beer   8
Rene's Sports Bar   13
Rock and Roll Taco   10
Senor Frog's   7

RESTAURANTS
Chabert's Restaurant &
  Mediterranean Cuisine   J
La Leña   3
Mexico Lindo II   1
El Nido   4
Ortega's Place   2
Ruben's Fish &
  Shrimp Stand   12
Susana's   5
Yaqui Tacos   9

ACCOMMODATION
Alamo   F
Brisas del Mar   E
Colonial   B
Festival Plaza   I
KOA Rosarito   A
Paraiso Ortiz   K
Pelicanos   D
Posada Don Luis   C
Rosarito Beach Hotel   J
Sonia   H
Villa de Lis   G

MEX 1   ● 13 ● K & Tourism Office ▼   ▼ Ensenada via MEX 1D toll road

and they resent the crumbling infrastructure and growing crime rate. But their concerns seem petty compared with those of recent immigrants from other parts of Mexico – their hastily built neighbourhoods have no plumbing, paved roads or city services, along with trickle-down violence from the border's drug turf wars.

Arrival and information

In town, the Mex 1 crosses under the toll road near its northern Rosarito exit and becomes the four-lane **Boulevard Benito Juárez**. Juárez splits Rosarito into the western beach scene and the factory and residential areas that are constantly expanding towards the east. Number addresses along Juárez go from very high (the 4000s) to the double digits as you move south. Mexicoach **buses** from Tijuana (US ☎619/428-9517) drop people off in the *Rosarito Beach Hotel* parking lot on the south end of town, while ABC coaches (☎664/621-2424) leave passengers at the southernmost Mex 1D.

The main tourist office, Km 28 Mex 1, is a good twenty-minute walk from the centre (daily 9am–7pm; ☎661/612-5222). There is a smaller office (Mon–Fri 9am-noon, 2pm-5pm; ☎661/612-0200) inside a building shared with a hair salon on Mex 1 2km south of the *Rosarito Beach Hotel*. Both offer brochures, maps and advice – the latter, though, is dependent on whether the friendly staff is on duty. The convention bureau has an office in the Centro Comercial Oceana Plaza on Juárez just across from *Señor Frog* (Mon–Thurs 10am–4pm, Fri & Sat 10am–7pm; ☎661/612-0396).

Banamex, Bancomer, Santander and Scotia Bank-Inverlat have branches on Juárez and have **ATMs** that dispense both US dollars and pesos. Baja Chat (Blvd Benito Juárez 23, ☎661/612-1008, ⓦwww.bajachat.com) in the *Rosarito Beach Hotel*'s merchant complex has dial-up **Internet** access for M$20 per hour.

Accommodation

Accommodation prices are highest during spring break (March & April) and the week after Christmas, but drop considerably the rest of the year. Throughout the year it's advisable to reserve at least a week in advance if you plan on staying Friday or Saturday night. Don't hesitate to try your hand at bargaining, either in person or over the phone; in the off-season you'll get lower rates (or at least a handful of free margarita coupons).

If you're traveling in a group larger than two and plan on staying longer than three nights it's a good idea to look into **renting a condo**. Absentee owners of the area's many condo developments rent out their units through both local real estate agents and web-based condo aggregators like ⓦwww.mexonline.com.

Alamo C Mar de Adriático 148 ☎661/613-1179, US ☎880/772-1393, ⓦwww.alamo-hostel.com. Stay in bunks or trailers at this rowdy and friendly non-HI affiliated hostel just a short walk from the beach. Transportation can be arranged from the downtown San Diego hostel *Alamo*. ❷

Brisas del Mar Blvd Benito Juárez 22 ☎661/612-2546, US ☎880/871-3605, ⓦwww.ventanarosahotels.com. With subtle pastel-colour palette, this remodelled motor court-cum-hotel wouldn't seem out of place in Palm Springs. The rooms, some of which are wheelchair-accessible, look out onto the pool or parking lot, which are preferable to the ones looking east to the residential neighbourhoods. There's a sand volleyball court, conference room and the only tapas joint in town. ❺

Colonial C 1 and C Primero de Mayo 71 ☏ 661/612-1575. You'll spend so much of your time on the nearby beach that you probably won't use the kitchenette or notice the worn rooms of this small motel. On weekends it's popular with partying groups who fill rooms with four or more. ➌

Festival Plaza Blvd Benito Juárez 1207 US ☏ 800/453-8606, ⓦ www.festivalbaja.com. If the howls of revellers haven't made this high-rise motel's purpose clear, the bright colours and a roller-coaster facade convey the message with a scream: this is Rosarito's home for margaritas and mischief. There are 207 rooms, all with views of the ocean and the pool and the Ferris wheel. The complex also includes nine cafés, restaurants and bars – including a tequila "museum" – a heated pool, Jacuzzis and an outdoor performance space. As rambunctious as it is, it's clean and well run. ➍

KOA Rosarito Km 22 Mex 1 D (exit San Antonio) ☏ 661/613-3305. RV park and campsite with hot showers, laundry and flush toilets starting at M$180 per night for tent camping with use of the showers. ➋–➌

Paraiso Ortiz Km 28 Mex 1, in between *Rene's Sports Bar* and the southernmost tourist office. ☏ 661/612-1020. Prices are low, and a room with a view of the ocean is almost assured at this single-storey budget motel south of town. ➌

Pelicanos C Cedros 115 ☏ 661/612-5545, ⓦ pelicanosrosarito.com. Oceanfront rooms and a restaurant/bar overlooking a native plant garden make up for rather lacklustre, frill-free rooms. Free parking. ➍

Posada Don Luis Blvd Benito Juárez 272, at C 5 de Mayo ☏ 661/612-1166. The prices are low and the rooms are clean, but at 2km north of town and with a long walk to the beach, it's not a good bet for those seeking nightlife. ➌

Rosarito Beach Hotel Blvd Benito Juárez 31 ☏ 661/612-0144, US ☏ 1-800/343-8582 ⓦ www .rosaritohtl.com. The hotel that gave the city its name is now a mini-village with the Casa Playa Spa (housed in a former mansion), restaurants, bars, two pools, time-share apartments, a racquet-ball court, craft shops, liquor stores, a history museum and an Internet café. Many of the rooms have ocean views but are otherwise without charm; request an older room with garden view – they've managed to retain some character. ➎–➏

Sonia Blvd Benito Juárez 783 ☏ 661/612-1260. Management is notoriously picky about how it runs this tiny hotel – no smoking, reservations or credit cards – but the rooms are at least spotless. ➌

Villa de Lis Calle Alamo at Costa Azul ☏ 661/612-2320. Basic motel rooms with cable and, on the second and third floors, views of the ocean. ➌

The City

All of the city's commercial activity takes place along **Boulevard Benito Juárez** with the majority of it happening on the west side around either the *Rosarito Beach Hotel* or *Festival Plaza*. City buildings and residential areas are between Juárez and Mex 1D, which runs parallel on the east. Only the western side of the Juárez has a fully paved sidewalk, which is why you can almost always find better deals and cheaper meals on the dirt-caked eastern side. Large restaurants, shopping centres and other businesses are in the less crowded northern half of town, shut off from the views of Playas de Rosarito by RV parks and condominium developments. Just about everywhere you'll want to go is either on Juárez or a twelve-block square warren of bar-laden streets that separates it from the beach.

Rosarito Beach Hotel

Rosarito's fortunes have been dictated by the whims of out-of-towners since Manuel Barbachano turned the young **Rosarito Beach Hotel**, Blvd Benito Juárez 31, into a regional hub in the late 1920s. It quickly became an exclusive escape for the Hollywood and international playboy set (see box, p.128). The family is still in charge of the hotel, and the current owner, Hugo Torres Chabert, is, like his uncle, the big man around town. Even if you're not staying here (see above), you should walk through at least a portion of the hotel to appreciate its history. The two-storey entryway is grand in a Golden Era kind of way, and the tilework and murals are reminders that an artisan's eyes were once considered valuable at the hotel.

Throughout the week the bar is a mini-town square for movers and shakers who come to curry favour with Chabert, as well as tourists looking for a scene where patrons are required to wear shirts and shoes. Regional dance groups and folk bands provide in-house entertainment every Friday and Saturday night in the Salón Mexicano ballroom, serving as a foil of sorts to the raucousness of the party scene just up the beach.

Festival Plaza

While it's old for Rosarito, the *Beach Hotel* is hardly a relic, even if that's what it looks like next to the brash twelve-storey **Festival Plaza**, a five-minute walk up Juárez. The Plaza is almost single-handedly responsible for the city's growing reputation as the poor man's spring break destination. A mini-city in itself, the upstart lures patrons on their way to the beach with seven restaurants and bars, including the pseudo museum El Museo Tequila Cantina. Although the hotel's guests have travelled for either sex and booze or a combination of the two, the *Plaza*'s restaurants and clubs have raised the bar on Rosarito's dining scene, forcing the other restaurants to come up with good reasons to lure Festival guests out of their cocoon.

Playas de Rosarito

People didn't start flocking to Rosarito for the cheap booze or party atmosphere but for its deep and wide beach, one of the two largest between Tijuana and Ensenada. Before 10 or 11am **Playas de Rosarito** has all the charm of a television commercial on retirement planning; locals stroll peacefully hand in hand as a graceful tide pulls out to reveal even more sand. By noon they give way to a small army of salesmen offering ATV rentals (M$200 per hour) and horse rides (M$150 per half-hour). From then until the end of the day (when

△ Beach volleyball, Playas de Rosarito

Rosarito's home to Hollywood's stars

Like Tijuana's *Agua Caliente Spa & Casino*, the **Rosarito Beach Hotel** was a destination in itself from the 1930s to the 1950s. It was never grand on the same scale, but Golden Age Hollywood stars, dictators and the international jet set crowd still flocked to its Spanish-style rooms for a bit of seclusion and one of the best beaches on the Pacific Coast. Their privacy was ensured at the time but the hotel now heavily publicizes their histories to tweak visitors' interest. During its heyday, the only access was via a dirt road from Tijuana, a private yacht or a beach runway. Without the gambling, it was this exclusivity that pulled in the names.

The bawdiest tales probably died with the perpetrators, but some gems have been passed along. There's the one about Kim Novak swinging from a lamp and sleeping with junior Dominican dictator Rafael Trujillo. The Shah of Iran's son Ali Khan brought girlfriend Rita Hayworth here for a week of long walks on the beach. On the tamer side, Paulette Goddard and Burgess Meredith walked down the aisle here to an audience that included Gregory Peck and Zsa Zsa Gabor. Orson Welles, Frank Sinatra, Marilyn Monroe, Mickey Rooney and a host of others made frequent trips to the hotel's *Beachcomber Bar*.

the action moves from the shore to the clubs on the other side of the sand), the beach throngs with pickup football and volleyball games and groups of kids wakeboarding. On the year's biggest weekends, it's too chaotic to be relaxing but during the rest of the year it has the nostalgic feel of a 1960s beach party.

Eating

Lunch and **dinner** crowds flock to Juárez's open-air stands for superb *al pastor* and *carne asada* tacos. It's relatively hard to get a bad meal at any of the restaurants along the boulevard unless you pick the more expensive ones.

Chabert's Restaurant & Mediterranean Cuisine Blvd Benito Juárez 31 ☎661/612-1111. You'll have to change out of your flip-flops and tank tops for *Rosarito Beach Hotel*'s fine dining spot. Oddly, the menu is haute continental (with prices to match) and flash frozen in the culinary sensibilities of the 1970s. Cordon bleu anyone?

La Espiga Panadería The three locations along Blvd Benito Juárez specialize in the region's sweet breakfast rolls and, with a cup of coffee, will start your day better than the heaping plates of *huevos rancheros* that come standard in hotels.

La Leña Blvd Benito Juárez 2500 ☎661/612-0826. This combo steakhouse, sports bar and piano bar has a menu that aims to please everyone, and does a pretty good job trying. Steaks are cheaper than those further south on the strip and tend to be more carefully prepared (New York Strip runs M$130), and while the margaritas are huge, there's no raucous bar scene.

Mexico Lindo II Blvd Benito Juárez 110 ☎664/613-5960. With a focus on rabbit, quail and chicken, this grill stands out among the many offerings along Blvd Benito Juárez. Whole chickens and quails cost less than M$100 and rabbits aren't much more; everything is served with tortillas and rice and beans. Take-out is even cheaper. Daily 8am–6pm.

El Nido Blvd Benito Juárez 67 ☎661/612-1430, ⓦ www.elnidorosarito.com. Wagon wheels, winding rope and enough Western memorabilia to decorate most of Texas make it quite obvious that this joint grills big steaks – which they do very well. Additionally, *Nido* raises free-range venison, quail, rabbit and lamb on its own ranch in the Valle de Guadalupe, then sautés them in garlic (like the quail and rabbit) or grills the chops and steak cuts (like the lamb and venison). Patrons can dine indoors or on a patio surrounded by native plants.

Ortega's Place Blvd Benito Juárez 200 ☎664/612-0022. Overlooking the ocean, this Rosarito outpost of a Puerto Nuevo restaurant of the same name offers a similar lobster-centric menu (M$130–220) of grilled langoustine accompanied by home-made tortillas and rice and beans.

Ruben's Fish and Shrimp Stand Blvd Benito Juárez 28, no phone. Settle into an outdoor booth for grilled or fried shrimp tacos, *ceviche*, deep-fried crab and by-the-pound fish dinners. Summer daily 6am–7pm, winter Thurs–Mon 8am–5pm.

Susana's Blvd Benito Juárez 4356 ⊕661/613-1187, ⓦwww.susanasinrosarito.com. There are multiple seating options – patios, private booths and a dining room – for enjoying the California-style cuisine such as Dijon salmon over grilled veggies (entrees M$120–200) and wide range of wines from the Valle de Guadalupe. Adds a bit of class to a block that's also home to *Senor Frog's*.

Yaqui Tacos Calle de la Palma at Av Mar del Norte. Ask any West Coast food fanatic, or better yet, someone on-line here, and they will agree: the city's best tacos come from this simple stand just a block off Blvd Benito Juárez. Giant marinated flank steak tacos topped with guacamole, grilled onions and salsa go for M$15.

Drinking

The **bars** and **clubs** that put Rosarito on the party map – mega club anchors such as *Papas and Beer* and *Club Maya* – either dot Avenida Costa Azul, one long block west of Juárez, or encircle the *Fiesta Plaza* complex. Cover charges of up to M$150 are the norm in high season, during a special event, or if you're a man, but for much of the year the clubs are free. For a less rowdy night out than what you'll inevitably find here, it's best to stick to the bar at *Rosarito Beach Club*, *Izu Tapas* or *René's Sports Bar*, a M$10 ride south.

Iggy's Av Coronado 11327 ⊕661/612-0537, ⓦwww.clubbiggys.com. *Iggy's* patrons shed the few inhibitions that keep *Papas and Beer's* customers from going all out. Alongside the cheap drinks and beach scene, *Iggy's* throws in daytime ATV rentals (M$150), bungee jumping and cages for go-go girls.

Izu Tapas and Vino Blvd Benito Juárez 22, inside *Brisas del Mar Hotel*. The low-key vibe here wouldn't be out of place in a large, cosmopolitan city, which makes the tapas bar *Izu* slightly disconcerting in this flip-flop town. While there is a large flat-screen television, the sound is turned off in favour of live DJs. Small plates start at M$30 and entrees run to M$100. A large by-the-glass wine list includes Baja selections alongside international ones.

Maya Eucalipto y Coronado 10102 ⊕664/995-3665, ⓦwww.clubmayarosarito.com. This massive open-air dance club and concert hall looks like a half-built Eastern European stadium, but it still pulls in massive crowds for sets by international DJs such as Mark Farina and Dmitri from Paris.

Papas and Beer Av Coronado 100 ⊕664/612-0444, ⓦwww.papasandbeer.com. If an 18-year-old were to build the ultimate party bar it wouldn't vary widely from the *P&B* formula. Dirt-cheap fruity drinks and beach access? Check. Foam room and mechanical bull? Check. Bikini contests and beach volleyball? Of course.

Rene's Sports Bar Km 28 Mex 1 ⊕661/612-1061. When this sports bar adjacent to an RV park isn't running boxing matches or baseball games on its 16 televisions, it's likely because there's a mariachi band playing. During the day they serve steaks and seafood.

Rock and Roll Taco Blvd Benito Juárez 1207. Once the site of the broadcast station of legendary 1960s and 70s DJ Wolfman Jack's, *Taco* now serves food during the day and turns into a concert hall and dance club at night. Its location next door to Festival Plaza brings in the gringo party crowd.

Senor Frog's Blvd Benito Juárez 4358 ⊕661/612-4375. Ostensibly a restaurant serving Americanized Mexican food, *Frog's* is more a rowdy bar fuelled by M$10 shots and giant margaritas.

Shopping

Rosarito isn't exactly brimming with **shopping** options, but you can find better deals here on pottery and housewares than you will in Tijuana or Ensenada. Many shops aren't outfitted with credit card scanners, so always bring cash. *Alex Curios*, Km 28.5 Mex 1 (⊕661/612-1175) anchors the merchant arcade in front of the *Beach Hotel* with a quirky collection of folk art and other handicrafts made by older artisans. You'll pay more at *Fausto Polanco*, Blvd Benito Juárez 2400 (☏ 661/612-2271, ⓦ www.faustopolanco.com.mx) than you would from the merchant herself but this regional chain is always a dependable stop for everything from handmade gifts to furniture. A second location at Km 35 Mex 1 (☏ 661/612-5424 & 25) is accessible directly from the toll road. You can't tell from the street, but *Mercado de Artesanías*, Boulevard Juárez at Calle Encino, is downtown's largest shopping arcade, with over a hundred stalls within its confines. Some of the crafts are from Asia rather than the Baja, and with a little bargaining you can get a deal on leather goods, carvings and ceramics.

Moving on from Rosarito

Bus riders continuing south to Ensenada and beyond can pick up long-distance ABC buses at the Mex 1D tollbooth on the south side of town, about 2km south of the *Rosarito Beach Hotel*. The cheap **taxis** that serve the region well up to this point will get you to Puerto Nuevo, but peter out beyond there. To get there, or back to Tijuana, flag down a *colectivo* on Boulevard Benito Juárez or use the stand directly across from the *Rosarito Beach Hotel*.

Drivers are hit with M$250 toll before going either direction on Mex 1D. Until you get to La Misión at Km 59.5 the toll and free roads run parallel and both have Pacific views of comparable quality. After the La Misión exchange, Mex 1 runs inland toward the Valle de Guadalupe before rejoining the scenic toll road 15km outside of Ensenada.

The coastal settlements

For most visitors, the **coastline** between Rosarito and Ensenada just rises above the level of a curiosity. Its residential nature and dearth of cultural sights makes it easy to cover quickly; a day's activity would consist of few hours at Fox's movie studio **Popotla**, lunch at the lobster haven **Puerto Nuevo**, and a breathtaking, leisurely drive south to Ensenada for shopping, dinner and a night's rest.

People do linger, though, spending days surfing and camping at secluded points like **Salsipuedes** or settling into one of the many one-hotel settlements that dot the coast and offer little more than great sunsets and generous bartenders. If you want to stop often along the way to or from Ensenada, take the free road (Mex 1) between Rosarito and **La Misión** and the toll road (Mex 1D) for all other travel.

Regular visitors tend to return to the same hotel year after year, and are likely to extol the virtues of their favourite with a vigour that can set up false expectations for the first-timer. For their part, the hotels are apt to describe themselves with terms like 'luxury,' 'five-star,' or 'resort' in instances where a more discerning hotelier would opt for the more appropriate 'quirky,' 'charming' or 'unique.' Whatever may be closest to the mark, the one unifying truth is the lure of the Pacific – the real reason people return to the area year after year.

There are no real towns along the coast, just a few stores and restaurant/bars clustered around a view or natural feature. Even though there's typically only one accommodation option to choose from at each settlement, you are never far from lodging suitable for every budget, from car camping and basic rooms to wedding suites. Some of the larger properties like *Hotel Las Rocas* and *New Port Beach Hotel* were built based on unbridled optimism, which means that room rates can vary wildly depending on vacancy level (bargain if these vast parking lots are empty). A recent surge in condominium and housing construction has closed some of the RV parks and campgrounds that had been around for years and may result in other changes to the coast's lodging options.

Popotla to Cantamar

Before **Fox Studios Baja**, Km 32.5 Mex 1, arrived in 1997, **POPOTLA** was a fishing village and RV park on Rosarito's southern fringe populated by a few hundred snowbirds and fishermen. Now it's given up a chunk of its wide, flat beach and ocean views with a fluctuating population of film industry workers, producers and movie stars.

Of course, some members of the community resent Fox's presence and its un-neighbourly act of cordoning off its 35 acres with a 2m high, 150m long wall; residents soon decorated its length with a colourful mural pieced together from fishing gear and found objects. The wall cuts off part of the beach and views of Fox Studios Baja's centrepiece, a seventeen-million-gallon oceanfront tank originally built to shoot the water scenes for the film *Titanic*. Filming went better than expected and Fox decided to stay, and subsequently used the giant tank for soggy flicks such as *Master and Commander* and *Pearl Harbor*. They've also built more soundstages for use in film and TV and, for a month in 2005, as a practice space for U2's world tour.

You can see much of the site – and eat at a bevy of US chain restaurants – on one of the **Foxploration** tours (Wed–Fri 9am–4:30pm, Sat & Sun 10am–5:30pm; ☎661/614-9444, US ☎866/369-2252; ⓦwww.foxploration.com; M$90–120), the only way to get onsite. There's a how-to exhibit about *Titanic* and pieces of the 95 percent scale ship (most of it's been packed away, though). If filming isn't taking place, you can take a very disorienting stroll along a recreated block of New York City's Canal Street. *Planet of the Apes* and *X-Men* are represented by a prop and make-up show for the former and a children's play area for the latter. Fox continues to install props from warehouses around Los Angeles, which explains the presence of the centrepiece fountain from *Hello Dolly* and other items that pre-date Foxploration's creation. Film buffs will appreciate the opportunity to wander a real working studio, especially since most US ones have now closed their doors to the public.

There's no hotel in Popotla, but the *Mobile Home Park* at Km 34 Mex 1 offers tent sites for M$200 per night and motorhome rentals from M$450 (☎661/612-1502, ⓔpopotla@telnor.net).

Calafia and Hotel Las Rocas

Moving southwards from Popotla along Mex 1 you'll soon see the dome and a cross of a mission, but once you turn off the road you'll notice that the chapel is more plaster than stone, and that it's merely the frontispiece to **CALAFIA**, a 70-room cliffside hotel at Km 35.5 Mex 1 (☎661/612-1580 & 1581, ⓦwww.hotel-calafia.com; ⑨) that's long been popular with families on weekend trips.

Bougainvillea and cobblestone lead into a lobby that gives way to a restaurant and bar overlooking the Pacific from its lofty perch, and there's an art gallery, craft shop and a mini-museum filled with replicas of Baja California and mainland religious artefacts. **HOTEL LAS ROCAS** sits a bit further south at Km 38.5. This whitewashed and slightly weathered multi-storey faux Moroccan resort offers ocean views from every room, two pools, a full spa and activities such as rope courses and rock climbing, depending on seasonal demand. (T661/614-0354, US T888/527-7266, Wwww.lasrocas.com; ⑥).

Puerto Nuevo

Calafia and *Las Rocas* are used as jumping-off points to explore the entire northwest coast in general and **PUERTO NUEVO** in particular. Once not much more than a dusty roadside settlement at Km 42, it is nowadays known the length of the

△ Lobster restaurant, Puerto Nuevo

peninsula for its near fanatical devotion to the local speciality that bears its name: Puerto Nuevo-style grilled Pacific lobster. Found off the coast and throughout the rest of the Pacific Rim, these lobsters don't grow as large as their Atlantic counterparts (actually, they're giant langoustines more closely related to shrimp) and they don't have claws, but they're just as delicious when smothered in butter.

Choosing where to sample the revered dish – and you must if you stop here – is made easy enough with the town's one-way street plan that juts to the west from Mex 1. Aggressive shell-pushers will attempt to herd you to the restaurant that's employed them, making window shopping difficult – even from the comfort of your car. Though every one of the more than two-dozen restaurants serves their lobster the same basic way – grilled and split in half with beans, rice and warm flour tortillas – *Puerto Nuevo #2* (☎661/614-1454), directly to your south on the second block, and *Ortega's Patio* at the southwest corner of the grid (☎661/614-1320 & 0345) are consistently good bets. Expect to pay M$120 at the former and up to M$200 at the latter, which will also get you ocean views, low lighting, a wood-beam ceiling and the best atmosphere in town.

Because there's nothing to do here but eat, many of Puerto Nuevo's visitors have driven or taxied in from Ensenada or Rosarito, and the two hotels on the south side of town are each larger than the crowds demand. The studios and villas of *Grand Baja Resort*, Km 44.5 Mex 1, sleep up to six people. The expansive property runs along the rocky coastline so even the standard rooms offer an ocean view, and there's a host of resort offerings, including a swimming pool, Jacuzzi, kids' playground and tennis courts (☎661/614-1488, US ☎877/315-1002, ⓦwww.grandbaja.com; ⑥). All 147 rooms in the four storeys of *New Port Beach Hotel* at Km 45 Mex 1 have a view of the ocean and the heated pool. Rooms have telephones, TVs, and there's in-room massage services and access to the Jacuzzi, tennis court and restaurant and bar (☎661/614-1188, US ☎800/582-1018, ⓦwww.newportbeachhotel.com; ⑦). There's a *colectivo* **taxi stand** directly across from the arch on the northbound side of Mex 1; the fare to Rosarito is M$20, the fare to Ensenada is M$150.

Cantamar

CANTAMAR, at Km 49 Mex 1, is a growing town bordered by sand dunes to the south and the Bahía El Descanso to the west. Although it's in the midst of a small building boom, it still retains the sleepy charm that's drawn campers and RVs to its shores for more than fifty years. A well laid-out dirt street system to the west of Mex 1 offers easy access to the beach and the northern half of the dunes. On the south side of the dunes, long-time residents and newcomers use the palapa-covered *The Palm Grill*, Km 53 Mex 1, as much as an unofficial town hall as to fill up on inexpensive steak, seafood and cold beer. Merchants in improvised structures to the west of Mex 1 cater to people needing ATVs, sandboards or other devices to scour the **dunes**, an unusual feature in the area.

San Miguel La Nueva

The dunes run along the coast for about 6km, breaking around Km 54. Here a dirt road leads east under Mex 1D and through a small village to the remnants of **SAN MIGUEL LA NUEVA** or **El Descanso Misión**. Missions don't have the best success story on the peninsula, but a view of the Pacific probably made Father Tomás Ahumada feel hopeful when he established it in 1817 as an alternative to the frequently flooded San Miguel de Arcangel nearby. In spite of his fervent hopes, Father Ahumada's mission was the penultimate the Dominicans established before giving up completely on the entire peninsula. Nothing from the 1817 structure remains, and what's left of a second adobe mission built in 1830 and abandoned four years later is something only a completist should seek out. The small foundation – built to accommodate two dozen parishioners – is covered by a corrugated steel shelter that's adjacent to a pink stucco church, which isn't looking much better than the adjacent ruins. If you've hiked here and have become too depressed by it all, there's a taxi stand at the road's junction with Mex 1.

The nearby tent campground *Medio Camino*, Km 56 Mex 1 (bathroom facilities; ②) is one of the oldest on the coast, but if you're not up for roughing it, take a bed in the nearby *Pyramid Resort & Condos*, Km 57 Mex 1 (☎646/155-0265, Ⓦwww .pyramidresort.com; ⑤–⑥). Some of the studios and one- or two-bedroom units have fireplaces, but none has a phone or TV. The Pacific is just steps away.

La Misión to San Miguel

LA MISIÓN, the closest approximation of a proper town in the area, consists of a popular surfing beach and coastal settlement starting at Km 58, a long swimming beach 3km south and a small town in the Río San Miguel valley immediately after Mex 1 turns inland away from its parallel track with the toll road. Swimming is possible at the northern end *Playa La Salina* (formerly *Los Alistos Trailer Park*), Km 58 Mex 1 (☎664/636-1169; tent camping with shower M$70 per car), but the waves are more popular with surfers who follow a day of hitting the breaks inside the two–storey beachside bar and restaurant *La Palapa Jose* (☎646/155-0339). The road rises south of here and gives the *Hotel La Misión*, Km 59 Mex 1, decent views of surfers below. The hotel is actually a modest two-storey motel with an attached restaurant/bar and a fireplace in every room (which you'll need here on winter evenings). Small mini-trailers that sleep up to six start at M$450. While they don't have the fireplaces or Jacuzzis in the suites, they're closer to the water and have small concrete patios (☎646/155-0333, US ☎562/420-8500, Ⓔptmision@telnor.net; ④).

The scene is positively swinging next door at *La Fonda,* Km 59.5 Mex 1 (℡646/155-0307 & 0308, ⓦwww.lafondamexico.com; ⓒ; cash only), a hotel with one of the most loyal clienteles in all of Baja California. In the 1970s and 80s, vacationing families and swinging singles rubbed elbows here with US senators and rock stars on a deck cantilevered above the crashing tide. The famous don't come as often anymore, but *La Fonda*'s enduring quirkiness still draws the curious. The hotel clings to the cliff side, with 26 rooms perched at different levels along the rock face. The pebbly beach below is accessed via a steep, twisting staircase. The rooms, all without phones, are comfy enough, with patios and some with fireplaces and wood-beam ceilings, but most of the action takes place on the deck, which serves as a bar and restaurant and hosts a popular Sunday brunch. There's also an on-site day spa offering massages, wraps and an assortment of beauty treatments.

If you're driving along Mex 1 and want to stick to the coastal route you'll need to enter Mex 1D just across from *La Fonda* – see the box below if you plan to continue inland on Mex 1. **Playa la Misión**, 1km to the south, is a gated members-only settlement, but just to its south along Mex 1D is the best public beach – complete with a rustic public bath and changing rooms – south of Rosarito. During the summer months merchants pack the kiosks separating the parking lot from the beach, some selling souvenirs or renting horses, but most serving finger food like fish tacos, and drinks like fresh coconut water. Park on either side of Mex 1D and use the pedestrian overpass if you're in one of the northbound lanes.

The beach has attracted some long-term visitors who've set up camp in one of two RV parks. The primitive campground *Rancho Mal Paso RV Park*, Km 71 Mex 1D, is only accessible from the southbound side and not very well marked either. Once you find it, pay at the shelter down the road and pick a spot; almost all are guaranteed to be peaceful (no phone; ⓞ). The campground is just down the beach from *Baja Seasons*, Km 72.5 Mex 1D, another combo RV park

Mex 1 to Valle de Guadalupe

The free and toll roads split at La Misión, with Mex 1 taking a swing southeast through the Valle de Guadalupe (see p.149) before merging with Mex 1D in San Miguel. The La Misión designation is owed to **Misión San Miguel Arcangel de la Frontera**, a Dominican settlement 5km from the toll road on Mex 1, that hasn't fared much better than El Descanso (see p.133). Founded in 1787 and abandoned in 1833, what's left of the structure amounts to the lone adobe wall held up by telephone poles. Locked gates protect the site year-round but also prevent visitors from viewing the detailed bilingual explanatory placards. If you could read them, they'd explain that the mission was the fourth along the Camino Real Misionero, and that the Spanish were preceded here by a Native American community called **Jakwatljap**, named after the eponymous nearby hot springs. During the mission's early years it was rather prosperous, collecting a good number of cattle and horses, but the Native Americans were killed off by disease, no one could tend to the livestock and the settlement foundered.

Although not nearly as beautiful as the coastal drive, the free road rises above the ocean and traverses a scenic stretch of farms for 27km. There's food and drink at *La Sinoalese*, Km 89, in the small settlement of **El Tigre**. The turnoff for the graded dirt road to Valle de Guadalupe at Km 92 is well marked from both directions, and once you're on it, follow signs to San Antonio de las Minas for 13km to get through to Mex 3 Ensenada–Tecate to the southeast. Despite the potential for washboarding at points, it's passable for any car driving under 30km/h.

and condo/hotel complex (☎646/155-4015, US ☎800/754-4190, ⓦwww .bajaseasons.com; rooms ❺). The twenty rooms share ocean views and amenities like volleyball and putt-putt golf with the RV park.

La Salina

One of the ports in the Mexican government's ambitious yet still unrealized maritime Escalera Nautica plan, **LA SALINA** is not much more than a dirt parking lot and a boat ramp. Still, this marina at Km 73.5 is one of the more easily accessible small-craft launches on the Pacific Coast. The young men working the entrance gate will walk you through the fee structure for your boat and parking. Just north of the marina is the stucco-gated entrance to *La Salina Beach Hotel & Cantina* (☎615/54 087, US ☎909/825-7364, ⓦwww.lasalinabeach.com; ❺). Each of the fourteen rooms has a patio or deck overlooking the beach and ocean. The cantina, which fronts the Pacific, is only open Friday to Sunday.

Bajamar

Billboards heralding **BAJAMAR** at km 77.5 Mex 1D dot the highway at regular intervals between Tijuana and Ensenada, so it's a bit anticlimactic to discover that it's a vast, largely vacant planned community, with cul-de-sacs clustered around the coast and the fairways of a 27-hole golf course (greens fees M$700–940). Still, it's the only course in the state of Baja California where golfers can tee off in sight of the Pacific, and for many that is reason enough to come here. Guests can stay in the secluded *Hacienda Bajamar*, whose seventeen rooms surround a courtyard with fountain, and there's a pool and generic Mexican–Continental restaurant onsite (☎646/155-0151, US ☎888/311-6076, ⓦwwwgolfbajamar.com; ❻).

El Mirador to San Miguel

From high above the shore at Km 83 Mex 1D, the rambling pastel-hued recreation area **EL MIRADOR**, with an expansive vista of Ensenada and Isla Todos Santos to the south, presents some of the most stunning views on either coast. Although the exit ramp is open, the chains blocking the parking lot are often locked. Follow the other cars' lead and park by the side of the road and step over the chains. There used to be a restaurant and bar in the complex, but the tables and hardware are gone now, leaving visitors to fend for themselves with picnics or barbecue at the remaining grill stations.

Salsipuedes

The small surfing community at **SALSIPUEDES**, Km 86 Mex 1D, is much more welcoming than either the name – which means 'leave if you can' – or the precarious dirt road you must negotiate to access it would suggest. The few dozen people who live here full time – either by choice or because they can't get their trailers back up the hill – welcome a collection of in-the-know Mexican and Southern Californians surfers who paddle out into the water for advanced breaks with good lefts and a long, heavy right. Don't come here if you're just learning how to surf – just getting to the water requires a good deal of agility and the waves here are by no means suited for beginners. Staying overnight costs M$100 for tents, M$400 for no-frills cabins (look for the caretaker, no phone). There's running water, but that's the extent of the amenities. If you want to park here for the day just to surf it'll cost you M$50, payable to the campground caretaker.

Playa Saldamando

If you want to camp near Ensenada but prefer to remain outside the city limits, the closest you'll get is the vast, rambling coastal campground at the foot of cliffs at **PLAYA SALDAMANDO**, Km 94 Mex 1D. Getting here is a bit like following a trail of breadcrumbs – in this case white painted rocks that line the dirt road accessible only from the southbound lanes. After you've meandered your way down a steep incline you'll enter a small settlement of permanent trailers and concrete slabs spaced well apart along the coastline leading to an expansive camping area that runs along the beach. Car camping begins at M$130 per night, motor-homes at M$150 and on-site trailers at M$300. Bathroom facilities are shared and other items (such as lanterns and boogie boards) can be rented or purchased (US ☎619/857-9242, ⊛www.playasaldamando.com; ❸).

Surfing

Though it has gained mythical status as the lifestyle of blond-haired, hedonism-seeking men from Southern California, **surfing** is an age-old sport. Reliefs discovered in coastal Peru, some over five thousand years old, depict native peoples navigating the waves on boards made from reeds. Hawaii has evidence of surfing in scenes carved into rock that date back 1500 years.

The practice was brought from Polynesia to Hawaii during a period of migration in the fourth century AD. It wasn't until the early twentieth century that Hawaiian duke Kahanamoku, an Olympic swimmer, actor and the greatest surfer of his time, popularized the sport internationally. Surfing took off in California and continued to evolve in board design and riding techniques. Californians crossed the border into Baja California to seek out some of its legendary waves, and the sport became established in Mexico.

There are different types of surfboards, which influence surfing style and performance. The longboard is over 2.5m long, has a single fin and rounded features. This traditional type of board is superior for cruising and is the easiest to stand on, but is difficult to manoeuvre out past the breaking waves. The shortboard is under 2.5m, has three fins and pointy front tip. These boards are easier to steer, but require more skill to gain your initial balance. Hybrid, mid-size boards, also referred to as funboards, are ideal for learning to surf.

Whatever board you choose to use, make sure you bring it and all your supplies with you, or rent them at the beginning of the trip. The best surfing spots in Baja are typically hundreds of kilometres from a surf shop.

Basic surfing terms

Close-out A wave that does not crest and gradually break to the left or to the right, but folds over at once and is almost impossible to ride.

Goofy foot Style of surfing with the left foot at the back end of the board. The back foot steers and, therefore, people typically favour the right foot.

Hang ten To stand on the front end (nose) of a longboard, thereby dangling all ten toes off the tip.

Kook An inexperienced surfer unfamiliar with surfing etiquette.

Leash The cord that attaches the surfboard to a Velcro strap around the ankle of the surfer.

Point break A wave that breaks at the tip of a promontory of land and continues down its side for a longer than average distance.

San Miguel

El Sauzal, on the outskirts of Ensenada, could very well be home to the biggest fish processing plant on the Pacific Coast. As harsh as the smell can sometimes be, the adjacent settlement of **SAN MIGUEL** is a surfing and camping spot popular with those who don't mind the whiz and whine of the nearby highway. Pull off the road just south of the toll plaza at Km 99 for both at *Villa de San Miguel* (T646/174-7948; ❶). The shower and bathroom facilities are rustic, but the surfing is advanced. If you're not prepared to camp, hike 2.5km east along Avenida L to *Hostel Sauzal*, Av L 344 (T646/174-6381, Whostelsauzal.tripod.com; ❷). Rooms are dorm-style, and bedding, breakfast and showers are included.

Ensenada and around

Flat, sea-level **ENSENADA** is the largest municipality in all of Mexico, with its southern limits stretching five hundred kilometres to Baja California Sur. Bordered by Bahía Todos Santos to the west, the Chapultepec Hills to the north, and Punta Banda to the south, the city lies at the confluence of several valleys, including the blossoming wine regions of Guadalupe and Santo Tomás. While Ensenada's short life as capital of the territory ended after only three decades, its massive size and position along the coast means that it still retains a great measure of control over the region.

Ensenada's attractiveness to both visitors and residents begins in the bay. Downtown streets radiate away from the port and, while the architecture isn't exceptional in any way, the scale of the city – aided by wide sidewalks in the shopping and eating district – encourages exploration by foot, a practice almost completely absent in most of the peninsula's other cities. Mornings typically begin with a trip to the raucous fish market, probably the best spectator sport in town. The malecón stretches out of the market for six blocks until the often-dry Arroyo de Ensenada, connecting pedestrians with tour boat operators, fishing piers, a movie theatre and small merchants along the way.

Southern Californians who have outgrown Tijuana but still want an easy day-trip or weekend getaway come for the clubs along Avenida Ruiz and the shopping on López Mateos. The city is the northernmost spot to watch the yearly whale migration, and is also a big base for sport-fishing expeditions. As well there are sights on the outskirts of town that are best experienced from a base in town; the Valle de Guadalupe's vineyards (see p.149) on one end, **La Bufadora**'s water spout on the other.

Perhaps the city's biggest draw is its thriving culinary scene – whether it's lunch in the fish market or a fancy dinner at a gourmet restaurant along López Mateos with a bottle of wine from the nearby Valle de Guadalupe. And of course there is the city's most lasting contribution to the world's tastebuds: the **fish taco**. Though you can find them throughout coastal Mexico and the US west coast, nowhere else is the standard as high as in Ensenada.

Some history

The Spanish explorer Juan Rodríguez Cabrillo was the first European to pull into Ensenada's bay when he came ashore here in 1542. Failing to notice any inhabitants, he left four days later after naming the bay San Mateo. The next foreign visitor was Sebastián Vizcaíno who arrived in 1602. He stayed long enough to rename the bay Ensenada de Todos Santos but, like his predecessor, didn't notice anyone on shore. The first Spaniard to stay for any length of time – at least long enough to notice the indigenous Kumai who fished regularly in the bay – was the Franciscan Junípero Serra, who rode through in 1769 on his way from Loreto to San Diego.

Modern Ensenada can trace its roots not to a mission settlement but to the rancher Alferez José Ruiz' purchase of the area from Baja California's governor in 1806 for a mere M\$2; eighteen years later he sold the entire 8600-acre plot to his son-in-law for three hundred times the price. With the exception of this ranching activity, Ensenada and its port were entirely ignored during the Dominican proselytising period that lasted until 1845. After the Treaty of Guadalupe Hidalgo, the city remained a blip on the radar until gold was discovered in 1872 nearby in Real de Castillo. The resulting rush created the need for a waterfront customs house and the tiny Ensenada was the best candidate. The gold vein died out almost immediately, but the town's leaders had a taste for power that, after much political wrangling, resulted in their relocation of the northern territory's capital to the Bahía de Todos Santos in 1882.

The city's real architects were immigrants like San Franciscan George Sisson and German Luis Hüller who used the depressed value of property to buy up land and subdivided the city and the outlying areas into parcels for both urban, agricultural and mining purposes. A short-lived building boom coincided with a similar one in San Diego and other parts of the southwest US. Shortly before this died completely the men sold their concession to a group of Englishmen seeking to expand mining claims throughout the region. English control coincided with multiple plots to annex the peninsula to the US or create an independent country, all of which failed. Foreign intrigue abounded because of both the isolated location and high percentage of non-Mexican residents, around seventy percent in the late 1880s.

Through the revolutionary tumults of the first quarter of the twentieth century, Ensenada managed to avoid upheaval. Although the city would eventually have its own casino, the town fathers looked down on the gaming industry in Tijuana and other cities, regularly protesting the illegal behaviour of regional leaders to officials in Mexico City – perhaps in an attempt to strengthen their case for moving the territory's capital back. Instead, they got a road to Tijuana. While it was being ignored by the power bases in the north, Ensenada created a mix of food, shipping and tourism-related industries that have allowed it to grow steadily and avoid Tijuana-style pandering to tourism or *maquiladoras* and their cheap labour. Although no hotbed of radicalism, it's been on the forefront of political change, electing Ernesto Ruffo in 1985 as the country's first non-PRI mayor in modern times; in 1988 Ruffo went on to become the first PAN governor in Mexico.

Arrival and information

From the north, **arrival by car** is straightforward. By 10km north of town, the southbound Mex 1, Mex 1D and Mex 3 (from Tecate and the Valle de Guadalupe) have all merged into one four-lane local road that, once downtown, becomes Boulevard Lázaro Cárdenas running along the waterfront. Prior to this, a bypass at the turnoff to Universidad Autonómica de Baja California

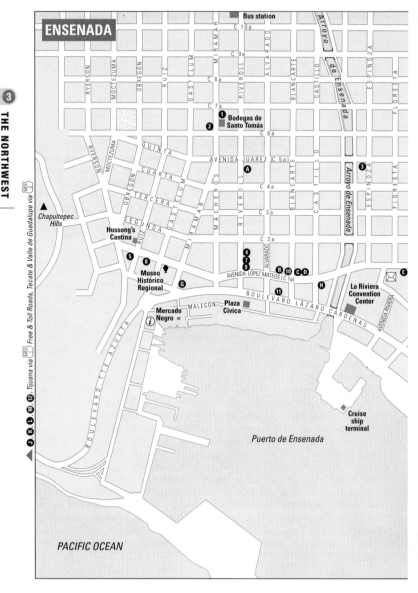

ENSENADA

Bus station

C 10a

C 9a

C 8a

C 7a

1 **Bodegas de**
2 **Santo Tomás**

C 6a

A AVENIDA JUAREZ (C 5a)

C 4a **3**

C 3a

Chapultepec
Hills

C 2a

Hussong's
Cantina

5 **8** **4**
7
9 **B 10 C D**
Museo **6**
Histórico AVENIDA LÓPEZ MATEOS (C 1a)
Regional **H** **E**
11 **La Riviera**
BOULEVARD LÁZARO CÁRDENAS **Convention**
Center
Mercado MALECÓN Plaza
Negro **i** Cívica

Puerto de Ensenada

Cruise
ship
terminal

PACIFIC OCEAN

allows drivers to skirt downtown via Calle 9a and provides a simpler link to
Avenida Reforma and Mex 1 towards San Quintín than does the marked Mex
1 through town.

On the other side of town, the west-bound branch of Mex 3 from San
Felipe descends into Ensenada along Calzada Cortéz. The signage won't
direct you downtown, but stay on Cortéz until Reforma, then take a left.

ACCOMMODATION

Best Western El Cid	B
Casa del Sol	C
Coral & Marina	J
El Cortez	D
Misión Santa Isabel	H
La Pinta	E
Paraiso las Palmas	I
Punta Morro	K
Quintas Papagayo	L
Las Rosas	M
San Nicolás	F
Santo Tomás	G
Del Valle	A

RESTAURANTS

Bronco's	6
Casamar	11
El Charro	8
El Cid	B
Las Conchas	5
La Cueva de los Tigres	13
La Enbotelladora Vieja	1
La Esquina de Bodegas	2
Manzanilla Restaurant	4
Mi Kasa	9
El Rey Sol	10
Sano's	12
Tacos Fenix	3
La Vendimia	7

Follow Reforma to Calle Diamante, take a right and another immediate right to access the southeast end of Avenida López Mateos.

Entering from the Valle de Santo Tomás and the south is somewhat messier. Mex 1 becomes Avenida Reforma and goes from two to four lanes at the turnoff to La Bufadora. To get downtown, turn left at Libramiento Sur or, missing that on Sanginés; the former becomes Lázaro Cárdenas, the latter runs into

Cruise ship operators

The following **cruise lines** offer service to Ensenada either as a sole destination or as part of multi-stop journeys.

Carnival US ☎800/327-9501, 🌐www.carnival.com. Ports of call Cabo San Lucas and Ensenada.

Cruise West US ☎800/888-9378, 🌐www.cruisewest.com. Ports of call Ensenada, Bahía Magdalena, Cabo San Lucas, La Paz, Loreto and Mulegé.

Lindblad Expeditions US ☎800/397-3348, 🌐www.expeditions.com. Ports of call Ensenada, Magdalena Bay, Cabo San Lucas, La Paz.

Royal Caribbean US ☎800/327-6700, 🌐www.royalcaribbean.com. Ports of call Ensenada, Puerto Vallarta and Manzanillo.

Searcher Baja Tours US ☎619/226-2403, 🌐www.bajawhale.com. Ports of call Ensenada and Cabo San Lucas.

Voyager US ☎800/451-5952, 🌐www.voyagercruiseline.com. Ports of call Ensenada and Cabo San Lucas.

it just before the waterfront. If you're staying to the north of town near Punto Morro, keep along Reforma before turning left on Calle 9a.

Cruise ships drop anchor in the harbour and shuttle visitors to the **Ensenada Cruiseship Terminal** on the south end of the malecón. Although taxis are lined up nearby, there are enough sights within very short walking distance to make them superfluous. If you're piloting your own **boat** into the port, you must pre-book a slip at the marina (☎646/173-4141, ✉reservations@ecpvmarina .com; from M$600 per day).

The **bus station** is at Calle 11a and Avenida Riveroll; coming out of the station turn right and head down Riveroll to reach the bay. This station serves ABC and Águila long-distance buses between Ensenada and mainland Mexico as well as points further south and San Felipe. Buses from Tijuana arrive every two hours at a second, smaller station two blocks down on Riveroll between C 8a and C 9a. There are no commercial airlines that fly into Ensenada's **airport**, which is part of the El Ciprés military base on southbound Mex 1 (☎646/177-4503).

The very helpful **visitors centre** (Mon & Tues 9am–5pm, Wed–Fri 9am–7pm, Sat & Sun 9am–5pm; ☎646/178-2411, 🌐ensenada-tourism.com) is at the southbound Mex 1 entrance into town at Cárdenas and Gastelum. The **secretary of tourism office** is at the southern end of the malecón at Cárdenas and Los Rocas (same hours; ☎646/178-8578, 🌐www.enjoyensenada.com).

Accommodation

If you're looking for somewhere to **stay** at the weekend book ahead or arrive early; during the week there should be no problem finding a room. Most of the hotels are on Mateos and Cárdenas between Riveroll and Espinoza, with the cheaper places closer to Riveroll. Rates are typically hiked by M$200 on weekends (when two-night minimums may also be enforced). Just one block northeast of this strip is a grubbier zone where the best deals are to be had, but the area is not as safe as Mateos. Wherever you stay downtown expect some street noise, especially on Friday and Saturday nights. Downtown hotels claim ocean views, but that's only with a high floor. Resorts to the north and south of town are directly on the water and, while most of the beaches are too rocky for swimming, you can still watch the waves roll in unobstructed.

Hotels

Best Western El Cid Av López Mateos 993 ☎646/178-2401, @www.hotelelcid.com.mx. Not glamorous, but clean and well positioned near restaurants and shops, which is why tour groups routinely fill many of the rooms. There's a two-night minimum stay during high-season weekends. ➍

Casa del Sol Blancarte 1001 ☎646/178-1570, @www.motelcasadelsol.com. Two-storey motor inn off Mateos with a heated pool at its centre and satellite TV in the rooms, half of which were recently remodelled; be sure to ask for one of these. ➌

El Cortez Av López Mateos 1089 ☎646/178-1503 @bajainn.com. The *Baja Inn* hotels are northern Baja's three-star stalwarts: rather plain, but always clean, and packed with basic amenities like a/c, TV, a gym and a heated pool. ➎

Misión Santa Isabel Blvd Lázaro Cárdenas 1119 ☎646/178-3616. *Isabel* was never a mission, but its relaxing courtyard and small pool do provide comfort. Rooms vary from small chambers to suites, some of which have been recently refurnished. ➍

La Pinta Av Floresta y Bucaneros s/n ☎646/176-2601, @www.lapintahotels.com/Ensenada. This chain's offerings are usually worn-down establishments on the outskirts of town, but this hotel is central and charming. Dark-stained trim and ceiling fans adorn the rooms, and a poolside bar adds a nice resort touch. ➎

San Nicolás Av López Mateos 1536 ☎646/176-1901, @www.sannicolas.com.mx. The closest hotel to the downtown waterfront has popular package vacations that include meals and deals with local aquatic outfitters. Murals by a protégé of Diego Rivera adorn many of the public spaces, and there's an Olympic-size swimming pool. ➎

Santo Tomás Av Miramar 609 ☎646/178-1503, US ☎888/226-1033, @bajainn.com. Its proximity to nightclubs means noise, but the cable TV and a/c can drown it out. Secure parking included and some rooms have balconies. ➎

Del Valle Av Riveroll 367 ☎646/178-2224, @ensenadahoy.com/delvalle/. You'll get the same features and style – TV, secure parking, a/c, tacky bedspreads – as the hotels on Mateos, but you'll save about M$200 a night (and get a quieter night's sleep) by bedding down at this 43-room motel three blocks to the north. ➌

Beach resorts

Coral & Marina Km 106.5 Mex 1 US ☎800/862-9020, @www.hotelcoral.com. Pull your boat into one of the private marina's slips and check into this all-suite spot that promises ocean views from every suite, as well as private bath, satellite TV and a/c. Full resort facilities, including a pool and tennis court, and an in-house spa. ➐

Paraíso las Palmas Av Sanginés 206 ☎646/177-1701, @www.paraisolaspalmas.com. This faded spot once had grand ambitions – with vaulted ceilings in the rooms and hand-carved wood detailing in the public spaces – but time has worn away some of the character and it only holds interest to those who like ageing quirks. Rooms have private bath, a/c and TV. ➎

Punta Morro Km 106 Mex 1 ☎800/526-6676, @www.punta-morro.com. The oceanview rooms have fireplaces, which may be why guests don't much mind the thirty-minute walk to downtown from *Morro*. Rooms also have satellite TV, a/c and sitting areas. There's an onsite restaurant for the nights you want to skip the downtown commute. ➏–➐

Quintas Papagayo Km 107.5 Mex 1 ☎646/174-4575; @www.hussongs.com.mx. The two-dozen or so charming one-storey bungalows here look like they were lifted out of 1950s Palm Springs. Rooms include kitchenettes and a parking spot in front. It's also adjacent to a *Hussong's Cantina* outpost. ➎–➏

Las Rosas Km 105 Mex 1 ☎646/174-4310, @www.lasrosas.com. This white and pink stucco building has balconies and ocean views from every room. It caters to the same clientele as *Punto Morro* and *Coral* and manages to differentiate itself with a small, onsite spa. ➏–➐

The City

The focal point for both municipal and tourist activity is the waterfront – almost all of Ensenada's attractions, such as the **Mercado Negro** fish market and marina, are squeezed into the streets near the **malecón**. The downtown is roughly a narrow rectangle running northwest to southeast and corresponding to the parallel Boulevard Lázaro Cárdenas and lively **Avenida López Mateos** (also Calle 1a). Along with the malecón, the zone is hemmed in by Calle 3a to the northeast, the **La Riviera Convention Center** to the southeast and the clubs and restaurants along Avenida Ruiz in the northwest.

The malecón

The six-block long **malecón** is where everyone comes to see and be seen. On weekend nights the crowds become especially thick, as locals take sunset strolls or gather en masse for special events like weddings and *quinceñeras* (a sweet fifteen-meets coming-out party for local young women), sometimes proceeding to the south end to hire horse-drawn carriages (M$100 for 30min). Everyone tends to congregate around the two-metre high bronze busts of the leaders Benito Juárez, Miguel Hidalgo and Venustiano Carranza that stare out from the waterfront's Plaza Civíca to the city.

Mercado Negro

During the day the prime attraction along the malecón is the **Mercado Negro** fish market, behind the Playa Marina shopping mall. Starting at around 8am over three-dozen merchants begin selling the day's catches. The diversity of what's on display – from squirming eel to giant abalone to even larger shrimp – is staggering, and you'll likely be drawn to eat at least some of what you're looking at. If you can't wait to cook it yourself, the surrounding food stalls lift their corrugated doors around 9am and start serving courses of prepared dishes. In addition to the fish taco, these vendors have perfected the fresh fish cocktail: large glasses loaded with tomato salsa, cilantro, lemon and your choice of fresh shrimp, clams, oysters, octopus or scallops; order a *campechana* – a generous helping – if you'd like to try a bit of everything. The hired fleets open for business at the same time, so it's easy to fill up on fish and then book a tour of the bay to see your meal in its natural habitat.

△ Mercado Negro

La Riviera Convention Center

The malecón ends at the white-washed, red-roof tiled **La Riviera Convention Center**, Boulevard Lázaro Cárdenas at Avenida Riviera (daily 9:30am–2pm & 3–5pm; ☎646/177-0594). The 1930 opening was an historic event, and for five years the centre drew an international clientele, Hollywood stars and friends of boxer Jack Dempsey, one of its original backers. Its life as a high-end casino was short lived, however; like the similarly fated Agua Caliente in Tijuana (see p.59) it faced the wrecking ball soon after President Cárdenas banned gambling. City leaders stepped in to save the Mediterranean-style structure – still the city's grandest building – and turned it into a cultural centre. The emphasis now includes hosting conventions and parties that complement seasonal events like the epic Baja 1000 off-road race. Works by muralist Alfredo Ramos Martínez are viewable inside the **Museo de Historia**, the centre's rather uninspired attempt at acknowledging the past (same hours as above; M$10).

Avenida López Mateos and downtown

On weekend evenings, **Avenida López Mateos**, the city's principal artery, is particularly crowded, especially when local youths cruise the street in tricked-out cars. Up towards Ruiz, the post-midnight hours are filled with the heavy beats of nightclubs, bars and the patrons that spill out of them. Some of the activity could be construed as purely historic interest: *Hussong's Cantina* (see p.147), at the intersection of Mateos and Ruiz, is the oldest continually operated bar in Baja California.

By day, **downtown** is a more staid affair with shoppers casually browsing the local crafts, silver and leather goods and duty-free beauty products. You can sample the region's wines at the outpost of Baja California's oldest winery, *Bodegas de Santo Tomás*, Av Miramar 666 (tours daily 11am, 1pm & 3pm; ☎646/174-0836; free) or the smaller *Cavas Valmar*, Calle Ambar 810 (tours by appointment; ☎646/178-6405; free). The **Museo Histórico Regional**, at Gastelum off Mateos (Tues–Sun 9am–5pm; donations suggested; ☎646/178-3692), documents what's known of the customs and plights of the area's pre-Columbian population as well as Ensenada history. Pay attention to the small section devoted to the city prison, now home to the museum you're standing in.

Eating

Even though **fish** is the big deal in town, be sure to sample the succulent local **farm-raised beef** at some point. Mateos has the largest share of straightforward options but steer away from cavernous spaces promising every kind of Continental indulgence and instead look for those that smartly pair wines with their courses. **Dinner** hour for locals begins after 9pm, and reservations on weekends are recommended.

Bronco's Av López Mateos 1525 ☎646/176-4900. The five blocks that separate *Bronco's* from the heart of the tourist district will save you a good M$100 on a steak (M$60). With spurs everywhere, the Wild West theme is over the top, but the spirit is genuine, and live bands on weekends add to the authenticity. Breakfast served.

Casamar Blvd Lázaro Cárdenas 987 ☎646/174-0417, ⓦ www.sdro.com/casamar. The marina views, rather than ambitious cooking, from this old-school seafood dining hall have made *Casamar* one of the more popular upscale dining choices for years. Lobster is more expensive (M$230) than in Puerto Nuevo, and the catch of the day (M$100) is almost always better.

El Charro Av López Mateos 475 ☎646/178-3881. Cheap, large and delicious portions of grilled rotisserie chicken and home-made

Street food

The same **street food** rules that apply elsewhere apply in Ensenada: eat only at crowded spots, pay attention to whether the ingredients are kept cool and out of the sun, and make sure the vendor doesn't take money and prepare food with the same hand. Although many of the vendors in the Mercado Negro operate out of permanent structures, you should approach them as if they were operating out of pushcarts.

The fish market stalls can open as soon as the day's haul is laid out, and almost all of them close shop by late afternoon. The best lunchtime spots away from the waterfront are located along Calle 5a near the local shopping strip. Foremost amongst these is *Tacos Fenix*, on calles Espinosa and Juárez, in front of Ferreteria Fenix, which does tempura-style fish tacos for M$9. During the evening you can always find cheap, safe options near the clubs on Avenida Ruiz.

guacamole are the popular choices in this rustic joint.

El Cid Av López Mateos 993 ☎646/178-1809. You can get by on the run-of-the-mill Continental cuisine but the specials, which include *chiles en nogada* (stuffed chilies in a walnut sauce) to crepes stuffed with grilled pork made tableside, are much better bets.

Las Conchas Av López Mateos 335 ☎646/175-7375. The best place in town to taste raw clams, oysters and cooked shellfish specialities matched with local wines. There's a sister restaurant and bar of the same name at Av Miramar 637.

La Cueva de los Tigres C Acapulco and Av Las Palmas ☎646/176-6450. This somewhat hard to find all-day restaurant off Mex 1 south of town is sought out in equal measure for its giant abalone and potent margaritas.

La Embotelladora Vieja Av Miramar 666 ☎646/174-0807. *Vieja*'s association with Santo Tomás Winery gives it an edge on rare and small-batch Baja wines – served by the glass and bottle – that are well-paired with the progressive Mexican-Mediterranean menu. Dinner only.

🏃 **Manzanilla** Av Riveroll 122 ☎646/1750-7073, ⊛www.rmanzanilla.com. The city's best restaurant is the unofficial home of local wine lovers and the region's growers. They come for the

convivial dining room, with its exposed brick and wood beams, and the dishes, such as *añejo* rib-eye and whatever the chef's doing to fresh tuna that day, which never disappoint. Wed–Sun. Dinner only.

Mi Kasa Av Riveroll 87 ☎646/178-8211. This cafeteria opens to a busy breakfast crowd and finishes with family dinners. In three meals you can get a broad sampling of Mexican home cooking, from *huevos con nopales* (eggs with cactus) in the morning, to chicken in mole at lunch and deep-fried tacos or *menudo* (stewed tripe and peppers) at dinner, all for less than M$80.

El Rey Sol Av López Mateos 1000 ☎646/174-0643. The city's first ambitious restaurant is consistently pleasing enough to say it's aged well over the past half century, but its take on mainly French Continental cuisine – heavy, butter-lathered dishes – tastes dated compared to the newcomers. Breakfast served.

Sano's Km 108 Mex 1 Tijuana–Ensenada ☎646/174-4061. The portions are huge at this US-style steakhouse, which is why fillets (M$275) and chicken in plum sauce (M$210) aren't such a bad deal. Most of the wines are from the Valle de Guadalupe.

La Vendimia Av Riveroll 85 ☎646/174-0969. Wine shop, bar and restaurant with tapas-style seafood dishes like marinated baby octopus and *bacalao* (salted cod).

Nightlife

Ensenada offers many of the same **nightlife** opportunities for clubbing and drinking as Tijuana but within a smaller area and without the same level of danger you get in a border town (although you should still exercise caution). Avenida López is at the centre of nighttime activities, especially after 10pm. The largest clubs on Avenida López Mateos are aimed squarely at the 18–25 year-old, jumbo margarita-pounding crowd and they don't miss the mark, while the wine bars on Avenida Ruiz offer more low-key entertainment. A word of caution: the city's strip clubs are barely distinguishable from the margarita joints; use a discerning eye particularly just north of Mateos on Avenida Miramar.

Abel's Bar Blvd Lázaro Cárdenas at Av Riviera. Regional touring acts pack in dedicated crowds at this *cerveza*-fuelled 18+ bar for Spanish rock and alternative music.

Capricho's Restaurant & Riedel Wine Bar Av Ruiz 138 ☎646/178-3433. Local vintner favourite Sé de Vino morphed into this more casual wine bar associated with the stemware company. The salads and small plates are good pre-dinner or late-night bites, when the bar is really humming.

La Esquina de Bodegas Av Miramar s/n, at C 6a ☎646/178-3557. This casual sister café/wine bar to *La Embotelladora Vieja* doubles as an art gallery and sometimes DJ lounge. Although the second-storey terrace doesn't have views of the sea, it's idyllic at sunset, when the surrounding buildings glow.

Hussong's Cantina Av Ruiz 113 ☎646/178-3210. Although it's a tourist destination with its own line of t-shirts, *Hussong*'s is still an honest bar packed with locals and gringos alike. The floors are covered in sawdust, the bands are *norteña*, and the drink of choice should always be the one invented here – a margarita.

Mango Mango Bar and Grill Av López Mateos 335 ☎646/178-1668. Salsa bands on weekends,

with dance lessons early in the evening, bring in a mix of locals and curious visitors.

Oxidos Cafe Av Ruiz 108 ☎646/178-8827. Wine bar and café is most popular late in the evening when local artists – some of whom have work on display here – gather.

Papa's and Beer/La Uh Discoteque Av Ruiz 102 ☎646/174-0145, ⓦwww.papasandbeer.com. This sister spot to Rosarito Beach's super-club doesn't have the Pacific at its front door, but the music is so loud and the lights flash so quickly that you'd never know what you're missing. Cover charge varies based on holiday and gender.

La Prisión Karaoke/La Uh Discoteque Blvd Lázaro Cárdenas and C Alvarado ☎646/178-2850. The Chippendales stop here when they're in town, and so do local Mexican folk bands – check ahead to make sure you're not coming on a theme night you don't want to be part of. The M$5 beers and M$15 mixed drinks add to the festive atmosphere.

La Tertulia Av López Mateos 448 ☎646/178-1952. After hours, this restaurant becomes one of the few places in the tourist area where Latin dance music is the *boogie franca*. Thurs–Sun nights only.

Listings

Banks US dollars are widely accepted along Mateos, but pesos are used more frequently everywhere else; this is the last city until Todos Santos in the Cape where dollars are so common. Most *casas de cambio* on the malecón and on Mateos do not readily accept travellers' cheques; those that do charge a heavy commission. For cheques you're better off with a bank, most of which are on Ruiz a few blocks north of Mateos.

Books The mini-chain Libros Libros Books Books, Av López Mateos 690 (Mon–Sat 10am–6pm; ☎646/178-8448) has a large selection of English-language magazines, a modest selection of paperback titles and driving maps of Ensenada and the peninsula. Also try Bookseller, Calle 4a 240, at Obregón (Tues–Sat 10am–6pm).

Events Information about the city's festivals and concerts is available online at ⓦwww.enjoyensenada.com and ⓦwww.bajaevents.com.

Hospital Blvd de las Dunas 22 ☎646/176-7600.

Immigration office Blvd Azueta s/n, just next door to the Harbour Master (☎646/174-0164). Stop here if you're travelling further into Baja and failed to get a tourist card after crossing the border.

Internet access Access at hotels, either through your own laptop or a terminal in the lobby, is becoming more common throughout the city. Browse the Internet at *Equinoxio*, Cárdenas and Miramar (Mon 9am–1pm, Tues–Sat 8am–10pm, Sun 10am–9pm; M$25/hr), where there's a fast connection, many terminals and a full café, or at Compunet next to Hertz (Mon–Fri 9am–10pm, Sat & Sun 10am–9pm; M$20/hr).

Movies The Playa Marina shopping mall, Cárdenas and Macheros, has a Cinema Star movie theatre. Locals prefer the cheaper Gemelos Balboa Multi-cinemas Av Balboa 2204, at Av López Mateos. (☎646/176-3616).

Newspaper *La Frontera* is the region's paid Spanish language daily. The weekly *Gringo Gazette* focuses on issues directly related to foreigners, while *Ensenada Tour* has information about goings-on around town; both are free and available from most establishments on Mateos.

Parking Two parking lots serve the malecón and fish market. The first, on the north side, is a dirt lot that's right at the intersection with Cárdenas and Blvd Azueta and costs M$10 per day. The more modern multilevel pay lot at Playa Marina is closer to the market and movie theatre but charges start at M$5 per hour.

Police Dial 078.

Post office Club Rotario 93 and Mateos, Mon–Fri 8am–7pm, Sat 9am–1pm.

Taxi *Colectivos* and standard taxis can be found on the southeast side of Cárdenas and Av Mancheros.

Telephones Telmex phone cards can be purchased in any corner store. Some phones take US quarters.

Theatre Teatro de la Ciudad, Av Diamante s/n (☎646/177-0392) and Teatro Benito Juárez, Av Guadalupe between calles 2 and 3 (☎646/176-3005).

Estero Beach and La Bufadora

Although Ensenada enjoys an enviable position on the Pacific, it lacks good beaches, and for a nice stretch of sand you'll have to head half an hour or so to the north (see p.134) or south. The first of these options in the latter direction, **ESTERO BEACH** at Km 15 Mex 1 (the intersection is marked from the north as Avenida José Morelos), provides a mix of activities for not a lot of money. Estero Beach – the community not the nearby development of the same name – is a beach settlement surrounding a small estuary directly south of a military hospital. Ensenada families drive down on weekends for a swim, packing their own supplies or picking up drinks and tacos from the vendors near the manicured square. *Taquería las Güeros*, Av Jose Morelos at C 2a and 3a (no phone) serves hefty tacos *al pastor*. Day-trippers continue on Morelos to the *Estero Beach Resort* (see Practicalities, below) on the water and simply set up on the beach.

Visitors who enjoy getting wet but don't want to bother with a bathing suit should go further south to the peninsula's most famous natural oddity, **LA BUFADORA** ("the whale hole"). Centuries ago, Pacific waters surging against the south side of the Punta Banda outcropping found a release through a deep-water shaft that rises up to a hole in the rock's surface. The combined action of wind, waves and an incoming tide periodically forces a huge jet of sea water up through this small vent – in ideal conditions, primarily the winter months, the spurt can reach 25–30m. Crowds pack the surrounding platforms and jockey for the best position so some of the cold ocean water can rain down on them. It's free, and there are vendors everywhere selling tacos and blown glass, among other food and trinkets. *Dave's La Bufadora Dive Shop*, just a two-minute walk southeast from the blowhole, (☎646/154-2092, ⓦwww.labufadoradive.com), has daily dive trips around Punta Banda and the nearby islands, equipment rental and tent camping for M$50 a person. Access to La Bufadora is along a 16km paved road from the Manadero turnoff from Mex 1 at km 21.

Practicalities

Accommodation options on the southern outskirts of Ensenada are good for those moving into Baja California Sur or looking for a hotel with beach access. There's only one good option for the latter, but plenty of cheap and safe ones for the former.

Estero Beach Resort, exit Km 15 Mex 1, turn left on Vita Novelo and drive to gate (☎646/176-6225, ⓦwww.hotelesterobeach.com; ⓺), is a self-contained multi-acre site that has spots for RVs, sells condos and homes and rents hotel rooms and camping slots near the beach. The facilities are slightly aged, and the resort is a distance from the city, but the beach is the centre of water sport activities in the region. Day-visitors are required to pay a fee for the benefit of accessible bathrooms and an onsite restaurant and may be charged a fee to park (typically around M$50), depending on who's working or how crowded it is.

Even though weekends are crowded at the beachside *El Faro Beach and RV Park*, exit Km 15 Mex 1, end of Estero Beach road (T646/177-4630; tent camping with showers; ❷), it's the closest place south of town where you can camp in peace. Like a setting from a trippy cartoon, *El Joker*, Km 12.5 Mex 1 Ensenada–San Quintín at Boulevard Technológico, crams a playground, karaoke bar and some RV slots within an orange stucco compound near the military base (T646/176-7201, F646/177-4460; ❸).

Moving on from Ensenada

Mex 3, towards Valle de Trinidad and San Felipe, is a scenic route through the northern ranges of the Sierra de San Pedro Mártir and primary access road to the Parque Nacional Constitución de 1857 (see p.113). It's reached at the eastern end of Avenida Cortés, itself an extension of Calle 5a. Much of the road was recently repaved, and many of the intersecting branches of roads entering and exiting the park have been regraded. There are few services between Ensenada and San Felipe – there is reliable petrol service at Colonia Lázaro Cárdenas – so pack essentials such as water and camping equipment if you plan on exploring off-road or staying in the vicinity of the park for any length of time.

Southbound **Mex 1** resets its kilometre count when Avenida Reforma intersects with Libramiento Sur again southeast of the centre of town, starting from zero toward San Quintín. The route to San Quintín (see p.158) begins in the vineyards of Valle de Santo Tomás before rising into the hills and traversing narrow, curvy roads before straightening out between San Vicente and Punta Colonet.

Both routes are best avoided at night, as is the trip through the Valle de Guadalupe, below.

Valle de Guadalupe

The vineyards of the **VALLE DE GUADALUPE** are so heavily drenched in hype that on first visit anyone but the most optimistic – or wine-soaked – visitor will be disappointed. A cynic would say the valley does a better job marketing its wine than making it, but the region is clearly on the right track, as illustrated by the growing number of vineyards that are experimenting with foreign vines and cross-breeding others. Small boutique wineries and epicurean-related ventures are riding on the coat-tails of the emerging industry, and farms that aren't devoted to vineyards grow olives, raise organically fed cattle or turn their milk into artisanal cheeses. These places aren't in tourist brochures but their creations can be enjoyed at stellar restaurants like *Laja* in the valley and *Manzanilla* in Ensenada. They can't, however, be easily sampled in the US or other countries, which is one reason why this valley isn't the next Napa or Sonoma; export taxes double the cost of the bottles abroad.

A total of 8600 acres in Valle de Guadalupe are currently devoted to wine production – about two-thirds that of Napa Valley in California. Though the valley lacks sufficient rainfall to permit the type of growth many of the area vineyards hope for, it does have vital factors leaning in its favour: the soil is a fortuitous mix

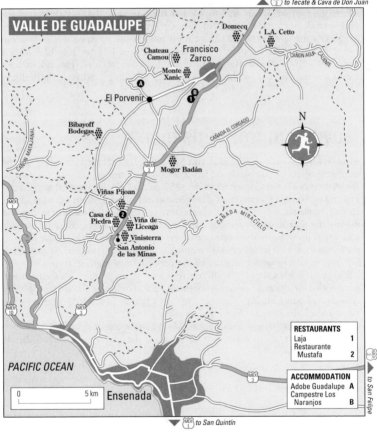

VALLE DE GUADALUPE

to Tecate & Cava de Don Juan

Domecq

L.A. Cetto

CAÑON AGUA CALIENTE

Chateau Camou

Francisco Zarco

Monte Xanic

A

B

El Porvenir

Bibayoff Bodegas

CAÑON MATAJANAL

CAÑADA EL CORGADO

N

Mogor Badán

Viñas Pijoan

Casa de Piedra

Viña de Liceaga

Vinisterra

San Antonio de las Minas

CAÑADA MIRACIELO

MEX 1

MEX 10

MEX 3

PACIFIC OCEAN

MEX 3

to San Felipe

0   5 km

Ensenada

RESTAURANTS	
Laja	1
Restaurante Mustafa	2

ACCOMMODATION	
Adobe Guadalupe	A
Campestre Los Naranjos	B

to San Quintín

of crushed granite and clay, and the intense daytime heat generates sugars in the grapes while the cool evening breezes aid tannin development.

The villages of **San Antonio de las Minas** in the southwest and **Francisco Zarco** and **El Porvenir** in the northeast are the centres of the valley's production; a sure sign of the relative infancy of the industry is the fact that there are more dirt roads in these towns than paved. One benefit of its youth and former obscurity was that vintners could experiment with blends that more established growers couldn't risk; it's not uncommon to find blends of Cabernet Sauvignon and Tempranillo or Chenin Blanc and Colombard. The diversity comes from the growers themselves, who reflect Ensenada's ethnically diverse past – a mix of Italians, Russians and Spanish.

The valley is not, however, without its share of growing pains. Some serious wine connoisseurs will tell you that fewer people know what they're doing here than in more established wine-producing regions. Also, the peninsula's heat makes proper storage and transportation difficult. Mostly, though, the success of the industry is hindered by the fact that wine consumption is not intrinsic to Mexican culture. Even for people with a love of wine, Baja California's climate and lifestyle are tailor-made for beer and margaritas, and something with such a high entry point – both economically and educationally – as wine can be a difficult sell.

Some history

Oddly enough, the seeds of the valley's burgeoning industry were planted by **Franciscan monks**. Though neither their religion nor their architecture made a praiseworthy impact in Baja California, the indomitable monks had a thing for wine and planted California's first vineyards around the same time they were attempting to convert the Kumai tribes in the region. In the eighteenth century, Franciscan friar Junípero Serra planted cuttings at missions across the peninsula as he journeyed north from Loreto.

For most of its life, the production and consumption of wine in Mexico has been linked directly to the sensual indulgences of the Catholic clergy and to its drinkers' desires to behave like proper Europeans. Small vineyards in the valleys around Ensenada flourished for years – almost solely to feed these specific needs – until **Bodegas de Santo Tomás** was founded south of the city in Valle de Santo Tomás in 1888. It survived the vagaries of Mexican liquor laws and US importation restrictions to become the country's second oldest continually operated winery. More often than not, though, vineyards in both the Santo Tomás and Guadalupe valleys were used solely to grow grapes to make brandy, and without local demand or the expertise to maintain them, vineyards faltered, were replaced with other crops or fell victim to disease following the revolutionary unrest of the early twentieth century.

The industry that the monks started got a kick in the pants from a group of pacifist Russian mystics whose names will be familiar to fans of Tijuana's Orquesta de Baja California. About two hundred members of the Molokan sect fled southern Russia following its revolution and settled south of Tecate. They were responsible for replanting the valley's dormant vineyards starting first with Santo Tomás in the late 1920s. By the 1930s and 1940s their influence spread to Guadalupe as they encouraged other local farmers to replant grapes, often going so far as to give away cuttings of European varietals. Although the Russians sustained it early on, modern Valle de Guadalupe owes much to Hans Backoff of Monte Xanic and other small planters who realized they could create a wine culture in the region – not just a crop for mass export to Mexico City (like Domecq and L.A. Cetto were engaged in). The Xanic vineyard's financial success – especially the way they negotiated new trade laws in the late 1980s – inspired others to follow suit. Nowadays the dozen established wineries produce more than eighty varietals and ninety percent of all Mexico's wines – about 1.5 million cases a year.

The wineries

With a few exceptions, the valley's vineyards are located on dirt roads that branch off a 25km stretch of Mex 3 Ensenada–Tecate, which, incidentally, is one of the most heavily policed stretches of highway in Baja California. After a rainfall, these roads can be hard to navigate for non-four-wheel drive or high-clearance vehicles. Since 2003 the Ensenada Association of Vinoculture has been posting and maintaining detailed signs that direct visitors how to navigate the unmarked dirt roads that link the vineyards. Even though reservations are not required at any of the valley's wineries, it is best to call ahead everywhere before visiting, especially if you're coming in the warmer months (July–Sept).

Bibayoff Bodegas from Mex 3, exit west at the sign to El Tigre, follow dirt road 4km and turn north, proceed 5.6km to Rancho Bibayoff ☎ 646/176-1008, ⊕ bibayoff@telnor.net. The Russians were responsible for resurrecting the wine industry, but this is the only one left that's open to the public. Bibayoff sells many of his grapes to other producers but keeps enough around to produce five estate wines, including a Nebbiolo and Colombard. Tours and wine tasting by appointment only.

Casa de Piedra Km 93.5 Mex 3, San Antonio de las Minas ☎646/155-3097, ⓦwww.vinoscasadepiedra.com. Although it's one of the tinier vineyards in the valley, Piedra commands a great deal of attention as well as high price tags for its bottles (around M$500). Winemaker and owner Hugo d'Acosta makes two types: Piedra del Sol, a small-batch Chardonnay, and Vino de Piedra, a mix of Cabernet and Tempranillo. In addition to tours and tastings, Piedra offers a yearly winemaking seminar and sells other small-batch wines.

Cava de Don Juan Km 28 Mex 3, Valle de las Palmas ☎664/621-8190. Although technically outside Valle de Guadalupe (it's on the border of Tecate), Rancho Don Juan produces a Chenin Blanc and has a cellar store that's one of the better sources for local olive oil, preserves and honey. Daily 9am–5pm.

Chateau Camou from Mex 3, follow main road into Francisco Zarco, turn north after 3km ☎646/177-2221, ⓦwww.chateau-camou.com.mx. two hundred acres of vineyards surround the mission-style building housing a modern winery and small tasting room. From here Camou turns out 30,000 cases of Bordeaux, Zinfandel and a dessert blend of Chardonnay, Chenin Blanc and Sauvignon Blanc. Reservations required; some tours include lunch. Tours from M$50; no credit cards. Mon–Sat 8am–3pm, Sun 9am–2pm.

Domecq Km 73 Mex 3, Francisco Zarco ☎646/155-2249, ⓦwww.vinos-domecq.com.mx. In 1972 Domecq was the first commercial winery to open in the valley, and it has steadily expanded from growing grapes for brandy to table wines and on to some smaller-batch, boutique wines. Like L.A. Cetto – with whom Domecq's wines make up eighty percent of the region's total output – its setup will be familiar to visitors used to California and Australia-style vineyard tours. Its massive scale accounts for the fact that it processes grapes from three other regions in Mexico. The tasting area also includes a store with merchandise. Free wine tasting and tours. Mon–Fri 10am–4pm, Sat 10am–3pm.

L.A. Cetto Km 73.5 Mex 3, Francisco Zarco ☎646/155-2264, ⓦwww.cettowine.com. Although the Cetto family has been bottling wine in Baja California since 1928, they didn't set up their current operation in the valley until 1974, though they're now the largest producer of table wines in Mexico. If the gaggle of the tour buses in the large parking lot aren't sufficient sign, a

15-minute drive through a few of Cetto's 2,500 acres will give you some sense how large the operation is. For first-timers, Cetto offers a great introduction to the process through its free wine tours and tastings; it's also one of the few wineries to have food and a dining area. Daily 10am–5pm.

Mogor Badán Km 86.5 Mex 3, San Antonio de las Minas ☎646/177-1484, ⓔabadan@cicese.mx. *Badán* is one of the valley's smallest wineries, turning out less than six hundred cases a year. It draws from fifty acres of old-growth vines to produce its red (a mix of Merlot and Cabernets Sauvignon and Franc) and turns to new growth for its Swiss-style Chasselas white. An on-site organic farm produces fruits and vegetables for some of Ensenada's better restaurants. Tours and wine tasting by appointment only. Daily 9am–sunset.

Monte Xanic from Mex 3, follow main road into Francisco Zarco, turn north after 2.7km ☎646/174-6769, ⓦwww.montexanic.com. Thirty thousand cases of wine from estate-grown grapes roll out of Xanic every year, some with price tags north of M$1500. A portion of Xanic's land contains old-growth vines planted by Molokans a half-century ago, and the vineyard expertly uses this pedigree to enhance its boutique-wine claim. Its speciality is Bordeaux, but it also bottles Chenin Blanc and Syrah, the latter used for cheaper wines. Wine tasting and tours by appointment. Mon–Fri 9am–4pm, Sat 8am–noon.

Viña de Liceaga Km 93 Mex 3, San Antonio de las Minas ☎646/184-1184, ⓦwww.vinosliceaga.com. This small, twenty-acre husband-wife operation deals only in Merlot and Cabernet Franc. It's relatively new, but has gained fans because of its lounge-like tasting room and proximity to Mex 3. Reservations required on weekdays. Mon–Fri 8am–4pm, Sat & Sun 11am–4pm.

Vinisterra from Mex 3, exit at paved road east to San Antonio de las Minas, turn left after one block, follow to end of street ☎646/178-3350, ⓔalmerico53@yahoo.com. The owner of Ensenada's *Las Conchas* restaurant set up this small operation in 2002. Vinisterra currently buys its grapes elsewhere which makes tours short, and the tasting room is central to the outfit. A small shop sells wine-related goods in addition to wines. Tours and tastings by appointment only. Daily 9am–sunset.

Viñas Pijoan from Mex 3, exit west at sign for El Tigre, follow the dirt road for 500m ☎646/178-3482, ⓔpau_pijoan@yahoo.com. Small, family-owned winery that's been experimenting with a mix of foreign and local grapes. Viñas has tastings in the cellar and tours of the vineyards. Weekends only.

Practicalities

To reach the valley **from Ensenada**, leave the city along Cárdenas and follow Mex 1 through El Sauzal and exit on Mex 3 towards Tecate, just prior to the beginning of the Mex 1D toll road north of San Miguel. The vineyards and stores begin in about 10km near the San Antonio de las Minas settlement. While the northbound approach from Ensenada is agricultural and industrial, **southbound** Mex 3 from Tecate and Mexicali runs through a scenic 50km of hills strewn with whitewashed boulders. While it is not as fast as the coastal route, the two lanes are in good condition. From this direction, wine country begins at km 75 with two of the area's bigger landmarks, L.A. Cetto on the left side of the road and Domecq to the right. The Pemex marked at km 30 on some maps is now closed. You can also approach the valley from a graded dirt road branching off the free Mex 1 (see box, p.135).

Companies and epicurean groups in San Diego and Tijuana organize day-trips to the valley that visit multiple vineyards and usually stop at a small museum connected to Bibayoff Bodegas (see p.151), which offers an account of the region's history of emigration, from the Kumai to the Molokan Russians. The trips will shuttle you from either your hotel in Tijuana or across the border in the US. Fees run from US$80 for day-trips to US$300 for overnight tours that arrange lodging in Ensenada.

Instead of **staying** in the valley, most visitors choose to stay overnight in Ensenada. Although there are no hotels, there are a few small inns and bed-and-breakfasts. The one that is open year-round is *Adobe Guadalupe* (☎646/155-2094, US ☎949/863-9776, ⓦwww.adobeguadalupe.com; ❾), a six-room inn on fifty acres. *Adobe* shares a vineyard manager with Monte Xanic (see opposite) who helps it produce small batches of three varietals: Kerubiel (blend of Syrah and Grenache), Serafiel (Cabernet and Syrah) and Gabriel (Merlot and Cabernet). The one-storey inn is situated around a central courtyard and both the dining room and pool look out over the vines. The sunlit rooms are very large, with decorations befitting a high-end hacienda. To get here, follow the main road into Francisco Zarco from Mex 3, turn north after 5.7km at the second stop sign in El Porvenir.

Unlike wine regions in Europe, the US and Australia, many vineyards here haven't opened adjoining restaurants, leaving few dining options in the valley. The best one – as well as one of the best on the entire peninsula – is ⅍ *Laja*, Km 83 Mex 3, Francisco Zarco (☎646/155-2556, ⓦwww.lajamexico.com; Wed lunch only, Thurs–Sat dinner. Reservations essential). Former *Daniel* and *Four Seasons* New York chef Jair Téllez along with partner Laura Reinert opened this prix-fixe destination restaurant in 2001 and continues to draw eager diners from nearby and across the border. Téllez continually experiments with seasonal ingredients, and relies on local farmers and artisans for staples such as olive oil, cheese, meat and fruits and vegetables. All diners eat a four-course meal picked by Téllez that can change daily; expect dishes like grouper with canellini beans, marinated Baja yellowtail or oven-roasted pig.

It's hard to compete with *Laja*, so the valley's other restaurants instead choose to complement it. *Restaurante Mustafa*, Km 93 Mex 3, San Antonio de las Minas (☎646/155-3095; lunch and dinner), serves Moroccan-influenced meals, including lamb kebab (M$100), as well as Mexican dishes and wine from the valleys. *Campestre Los Naranjos*, Km 82.5 Mex 3, Francisco Zarco (☎646/155-2522; lunch and dinner), is the most consistent budget option, serving local game such as quail (M$65).

San Quintín to the Desierto Central

The region south from Ensenada to the border with Baja California Sur is largely devoid of sights of interest to visitors – or locals for that matter. Within the **Valle de Santo Tomás** and feeder valleys, the Mex 1 highway is a narrow band of two lanes punctuated with twists and a near-constant fleet of lorries and RVs roaring by. To the west is the **Pacific Ocean**, whose craggy rocky coast rises thirty metres from the crashing waves below, off-limits to all but the most adventurous surfers yet still enormously scenic at sunset.

On the other side of the Transpeninsular Highway, **Parque Nacional Sierra de San Pedro Mártir** expands into the mountains, rising up into formidable peaks and rocky slopes, providing stark challenges to anyone who's not a seasoned outdoorsman. The largest settlement in the area is **San Quintín**, a very dusty highway town that runs for 5km on either side of Mex 1. It's thoroughly unpleasant along the highway, but can be completely relaxing if you make for the fishing camps, especially the one centred around an old cannery, along the bays to the west.

Santo Tomás and San Vicente valleys and the coast

Mex 1 Ensenada–San Quintín changes from four to two lanes at **Maneadero**, an agricultural centre just south of the road to La Bufadora. The topography around the highway shifts from suburban sprawl to farmland and then into curvy, hilly passes that are frightfully narrow, especially considering the number of large lorries passing through the area. Once you've dropped into the **Santo Tomás** valley below, the soothing sight of rows of grapevines stretches out before you. Almost the entire valley is farmed, although the water supply can only sustain about half of the area at a time, which explains why the other half lays fallow.

When the first Dominicans arrived here in 1785 there were over a thousand natives minding sheep and cattle in the valley. The newcomers established a mission near an oak stand and set to farming corn. The regional governor, though, didn't like the initial site, and the Misíon Santo Tomás de Aquino

---

Military checkpoints

The military checkpoints from here to the border with Baja California Sur almost exclusively stop northbound traffic. The stop at Km 45 Mex 1 Ensenada–San Quintín is located after a curve at the top of a hill, making it rather dangerous from either direction. If you are stopped, you'll be asked where you've come from, where you're going and will possibly have your vehicle searched. The soldiers conducting the search are almost exclusively in their late teens and early twenties yet should be treated with the utmost respect to avoid hassles.

was built at the lower end of the valley in 1791. Disease took a toll on both the missionaries and the locals – the governor's preferred plot was next to a mosquito-filled marsh – and they were forced to move three years later to the site of present-day **Santo Tomás**. The mission fell into such disrepair that no one's quite sure where it originally stood, even though certain structures and piles of rubble are often given credit.

Religion never really took off here, but the vineyards that the Dominicans planted did, and the valley began an industry that's long outlived the abandonment of the mission in 1849. Rancho Dolores winery began operating commercially after the federal government sold off seized religious property in 1857 and, after changing hands three decades later, became **Bodegas de Santo Tomás**. The visual centrepiece is Bodegas' high-tech gravity-flow winery sitting at the bottom of the descent into the valley. But for visitors, there's no reason to stop around Santo Tomás – Bodegas hosts all its public tours in Ensenada.

The Dominicans who settled in the **Valle de San Vicente**, 38km south of Santo Tomás, had more luck maintaining their mission, and it's worth a pit stop both for the surviving ruins and nearby rock paintings. Like Misión San Miguel Arcangel de la Frontera on the northwest coast, **Misión San Vicente Ferrer** (follow signs at Km 90 on the north side of the sleepy town of San Vicente) is an adobe brick shell of its former self. The placards, though, detail the area's history, which included a stint as the territorial military and administrative hub during the last two decades of the eighteenth century. During its heyday between 1780 and 1833, Ferrer was the largest Dominican mission, presiding over 320,000 acres and consisting of several large adobe buildings, including a dormitory and prison.

Most of the **rock painting** sites on the peninsula can only be reached with the help of a guide or pre-approval from the Instituto Nacional de Antropología e Historia (INAH), which is why the site 6km west of San Vicente is a welcome exception. Red and black humanoid and animal figures, as well as abstract shapes, cover a ten-metre high rock wall on the La Llave ranch on the south side of the Río San Isidro. You can get here on your own, but you'll understand more of what's going on if you stop by the **Cucapá Museo Communitario** first and get advice from an expert (Mon–Fri 9am–3pm, Sat 10am–2pm). The museum, located on San Vicente's central square next to the library, has a collection of frontier furniture, a rebuilt Cucapá Indian home and implements used by the Pai-Pai tribe prior to the influx of missionaries.

The best base to explore the area is Ensenada, but there is tent and cabin camping at *Las Cañadas*, Km 31.5 Mex 1 Ensenada–San Quintín (☎646/153-1055, Ⓦwww.lascanadas.com; tent camping M$160, cabins M$700 for up to 6 people plus M$160 per person). The cabins have electricity and hot water but don't come with sheets or, in the case of the bunks, mattresses. In the morning you're likely to rub shoulders with Ensenada school kids who arrive in buses for the nature education classes and lake and water activities, which are included in the camping fees. You can buy some staples from markets along the highway, but there are no proper restaurants in the area.

The coastal settlements

Small, relatively accessible settlements dot the Pacific coast from the mouth of Río Santo Tomás in the northwest to the town of Eréndira in the south. While there are practically no services, this stretch is popular with skilled surfers. From Mex 1 Ensenada–San Quintín there are four western exits. The first at Km 47 leads about 30km along a packed dirt road to the fishing settlements of **La Bocana**, **Punta China**, and **Punta Santo Tomás**, the last a site favoured by divers. Dropping a boat here is difficult but *pangas* – a basic fishing boat used throughout the peninsula – are available along the coast from around 7–9am every morning from local fishermen.

A dirt road at Km 51 in Santo Tomás and a paved road at Km 78 heading south to **Eréndira** lead to a line of sleepy coastal towns that typify the area. The dirt and coastal roads are slow going so it's best to take the paved road first and move northwest from Eréndira. Overnight visitors can either find a location to camp along the coast or stay at *Coyote Cal's Beach Resort*, exit Km 78 Mex 1 Ensenada–San Quintín and drive west 12km to Eréndira until you see the hostel (☎646/154-4080, ⓦcoyotecals.com; shared rooms, including breakfast ②). From here it's easy to get to surf-spots near Punta Cabras, and *Cal's* has a bar, kitchen facilities and the best local knowledge you can get on surfing the northwest coast.

There's nothing but a couple of *tiendas*, trailers and waves at **Cuatros Casas** (aka Shipwrecks or Freighters), a surf-spot at the end of a dirt road twenty-five minutes south of the Km 150 Mex 1 turnoff; bring cash and any supplies you'll need for your stay. There's camping on the beach along with rooms at *Campo Cuatro Casas Hostel*, a two-storey ramshackle affair popular with young skateboarders – who roll in the skate pool – and surfers (☎616/165-0010; ①). Food and drink are limited to what's available at the *tiendas* and items your guests and hosts will be willing to part with.

Parque Nacional Sierra de San Pedro Mártir

With 160,000 acres containing trout-filled streams, alpine lakes, evergreens stands, granite cliffs and, during the winter, snow, **PARQUE NACIONAL SIERRA DE SAN PEDRO MÁRTIR** is a striking change from the cacti and coastlines that dominate the peninsula. The road through the park ends at 2831 metres, just shy of the **Observatorio Astronómico Nacional** (ⓦwww.astrossp.unam .mx), which is home to the largest telescope in the country. Looming at the

△ Parque Nacional Sierra de San Pedro Mártir

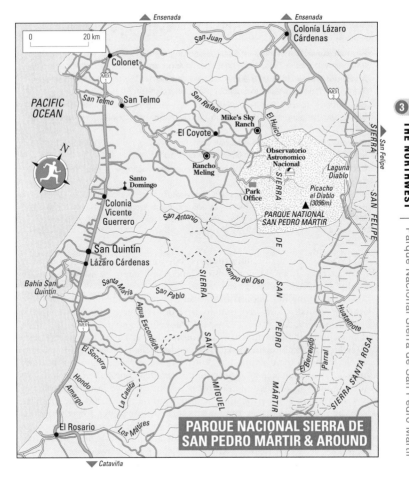

PARQUE NACIONAL SIERRA DE
SAN PEDRO MÁRTIR & AROUND

▼ Cataviña

park's centre, **Picacho del Diablo** (Devil's Peak) is, at 3096 metres, the highest peak on the peninsula and a solid challenge if you're an experienced climber. The approach is typically from the west, and most stretch the climb over at least two days. Less demanding is **El Altar**, a scenic overlook that's accessed after a 2km hike from the observatory's parking lot. From here you can take in much of the park as well as both the Pacific Ocean and the Sea of Cortez.

Practicalities

The only way to reach the park by car is by taking the paved road turnoff at Km 141 on Mex 1 Ensenada–San Quintín, which leads to the settlement of **San Telmo**, a place not likely to pique your interest. Though it does have a few shops, if you're headed into the park for an overnight trip it's better to stock up at either the supermarket in San Quintín or one of the many large stores in Ensenada. The pavement ends on the outskirts of San Telmo, and then it's another 60km to the entrance to the park; the observatory is a further 21km along the same road. There are rustic **campsites** near the entrance and off

③

Park guides

Any real exploration of the park requires **booking a guide** ahead of time. The operators below, based in Tijuana or Ensenada, have general and targeted itineraries.

Andiamo Travel ☏646/178-8909, US ☏1-800/661-1325, ⓦandiamo-travel.com. Single and multi-day tours throughout the northern state,

Baja Motion Tours US ☏1-877/246-2252, ⓦwww.2gobaja.com. Multi-day hiking, biking and camping tours to Picacho del Diablo and the observatory, starting at US$175.

Cucapah ☏664/686-6385, ⓦcucapah.com. Small-group, multi-day camping trips to the observatory and Cañon de Guadalupe (see p.116).

Ecobajatours ☏646/623-8875, ⓦecobajatours.com. Sightseeing tours of the park, including visits to the observatory.

Ecotur ☏646/178-3704, ⓦmexonline.com/ecotur.htm. Mountain bike to La Llave (see p.155), backpack to hidden waterfalls and climb Picacho del Diablo for about M$150 for two-day trips.

the sides of the dirt road within the park, but you will likely be on your own; the ranger force is almost non-existent, and you'll rarely be asked to pay for camping.

Beyond the campsites, **accommodation** choices around Sierra de San Pedro Mártir are limited. A forty-five minute drive from the park gates, *Rancho Meling* (☏619/758-2719, US ☏858/454-7166, ⓦmelingguestranch.com; ❻, meals and horseback riding included) is the most comfortable and convivial place from which to explore the park. The wood-panelled, 1930s-era rooms only have electricity in the evenings but do have running water and wood-burning fireplaces. Meals are taken as a group in a covered area near the main house. If you make plans in advance the ranch can organize guided horseback tours of the western edges of the park along with portions of the 10,000-acre property. There's also an airstrip that accommodates small private planes. To get to *Rancho Meling*, a two-hour journey from Mex 1, turn south at the signs 50km east of the highway and drive a further 2km. About 30km from *Meling* as the crow flies, *Mike's Sky Ranch* (☏646/681-5514; ❻) on the northwest border of the park, is a tough haul from the southwest and rather impossible to reach with anything but a high-clearance vehicle. A route to the ranch connects with the San Telmo road 48km from Mex 1, and there's an easier road to follow directly opposite the *Rancho Meling* turnoff; either will bring you to the settlement of El Coyote before leading up a steep, thirty minute-drive to *Mike's*. The ranch, similar in spirit to *Meling*, is in the San Rafael Arroyo, a hunting and fishing-rich area that borders the park. Guests can camp in a large meadow or take rooms in cabins; wherever you stay you'll be eating communally at the large table that's the ranch's unofficial centre.

San Quintín and around

With its streets straddling the Transpeninsular Highway, **SAN QUINTÍN** is, if nothing else, convenient if you're on your way to the Desierto Central or heading north to Ensenada. For northbound travellers it's the last gasp of rural Baja California; for those journeying south it's the first real rest available from a highway packed with eighteen-wheelers and agricultural vehicles.

Its usefulness as a refuelling point aside, everything that's charming about the area lies to the west of Mex 1: namely the **bays** and the **beaches**. For all intents and purposes, San Quintín incorporates everything in the 25km stretch between the Mex 1 turnoff to **Playa Santa María** south of town up through **Lázaro Cárdenas** and to the tourist information centre in **Ejido Padre Kino**.

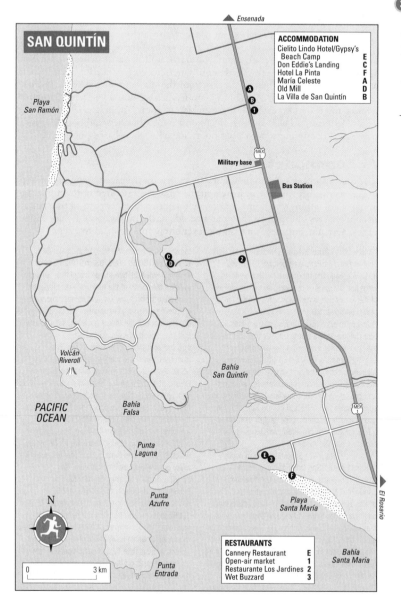

▲ Ensenada

SAN QUINTÍN

ACCOMMODATION
Cielito Lindo Hotel/Gypsy's
  Beach Camp   E
Don Eddie's Landing   C
Hotel La Pinta   F
María Celeste   A
Old Mill   D
La Villa de San Quintín   B

Playa
San Ramón

Ⓐ
Ⓑ❶

MEX 1

Military base

Bus Station

Ⓒ
Ⓓ

❷

Volcán
Riveroll

Bahía
San Quintín

PACIFIC
OCEAN

Bahía
Falsa

MEX 1

Punta
Laguna

Ⓔ❸

Ⓕ

► El Rosario

N

Punta
Azufre

Playa
Santa María

RESTAURANTS
Cannery Restaurant   E
Open-air market   1
Restaurante Los Jardines   2
Wet Buzzard   3

Bahía
Santa María

0   3 km

Punta
Entrada

Arrival and information

Buses from Ensenada stop at **Lázaro Cárdenas**, 5km south of town. Although the sign is on the west side of the road, the station is on the east, set back about one hundred meters.

The **tourist office**, Km 178 Mex 1 Ensenada–San Felipe (Mon–Fri 8am–5pm, Sat & Sun 10am–3pm; ☎616/166-2728), can put you in touch with local guides and fishing companies, as well as ply you with brochures for hotels from here to the state border.

There are four **Pemex** stations in the area, the last one about 3km north of the Old Mill turnoff on the south side of town. Although filling your petrol tank isn't absolutely imperative until you arrive at El Rosario an hour south, San Quintín does have the last **ATM**s until Guerrero Negro. HSBC has a branch at Av Ignacio L Alcerriga 150, across from the dusty town square; Bancomer has a branch at Km 197 Mex 1 in Lázaro Cárdenas. Should you need **Internet access**, there are two cafés on the west side of Mex 1 near Km 195. Both use yellow lettering on blue awnings to announce their business and both locations have several computers (M$15 per hour) and allow web-based phone calls.

Accommodation

The one advantage of being not much more than an oversized highway rest stop is that there are a number of **hotels** in the M$200–300 range in town that are as good as anything you'll find for double that price in other parts of the state. A handful of very cheap hotels line the west side of the highway on the north side of San Quintín, but these cater almost exclusively to long-haul truckers.

Cielito Lindo Hotel/Gypsy's Beach Camp Next door to *Hotel La Pinta* (see below) ☎616/162-3012. Although the rooms are rather bland and worn and the water's brackish, its beach and one of the area's better restaurants help make this a gringo paradise. ❹

Don Eddie's Landing exit west from Mex 1 San Quintín–Punta Prieta directly across from the transformer station on the south side of Lázaro Cárdenas ☎616/165-6061, ⓦwww .doneddies.com. The first of two motels along the Bahía San Quintín that caters to fishermen and groups of budget travellers. Each otherwise sparse room has a TV and ceiling fan, and there's use of cleaning facilities for caught fish. There's a free continental breakfast and, when there's a crowd, a bar. ❸

Hotel La Pinta Playa Santa María, turn south at Km 11 Mex 1 San Quintín–Punta Prieta ☎616/165-9008, ⓦ www.lapintahotels.com/SanQuintin. If you want a place to stay on the beach, *Hotel La Pinta* is the high-end option, right on Playa Santa María. Like a few other locations in the Baja-based chain, this *La Pinta* is upgrading its rooms one at a time and may have sections of the hotel closed for long periods of time. The restaurant here has a lovely view of the ocean and rote interpretations of Mexican basics. ❺

Maria Celeste Km 189 Mex 1 Ensenada–San Quintín ☎616/165-3999, US ☎619/207-4284. This whitewashed, two-storey motel tries valiantly to block the sound of the highway with plexiglass panels on the breezeways, and actually succeeds in keeping dust out of its rooms. Like the *Villa* down the street, the rooms have a/c, satellite TV and high-speed Internet access. ❸

The Old Mill follow directions to *Don Eddie's* from Mex 1 until the marked turnoff to the *Mill* US ☎800/479-7962, ⓦwww.oldmillbaja.com. Rooms at *The Old Mill* range from doubles to suites and, although they're not exactly fancy, they're the most sought-after in town, both for their price and the hospitality of the owners. Most rooms have a kitchen and grill area in the front, along with outdoor tables and chairs. There are no TVs or a/c, which is just fine as most guests chat the evenings away outside with their neighbours. ❸

La Villa de San Quintín Km 190 Mex 1 Ensenada–San Quintín ☎616/165-1800, ⓔvillasanquintin@hotmail.com. Convenient to Mex 1, this sixteen-room motel is run by the family that owns Tijuana's *Hotel La Villa de Zaragoza*. The rooms, all of which have free high-speed Internet access, a/c, satellite TV and secure parking, are set thirty metres off the highway and behind the motel's restaurant. ❸

The town and the coast

San Quintín's ramshackle two-storey buildings lining the highway practically scream unplanned urban expansion, which is exactly what's happened here since this freakishly straight stretch of the paved Transpeninsular Highway was laid down in the 1970s. The original town was a small colonial affair situated around Bahía San Quintín, one of the area's three bays (the others are Falsa and Santa María). During the early nineteenth century American smugglers hid out in the bay and later, in 1885, an Anglo-American company began building a railroad from the bay and lured Englishmen to come here to grow wheat; a decrepit bayside cemetery is filled with markers bearing their names. After the farming and railroad failure in the late nineteenth century, San Quintín remained largely deserted until the highway was paved, at which point businesses catering to local farmers and stationed military personnel popped up. These days there's nothing to detain you unless you need to do some grocery shopping or catch up on email at one of the Internet cafés.

You won't find many fellow travellers along San Quintín's appealing **Pacific coast** beaches – a good twenty-minute drive (there are no buses) atop dirt and sand roads can be quite a deterrent. The largely unpopulated coast is reached from the road bordering the southern side of the military camp at Km 188 Mex 1. There's no street sign (nor is there one along the route) but northbound drivers with a pilot's vision may be able to make out a faded sign mounted high on a lamppost that reads "*Zona Turística/Attractivos Natural/Bahía Falsa.*" The beach road is a graded gravel road for the first 5km and then turns to a mix of dirt mixed with volcanic ash just shy of a Fork in the road. A left turns leads around Volcán Riveroll – one of five volcanoes in the area – to the west side of Bahía San Quintín and the oyster farms on the north side of Bahía Falsa. Except on very cold or rainy days, you can purchase oysters directly from the fishermen along the bay; bring cash and expect to pay about M$10 each. A right turn at the fork leads to a few fishing encampments and the wide, shell-strewn beach of Playas San Ramón, one of the best places for surf fishing in the area (which does not require a licence). Virtually any time of year you'll have the beach largely to yourself, both for fishing and for

---

Sport-fishing guides

If you're looking to **fish** in Baja California but don't want to spend a ton of cash, find a **guide** in San Quintín. From Mex 1, follow signs to *Don Eddie's* and the *Old Mill* to get to the Bahía de San Quintín boat launch. Both of the motels have their own, in-house fishing guides who also double as independent operators. For first-timers, the motels, along with Pedro Pangas, offer the easiest introduction; on subsequent trips book directly with the boat's owner. Expect to pay about M$800 per person, per day, including food and drink. Some of the area's more regarded guides are listed below.

Bertoldo García ☎616/165-3372, ⓦgarciaspangas.8m.com.

Don Eddie´s Landing ☎661/165- 6061, ⓦdoneddies.com.

Ernesto Alonso Aguayo ☎616/165-6012.

Jaime García ☎616/162-2060.

Kelly Catlan ☎616/162-1716, ⓦwww.elcapitan.us.

Old Mill Sport Fishing ☎616/165-6034, 163-2911, ⓔoldmillsportfishing@hotmail .com.

Pedro Pangas ☎616/159-8626, US ☎1-888/568-BAJA, ⓦwww.pedropangas.com.

Tiburón Pangas ☎616/165-6003.

swimming. It's easy to lose track of the road you took to get to either the bay or the beach, so never drive out within a few hours of sunset.

If you want to visit any of the bays without packing a lunch and compass, head to the site of the **Old Mill** on the south side of Lázaro Cárdenas. Access is along a 6km-long dirt road at Km 1 Mex 1 San Quintín–Punta Prieta, directly across from a power transfer station; look for the large sign for *Don Eddie's Landing*. This was the site of the original colony, and all the bay's commercial activity is situated around the remnants of the nineteenth-century settlement. The mill itself has been converted into a restaurant and bar (see below), and scattered remains of industrial machinery decorate a landscaped area between the restaurant, waterfront and adjacent motel. Although there are sport-fishing outfitters down here, you're better off booking ahead to ensure you're properly licensed and can get a *panga* or other boat rental (and room) when you arrive.

Eating and drinking

The **restaurants** and **bars** along Mex 1 cater primarily to the long-haul truckers taking away the area's agricultural products, and the bars especially are not recommended for female travellers. For an inexpensive taste of local **seafood**, seek out one of the palapa-covered stalls on either side of Mex 1 in the gully between San Quintín and Lázaro Cárdenas (just south of *Hotel la Villa de San Quintín*). Although there's a supermarket to the south, this is the region's most popular food and clothing **market** (10am–dusk), with vendors hawking fresh fruits and vegetables, as well as raw seafood and ready-to-eat fish tacos and clams, oyster and other seafood cocktails.

The unappetizingly named *Wet Buzzard* bar and restaurant at *Cielito Lindo*, adjacent to *Hotel La Pinta,* is justly famous for its large cracked-crab plate and other seafood dishes, all around M$120 a person. The *Cannery Restaurant*, right next to the *Old Mill* (☎616/162-1796), has a happy hour that starts at 5pm and, although the prices change at 7pm, carries on until the fishermen remember they have to get up early the next morning. The meals here aren't as seafood-centric or good as you'd expect, but the service and scenery make up for the kitchen's shortcomings. *Restaurante Los Jardines* is a green oasis halfway between Mex 1 and the *Cannery* (once you're on the road look for the painted signs with arrows). In warmer months you can eat your clams and seafood in the garden and escape the TV noise.

If you have an urge to go **dancing**, *Discotheque Tomatoes & Beer* directly across from the military camp is the safest bet, but go early to suss out the scene.

Around San Quintín

The outlying areas south of San Quintín are planted with tomatoes for export to the US. At around Km 35 Mex 1 San Quintín–Punta Prieta, a 20km-long line of cliffs and dunes separates the road from the Pacific Ocean. At the southern end, just before the turn inland towards El Rosario, you can access the beach through the town of **El Socorro**, the site of a new housing development.

Mex 1 kilometre markings

The **Mex 1 kilometre markings** heading south are reset at zero in Lázaro Cárdenas and are listed as Mex 1 San Quintín-Punta Prieta. Northbound traffic traverses Mex 1 along the Ensenada–San Quintín segment, which counts down towards zero from Km 195.

This was once a popular spot for beach camping, but reports of robberies over the last few years have scared visitors away.

Travel details

Buses

Ensenada to: Guerrero Negro (2 daily; 9 1/2hours); San Quintín (3 daily; 4 1/2hours); Tijuana (via Rosarito, every 30 mins; 1 1/2 hours).

San Quintín to: Ensenada 3 daily; 4 1/2hours); Guerrero Negro (2 daily; 6 hours); Tijuana (3 daily; 6 hours).

The central deserts

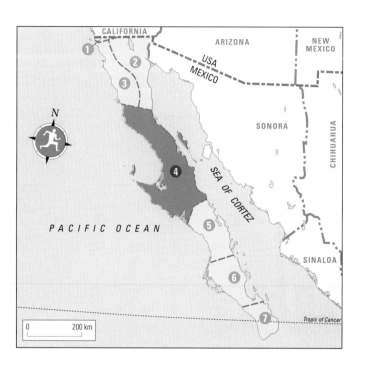

CHAPTER 4 # Highlights

* **Cataviña's landscape** Eerie rock fields and trippy cacti will take your breath away. See p.170

* **Bahía de los Ángeles** Laid-back, Sea of Cortez haven designed for the lazy and the sportsman alike. See p.172

* **Punta Abreojos** Off the coast of the isolated Peninsula de Vizcaíno, this dramatic, hidden surf spot is well worth a side-trip. See p.181

* **Cave paintings in the Sierra de San Francisco** Give yourself at least two days to explore the peninsula's most extensive collection of cave paintings. See p.182

* **Laguna San Ignacio** Each winter the pristine Laguna de San Ignacio plays host to migrating gray whales that journey from the Arctic Circle to nurse their calves in the warm waters. See p.186

△ The Desierto Central

The central deserts

Though its 3200 kilometres of coastlines tend to receive more attention, more than a third of Baja California is consumed by the two sprawling deserts that dominate its centre. Though they share essentially the same climate – a searing heat by day and a still coolness at night – their landscapes are very much different: the northerly Desierto Central is coloured by twisting cacti, immense boulders, volcanic mesas and mountain ranges, while the southern Desierto de Vizcaíno is largely a flat expanse of sand and salt that runs east from the Peninsula de Vizcaíno to the foot of the **Sierra de San Francisco**.

Harsh and spectacular, the vast **Desierto Central** stretches over 300 kilometres from north to south. For all its beauty, it is sparsely populated, and most of the region's inhabitants confine themselves to two towns just beyond the desert's reaches: the historic transpeninsular staging point **El Rosario** in the northwest and the remote village of **Bahía de los Ángeles** on the Sea of Cortez. At the desert's centre, just beyond the wind-blown settlement of **Cantaviña**, is the otherworldly **Valle de los Cirios**, an expanse of rocks and cacti that looks not unlike an album cover by a psychedelic rock band from the 1970s. The **Sierra Columbia** on the western coast blocks access to the Pacific Ocean and much of its moisture from providing relief from the desert heat. To the east, the **Sierra Calamajué** cuts apart the central desert plain from the Sea of Cortez with a series of almost impassible rises and arroyos.

The **28th parallel** divides the peninsula into two states, and roughly serves as the transition point from the Desierto Central to the **Desierto de Vizcaíno**. Whereas the northern state is relatively young and shares economic, historical and familial ties to the US, **Baja California Sur** shares a colonial history more in line with that of the rest of Mexico, as well as direct economic ties with it across the Sea of Cortez. The south is also where ecotourism has really gathered energy, charged by the yearly migration of **California gray whales** to the lagoons of the **Reserva de la Biósfera El Vizcaíno**, Mexico's largest protected area. Of Baja California's three whale breeding areas, two are in the Vizcaíno biosphere; **Laguna Ojo de Liebre**, just across the salt flats of industrial **Guerrero Negro**, and **Laguna San Ignacio**. In addition to the cetaceans and those who make the annual pilgrimage to come watch their movements, kayakers, cyclists, surfers and fishermen make personal playgrounds out of the largely uninhabited lands and waters around the biosphere. Near the Laguna San Ignacio is the Jesuit settlement of **San Ignacio**, an ideal base for jumping off into the **Sierra de San Francisco** to view the mountains and their wealth of **cave paintings**, some of the oldest works of art in the western hemisphere. And although they aren't quite works of art, Baja California Sur's **missions**, like the one at **Santa Gertrudis**, begin to make up for the uninspired attempts in the north.

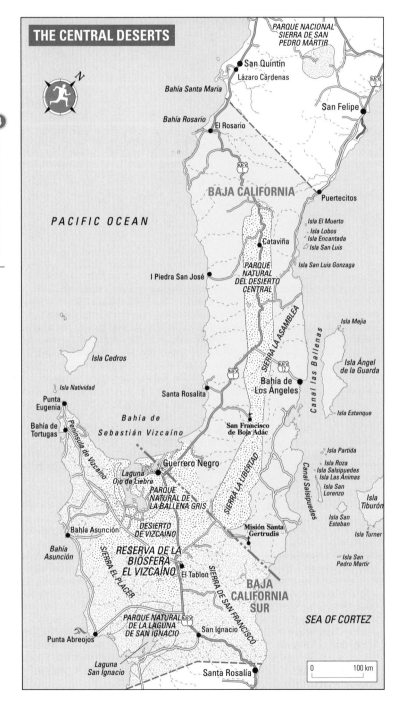

El Rosario and the Desierto Central

Heading south on Mex 1, **El Rosario**, with its petrol station and handful of restaurants, is the last stop before modern conveniences get stripped away by the unforgiving **Parque Natural del Desierto Central**. There isn't a lonelier place in all of Baja California than the segment of the Transpeninsular Highway between **Cataviña** and the small settlements north of Guerrero Negro on the other side of the state border; you will encounter few people – and no dependable petrol pumps – for a few hundred kilometres. It's a daunting stretch to be sure, yet one that can be mercifully interrupted around the halfway point by taking a side trip along Mex 12 to idyllic **Bahía de los Ángeles** and the Sea of Cortez.

El Rosario

Before the Transpeninsular Highway was completed, **EL ROSARIO** was the end of the road for those heading south; it's now the last place you can fill your petrol tank for 310km. The town begin its life in 1774 as the site of the first Dominican mission in the state. Flooding and other troubles forced them to move the site a few times, but even relocation couldn't keep it from suffering the same fate as most other missions: disease, death and abandonment; although unlike the other Dominican and Franciscan missions in the region, it still stands and has a museum attached. Today, the town is actually two settlements: Rosario de Arriba, which hugs the highway, and Rosario de Abajo, accessed by going south at the Mex 1 dogleg. Other than petrol, the only reason to linger here is to enlist the services of a guide to Las Pintas cave painting site, a good hour and a half to the southeast via dirt roads (see p.170). Guides can be found at the El Rosario Community Museum (Mon–Fri 10–3pm) 2km off the highway next to the mission and the mission itself.

The recently remodelled *Baja Cactus Motel*, km 55 Mex 1 San Quintín–Punta Prieta (☎616/165-8850; ⓦwww.bajacactus.com; ❸) has relatively quiet **rooms** with satellite TV and wireless Internet access. It's conveniently positioned between the Pemex Station and *Mama Espinosa's* restaurant and cabanas (☎616/165-8770; ❹). *Espinosa's* is one of the oldest **restaurants** on the peninsula and serves as the unofficial town hall. The famed lobster tacos are rather dry and expensive, but everything else – beef and pork tacos and big burritos – qualifies as the best food between here and Bahía de los Angeles. The ten-room *Motel Sinai*, Km 56.5 Mex 1 San Quintín–Punta Prieta (☎616/165-8818; ❸), at the town's southern edge, is quiet and clean. A few kilometres farther along the outskirts, *Baja's Best*, Km 60 Mex 1 San Quintín-Punta Prieta (☎616/165-8656; ❸) is a combo café and bed-and-breakfast on the outskirts of town. The three rooms are part of the proprietor's home, but they do offer private baths. The attached café makes a claim to serving one of the world's most remote cups of Starbuck's coffee.

Las Pintas

One of two primitive rock art sites in the northern state that's open to the public, **Las Pintas** is a fascinating collection of a few hundred petroglyphs and paintings that decorate a cluster of boulders at the end of a canyon. Although you can reach the site without a guide, one can be arranged at El Rosario's community museum or by asking around at *Mama Espinosa's*. If this is the only rock art site on your itinerary, go ahead and spend the M$600 for the guide; otherwise, brave it with at least one other person and save the cash for a guided trek into the Sierra de San Francisco (see p.182).

The turnoff to Las Pintas is 23km east of El Rosario at a marked dirt road going to Abelardo L Rodriguez. Follow this about 35km south until you reach Rodriguez, then turn northwest and follow a rougher dirt road along the Arroyo San Fernando for another 16km. The last 6km must be taken by foot. This is a day-trip; allow yourself three hours of travel each way and take food and plenty of water.

Parque Natural del Desierto Central

From the north, bulbous grey boulders signal the unofficial start of the **PARQUE NATURAL DEL DESIERTO CENTRAL** soon after El Rosario departs from the rear-view mirror. The transition from the south is more gradual; cacti begin to inch out of the ground and eventually rise three storeys high. A eerie landscape of desolate mountain ranges, yucca, towering cardon cacti – the world's largest species of cactus – abandoned RV parks, shuttered Pemex stations and vultures circling overhead, the Desierto Central is not a place to be taken lightly. At the desert's southern extremes, the understated elegance of the **Misíon San Borja** speaks clearly through weathered stone about the trials of the desert.

Pit stops within the desert's 300km expanse are almost non-existent, limited to a side-trip to **Bahía de los Ángeles** (see p.172) and **CATAVIÑA**. The latter isn't so much a town as it is the only dependable place to take a break, get a bite to eat, stay overnight, or if you're desperate and have the right timing, buy petrol from the back of a local entrepreneur's pick-up truck. With such slim options it is fortuitous to find **accommodation** in the form of *La Pinta Hotel* (☎200/124-9123, ⓦlapintahotels.com/Catavina; ➎) – the best one in the chain, at that. The hotel rooms and **restaurant** are situated around two breezy courtyards, one with a pool. The restaurant serves standard pan-Mex dishes, and the large, carved-wood **bar** opens at noon.

The desert's strangest sight is the *cirio*, or *boojum*, a cactus strain abundant around Cataviña that would seem more

△ The Cataviña landscape

El Mármol

For 58 years, the onyx mine at **El Mármol** churned out a hefty chunk of the world's supply, eventually growing into a large village. When the demand for onyx dried up, so did the mine's prospects, and it was abandoned in the mid-1950s. Stacks of large slabs of golden onyx remain, as does a roofless, eroding schoolhouse made entirely of unpolished onyx, giving the settlement an old glow.

El Mármol is worth a side trip if you're certain you have enough petrol in the tank; exit the Mex 1 at Km 143 and proceed east for 15km.

appropriate in a dreamland or a set designer's sketchbook; fittingly it was named after a mythical creature from a Lewis Carroll tale. Shaped much like a carrot, the *boojum's* narrow shaft grows over 18m tall in every possible direction. Around Cataviña these oddities appear all the more unearthly when juxtaposed by the massive grey boulders that were seemingly tossed throughout the hills and flat areas. The graffiti adorning some of these rocks seems like a desperate attempt by humans to leave their mark, but not much endures in this harsh climate.

Earlier inhabitants or nomadic groups left some modest marks on the landscape too, which you can see off of Mex 1 by taking the Km 171 exit, just before Cataviña. **La Cueva Pintada** has two relatively unimpressive collections of images, one set on the sun-drenched surface of a huge rock, the other in the tiny cave beneath it. The compositions are almost predominantly of circles, dots, sunbursts and stick figures.

The scenery along the winding and white-knuckle-inducing Transpeninsular Highway changes little for the rest of the Desierto Central. Roadside *tiendas* at Km 190 and Km 195 sell beer and packaged food and have telephones for in-state calls.

San Francisco de Borja Adác

The only mission in the state of Baja California that is worth stopping for on its own merit is the Jesuit, Franciscan and Dominican team effort at **San Francisco de Borja Adác**. The natural spring at the site had been drawing a steady stream of Cochimí Indians for years, so when the Jesuits showed up in 1758 and laid claim to the site they didn't have trouble keeping the Indians interested. The Jesuits were kicked out of Mexico ten years later, to be followed for a three-year stint by the Franciscans. The architecture here should be credited to the Dominicans, though, who completed the still-standing, two-storey structure in 1801. Disease soon reduced the population, and the mission was abandoned in 1817.

Unlike their other adobe missions, the Dominicans built this one out of cast-stone style akin to sixteenth-century Spanish missions. The builders' whimsies were made possible by the financial backers, the Italian Borgia family. The front door is flanked by columns and a carved lintel, while the interior is a rather simple affair, unadorned except for stone columns and wooden benches, and lit by clerestory windows (although there is a second-storey choir loft). In addition to the chapel, ruins of outbuildings are situated throughout the area.

San Borja is open to the public Mon–Fri 8am–3pm, but from July–Sept the desert is quite hot and the mission may close periodically. If you're coming the long way from Bahía de los Ángeles (see p.172), ask around in town about its status before making the journey. The mission does take some work getting to: from Mex 1 Punta Prieta–Guerrero Negro, exit east at the settlement of Rosarito and drive about 45km along a bumpy dirt road. If you're coming from the Bahía de los Ángeles, there is an exit from Mex 6 at Km 21. Drive 35km south along a slightly better road.

Bahía de los Ángeles

Striking though the Desierto Central is, after driving through its stifling heat for a few hours, the lure of the coast will once again be strong. There can therefore be few sights that would be more welcome than the crisp, blue waters of **BAHÍA DE LOS ÁNGELES**, reachable at the end of the 69km trip east along the recently resurfaced two-lane Mex 6. Occupying one of the Sea of Cortez's more stunning settings, the eponymous town has a lazy, frontier vibe, though RV parks have arrived and taken up some of the choice waterfront real estate. Despite this, the bay still exerts an almost mythical allure, and the local mix of Mexicans and gringos is exceedingly amiable.

The town and the bay

Taking in the scenery and, from time to time, heading into the bay to fish or kayak, are the primary activities here. The one exception would be the small bilingual **Museo de Naturaleza y Cultura**, two blocks west of the main drag (daily 9am–noon & 2–4pm; M$15 suggested donation). Its location is marked by a narrow-gauge locomotive, a relic of the gold and copper mines that first attracted Europeans to the area. Mining history and that of the local ranchero life is well covered, along with details of sea life in the bay.

Isla Ángel de la Guarda, the largest island in the Sea of Cortez, dominates the bay and is the focus of the settlement's activities; it's the best place on the sea's northern coast for diving and kayaking trips. So far, there aren't any specialty operators in town, and any activity you'd like to indulge in – kayaking, fishing or off-roading – is typically arranged through the campground or motel you're staying at. If your hotel doesn't handle it directly, they'll direct you to someone who does. *Camp Gecko* rents kayaks and snorkelling gear for M$30 per hour and can fill up your scuba tank; *Costa del Sol* and *Villa Vitta* (see Practicalities for both, below) do the same for their guests, along with anyone else on their side of the shore.

Practicalities

Because of the difficulty in getting supplies to the bay, lodging and food are more expensive than you'd expect, but still cheaper than Ensenada or La Paz. Two of the best **places to stay** are just off crumbling asphalt roads on the north side of town. ⚞ *Larry and Raquel's Motel on the Beach*, 3km north on the La Gringa Road (☎619/423-3454, ✉bahiatours@yahoo.com; ❸) has nine rooms in a two-storey motel just 50 metres from the sea. The rooms are spare and clean, without phones or TVs, though the restaurant does have satellite TV and an Internet connection. *Camp Daggett's*, between *Larry's* and the town (☎200/124-9101, ⓦcampdaggetts .com; tent camping ❶, cabins ❸), is primarily an RV community, but they've reserved the beachfront for palapa-shaded plots for campers. There are also simple cabins with hot-water showers next to the restaurant.

There are three motels and parks in town directly off the paved road, each offering a handful of basic rooms, along with attached restaurants and short walks to the shore. As you approach from the highway, the first of these, *Costa del Sol* (☎200/124-9110, ✉costadelsolhotel@hotmail.com; ❹), has seven rooms and a pool. The forty rooms at *Villa Vitta* ☎200/124-9103, US ☎619/454-6101, ⓦwww.villavitta.com; ❹), are a bit worn, but the motel has a pool, Jacuzzi and boat ramp to keep you occupied. Next door, *Casa Díaz* (☎617/650-3206; ❸) has fourteen very basic rooms on the beach, and if you're a guest you're free to camp outside. *Guillermo's Trailer Park* also has five hotel rooms that sleep up to

△ Kayaking in Bahía de los Ángeles

eight in queen-size beds (☎200/124-0104, ⓦwww.guillermos.com; ❹). These are typically packed with fishermen, so book ahead.

The south side of the bay has a number of smaller operations, most of them without electricity or telephones. *Camp Gecko* (no phone, ⓔgecko@starband .net, ⓦwww.campgecko.com; campsites ❶, cabins ❸) is really bare bones, with beds and worn sheets in its cabins.

Many of the hotels have **restaurants**, but *Guillermo's* has one of the better locations, with palapas right on the beach and basic Mexican dishes around M$80 per person. Raquel, of *Larry and Raquel's* fame, makes the best fish tacos between Ensenada and San Jose del Cabo. The motel's second-storey dining room looks out onto the bay from interior and exterior dining tables. Larry, who's typically behind the bar, does a mean margarita.

The Pemex station near the intersection with Mex 6 has been known to close for long periods when **petrol** is not delivered; when this happens you can often find petrol by asking at one of the hotels – but don't depend on it.

The Reserva de la Biósfera El Vizcaíno

The **RESERVA DE LA BIÓSFERA EL VIZCAÍNO** offers a bit of everything that makes the peninsula's landscape so enthralling: two rugged coastlines, a vast, unforgiving desert, commanding mountain ranges and long-dormant volcanoes. Looming over the Sea of Cortez on its eastern side, the **Sierra de San Francisco** contains spectacular **cave art** whose origins and purpose continue to vex scholars. Smaller mountain ranges like **Sierra Santa Clara** and **Sierra Vizcaíno** are virtually unexplored as well as wholly unwelcoming to visitors. Spreading west from the Sierra de San Francisco is the **Desierto de Vizcaíno**, home to the Pronghorn antelope and the barrel-shaped Biznaga cactus. At its western reaches, the wedge-shaped **Peninsula de Vizcaíno** juts out into the ocean like a horn, around which migrating **California gray whales** swim every winter to mate and spawn.

To visit the biosphere, you'll need to set up base in the salt-blown company town of **Guerrero Negro** or, more appealingly, in sleepy **San Ignacio**, a veritable oasis packed with date palms to the south. As an entry point into the southern state – which Guerrero Negro is for anyone on a Transpeninsular jaunt – the city itself offers little but is an essential stop if you want to explore the natural wonders within the region. Tours of Laguna de Ojo Liebre, the northernmost whale breeding ground, originate from here, and its location is ideal for exploring the Peninsula de Vizcaíno's isolated Pacific coast. San Ignacio appears as a mirage and maintains an ethereal, oasis-like quality throughout. Its mission is an odd blend of now-disappeared indigenous culture and Jesuit ambition. The similarly named lagoon south of the town contrasts sharply with Ojo de Liebre, here the coastline is packed with mangroves and rich animal and bird life.

Getting around the biosphere is both logistically and financially much more manageable if you're doing the driving; you'll pay a great deal more for everything if you don't have your own set of wheels. Flights into Loreto (see p.205) are the easiest way to get here if you're not on a peninsular tour, but you'll need to rent a car to get Guerrero Negro, San Ignacio or anywhere else in the area in a decent amount of time. If you come **by bus**, guided tours can be organized to just about anywhere, but you'll have to hire the guide's car as well and this is never cheaper than renting your own.

Crossing the state border

You'll have to set your watch forward an hour when you cross the border into Baja California Sur, unless the peninsula is on **daylight saving time** (April–Oct), in which case there's no change.

When you cross the border heading south officials will spray the bottom of your car with a pesticide and tell you to throw away any fruit or vegetables. There's a M$10 charge and they will give you a receipt. Roll the windows up to avoid the fumes.

Guerrero Negro and around

Despite a colourful name, flat and fly-blown **GUERRERO NEGRO** is, with the exception of the occasional enormous salt dune rising from the horizon, rather dull. Most of the ten thousand or so people who live here work at Exportadora de Sal (ESSA), the mining company that created the town in the 1950s. The business is based on flooding the surrounding saltpans – the world's largest – with ocean water and waiting for the water to evaporate so that trucks can haul away the salt for export. While that's certainly fascinating to some, for travellers, Guerrero

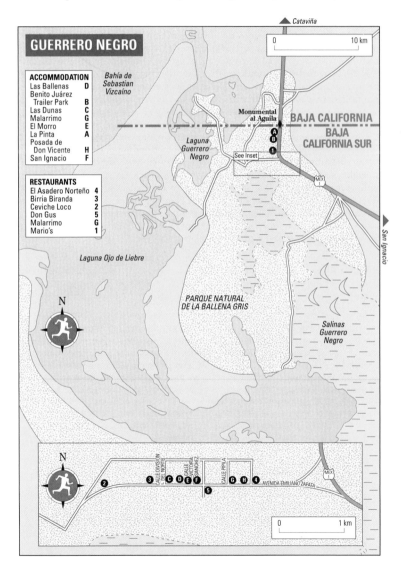

GUERRERO NEGRO

ACCOMMODATION
Las Ballenas   D
Benito Juárez
   Trailer Park   B
Las Dunas   C
Malarrimo   G
El Morro   E
La Pinta   A
Posada de
   Don Vicente   H
San Ignacio   F

RESTAURANTS
El Asadero Norteño   4
Birria Biranda   3
Ceviche Loco   2
Don Gus   5
Malarrimo   G
Mario's   1

Cataviña

0   10 km

Bahía de
Sebastian
Vizcaíno

Monumental
al Aguila

BAJA CALIFORNIA
BAJA
CALIFORNIA SUR

Laguna
Guerrero
Negro

See Inset

MEX
1

San Ignacio

Laguna Ojo de Liebre

N

PARQUE NATURAL
DE LA BALLENA GRIS

Salinas
Guerrero
Negro

N

CALLE DIVISIÓN DEL NORTE
CALLE VICTORIA SÁNCHEZ
CALLE PIPILA

AVENIDA EMILIANO ZAPATA

MEX
1

0   1 km

Negro for eight months out of the year is little more than a well-supplied pit stop along the Transpeninsular Highway. Winter sees an influx of visitors gearing up for a **whale-watching tour** of the Peninsula de Vizcaíno lagoons, where everyone hopes to get close to the gray whales that congregate to calve just off the coast.

Arrival and information

The town lies 6km south of the state border and halfway between an elbow-like bend in Mex 1 and Laguna Ojo de Liebre to the west. Salt ponds bump up against the southern side of Avenida Emiliano Zapata, its main thoroughfare. The commercial district, which includes the **bus station** and many of the motels and restaurants, occupies a ten-block length of Avenida Zapata. Private planes and the small, coop-owned operator Aero Cedros are the only craft that use Guerrero Negro's **airport** just north of the state border; the closest commercial airport is in Loreto (see p.205), a five-hour drive to the southeast.

There is **no official tourism office**, but the *Malarrimo* motel complex (see below) at Emiliano Zapato and Calle Pipila has free brochures about whale watching along with a collection of hard-to-find and small press books about the lagoons, desert, missions and the southern state. The bus station (☎615/157-0611), more of a glorified kiosk actually, sits across from *San José* motel.

A half-dozen **Internet** cafés (typically open Mon–Sat only; M$10–20/hr) such as Café Internet Las Ballenas, TechNet (open on Sundays) and Cyber Guerrero Negro line Zapata and the adjacent blocks between the *Malarrimo* and *El Morro* motels. The Banamex next to the Essa company store – a good fifteen-minute walk west on Zapata – has the only **ATM** between San Quintín and Loreto. The bank also has a Western Union inside. There are two **Pemex** stations at the western end of Zapata and another one south of the border crossing.

Accommodation

With the exception of *La Pinta* near the military base, all of Guerrero Negro's **hotels and motels** are strung out along the north side of Zapata. Since most guests come during the more mild winters, few rooms have air conditioning but almost everywhere will have fans to keep you cool, and none could honestly be called anything more than one star.

Las Ballenas C Victoria s/n, at Av Zapata ☎615/157-0116. Tiny Motel option with very basic yet quite well-maintained rooms with TVs and private baths. ❷

Benito Juárez Trailer Park Km 220 Mex 1 Guerrero Negro–Santa Rosalía, adjacent to *La Pinta* ☎615-157-0025. These tent and RV sites are bland and sand-swept, but they're also near the military base and entirely safe. The camping fee includes use of hot showers, and there's an on-site shop. ❶

Las Dunas Av Zapata s/n, at C División del Norte ☎615/157-0650. A simple, clean and friendly motel, though sometimes a little noisy because of street traffic. ❸

Malarrimo Av Zapata, at C Pipila ☎615/157-0250, ⓦwww.malarrimo.com. The town's informal tourist information centre (see above), *Malarrimo* offers perhaps the best beds in Guerrero Negro. The rooms themselves, all concrete and tiles, aren't the most comfortable you'll find, but there's heat in the winter and TV year-round. There's also a restaurant and shop onsite and an additional sixty-five RV hook-ups are at the back of the complex. ❸–❹

El Morro Av Zapata s/n, at C Victoria ☎615/157-0414. A good, yet almost antiseptic hotel at the centre of Zapata's street life. All rooms have fans and cable TV. ❹

The **kilometre markings** on Mex 1 begin anew at the border and from this point on, count down towards zero as the highway moves southwards. This stretch begins at Km 221 and ends, to be reset again, in Santa Rosalía.

La Pinta Km 220 Mex 1 Guerrero Negro–Santa Rosalía ☎615/157-1304, ⓦlapintahotels.com/GuerreroNegro. Located just south of the state border, this is the nearest approximation to a luxury option in the region. The rooms haven't been refurbished since the early 1990s, and have satellite TV and room service. ❺

Posada de Don Vicente Av Zapata s/n, 1.5km from Mex 1 ☎615/157-0288. A two-storey structure built around a courtyard. Like *Malarrimo*, they'll help you plan whale outings. Second-storey rooms facing south have views of the salt flats. ❸

San Ignacio Av Zapata s/n, at C Victoria ☎615/857-0270. Offers older, stuffy, sink-in-the-bedroom motel lodging as well as a modern, pricier section that has more comfortable rooms with full bath. ❸

The Town

Such is the dearth of attractions in Guerrero Negro that the **Monumental al Águila**, a massive, abstract steel eagle sculpture smack in the middle of Mex 1 just north of town, is considered a sight of some visual significance. It is, however, with the exception of some of the new coastal developments, the largest eyesore in either state. It does, though, adequately delineate the peninsula's time zones and the border separating the states of Baja California and Baja California Sur. In town there's a two-block long shopping area at right angles to Avenida Zapata near the Calle Quintana Roo intersection. This packed dirt road bustles in the late afternoon with shoppers fingering goods at outdoor clothing markets, second-hand shops, a nice stationery shop and a frozen fruit café. In the evening, street vendors hawk tacos and sweets from stalls along Zapata, creating a lively scene for the strolling townsfolk.

During whale-watching season (Dec–April), the town is flush with foreigners preparing for day or overnight trips to **Laguna Ojo de Liebre** (see box, below). All prices rise during this period, and hotel rooms and space on buses become difficult to come by; organized trips get around this by taking guests directly to temporary camps on the shore of the lagoon and bypassing the town altogether.

Whale-watching trips from Guerrero Negro

Whale-watching tours originating in Guerrero Negro take place at the nearby Laguna Ojo de Liebre. Just about anyone in Guerrero Negro will sell you a whale-watching trip, but it's worth the extra legwork to book with a reputable guide. During the official season Dec 15–April 15, the tours from respected operators fill up quickly; call ahead to book a place. For day-trips, expect to pay about M$480 for transportation, guides, the boat and a meal. Bring your own jackets and binoculars. For US-based operators with package tours, see Getting There, pp.23–24. More information about the lagoon is available on p.178.

Guides

Ecotours Malarrimo Av Emiliano Zapata ☎615/157-0100, ⓦmalarrimo.com. Malarrimo may be the most expensive operator in town, but it's with good reason: they're home to the best guides in the region and are consistently the most reliable. They arrange tours of the nearby rock art, missions as well as the lagoons, and they can also arrange custom trips.

Laguna Tours Av Emiliano Zapata ☎615/157-0050, ⓔelaguna@intecnet.com.mx. In addition to lagoon trips, Laguna arranges visits to rock art sites and the salt plains.

Mario's Tours Km 217 Mex 1 Guerrero Negro–Santa Rosalía ☎615/157-0120. Located inside *Mario's Palapa Restaurant*, just south of the border crossing. Good resource for spur-of-the-moment trips.

△ Salt dunes around Guerrero Negro

Eating and drinking

Guerrero Negros doesn't make any attempt to impress when it comes to **dining**, and there is little to distinguish most of the dozen or so restaurants along Zapata. The only sit-down standout is *Malarrimo*, an Italian-tinged seafood restaurant in the motel/RV/tour complex of the same name (see p.176). The price is high (about M$200 for dinner), but the breezy patio, low-lit dining room and large portions make it worth the extra pesos; an adjoining bar is one of the few places in town where you can grab a beer and watch a game on television. There are cheaper options three blocks west on Zapata at *El Asadero Norteño*, where *carne asada* and more grilled meat tacos go for M$12 each. Next door to the bus station, you can eat huge M$160 shrimp platters and gaze at one of the region's salt flats from the motel *Don Gus*' restaurant (☎615/157-1611). *Ceviche Loco*, behind the Pemex on the north side of Zapata, has tacos *pescado* for M$8 as well as ceviche for M$17. On Saturday and Sunday, the town rids itself of its hangover with a bowl of goat stew at the busy, semi-permanent *Birria Biranda* cart on Zapata just east of the TechNet Internet cafe. *Supermercado La Ballena* on Zapata has a large stock of vegetables, fruits, breads and other staples you'll want to have in the car if you're continuing south on Mex 1. *Mallarrimo*'s only real rival is *Mario's*, Km 217 Mex 1 Guerrero Negro–Santa Rosalía (☎615/157-0788) near the border and *La Pinta*. The seafood-centric menu does basic Baja dishes like *ceviche* and tacos *pescado*, but at lower prices. There's a big beans and meat breakfast spread that's popular with Mexican truckers coursing the Transpeninsular.

Laguna Ojo de Liebre and Parque Natural de la Ballena Gris

The Vizcaíno biosphere's biggest attractions are the California gray whales that gather at **Laguna Ojo de Liebre**, outside of Guerrero Negro, and San Ignacio to the south. For thousands of years, the whales have made a yearly, 20,000km migration from the icy Bering Sea to calve in these shallow lagoons. **Parque**

Natural de la Ballena Gris, which surrounds the Laguna Ojo de Liebre, is nominally designed to protect the whales, but its shores fill up with increasing numbers of visitors each year, eager to ride out in *panga*s while more watch from towers along the coast.

Fortunately, the attention is largely benign, though it wasn't always the case. The grays had the lagoon to themselves until the whaling captain Charles Melville Scammon found a safe way into the lagoon in 1857. He quickly tore through the whales' baby calf nursery and killed every cetacean he could harpoon. Plenty of whalers rushed in, one of them being the *Black Warrior*, an overladen whaling ship that sank in 1858, spawned a dozen legends and gave the nearby town its name a hundred years later. After a dozen years of wanton slaughter (and amazing profits), Scammon became a naturalist – perhaps because he'd killed so many whales it was no longer a viable industry.

During the season there are organized **whale-watching trips** and observation towers that guarantee at least a distant sighting. Although every year talk turns to restricting numbers or banning tour boats altogether, there are currently more tour operators running **boat trips** than ever. If you can take one, then do so – it's an exceptional experience, and many visitors actually get close enough to touch the curious whales as they come right up to the bobbing vessels.

Practicalities

To get to the lagoon on your own, take Mex 1 Guerrero Negro–Santa Rosalía to Km 207, where a billboard with a whale on it heralds the exit. Drive 6km southwest to a salt company checkpoint and sign in; you're actually driving next to their saltpans at this point. In another 16km, turn right at the Y in the road and pay M$30 at the kiosk to enter Parque Natural de la Ballena Gris (park information ☎615/157-0025). To **watch the whales from the shore** you'll need to get up early or stay late, as they move out to the deeper water in the middle of the day. The observation towers are within walking distance of the parking lot, and they all provide good views of the lagoon, but their actual success depends upon where the whales end up congregating. If you'd like to go out in the lagoon, you can almost always find a *panga* boat pilot up along the shore who will take you out for around M$200 for two hours. There are rustic **campsites** along the southeast coast of the lagoon, but you'll need to bring everything you want to eat, drink or sleep in with you (M$30; pay at the park entrance when you arrive).

Santa Gertrudis

Many of the missions of Baja California Sur probably would not hold much interest elsewhere, but in comparison to those in the north, they're fascinating. And to be fair, in conjunction with the cave paintings in the Sierra de San Francisco, missions in the southern state such as the weathered yet solid **Santa Gertrudis** are some of the most significant remaining links to the peninsula's pre-18th century history.

Misión Santa Gertrudis, set in the foothills of the Sierra de San Francisco, was an offshoot of the successful Kadakaamán mission in San Ignacio (see p.184). The initial settlement was founded by a Jesuit and a blind native convert named Andres Comanaji Sistiaga. Their work in the area attracted a large number of Cochimí converts and convinced the leaders in San Ignacio that they should establish a more permanent presence. The Jesuits began constructing the mission complex in 1752, and the Dominicans finally finished the chapel in 1796. Disease eventually decimated the Indian population, and the site was abandoned in 1822 before the complex was finished.

The building identified as the chapel was originally a dispensary converted into a church after the original adobe chapel fell apart. For a dispensary in the desert, it's not too shabby: it's still adorned with the painted wooden confessional and fonts for baptisms and holy water. Carvings that mix Jesuit and Dominican symbols surround the doorways and exterior walls. A three-storey-high bell tower stands 50m from the mission, a cracked bell hanging from the crossbeam.

Getting to Santa Gertrudis requires a two-and-a-half-hour drive northeast off of Mex 1 Guerrero Negro–Santa Rosalía. Follow the exit to El Arco at Km 189 and drive 35km to El Arco. At the settlement, turn right and drive another 30km to the mission.

Moving on from Guerrero Negro

Buses from Guerrero Negro's bus station are irregular and often full upon arrival; buy your ticket at least a day in advance. The six services (one local) which head **north** to Tijuana (M$390), and the one to Mexicali, leave at night and early morning; the eight **southbound** services – two local, running all the way to La Paz (M$420) – depart either early in the morning or in the late afternoon and evening. The **taxis** at the stand in front of the blue and yellow Mercado Tianguis supermarket on Zapata adjust their rates depending on how long you'll have to wait for a bus – a ride to San Ignacio is about M$300 per person.

The Peninsula de Vizcaíno

Thanks to its relatively remote location, the **Peninsula de Vizcaíno** has remained largely undeveloped. Those who know its secrets – surfers, fishermen and boaters – don't talk about it a great deal, most likely because they know few people will make the considerable effort required to get to the **coast** or one of the nearby **islands**. If, though, you have either the time or the money to make it to the peninsula via a well-packed truck or your own boat or plane, there are kilometres of unspoilt beaches and world-class surfing and fishing. There are virtually no services, however, so come with plenty of food, water, camping equipment and at least one good spare tyre.

The coast

Two roads head west to **the coast** from Mex 1 Guerrero Negro–Santa Rosalía, one at Km 144 from the small town of Vizcaíno and another to the south at Km 102. The first route is a partially paved, three and a half hour slog westward to **BAHÍA DE TORTUGAS**, a refuelling station for boats plying the Pacific coast; the two thousand or so people who live here cater to boaters travelling either to or from Los Cabos and the US. The ramshackle town is a lifeline to not only US and Mexican boaters but to the tiny fish camps that line the coast here, attempting to haul in lobster, abalone and seaweed for export, and is worth a visit if you're after the ethereal "Baja experience". It's not advisable to drive out and back the same day, so book a room at either the a/c-free blue cinderblock *Motel Nancy*, Independencia 19 (☎615/158-0100; ❶) or slightly more appealing *Hotel and Restaurant Veracruz*, Av Juárez 43 (☎615/158-0410; ❷), where there are fans to keep you cooler. There's a small **airstrip** here and, if you're lucky, the **Pemex** station might have petrol. Dedicated surfers continue past Tortugas another 25km to **Punta Eugenia**, where they hire fishermen to take them to Isla Natividad's formidable breaks (see p.182). The northern coast, lined by the

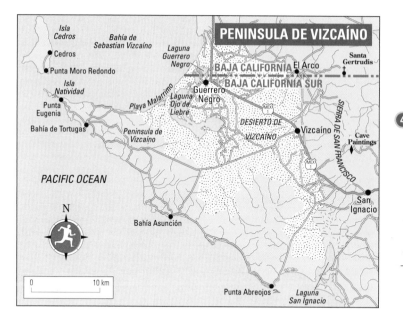

driftwood-strewn **Playa Malarrimo**, is a good hour-long drive northeast from Bahía Tortugas along a dirt and sand road. Because of ocean currents and the shape of the peninsula, the beach here attracts so many foreign objects it looks like a driftwood-strewn junkyard. This makes it rather unappealing to swim at, but people make the journey in hopes of finding messages in a bottle, a legend locals encourage. Fill up with petrol in **VIZCAÍNO** before moving on or, if you arrive after sunset, stay off the road at night and book a rooms at the recently expanded *Motel Olivia* (☎615/156-4524, ℱ615/154-0127; ❸) next door to *Restaurante Martha Seafood* and the open-air Sunday night market.

The second coastal route leads directly to **PUNTA ABREOJOS** after a 100km jaunt along a relatively well-paved road passable for every vehicle at the right speed. Abreojos, a town of 1200, began life in the 1930s as a fishing village with a handful of San Ignacio immigrants. In 1995, ESSA announced plans to built a concrete pier here and begin mining salt from the nearby Laguna San Ignacio. US environmental groups turned the proposal into a worldwide eco-battle, and after five years the Mexican government scrapped the project. Town residents were mixed about the result, but surfers certainly rejoiced. They come for the 300-metre rides, the right swells and east-facing breaks at Burgers and Razors, just off the shore in town. The beaches here are as lovely as they are remote, but you'll need a 4WD if you want to go any distance out of town to the more far-flung, equally scenic expanses of sand. The area immediately north of town is the most accessible, freer of *pangas* and, if you have a tent, a fine place to do some rustic camping. If you're not a surfer, there's nothing to keep you here but wave watching and shore-based whale watching. **Lodging** at Punta Abrejos is a casual affair. If there's nobody at *Campo René*, the only accommodation in town (no phone; ❸) when you arrive, just wait or wander into town and ask around for the owner. He'll gladly put you up in one of the twelve clean yet shack-like rooms and fill you with some of the freshest lobster and abalone from the nearby, protected fishery.

The islands

ISLA NATIVIDAD, a small island off the western tip of the peninsula, is home to a fishing cooperative of about eight hundred who sustain themselves with lobster and abalone catches off the island's coast. The only other business comes from the surfers who fly or boat in from May to October when southern swells produce beach-breaking barrels on the southeast corner of the island at Open Doors. Baja Air Ventures (Ⓦ www.bajaairventures.com) organizes fly-in trips from San Diego, but you can also hire a boat from Punta Eugenia for about M$600 a day. As with the peninsula, bring everything you need with you.

Barges from Guerrero Negro float out to **ISLA CEDROS**, about 20km northwest of Punta Eugenia, to transfer their cargo to freighters harboured in the island's deep-water port, Mexico's third largest. In addition to running the port, the islanders run a handful of restaurants and hotels popular with ESSA workers, fly-in guests, fishermen and organized eco-tourist groups. Though the island is no longer home to the cedar tree it was named after, the rare Cedros mule deer pretty much have free reign of the island, which is only populated in the southeastern villages of Punta Morro Redondo and Cedros. The biggest event on the island is the annual **Torneo de Pesca** yellowtail fishing tournament, held the first week of every July. Unless you're flying in your own plane, you'll need a place to stay between flights on Aero Cedros (from Ensenada and Guerrero Negro on Tuesdays and Fridays; ℡615/157-1626). *Hotel Zam-Mar*, Primero de Mayo 19-C (℡616/158-5527, Ⓦ www.qbrandi.net/zammar; ❸) offers seven rooms in the centre of Cedros, not far from the airstrip. Three rooms are singles and the four doubles have TV, two of them with Internet connections. Next door, *Restaurant El Marino* serves seafood caught by the local cooperative, including abalone when in season.

The Sierra de San Francisco

The black, white, yellow and rust-coloured *pinturas rupestres* (cave art) that adorn remote cave and mountain walls throughout Baja California remain, thousands of years after their creation, the peninsula's best-known artworks. The most extensive and compelling collection of drawings and paintings that's open to the public is on the eastern side of the Vizcaíno biosphere in the **SIERRA DE SAN FRANCISCO**. A UNESCO World Heritage Site since 1993, the mountain range contains over three hundred sites. It's impossible, though, to see more than a small sampling on one trip – attempting to visit more would require a series of guides who specialize in one section or another, not to mention enough water supplies for a few months in the wilderness.

Heat overwhelms the Sierra de San Francisco and the rest of the desert from July to mid-September; planning a tour during this time is a proposition best reconsidered. Guide-groups tailor visits to short, one-day tours or, for hardy travellers, multi-day treks that require camping. The one-day tours are exhausting and, if you're at all intrigued by what you see, will leave you feeling short-changed, as it takes a day and a half of hiking to begin to appreciate the vast scale of the paintings. If you have the time, money and strength for the journey, focusing an entire week-long tour of the area with an academic group is the best way to see the region.

That said, there are three very good sites that can be seen on a short trip. The most popular route leads to the 12 metre-long **Cueva del Ratón**, the most easily accessible site, and then along the Cañon de Santa Teresa to **Cueva de las Flechas** and on to the monumental **Cueva Pintada**, a 150 metre-long mural rising 50m high. Groups of black and red human figures gaze upon sheep, rabbit,

Art in the Sierra de San Francisco

All the studies of the **paintings** in the **Sierra de San Francisco** and elsewhere in Baja California have taken place within the last fifty years, and everyone seems to have their own idea about who created them and how old they are. A few of the murals in this part of the peninsula were written about by late-18th-century missionaries; at that time, the Cochimí Indians told them they were created by giants. The paintings were largely ignored until an amateur archaeologist named Harry Crosby started exploring them in the 1960s and subsequently publicizing his findings. *The Cave Paintings of Baja California*, Crosby's photo-heavy book chronicling his journeys, is essential reading prior to any trip of length.

Crosby's cheerleading eventually led to studies in 2003 by a team backed by the National Geographic Society. They concluded the paintings in the Sierra de San Francisco region were about 7500 years old – predating the Aztecs and any other known Mexican societies. This finding has sparked more interest in the paintings and has led to the discovery of hundreds of previously unknown sites, the majority of which are known only to archaeologists.

deer and other animals, and a few figures that resemble whales and turtles. As you penetrate further into the mountains, renderings of giant snakes, interpretive drawings of planets and stars, and rock engravings crop up with eerie precision.

Not getting lost is your first matter of concern; book a trip in advance through established and respected outfits like Kuyimá in San Ignacio (Ⓦ kuyima.com; all-inclusive tours for one day at M$720 and three days at M$4500) or Malarrimo in Guerrero Negro (see box, p.177; all-inclusive one-day M$900, three days M$4500). The solo yet not necessarily cheaper route involves registering for and obtaining a guide in San Ignacio at the INAH office next to the mission (Mon–Sat 8am–3pm; ☎615/154-0215). The cost of doing this depends on your negotiating skills and whether you have your own means of transportation to the mountains; it can be as little as M$400 per day if you have all the equipment you need, otherwise it gets into custom-tour territory and you will end up spending a lot without the peace of mind an established operator can provide. Organized trips will have their own transportation to the town of **SAN FRANCISCO** and up into the mountains. Once you arrive in the mountains you'll be walking or riding a donkey most of the way; never turn down the chance to load up your gear on a donkey.

The exit for San Francisco is clearly marked at Km 118 with an enormous sign as well as a clear path into the hills. From here it's another 37km along a dirt road to San Francisco itself, where you begin your hike into the sierra or, if you're spending more than one day here, loading up your backpack or pack mule for the journey. You can get basics here, but all real stocking should be done prior to arrival.

San Ignacio

Set in a valley crowded by date palms, **SAN IGNACIO**'s appeal is immediate even from a distance. Gone is the dust and concrete that defines the peninsula, replaced by green hues and a cool breeze; it's an oasis any desert traveller would hope for. In town, the central **Plaza Ecotourismo** plays hosts to concerts, festivals and children's soccer games, and is dominated by **San Ignacio de Kadakaamán**, a mission constructed of lava-block walls – carved out of the output from Volcan las Tres Virgenes to the east – over one metre thick.

Once the initial daze has worn off, San Ignacio still charms, but its limits can be quickly discerned. The streets are shaded but still paved with dirt, and

Whale-watching trips from San Ignacio

Visitors to Laguna San Ignacio must pass through the town of the same name, and all of the tour operators conducting **whale-watching trips** are conveniently located around its central plaza. Like in Laguna Ojo de Liebre (see p.178), the season begins in December and runs to the beginning of April. The going rate for a boat tour is M$450, but it quickly rises when you add food and transport from San Ignacio. More information about the lagoon is available on p.186.

The most respected operator in the region is **Ecoturismo Kuyimá**, C Morelos 23 (☎615/154-0070, ⓦwww.kuyima.com). They have a camp at the lagoon, with tents and clean palapas huts with solar power, three meals a day and mountain bikes and kayaks when you're sick of whales. The per-night fee is high (M$1800) but multi-night packages bring the price down, and include transport from San Ignacio.

a significant portion of the economy is dependent on tourists heading to the eponymous lagoon 60km away or to the Sierra de San Francisco. With the exception of its July festival celebrating patron saint San Ignacio de Loyola, the town is too low-key to keep your interest for long.

The first Spanish settlement on the site was founded by the Jesuit Juan Bautista Luyando in 1728, but the area had long been settled by the indigenous Cochimí, who knew enough not to set up camp in areas that would be swept away when the tiny stream flooded the valley. Once the missionaries found higher land, their settlement prospered and became the base of exploration for establishing missions farther north. Underneath the surfaced road between the highway and town is the small dam that the settlers built to form the lagoon that still sustains the town's agricultural economy, mostly based on the Mediterranean staples of figs, grapes, olives, limes and oranges and the now-ubiquitous date palm, first planted in 1765.

Life these days centres on the plaza and the seasonal traffic going to the lagoon. If you're stuck in town looking for something to do, there is some good hiking to the northeast on the **Mesa de la Cruz**, a small, well-shaded mesa between San Ignacio and the highway.

Misión San Ignacio Kadakaamán

Not only did the Jesuits who arrived here get along quite well with the Cochimí, but the newcomers incorporated the locals' own settlement name, Kadakaamán, into the church that they started in 1733 and the Dominicans finished in 1786. Like the name **Misión San Ignacio Kadakaamán** (daily 8am–4pm, mass Sun 11am; ☎615/154-0222), the final result is a mismatch of styles and materials, with lipstick red lines drawn on plaster to mimic bricks and a peeling facade, even though it was renovated in 1976 after the completion of the Transpeninsular Highway brought the town more attention.

Inside, the refreshingly bright chapel, aided both by stained-glass free transom windows and white-washed walls, is dominated by a gold altarpiece that reaches to the ceiling. Set into the altar are seven oil paintings, including one of the Virgin of Pilar, and a workmanlike execution of the church's patron saint San Ignacio de Loyola done in statue.

The INAH **Museo de Pinturas Rupestres** (Mon–Fri 8am–3pm, free; ☎615/154-0222) occupies an old church building immediately to the right upon exit. Large-format photographs mounted on light boxes and a half-scale replica of Cueva La Pintada illustrate the Sierra San Francisco and Sierra Giganta's compositions and offer a decent glimpse if you don't have the time to ride a donkey into the desert to see the real thing. There's also a small, permanent collection of exhibits related to the town's history. If you're inspired by the art, you're in luck; this is also where you get permission to visit the cave painting sites in the Sierra de San Francisco (see p.182).

Practicalities

San Ignacio is hidden by a sea of inviting, mirage-like green palm fronds from its exit at Km 74 of Mex 1 Guerrero Negro–Santa Rosalía – the town lies almost 3km south of the highway. If you've taken the **bus**, you're let off at this northern junction, and it's a good thirty-minute walk into town; the stop is actually San Lino, a little settlement anchored by the campground and restaurant *Rice & Beans,* just west of the intersection along a road parallel to the highway (☎615/154-0283; ❹). There are clean yet old rooms here, with hot showers, and outside, plenty of space to **camp** (M$50 per car and all passengers, M$110 if you want to use the showers). The hospitable owner is a long-time resident, and can organize numerous activities in and around San Ignacio. The restaurant serves an ample menu of excellent seafood and traditional Mexican dishes, from morning until night. Try the house speciality, *caldo de pescado*, a fish soup made from fresh local catch. If you just need a place for the night and can't make the trip into town, there's *Baja Oasis Motel*, Km 72.5 Mex 1 Guerrero Negro–Santa Rosalía (☎615/154-0111; ❸). Highway noise permeates the ten rooms, but you can drown it out with the a/c and TV.

Camping at *Ignacio Springs Bed and Breakfast* on the northern shore of Río San Ignacio (☎615/154-0333, ⓦignaciosprings.com; ❹ includes breakfast and kayaks) is a rather glamorous and comfortable affair. The well-appointed yurts have queen-size beds, tile floors, a/c and patios; some even have their own bath. Guests have use of kayaks and easy access to the only espresso in town. The ever-present *La Pinta* pops up between the river and plaza (☎615/154-0300, ⓦwww .lapintahotels.com; ❺). Rooms here are a bit more worn than in Guerrero Negro, but there's a pool. Some of the **trailer parks** along the highway and on the road into town have camping space; the most useful, *El Padrino* (☎615/154-0089), almost opposite the *La Pinta*, charges M$50 per person and has a pit toilet. In town, the unmarked *Posada San Ignacio*, Calle Carranza 22 (☎615/154-0100; ❸) is southwest of the plaza. Rooms are very simple, but the owners know the area quite well and can facilitate good whale-watching trips. If you can get in, the most enjoyable rooms in town are at the three-room *Casa Lerré* guest house, Calle Madero s/n (☎615/154-0158, ⓦwww.prodigyweb.net.mx/janebames/ index.html; no credit cards, ❸), you can't miss the bright blue exterior, and even if you don't stay here you wouldn't want to miss the little bookstore and the years of local wisdom packed in it. The guesthouse rooms are little more than clean, brightly painted rooms looking out on a courtyard, which has chickens.

For **food**, *Restaurant Chalita* on the central plaza has *chiles relleno* and locally raised beef. *Rene's*, just past the plaza on La Correa, serves *desayuna* to gringos' liking (scrambled eggs and French toast) along with *chilaquiles* and *huevos rancheros*. The *El Padrino* campground on the lake serves seafood-centric dishes on the waterfront for about M$85 per person.

There are **no banks** in town, few places accept credit cards and people are reluctant to take travellers' cheques. There is, though, **Internet access** on the north side of the plaza at *Internet Café & Tour Service*. The Tienda Nuevos Almacenes Mesa general store, on the main road one block north of the square, sells hats, drinks, maps, machetes, camping gear and anything else you'd need before heading down to the lagoon or into the Sierra de San Francisco.

Parque Natural de la Laguna de San Ignacio

Because it's free of industrial operations and the sight of any permanent human settlements, the marshy **PARQUE NATURAL DE LA LAGUNA DE SAN IGNACIO** is a better place to witness the biodiversity of the Vizcaíno biosphere than Laguna Ojo de Liebre to the north. The lagoon's total coastline is just shy of 400km, over three-fourths of which are covered with mangrove trees and palm trees. The shores attract green sea turtles and pronghorn antelope on land, and osprey, peregrine falcons and over two hundred more bird species nest in the trees around its shores. The real attraction, though, are the gray whales that migrate here annually from December to early April to give birth and to feed and nurse their calves in the lagoon's shallow waters.

Like Laguna Ojo de Liebre, Laguna San Ignacio is best visited with a guide (see box, p.184). The lagoon is reached from a rutted dirt road that runs 65km south from San Ignacio's southeast corner. Instead of going back into San Ignacio to reach Mex 1, you can drive southeast towards San Juanico. This **alternate coastal route** along the Pacific used to be the main road, and there's always talk that it will one day be paved to provide a secondary route to Mex 1. For now, it's just dirt and sand for 142km until La Purísma (see p.213), where the paved BC 53 takes over for another 85km until it hits Mex 1 at Ciudad Insurgentes.

If you'd like to stay overnight, the area's numerous birds and frogs produce a rather surreal, rainforest-like soundtrack in the middle of a desert. The Kumiyá campground (see box, p.184) accepts drop-ins for M$110 for four people tent **camping** with your own gear, M$440 for two if you need to use theirs. It is possible to drive in for the day, park on the shore and watch from there without paying a thing, but your visiting time will be restricted by the commute back to your accommodation – and whales don't always stick to schedule.

Travel details

Buses

Both Guerrero Negro and San Ignacio have bus stops; in the former it's conveniently located on the main drag, in the latter it's on Mex 1, a thirty-minute walk to town. From both towns, travellers sometimes have to wait a day or two for a bus with available seats. All buses stop in both towns and follow the same path along Mex 1 with final stops in Tijuana or Los Cabos.
Guerrero Negro and **San Ignacio** to: Northbound towns (6 daily; from Guerrero Negro 9 ½ hours to Ensenada, 13 hours to Tijuana), southbound towns (8 daily; from Guerrero Negro 6 ½ hours to La Paz; 8 ½ to San José del Cabo)

Flights

There are no commercial flights from either Guerrero Negro or San Ignacio; Loreto is the closest commercial airport. Charter flights, often with Aereo Calafia (☎624/143-4302, ⓦaereocalafia.com) depart from Guerrero Negro's airport for Isla Cedros, Santa Rosalía, Bahía Magdalena, Loreto and Los Cabos.

The central coast

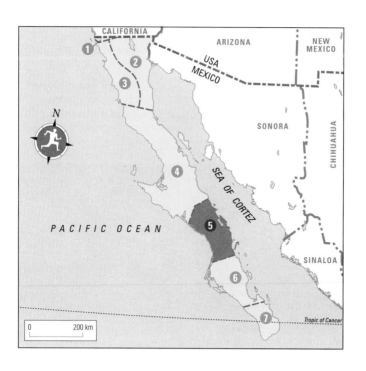

CHAPTER 5   # Highlights

△ Mulegé

5

The central coast

The **central coast** between Santa Rosalía and Loreto – California's first Spanish and indigenous town – captures the spirit of Baja better than anywhere else. Nestled between the Sea of Cortez and the **Sierra de Guadalupe** and **Sierra de La Giganta** mountain ranges, the region is defined by the crisp turquoise waters of the sea and the drama of the peaks to the west.

The principal towns along the coast – **Mulegé** and **Loreto** – may not have the most cosmopolitan restaurants, hotels or shops, but they deliver customizable experiences that fit a wide array of budgets. You can snorkel with dolphins in the morning, hike to a cave-painting site in the afternoon and dance the night away before hitting the sack at either a campground or a lavish hotel. Both towns were constructed before the car replaced the pedestrian, and walking remains the preferred method of seeing what each has to offer. With one of the peninsula's best museums, Loreto has embraced its missionary past while Mulegé's done not much more than kept the colonial downtown free of such modern intrusions as ATM machines and reliable bus service.

These towns are joined on the coast by **Santa Rosalía**, located right where the southbound Transpeninsular Highway runs up against the Sea of Cortez for the first time. A former regional mining powerhouse, Santa Rosalía now has the look and feel of a forgotten Caribbean colony; immediately evident in the architectural traces of its past, from the still-occupied workers' shacks built in a ravine to the grand mansions on the town's mesa. **Bahía el Islote de San Lucas** between Santa Rosalía and Mulegé and **Bahía Concepción** farther south are kayaking meccas as well as ideal locales to camp with little interference from the outside world. The glassy, blue waters of Bahía Concepción are spoken of in reverent terms by its visitors, much more so than any of the area's dismal cultural offerings could match. To the south in **Parque Nacional Bahía de Loreto** – Mexico's largest marine park – *panga* boats headed to one of the islands' snorkelling sites are likely to be trailed by dolphins. Inland, the little-visited mission of **San Javier** and the ignored towns of both **Comondú** and **La Purísima** are welcome reminders that all life doesn't take place near Mex 1.

Santa Rosalía and around

The brown of the surrounding land is eclipsed by the stunning blue hues of the Sea of Cortez, as Mex 1 takes a windy and precipitous descent for 3km – a segment known as *Cuesa del Infierno* ("Grade to hell") – before emerging on the coast just north of **SANTA ROSALÍA**. An odd little town wedged in the narrow river

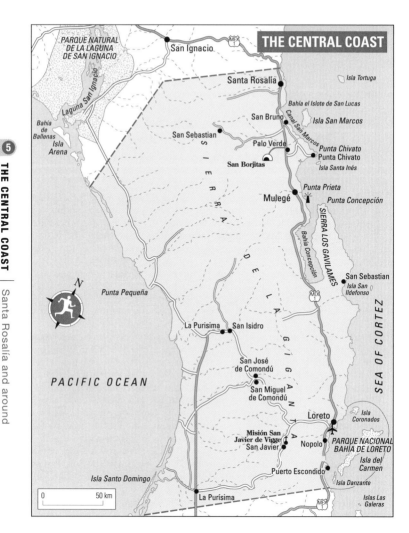

THE CENTRAL COAST

PARQUE NATURAL DE LA LAGUNA DE SAN IGNACIO

San Ignacio

Santa Rosalía

Isla Tortuga

Bahía el Islote de San Lucas

San Bruno

Canal San Marcos

Isla San Marcos

San Sebastian

Palo Verde

Punta Chivato
Punta Chivato

San Borjitas

Isla Santa Inés

Bahía de Ballenas

Isla Arena

Laguna San Ignacio

Punta Prieta

Mulegé

Punta Concepción

SIERRA

Bahía Concepción

SIERRA LOS GAVILANES

DE

San Sebastian

Isla San Ildefonso

N

Punta Pequeña

LA

GIGANTA

La Purisima   San Isidro

San José de Comondú

San Miguel de Comondú

Loreto

Isla Coronados

PACIFIC OCEAN

SEA OF CORTEZ

Misión San Javier de Vigge
San Javier

Nopolo

PARQUE NACIONAL BAHÍA DE LORETO

Isla del Carmen

Puerto Escondido

Isla Santo Domingo

0   50 km

La Purísima

Isla Danzante

Islas Las Galeras

valley of the Arroyo de Santa Rosalía, it was built in 1885 around a port used to ship copper from the nearby hillside mines of the French-run El Boleo company (see box, p.193). The French left in 1954, and nowadays the mines are virtually exhausted and the smelters stand idle, though much of the massive equipment lines Mex 1 and the surrounding hills, including parts of a rusting narrow-gauge railway. The government has long claimed to be developing a plan to employ modern techniques to extract the last of the ore from the five million tonnes of tailings, a move that would provide a much needed financial boost to a community that subsists on revenue from fishing and the gypsum mines on the Isla de San Marcos to the south. To date, however, little real progress has been made on this front.

Santa Rosalía has somewhat of a transient feel, like a Wild West town in freeze-frame. The town's undeniable charm is largely successful at luring tourists for a day or so as they make their way across the peninsula. The one-way streets are narrow and crowded, and conceal small architectural delights, such as a **nineteenth-century pre-fab church**. Former miners' houses and small businesses catering to locals constitute the bulk of the town, filling the river valley running at right angles to the coast. Known as La Playa, the neighbourhood resembles a colonial Caribbean village, with cheap, clapboard panelling and low-angled zinc and steel roofs over hibiscus-flanked porches. Historic yet shuttered mining buildings and formerly grand residences of the managers rim the expanse of the Mesa Francia hill above town. Every year, the city holds the **Festival Fundadores**, a two-week-long birthday celebration at the end of October that takes over the downtown streets with carnival rides, stages for bands and every food vendor within 200km.

Arrival and information

Mex 1 enters Santa Rosalía in both directions from along the coast, passing between Santa Rosalía's harbour and the eastern border of the triangle-shaped **Parque Morelos**. Five avenidas – the main commercial drag Obregón, along with Constitución, Carranza, Sarabia and Montoya – run inland from the coast, crossing the numbered *calles* that intersect at right angles.

The **ferry terminal** lies two minutes' walk south of Parque Morelos; the ferry arrives from Guaymas in Sonora on Tuesday, Wednesday, Friday and Sunday mornings. The terminal also serves as the town's transport and **information** hub: **taxis** wait here and ABC and Águila **buses** use the parking lot to drop off and receive passengers. **Bus** riders are dropped here too, which makes it one of the few centrally located stations on the entire peninsula.

Accommodation

Nothing is too expensive in Santa Rosalía, and paying M$50–100 a night will make a real difference in the quality of the level of **accommodation**. For a

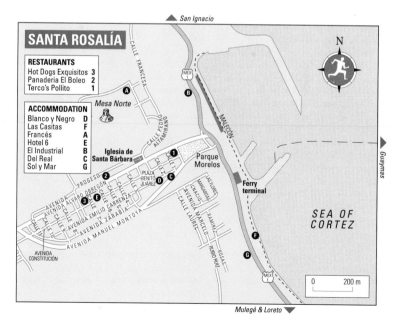

SANTA ROSALÍA

San Ignacio

N

RESTAURANTS
Hot Dogs Exquisitos 3
Panaderia El Boleo 2
Terco's Pollito 1

ACCOMMODATION
Blanco y Negro   D
Las Casitas   F
Francés   A
Hotel 6   E
El Industrial   B
Del Real   C
Sol y Mar   G

Mesa Norte

Iglesia de
Santa Bárbara

Parque
Morelos

Ferry
terminal

SEA OF
CORTEZ

Guaymas

0   200 m

Mulegé & Loreto

view of the water, stay on Mex 1 or the mesa north of town; the downtown rooms can get pretty hot in the summer months.

Blanco y Negro C 3a at Av Sarabia ☎615/152-0080. The cheapest rooms at this longtime backpacker's favourite share a bathroom, and the more expensive ones have televisions and full baths. ❸

Francés C Jean Cousteau 8 ☎ & ☏615/152-2052. Built in 1886 at the top of Mesa Norte, this hotel is one of the few historic buildings the public can get into (but it'll cost you M$15 if you're not a guest). The wood panelled lobby smells of pine oil and antiques and the rooms, seventeen matchless creations featuring more stained wood as well as upholstered wall panels, are worth the little bit extra for their relative luxury. ❺

El Industrial 1km north of Parque Morelo on Mex 1 ☎615/152-1078. Across from the malecón, this basic motor inn has a western theme going on the exterior and rooms with a/c and TVs; there's also a gated parking lot. ❸

Las Casitas Km 195 Mex 1 Santa Rosalía–Loreto ☎615/152-3023, ⓦsantarosaliacasitas.com. It's a short, ten-minute walk from downtown, but the excellent views of the sea from its hillside perch make the trip worthwhile. The large, ceramic tiled rooms have modern amenities and large windows overlooking the water. ❹

Del Real Av Montoya at C Playa ☎615/152-0068. Trusty combination of cheap and charming; rooms have TV and a/c, and coffee be taken on the plantation-style front porch. ❸

Sol y Mar Km 195.5 Mex 1 Santa Rosalía–Loreto ☎615/152-2025. A pink stucco exterior manages to provide some distinction for this one-storey motor inn and its plain yet clean rooms. There's off-street parking, a *taquería* and views of the port. ❸

The Town

Except when a ferry is arriving, Santa Rosalía has surprisingly little waterfront activity for a port town. Instead, people busy themselves along the narrow and lively one-way streets and small plazas inland. Crammed in a narrow valley, the grid of one-way streets moves inland from the coast and forms a long, thin downtown area. To orientate yourself, start in Parque Morelos and walk down Obregón, a one-way, one-lane street that goes away from the water. At Obregón and Calle 5a you'll find the city's favourite *boulangerie*, the **Panadería El Boleo** with a small museum in a former warehouse next door that has a permanent exhibit of faded photographs from the early twentieth century; the bakery's rolls are the more diverting of the two.

Alexandre-Gustave Eiffel's prefabricated iron church, **Iglesia de Santa Bárbara**, Obregón at Calle Altamirano (daily 8am–10pm), was originally a prototype displayed at the 1889 Paris World's Fair. He had hoped to manufacture and sell them as missionaries sought ever more converts in new colonial territories in Africa and Southeast Asia. The colonial powers weren't buying, though, and Eiffel's church in a box went back in the box until a Boleo mining exec heard about how he could get a cheap church for his workers in Santa Rosalía. The exterior filigrees and eaves look like they were fashioned in a giant metal punch press; trompe l'oeil mixed with a movie set. Inside the church has the appearance of an upturned boat backlit by stained glass. Still, the town is proud of its church, and it regularly serves as the backdrop for parties in the adjacent square.

Central Santa Rosalía is too crowded to permit many reminders of its mining past, though remnants of the French mining town overlook downtown from atop the hill. With the exception of *Hotel Francés*, none of the buildings is open to the public, but it's still worth the stroll, if only for the stunning views of the town below, the mining project to the west, and the sea to the south. To get to the hilltop, turn right at the church and walk up the brightly coloured staircase near the school until you hit the curvy, climbing Calle Pedro Altamirano. The street dumps you off on a quiet cobblestone boulevard lined along its centre with vintage smelting pots, locomotives and transport cars.

The ocean and the sea

Providing the perfect foil to Baja California's arid interior, the pristine waters that surround it are supremely inviting any time of the year. Never far away no matter where you are on the peninsula, the Pacific Ocean and the Sea of Cortez beckon adventurers with spectacular surfing, serene kayaking, and some of the world's best spots for whale watching. And with 3300 kilometres of coastline, Baja California offers near limitless opportunities to get on and go under the water.

Whale watching

Each December **California gray whales** migrate to lagoons along Baja California's western coast and stay in the area until late March or early April, when they return home to the Bering Sea, some with a newly born calf in tow. The arrival of the whales in the placid warm waters near Guerrero Negro, San Ignacio and Bahía Magdalena heralds the start of the peninsula's renowned **whale-watching** season. Numerous companies based in California, northwest Baja California and the central coast arrange multi-day **camping excursions** to the lagoon's coasts where visitors board shallow *panga* boats and motor into the middle of the waters to observe mother whales coaching their young calves. For the leery, there are observation towers along the shore, while larger boats depart

The flukes of gray whales off the coast of Baja California

Ensenada in the early winter and early spring to follow the migrating whales. And there's always the sunset margarita and whale-watching **cocktail hour** at the top of the *Finisterra Hotel* in Cabo San Lucas.

Choosing a tour company that operates out of San Ignacio is often the best route to take if you want to see the whales and are able to plan ahead: a number have camps they return to each year and are much more dependable and easier to sort through than the legion of independent operators – who aren't necessarily bad – that you'll find if you want to take a day-trip.

Underwater

There are men and women who've spent a lifetime **scuba diving** and **snorkelling** around the peninsula and its islands, and it's safe to say that they have seen Baja California's wonders as no landlubber ever will. These explorers, a diverse mix of divers from all over the world, know about underwater sandfalls, the giant manta rays of the remote Islas Revillagigedo and the playful sea lion community of Isla Espíritu Santo. Most of the underwater action takes place in the placid Sea of Cortez, which is home to two protected marine parks. Over eight hundred species of marine life thrive in the larger of the two parks, **Parque Marino Nacional Bahía de Loreto**, which takes in the equivalent of half a million acres of water around Loreto and

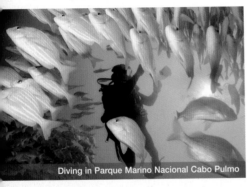

Diving in Parque Marino Nacional Cabo Pulmo

five large islands. Further south, at **Cabo Pulmo** along the eastern cape, lies North America's largest living Pacific **coral reef**, where underwater visibility can range up to 100 feet. It's remote and difficult to access even by Baja standards, and tends to keep away all but the most devoted.

Anyone who **dives** in the Sea of Cortez will tell you that Mulegé, Loreto and La Paz have some of the most helpful dive instructors as well as realistic pricing for what you'll be doing. There are places to rent equipment in each town and plenty to keep you busy while you plan your next trip underwater.

Kayaking the Sea of Cortez

The possibilities of gliding through the aquamarine waters of the Sea of Cortez on a **kayak** range from the relaxing to the epic. Below are a few of the best, but you can't go wrong anywhere on the coast.

Best extended trip: Mulegé to La Paz. Plenty of kayakers do a portion of this journey, but only hardcore kayakers know how to pack enough water and gear for this nearly 200km-long journey along the peninsula's most beautiful stretch of coastline.

Best island tour: Isla Carmen circumnavigation. It usually takes a week of camping and paddling to make the 100km journey around the largest island in the Parque Marino Nacional Bahía de Loreto.

Best place to learn: Bahía Concepción. The appeal of kayaking will be immediate in the glassy waters of Bahía Concepción, and once you've got into the swing of it, there's a tranquil bay full of tiny islands to explore just a few leagues away.

Best place to see wildlife: Bahía Magdalena. The peninsula's largest saltwater bay is filled with migrating birds, dolphins and, in the winter, breeding gray whales – all of which you stand a good chance of paddling alongside.

On the water

With its powerful, erratic waves and unpredictable undercurrents, the Pacific Ocean is largely the exclusive domain of **surfers**. Finding the right impact zone along this rugged coastline requires both research and word-of-mouth insight. There are, however, a few easy-to-get-to spots – Salsipuedes in the north and Todos Santos in the south – and in between you'll need to hook up with a regular (or read the right surfing websites) to discover the best time to hit the hidden locales off the Peninsula de Vizcaíno. To ensure that your only worry is the waves once there be sure to prepare like the locals

Catching a wave, Isla Natividad

Bahía Concepción

and bring first-aid kits, food and water to last for days, camping gear and a 4WD that can handle off-road tracks.

Kayaking is perhaps the most inviting activity on the peninsula for the water novice; rentals are relatively cheap and the tranquil waters of the Sea of Cortez are generally accommodating. Bahía de Concepción south of Mulegé and Bahía de los Ángeles halfway between San Felipe and Santa Rosalía are the calmest and most enjoyable places to ease into the water, and you could ply the waters here for months without ever tiring of the scenery. The Sea of Cortez can whip up some pretty mean, unexpected storms, though, so be sure to speak to experts before heading out and heed their advice.

The growing popularity of **sport fishing** in the 1980s and 1990s created a genuine threat to the aquatic life you'll encounter in the Sea of Cortez. Though the threat hasn't disappeared, it has dissipated since a large number of local operators between Loreto and the eastern cape began instituting catch-and-release policies in the late 1990s. For amateurs,

Panga, Cabo Pulmo

sport-fishing charters can be daunting due to high prices and plain unfamiliarity with the process. Fortunately, outside of Cabo San Lucas, there are a number of reputable local operators that run affordable group trips with equipment and licence fees included, usually in conjunction with a US-based package company. **Pros** also tend to stay away from Cabo, opting either for some of the same trips that work well for amateurs or for longer, more involved tips to distant Pacific waters.

Santa Rosalía's copper mines

While walking in the hills in 1868, local fisherman José Villavicencio chanced upon a **boleo**, a blue-green globule of rock that proved to be just a taster of a mineral vein containing more than twenty percent **copper**. By 1880 the wealth of the small-scale mining concessions came to the notice of the Rothschilds, European über-capitalists who provided finance for the French El Boleo company to buy the rights and found a massive extraction and smelting operation. Six hundred kilometres of tunnels were dug, a foundry was shipped over from Europe, and a new wharf was built to transport the smelted ore north to Washington State for refining. Ships returned with lumber for the construction of a new town, whose houses were laid out in a manner proportionate with their occupier's status within the company. Water was piped from the Santa Agueda oasis 15km away and labour was brought in: Yaqui from Sonora as well as two thousand Chinese and Japanese who supposedly found that Baja was too arid to grow rice and soon headed off to the Mexican mainland. By 1954, falling profits from the nearly spent mines forced the French to sell the pits and smelter to the Mexican government who, though the mines were left idle, continued to smelt ore from the mainland until the early 1990s.

If you fancy a short desert walk, pick a cool part of the day and make a circuit of what remains of the mining equipment and the tunnels that riddle the hills to the north. None of the mines is fenced, so take a flashlight and explore cautiously. Following Calle Altamirano from the Iglesia Santa Bárbara, you reach the massive kilometre-long above-ground duct, built of furnace slag, which once conveyed fumes from the smelter to the hilltop stack. You can walk along the top of it to the chimney for a superb view of the town and surrounding desert. From here, choose one of the numerous paths that head away inland to a series of gaping maws in the hillside. You can return the same way or pick your way straight down to the town or, with enough time, continue among the low cacti on the mesa, working your way down to the top end of Santa Rosalía.

Eating and drinking

Sadly, no French restaurants remain, but the *Panadería El Boleo* on Obregón produces some of the better baked goods in these parts, even if the baguettes aren't as crisp as the real thing. In general, though, Santa Rosalía's **restaurants** offer much less than other towns of the same size and focus on simple executions of street-food basics. You can eat large and inexpensive portions of grilled chicken at *Terco's Pollito*, Obregón at Calle Playa. The porch of the *Hotel del Real* is a wonderful spot in the mornings, with a good coffee and breakfast selection; they will prepare *huevos* any way you like them. Several inexpensive places are scattered along Obregón, many selling basic fish and seafood tacos. Try *Hot Dogs Exquisitos* on Calle 6 just down from the *Hotel 6*, where you can enjoy a filling evening meal as you watch TV outside with the family who runs the joint. *Restaurant Regio*, on the highway just as you come into town, serves as the local truck stop; they have tacos and quesadillas for M$10.

Listings

Banks Banamex and Bancomer stand on opposite corners of Constitución at C Vicente Guerrero. Both have ATMs. Bancomer changes cheques until noon, and Banamex accepts only bills until 1pm. If you are heading south, note that Mulegé does not have a bank and that Santa Rosalía will be your last chance to withdraw money until Loreto.

Books Librería Nuñez Brooks, C 3a at Obregón, has books and magazines in English.

Internet access *Café Internet Vision*, on C 6 just off Obregón (Mon–Sat 10am–2pm & 4–10pm; M$15/hr), and its sibling *Café Internet*, on Obregón and Playa (Mon–Sat 9am–9pm; M$15/hr).

Phones There's a public phone outside the *Hotel del Real*.

Post office Constitución at C 2.

Moving on from Santa Rosalía

If you're leaving town by **car**, filling up on petrol isn't essential; Mulegé is only 60km to the south. The **ferry** leaves for Guaymas in Sonora Tuesday and Thursday at 9pm and Friday and Sunday at 8pm. Although there are sometimes specials at M$400, typical fare is M$650 (reservations ℡615/152-1246, US℡1-800/505-5018, ⓦwww.ferrysantarosalia.com). Buy your ticket in advance and, if you're taking your car, ensure that your papers are in order for the mainland (see Basics on p.22). If you've got your own boat, the town's **marina** has fifteen slots for guests (℡615/152-0011).

Bus riders can cool their heels at the ferry terminal; only the daily 5pm to Tijuana originates here. All others are *de paso* – you can only buy tickets on board, not in advance – and may at times be full, though if you arrive early enough the friendly staff can generally call ahead to locate a seat for you. Northbound buses call in the evening or very early in the morning, while those heading south stop mostly in the late morning and late evening. Getting on buses from central Baja California is always difficult and makes an otherwise quite pleasant transpeninsular bus ride very frustrating. If you cannot get a bus, one popular – and sometimes faster – option if you're going to other parts of the US or Mexico is to take the ferry to the larger Sonoran city of **Guaymas** and then a bus north to Arizona or south along the coast to the Pacific beaches. Guaymas' station is at Calle 14 and Rodríguez, and serves the Tres Estrellas, Norte de Sonora and Baldamero Corral lines (℡622/224-2949).

Santa Rosalía to Mulegé

Although not as breathtaking as Bahía Concepción farther south, the coast between Santa Rosalía and Mulegé has a handful of campsites that offer south-bound travellers their first opportunity to swim, fish and kayak since Bahía de los Ángeles. The rocky shores directly adjacent to Santa Rosalía are poor options for campers, and anyone who wants to be near the water comes down to **Bahía el Islote de San Lucas**, where there are two big RV parks as well as a smaller one that's more hospitable to tent campers. The first, and most comfortable option, *RV Camacho*, is reached by exiting at Km 181 Mex 1 Santa Rosalía–Loreto and taking a left at the fork. The RV park has a store, hot-water showers and toilets (℡615/155-4063; ❶). Taking a right at the fork brings you to *RV Park San Lucas Cove* (no phone; ❶), which has a better position on the bay and a longer beach than *Camacho*. Just down the road at Km 178, *Playa Dos Amigos* (℡615/152-1020; ❶) has a wide beach and fewer trailers than its northern neighbours.

Heading south, Mex 1 hugs the coastline and then cuts inland as **Punta Chivato** juts directly eastward into the Sea of Cortez. With the exception of the *Posada de las Flores* (see opposite) resort, lodging here is limited to tents or trailers and you'll need to bring one of those (as well as all your supplies) if you want to stay overnight. It is, though, close enough to both Santa Rosalía and Mulegé to allow for a short dip or paddle in the morning or afternoon before heading to either town for dinner or night's sleep. Although there are no outfitters renting equipment, it is possible to approach long-term residents and, if they like the look of you, strike a bargain for a day's rental of a kayak.

5

Two roads ply the rocky distance out to the tip of Punta Chivato: the first is rough but well marked, the second is better but easy to miss. The first route is accessed at the turnoff to San Bruno and near a small settlement with palm trees, homes by the water and an RV park. There's a picturesque view of Isla San Marcos and the ships that pass between the island and mainland along the Canal Marítimo San Marcos. The scenic yet bumpy coastal route meets up with the second Punta Chivato road after 20km and a handful of left turns. This second road isn't well marked at its junction with Mex 1, so keep your eyes peeled for eastbound roads when passing through the village of Palo Verde. *Posada de las Flores*, Km 155 Santa Rosalía–Loreto, after 3.5km turn right at the fork (☎615/153-0188, ⓦposadadelasflores.com; breakfast, dinner and room ❾) is 17km from the highway along a bumpy dirt road. Few trailers make it this far out, so the campground – another 1km past the resort – cedes the better plots to tent campers. The resort itself is made up of eighteen rooms and suites, and offers a pool, restaurant, satellite TV, Internet access and free use of sporting equipment, which includes mountain bikes, kayaks and tennis racquets.

There is a small **cave painting site** found by exiting Mex 1 at the sign for Santa Aqueda at Km 189. Follow the road 35km to *Rancho Candelaria* and upon arrival ask if a staffer can take you to the site.

Mulegé

Tucked into a lush valley at an elbow bend in Mex 1, the dirt streets and low-slung buildings of **MULEGÉ** reach around both sides of the Río Mulegé estuary toward the Sea of Cortez. Palm trees bestow Mulegé with a discernible tropical air, and the laid-back lifestyles of its inhabitants reinforce this first impression. The town's orchards and farms produce much of the region's fruits and vegetables, while the sea and estuary cater to kayakers and divers who prefer its vibe to the comparatively hectic pace of Loreto or La Paz to the

△ Río Mulegé

south. There's a healthy sense of history, too, from the restored mission that looks over the town from a hill on its west end to the tours of the cave paintings in the nearby Sierra de Guadalupe.

The area around the mouth of the Río Mulegé had long been settled prior to the arrival of the Jesuits in 1705. The original Cochimí settlement of about two thousand people was called *Caamanc-ca-galejá*, roughly translated as "big ravine of the white mouth", and they survived largely on fishing and small-scale agriculture. The first Spaniard to see it was Loreto's founder Juan María de Salvatierra, who passed through on his way back from Sonora to his city in 1702 and decided to build a mission west of the estuary. By 1782 disease had decimated the Cochimí's numbers, and the town no longer held much importance for missionaries. Its enviable location alongside fresh water and amidst fruit-bearing trees, however, ensured that it remained an important settlement. In 1847 during the US–Mexican War, the US army occupied the city for a day after a brief battle near the mouth of the estuary. History since then has been uneventful, so much so that many accounts of the city, from John Steinbeck to Walt Wheelock (see Contexts, p.293), refer to the firm belief amongst outsiders that the entire town's population suffers from a local strain of malaria.

Arrival and information

Part of Mulegé's charm comes from its narrow, one-way dirt streets that branch eastward from Mex 1 and surround both sides of the estuary. Although it's difficult to find where you're going at first crack, the town's compact layout will keep you from wandering lost for too long. The streets' slimness prevents large trucks or cars with trailers from operating easily, or at all, in the town itself; scout your route ahead of time if you're driving in anything larger than an SUV. There are two **Pemex** stations in and around town: one in town on Avenida Martínez and another 2.5km south of town along Mex 1.

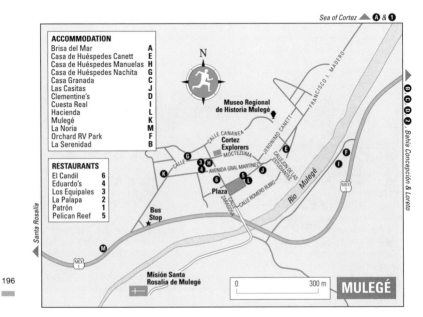

ACCOMMODATION
Brisa del Mar	A
Casa de Huéspedes Canett	E
Casa de Huéspedes Manuelas	H
Casa de Huéspedes Nachita	G
Casa Granada	C
Las Casitas	J
Clementine's	D
Cuesta Real	I
Hacienda Mulegé	K
La Noria	M
Orchard RV Park	F
La Serenidad	B

RESTAURANTS
El Candil	6
Eduardo's	4
Los Equipales	3
La Palapa	2
Patrón	1
Pelican Reef	5

Sea of Cortez ▲ Ⓐ & ❶

Museo Regional de Historia Mulegé

Cortez Explorers

Plaza

Bus Stop ★

Misión Santa Rosalía de Mulegé

0 — 300 m

MULEGÉ

Santa Rosalía ◀

Río Mulegé

▶ Ⓑ Ⓒ Ⓓ ❷, Bahía Concepción & Loreto

The **bus stop** is at the triangle junction of Mex 1 and Martínez, a good ten-minute walk southwest of downtown; to get to the centre, follow Mex 1 to the right fork onto Martínez, then a second right onto Zaragoza and the plaza.

Accommodation

While **places to stay** in Mulegé are not plush, their proprietors are armed with a body of local knowledge and are able to provide expert advice on dive sites, kayak rentals and local tour guides. Geographically, the options are spread across town, though any place with a pool is likely to be off Mex 1 on the south side. There are sometimes too few beds to meet the weekend demands during high season, so be sure to book ahead if you're travelling between November and April. Cash is the preferred method of payment at the smaller inns and guesthouses, but many accept major credit cards.

Brisa del Mar 2km from town square on the north side of the Río Mulegé ☎615/153-0089, ✉hotelbrisadelmar@prodigy.net.mx. This imposing 16-room hotel set on a hill near the sea on the fringes of town offers excellent views and a cool breeze. Rooms have a 1970s feel, as well as private bath, a/c, TV and views of the river or sea. ❸

Casa de Huéspedes Canett C Playa s/n ☎615/153-0272; **Casa de Huéspedes Manuelas** C Moctezuma s/n ☎615/153-0175; **Casa de Huéspedes Nachita** C Moctezuma s/n ☎615/153-0140. These three guesthouses offer the same level of comfort as a basic youth hostel; each one has a handful of rooms with shared baths and no a/c. The service, though, is quite hospitable. ❶

Casa Granada Estero de Mulegé 1 ☎615/153-0688, ⓦwww.casagranada.net. This four-bedroom B&B on the south side of the estuary is the closest accommodation to both the sea and the estuary. Rooms, with exposed brick walls and tile floors, have full baths, a/c and unobstructed views of the sea. ❺

Las Casitas C Madero 50 ☎615/153-0019, ✉lascasitas1962@hotmail.com. The former home of Mexican poet José Gorosave has its charms, like a fruit-tree-packed yard and dribbling fountains. The restaurant is excellent and the staff can help arrange dive and kayak trips in the estuary and sea. ❸

Clementine's Estero de Mulegé 507 ☎615/153-0319, ⓦclementinesbaja.com. This B&B has four rooms with private baths, in addition to two houses that rent by the week or month, all with high-speed Internet access. Guests have unlimited use of the kitchen, docks, bicycles and kayaks, as well as grills that dot the property. ❹

Cuesta Real Km 132 Mex 1 Santa Rosalía–Loreto ☎615/153-0321. Well-kept 1970s-style motor inn on the south side of town and steps away from the estuary. The white-tile floor rooms have a/c and TV, and outside there's a pool, a small restaurant near the water and Internet access in the office. ❹

Hacienda C Madero 3 ☎615/153-0021. A family-run hotel with 23 simple doubles with private bath and a/c in modest surroundings as well as modest prices, considering there's also a small pool, pleasant courtyard and parking. ❸

Mulegé C Moctezuma 15 ☎615/153-0090, 615/153-0555. Recent renovations and the addition of a bar have given life to this older standby with less-weathered furnishings and a/c. Although it's at the beginning of the main street into town it remains rather quiet. ❹

La Noria Mex 1 at Domingo Conocido ☎615/153-0195. Sixteen very bland, somewhat dusty rooms with a/c face a noisy bend in the highway. It's the closest hotel to the bus station and best as a late-hour option on crowded weekends. ❷

Orchard RV Park Km 133 Mex 1 Santa Rosalía–Loreto ☎615/153-0300, ⓦwww.orchardvacationvillage.com. Permanent and temporary trailer residents pack *Orchard's* shaded park, and there is a separate area for tent camping. The park rents out canoes and other equipment, and also has deals on one- and two-bedroom *casita* rentals by both the night and week. Camping ❶, *casitas* ❸

La Serenidad Km 139 Mex 1 Santa Rosalía–Loreto ☎615/153-0530, ⓦserenidad.com. Anyone who's been coming to Mulegé for a while likely started off by staying at *Serenidad*, the town's first hotel bigger than a *huésped*. The fifty, *casita*-style rooms are arranged around a palm-studded central courtyard and pool. The restaurant is the town's social centre on weekends when the band plays and the kitchen roasts a pig. Closed Sept. ❻

The Town

Even though there's not much in the way of historic sights or cultural activities, Mulegé's lovely to stroll around in, one of just a handful such towns in Baja California. Its colonial-era architecture is a welcome respite from the all too common sight of hastily thrown-up concrete block buildings along Mex 1 in the peninsula's younger towns.

Though wandering the narrow streets is a pleasant enough diversion, there are only two destinations within town that warrant closer inspection: the unkempt **Museo Regional de Historia Mulegé** and the **Misión Santa Rosalía de Mulegé**.

Museo Regional de Historia Mulegé

Follow Calle Zaragoza north to Calle Cananea to reach the **Museo Regional de Historia Mulegé** (Mon–Fri 9am–1pm; M$15 suggested donation), set on a hillside above town. The museum has spent the majority of its century-long life as an unorthodox prison. Known as the "prison without doors", the jailers allowed inmates to work in town in the mornings and afternoons as long as they returned every evening by nightfall when the doors were then locked. The unique arrangement led to many prisoners maintaining a home in town for their families even though they stayed in their cells for the duration of their sentence. Escapes were few, not only because being sentenced to Mulegé wasn't all that bad, but if anyone split they'd have the desert to contend with as well as their fellow inmates who were used to hunt them down. This novel approach to incarceration was effective until the Transpeninsular Highway was built and seclusion could no longer guarantee compliance. Nowadays visitors can enter the prison cells and view exhibits about Mulegé, such as family artifacts, old industrial objects and a sea turtle preserved by taxidermy. They're far from fascinating, but the descriptions are in English, and it's the only place in town that attempts to put its history into context.

Misión Santa Rosalía de Mulegé

Like the museum, the imposing, well-kept **Misión Santa Rosalía de Mulegé** overlooks the town below, albeit from a hill on the other side of the river. The Jesuit fathers Juan María Basaldú and Juan Ugarte picked the original site in 1705, three years after Salvatierra decided the estuary would make a good spot for a permanent mission. The present stone building followed one started by father Francisco Escalante in 1758 and finished after just eight years. A flood destroyed it four years later and the church elected to build the next one on higher ground. Though floods were no longer a concern, the Cochimí population that the missionaries sought to convert was subsequently devastated by disease. The mission was abandoned in 1828 and went through years of neglect until restorations began in the 1980s.

The altar is gone now, and the church's interior resembles a wine cellar with slight religious imagery. The church only opens for the occasional mass, but it's still well worth the hike up for the spectacular view from above the palms.

To reach the mission, follow Zaragoza back past the plaza, under the highway and back up a hill along a stone-block stretch.

Activities around Mulegé

Mulegé mainly serves as a staging point for tours of the **cave painting** sites in the Sierra de Guadalupe and **kayak**, **diving** and **snorkelling** trips in the Sea of Cortez, and compared to the movement along Mulegé's sedate blocks, the sea, river and nearby mountains are alive with activity. The proximity of Bahía

Concepcion (see p.200) to the south makes day-trips there possible, though you'll experience the bay better by **camping** along its shores.

Diving and snorkelling

What Mulegé's lacks in terms of cultural offerings it more than makes up for with some of the best **diving** and **snorkelling** in the Sea of Cortez. You're likely to have a nice stretch of the sea all to yourself, prices are about half of what you'd pay in Los Cabos, and the local operators are eager to assist first-timers.

Even though many RV parks and hotels can arrange guides or recommend sites, everyone headed to the water should first pay a visit to Cortéz Explorers, Moctezuma 75-A (☎615/153-0500, ⓦCortéz-explorers.com; daily 4–7pm). The knowledgeable dive shop rents pretty much any equipment you'd need to enter the water, and they provide expert advice on what to expect at the area's hot spots.

There are a handful of established sites in the waters around Mulegé. **Punta Prieta**, a short walk north from town past the lighthouse, is a relatively little known gem, even though it's really the only place you can reach from shore. Cortéz has day-long trips to more popular sites like **Punta Concepción** and **Punta Chivato**, both about an hour away by boat, and can offer help on getting to the reefs of **Isla San Ildefonso**, a three-hour boat ride around the Peninsula Concepción.

Basic shore dives start around M$300 and snorkelling trips start at M$350. First-time divers can have a resort course, a half-day affair that teaches the basics, for about M$600.

Cave paintings

Cave art in the **Sierra de Guadalupe** range is spread out over more than twice the area of the art in the Sierra de San Francisco to the north, and getting in and out of most sites requires detailed planning, an experienced guide and a few days to devote to the undertaking. Two of the more worthwhile sites within this range that can be reached from Mulegé on a day-trip are **San Borjitas** and **La Trinidad**. The Jesuit Francisco Escalante was the first outsider to account for San Borjitas – "well preserved, clear and perceivable" was his straightforward assessment – which he was led to by locals in the mid-eighteenth century. The dominant feature of this site is a thirty-five by twenty-five metre mural of interlocking black and red human figures. More varied in appearance, La Trinidad is a mix of white handprints, giant red deer and a vast menagerie of desert and aquatic creatures.

Both are accessed via rough dirt and rock roads, followed by either a hike or mule ride. It's essential to have a guide for either, and the best ones can be found in town at *Las Casitas*, C Madero 50, where Salvador Drew runs Mulegé Tours (☎615/153-0232, ⓦMulegétours.com). As with the sites in San Francisco, having your own car will save you at least half the cost of a visit. Tours from Mulegé are full-day affairs that cost around M$400.

La Trinidad is accessed along a 30km long drive from Km 136 Mex 1 Santa Rosalía-Loreto. Once you reach the Rancho la Trinidad, it's another 7km of hiking, wading and maybe even swimming to get to the artwork. San Borjitas is easier to get to, but timing can be an issue. Exit Mex 1 at Km 157 and drive 28km to Rancho las Tinajes. Ranch hands will provide your guide with keys that allow you to pass through a series of gates and get to within a 2km walk to the caves.

Eating and drinking

Mulegé doesn't offer a wide array of **eating and drinking** options, but what it does have is serviceable, and the prices are so very low that you'll never walk away feeling hungry and ripped off.

El Candil C Zaragoza s/n, at the plaza. A cheap and informal gringo rendezvous spot that does excellent breakfasts of fruit, eggs, ham, bacon, toast and potatoes for M$30. They have dining around the large bar – which plays big international sports matches via satellite – and in a bougainvillea-covered patio in the back.

Las Casitas see p.197. The majority of the long-term North American visitors and a good many Mexicans gravitate towards the decent and reasonably priced restaurant and bar at *Las Casitas*, which in addition to standard Mexican fare, has a popular Friday night feast with live music.

Eduardo's Av Martinez s/n ☎615/153-0258. If you happen to be around on Sunday night, head to *Eduardo's* for some of the best inexpensive Chinese food on the peninsula; expect to wait some time for service.

Los Equipales C Moctezuma and C Zaragoza. A mid-range steak and seafood place serving large portions; a steak with soup, salad and potatoes costs M$100, while barbecued quail goes for M$90. The second-storey dining room overlooks the busy street and is a good spot for people watching.

La Palapa Km 136 Mex 1 Santa Rosalía-Loreto. Most visitors on their way out of town stop here first for hearty breakfasts of huevos rancheros and chorizo omelettes.

Patrón Av Madero s/n, next to the lighthouse. Mulegé's only waterfront restaurant and bar, *Patron* is one of the better places in town to be on a hot summer night. Dine on *ceviche* and wash it down with cold Coronas and margaritas.

Listings

Banks Mulegé has no banks, although *Rosario's Patio*, on Moctezuma two blocks off the plaza (Mon–Sat 9am–1pm & 4–8pm), serves as a *casa de cambio*. If you're travelling with dollars there's typically no need to spend the time or fees switching over, while travellers' cheques are not widely accepted in town. If you're strapped for cash, try La Tienda, on Martínez, which primarily sells books and film plus diving and fishing accessories. They accept payment by ATM cards and, for about a 6–8 percent fee will give you cash back. The owners are also a great source of local information, which is particularly helpful since there's no official tourism office.

Buses A schedule of *de paso* services (the only way out of town) is posted at the café adjacent to

the bus stop, just beneath the "ABC" sign. Heading south, all services currently pass through during late morning or late evening; northbound buses mostly pass in the afternoon.

Internet access There are a few Internet cafés on Moctezuma, three blocks from the bus stop (Mon–Sat 9.30am–8pm & Sun 10am–2pm; M$20/hr).

Laundry Lavamática Claudia, at Zaragoza and Moctezuma, washes, dries and folds your clothes for about M$40 per load.

Phones There are long-distance phones outside the post office; there are also some at the Padilla grocery store at Zaragoza and Martínez.

Post office Along Martínez on the square.

Taxis There's a taxi stand on the square.

Bahía Concepción

Any mention of Mulegé is quickly followed by gushing praise for the Sea of Cortez's largest bay, **BAHÍA CONCEPCIÓN**, a half-hour drive to the south. Its alluring turquoise waters notwithstanding, most of that adulation comes from paddlers – there are few places better than Bahía Concepción to **kayak**. Its protected coves and smaller bays are placid and easy to negotiate and its multiple islands and long, navigable spaces allow for extended touring. The land that fronts the bays slopes down from the coastal highway into wide, deep beaches that are relatively undeveloped – though you will at times find teams of RVs lining the waters – and it's an inviting place to break your journey for a day or so before continuing on in either direction. At night, it's hard to see that there's any life on the beaches around the bay; the generators typically flip off at nine or ten in the evening and the only illumination comes from the moon and stars.

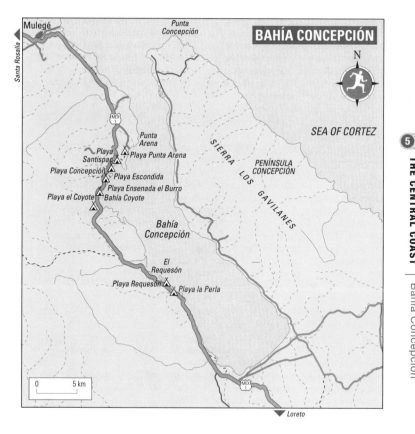

The best stretches of sand are around **Bahía Coyote** beginning just past **Playa Punta Arena** at Km 118, where basic palapa shelters provide shade during the day. **Playa Santispac**, some 5km further on, is right on the highway; despite the early stages of development and occasional crowds of RVs, it's a good option for both swimming and kayaking. **Playa Concepción**, just south of Santispac, also shows signs of development on the cliffs overlooking the bay. *EcoMundo*, at Km 111, rents out kayaks and snorkelling equipment for a day or longer (from M$260 per day, reservations a must; see p.202) and will provide maps of the bay. Facilities also include a barbecue pit, an excellent little bookstore and a bar.

Further south there are few facilities for anything other than camping. At **Playa el Coyote** there's also a hot spring, and at **Playa el Requesón**, another couple of popular, beautiful beaches. When the tide is low, it's possible to walk from the beach to the island of **El Requesón.** Note that there's no fresh water available at either, but locals drop by in the early morning and afternoon selling everything from water to fresh shrimp. Your other best bet is renting kayak, snorkelling or scuba equipment either from *Las Casitas* or *El Candil* (see opposite) or from the reputable Las Parras Tours in Loreto (see p.208).

Practicalities

Just about every beach has a privately-run campground or a place where you can throw down a bag and pitch a tent. With the exception of *EcoMundo* (see below), you'll need to bring your own gear to camp and explore the water. *Playa Punta Arena*, Km 118, turn right at the fork (no phone; free), is on the south side of the point that fronts the bay. There aren't any showers, but there are pit toilets, and the beach is less crowded than Bahía Coyote's.

Playa Santispac, Km 114 (no phone; ❶), is the best-outfitted beach, but tends to get crowded. The tent camping area is to the right after you pass the gate where fees are collected. There are two restaurants here, the excellent *Ray's Place* and passable *Restaurant Bar Anna's*. 🍴 *Ray's* is a small palapa hut with indoor and outdoor seating and a mouth-watering menu of seafood and, oddly, a wonderful hamburger. *Anna's* pales in comparison – the harsh flourescent lights make it feel like a truck stop – but it's open on Sunday nights when *Ray's* is closed.

🍴 *EcoMundo* (no phone, ⓦ www.ecomundobaja.com; camping ❶, palapas ❷) is an environmentally minded place offering standard palapa and tent accommodation directly on the beach. There's a shared bathroom and shower compound with pay showers and waterless toilets. Guests get first crack at kayak and other rentals. If you keep to the right on the *EcoMundo* road you'll go over a hump 1km to the rather secluded *Playa Escondida* (no phone; ❶). Few trailers can make it over the hump, so the campground is more hospitable to tent campers. It is rustic (cold showers and outhouses) and there are no services. Both *Playa Ensenada el Burro*, at Km 111 and *Playa El Coyote*, Km 107 (no phone; ❶) have pit toilets and good plots for tents. *Burro* also has a restaurant and, just across the highway, a *tienda*.

The only non-camping option on the bay is the *Hotel San Buenaventura*, Km 94 (☎613/104-4064, ⓦ www.hotelsanbuenaventura.com; rooms ❺, camping ❶). Its eighteen rooms aren't plush, but there is a restaurant onsite and the beach is enormous. The last two dependable campgrounds are *El Requesón* at Km 92 (no phone; ❶) and *Playa La Perla* at Km 91 (no phone; ❶). Both have pit toilets and are about half a kilometre from the highway.

Loreto and around

Although Cortéz first set foot on the peninsula near modern-day La Paz, **LORETO** is Baja California's oldest city and the one that has most visibly retained its colonial past. Despite development, repeated natural disasters, abandonment and then neglect, the physical layout of the city miraculously survived the last three centuries and remains much how the Jesuits designed it in the late 1600s.

It's a vibrant town, thanks largely to the current generation of local leaders and outside developers who are taking advantage of an infrastructure created in the 1970s and subsequently squandered by the tourism agency FONATUR (Fondo Nacional de Fomento al Turismo). It has natural assets working in its favour, too. Mexico's largest marine park, **Parque Nacional Bahía de Loreto**, lies just offshore, while the Sierra de La Giganta hems in the city from the west, providing a dramatic backdrop to the colonial street grid that makes up the core of the town.

South of town, FONATUR's failed Cancún-like master plan for the new 'town' of **Nopoló** has mushroomed into the **Villages at Loreto Bay**, the largest residential development by a foreign builder in Mexico. Loreto Bay's success, although providing a massive economic boost to the entire region, threatens to overwhelm the already limited water supply and upset the delicate desert ecosystem.

The **Sierra de La Giganta** mountains that hem in Loreto along the coast also separate it from small towns and villages that played a vital role as mission and farming centres in the peninsula's early history. The otherwise sleepy village of **San Javier** is home to arguably the most impressive of the peninsula's remaining missions. And while the missions of **Comondú** and **La Purísima** turned to rubble generations ago, the settlements – with their date palm and other fruit farming – are a testament to the early ambitions of the missionaries that filled in streams and moved earth to cultivate the area three centuries ago.

Some history

In 1697 a group of **Jesuit missionaries** established the town and made it the capital of their California empire, which soon expanded past present-day San Francisco. From the start, California was going to be different from the rest of Mexico. Not only were the Jesuits not going to enslave every native they came across, they began their religious incursion by incorporating objects of value to the local tribes into the Catholic ritual. The Jesuits were also to have complete control over the territory: nobody was allowed into California – especially not soldiers – without their permission. Unfortunately, disease stuck to its old strategy and over the next half century wiped out Loreto's Cochimí Indians and every other native group in Baja California Sur – the only Mexican state without an indigenous population.

With the exception of today's real estate land grab, Loreto's headiest days were during its first seven decades when it bustled as the launching pad for nineteen other Jesuit missions in the region. The city's first mission was a simple affair built not far from the mouth of Río Las Parras, and the newcomers planted laurel trees in honour of the city's patron saint, Nuestra Señora de Loreto. Unlike other parts of Mexico, the main interest was in spreading religious teaching rather than mining for gold and other precious metals. While this worked for a while, the Spanish crown got fed up with the expense and the lack of payoff. They also believed the Jesuits were squirrelling away a fortune somewhere in their private territory. After some lobbying by rival religious orders, the Jesuits were kicked out and replaced by a gaggle of Dominican friars and a legion of soldiers.

Even without the Jesuits around, it remained the active administrative capital of the entire territory until a devastating **hurricane** struck in 1829. Most everything was flattened and the townspeople packed up what remained and moved themselves and the capital to La Paz. Loreto was largely abandoned until a collection of landless US Civil War veterans stumbled on the site in the late 1860s and began to rebuild the town. This helps explain the preponderance of sixth-generation Mexicans with names like Cunningham.

For years it hobbled along as another middling fishing centre on the sea, albeit one with more gravitas than many other coastal towns. In the 1970s, **FONATUR** planned a super-resort along the lines of Cancún some 10km south of town in the newly created neighbourhood of **Nopoló**. The agency built an international airport, constructed a road system, laid an electrical and plumbing grid and put in a tennis and golf centre. Soon after the groundwork was laid, one of the largest private investors involved in the project pulled out and priorities were shifted elsewhere and it sat dormant for three decades. Nowadays it's enjoying something of a renaissance, boosted by that new master plan and development of southern Baja California as a whole.

Arrival and information

Three avenidas from Mex 1 lead into town: Avenida Salvatierra, Paseo Pedro de Ugarte and Avenida Independencia. Once they reach the centre, each of these streets either ends at or intersects with avenidas Benito Juárez or Miguel

▲ Mulegé

LORETO

0   500 m

N

MEX 1

SEA OF CORTEZ

PREPARATORIA

FRANCISCO I. MADERO

AV CONSTITUYENTES

INDEPENDENCIA

See 'Central Loreto' Map

PASEO JUAN MANUEL BASALDÚA

MARQUÉS DE LEÓN

CALLE DE LA PLAYA

PASEO PEDRO DE UGARTE

HÉROES DE LA INDEPENDENCIA

MARQUÉS DE LA INDEPENDENCIA

BENITO JUÁREZ

SALVATIERRA

DOBLADO

❶

ℹ

AV MIGUEL HIDALGO

FRANCISCO I. MADERO

MEX 1

SALVATIERRA

Bus Station ★ ✉

Baseball Stadium

Ⓐ ❷

Río Loretzo

▼ Airport, Popotla, Cd. Insurgentes, Ⓑ & Ⓒ

CENTRAL LORETO

0   200 m

N

ANASTACIO   CARRILLO

FRANCISCO I. MADERO

CALLE DAVIS

Ⓓ   AGUA DULCE

JOSÉ MARÍA PINO SUÁREZ

Ⓔ   BENITO JUÁREZ

MISIONEROS

ROSENDO ROBLES

SEA OF CORTEZ

EMILIANO ZAPATA

INDEPENDENCIA

BENITO JUÁREZ

CALLE DE LA PLAYA

SALVATIERRA

❸

❹

❺   Plaza Cívica

Misión Nuestra Señora de Loreto Conchó   ℹ   Ⓕ ❻ ❼

Museo de las Misiones   Ⓗ   Ⓖ

EL PIPILA

Ⓘ ❽

FRANCISCO I. MADERO

MALECÓN

SALVATIERRA

❾ ❿ ⓫ ⓬   AV MIGUEL HIDALGO   ⓭

FERNANDO JORDÁN   Ⓘ

Ⓙ   JOSÉ MARÍA MORELOS

IGNACIO ZARAGOZA

Ⓚ   BAJA CALIFORNIA   Ⓛ

ACCOMMODATION
Las Cabañas de Loreto	**J**
Coco Cabañas	**D**
Hacienda Suites	**A**
Iguana Inn	**E**
Inn at Loreto Bay	**B**
El Junipero	**H**
Oasis	**L**
Palmas Altas	**K**
Plaza Loreto	**G**
Posada De Las Flores	**F**
Sukasa Bungalows	**I**
Whales Inn	**C**

RESTAURANTS & BARS
Café Olé	6
El Canipole	5
Coco Loco	1
Macaws	8
McLulu's	10
Mike's Bar	13
El Nido	2
Playa Blanca	11
El Rey del Taco	3
El Taste	4
La Terraza	7
Tiffany's Pizza Parlour	9
Tío Lupé	12

Hidalgo, two streets which run towards the sea and frame the pedestrian-friendly town square and mission complex. Calle de la Playa traces the edges of the shore and takes in the **malecón**, marina and beach. Street addresses are rare and, when they do exist, don't offer any helpful point of reference; most addresses will include the nearest cross street.

Loreto's **airport** (⊕613/135-0454) is 5km south of town off of Mex 1, halfway between Nopoló and Loreto. AeroMexico, Mexicana Air and Alaskan Air have desks here and there are Hertz, Avis and National rental counters at the entrance. **Taxi** shuttles to downtown run M$60–80; there's no regular bus service to or from the airport.

ABC and Áquila lines use Loreto's **bus station**, Avenida Salvatierra and Paseo Pedro de Ugarte (⊕613/135-0767), just in front of the baseball field. It's a fifteen-minute walk east along Salvatierra to the Plaza Cívica, and a further five minutes in the same direction to the beach.

Though it's easy enough to get around town **by foot** there's a local **bus system** that runs along the major streets for a M$5 flat fee. There are three downtown **car hire** locations: Budget (⊕613/135-1090) is on Miguel Hidalgo, right before it hits the malecón; Hertz (⊕613/135-0800) is just at Salvatierra, west of Independencia; and Europcar (⊕613/109-0096) is at Hidalgo and Independencia. Getting around via **taxi** is both easy and cheap. The stand at Salvatierra near the plaza serves both Sitio Loreto (⊕613/135-0424) and Sitio Juárez (⊕613/135-0915).

The English-speaking **tourist office** (Mon–Fri 9am–3pm; ⊕613/135-0411) is located in the Palacio de Gobierno at Madero and Salvatierra, on the west side of the pedestrian **Plaza Cívica**. BBVA Bancomer, just across the street, has the **only ATM** between Santa Rosalía and Ciudad Insurgentes; the staff will change travellers' cheques Mon–Fri from 8:30am–3:30pm. The **post office** is on Deportiva 13, just off Salvatierra on the way into town, behind the Cruz Roja building.

More spots in town are adding wireless **Internet** access; if you have the right gear you can walk the streets and plop down on a bench with your laptop once you've picked up a signal. Established locations include *Caseta Soledad Internet Café* on Salvatierra just as it meets Hidalgo (Mon–Sat 8am–9pm & Sun 9am–1pm; M$30/hr), *Ram 64* on Juárez (daily 9am–9pm; M$25/hr) and *.Com Café*, Madero at Salvatierra (Mon–Sat 9am–10pm; ⊕613/135-1847; M$25/hr), which also has wireless access.

Accommodation

Loreto has a wide range of **accommodation** available, from cute B&Bs to four-star resort-style hotels, and waterfront lodging isn't limited to visitors with big bucks.

Hotels and motels

Hacienda Suites Av Salvatierra 152 ⊕613/135-0202, ⊛haciendasuites.com. The newest downtown hotel looks like a suburban US chain operation, but its courtyard pool, bar and café give it plenty of character. Rooms have tile floors and the standard suite of TV, a/c and private bath. ❹

Inn at Loreto Bay Blvd Misión de Loreto s/n, Nopoló ⊕613/133-0010, ⊛innatloretobay.com. Built as a part of the Camino Real four-star chain, the *Inn* was bought up by the Loreto Bay developers who quickly set about remodelling the two-year old property to make the restaurant, bar, pool and all public spaces eco-friendly. The tiled rooms are large and have a/c, TV, private patios and sea views. In addition to a private beach, there's a giant pool with a swim-up bar at the centre of the property. ❽

El Junípero Paseo Hidalgo s/n ⊕613/135-0122. *Junípero's* location just off the plaza is its best asset; rooms are rather plain and sparse, but each comes with a/c and a private bath. ❹

Oasis C de la Playa s/n at Zaragoza ⓣ613/135-0211, ⓦhoteloasis.com. Opened in the 1960s, *Oasis* is a family-run affair whose palapa-covered buildings and a prime end-of-the-malecón location evoke a posh *Gilligan's Island*. The large rooms and suites have views of either the sea or pool, and all rooms have a/c and coffee makers. Rooms with TV and phone are available on request, as are pre-departure fishing packages done in tandem with local partners that will park their *pangas* just across the street from the motel. ⑥

Palmas Altas Nicolas Bravo s/n, at C Baja California ⓣ613/135-1429. The landscaped courtyard and pool add a bit of luxury to the otherwise bland surroundings. Rooms have TV and private bath but are otherwise rather bare. ②

Plaza Loreto Paseo Hidalgo 2 ⓣ613/135-0280, ⓦwww.loreto.com/hotelplaza. This two-storey mission-style hotel occupies a prime position across from most of the town's tour operators and restaurants. The plain brown rooms haven't seemingly seen a remodelling since the 70s, but they

have a/c and TV and there's Internet access in the front office. ④

Posada de Las Flores Av Salvatierra, at Madero ⓣ613/135-1165. One of a handful of hotels on the peninsula that can make a valid claim to boutique status, *Posada* is the swankest spot in town. The courtyard is lit by natural light streaming through the rooftop glass-bottom pool and a plaza-level bar attracts local business owners and better-dressed tourists. The twenty rooms and suites are decked out with mini-bars, satellite TV, a/c and other luxuries, but make sure you ask for one with plenty of natural light. ⑧

Whales Inn Blvd Misión de Loreto s/n, Nopoló ⓣ613/133-0700, ⓦwww.whalesinn.com. Poor *Whales Inn* was the only hotel built during FONATUR's early development of Loreto and its age shows. Although it's outgrown its clothing-optional days (not a good idea when everyone's a fisherman), it's still adults-only most of the year. Rooms are worn three-star affairs and the required all-inclusive packages give you access to ho-hum food. ⑥

Bed-and-breakfasts

Las Cabañas de Loreto C Moreles s/n, at the malecón ⓣ613/135-1105, ⓦlascabanasdeloreto .com. The four cabanas with a/c, kitchenette, TV and video are situated around a central, gated courtyard. Guests share hammocks and a barbecue grill, as well as free Wi-Fi access. ⑤

Coco Cabañas C Davis s/n, at C Constituyentes ⓣ613/135-1729, ⓦcococabanasloreto.com. All eight cabanas surround a patio with a sunken pool and barbecue area. The rooms have kitchens and private baths but no TV. If you've caught your dinner in the sea, there's a cleaning area off the patio. ⑤

Iguana Inn Blvd Juárez s/n, at C Davis ⓣ613/135-1627. Another friendly, small

inn near the centre of town. The owners live in the front house, guests stay in the four spotless cabanas situated around a gurgling fountain and courtyard at the back. The relatively modern rooms, with tile floors, a/c, TV and ceiling fans, have kitchenettes and private baths. ③

Sukasa Bungalows C de la Playa s/n, at C Jordan ⓣ613/135-0490, ⓦloreto.com/sukasa. Small, family-run inn just across the boulevard from the malecón. The large bungalows have separate living and sleeping areas, as well as kitchen facilities and private patios. A separate, two-storey home can be rented by the week for US$750. ⑤

The Town

Neat and tidy, Loreto has a strong sense of history and a handful of solid restaurants that serve locals and visitors hungry after a day of working at sea. The town is shaped roughly like a triangle pointing west from the malecón and the edges of the Sea of Cortez; all points of interest are near the wide end nearest to the shore. Salvatierra turns into a **pedestrian mall** at Independencia and every building of note in town is along this six-block-long promenade to the sea, including the **Misíon Nuestra Señora de Loreto Conchó** and **Museo de las Misiones** at Calle Misioneros. The last two blocks of Salvatierra are a promenade of laurel trees that sometimes serve as the passageway from the odd cruise ship that drops anchor here.

    The large Palacio de Gobierno building on the western edge of the plaza houses the tourism office and the local treasury. The plaza is anchored by a fountain and gazebo, the latter serving as a mini-stage for musical and social events and holidays, as well as an ornamental bell. The latter is a gift from the city of Hermosa Beach, California to recognize Loreto's role in originating the Camino Real.

Misíon Nuestra Señora de Loreto Conchó

The town's mission grounds that served as the centre of religious activity and government seat were destroyed by fire and hurricanes on several occasions during their three-century-long history, but you wouldn't be able to tell this from the present state of the immaculate **Misíon Nuestra Señora de Loreto Conchó**. Although the mission site has been in continual use since the beginning of the eighteenth century, formal construction of the church did not begin until 1740 and took twelve years to complete. Solid and simple, the original **mission church**, though heavily restored after repeated damage, is little changed, and it's rough enough around the edges to appear authentic rather than gussied up. The facade of seashells mixed into the concrete remains intact, as is the rebuilt bell tower, replete with a set of bells from the mid-eighteenth century.

The inscription over the door, which translates as 'The head and mother church of the missions of upper and lower California,' attests to its former importance, as does the Baroque altarpiece originally transported here from Mexico City. The altar, like much of the structure, was reconstructed in the 1960s; the oil paintings represent Saint Peter, Jesus and his parents, Saint Paul, Saint Ignacio and Saint Javier. A reproduction of the seventeenth-century Virgen de Loreto occupies the altarpiece while the original is being restored. The chapel's interior is a long and narrow space with whitewashed walls and a wood beam ceiling sectioned off by three stone arches. Shallow wood benches line the simple red tile floor. Outside the mission stands a large, bronze bust of the Jesuit Juan María Salvatierra, considered the city's founder and the brains behind the early religious strategy in California. His legacy competes with the Dominican Junípero Serra, who began his trans-California trek from here in 1769, eventually planting missions in San Diego, Sacramento, Monterey, Santa Barbara and San Francisco.

Museo de las Misiones

Next door to the mission, in a former storage house and courtyard complex, stands the thorough and engaging **Museo de las Misiones** (Tues–Sun 9am–6pm, ☎613/135-0441; M$30). The museum chronicles the early conversion and colonization of Baja California in five rooms that are accessed via a covered walking path. The museum is filled with religious artefacts, such as an eerie prostrate Christ in a glass box, eighteenth-century carved wood statuettes covered in porcelain, as well as a seventeenth-century declaration of Loreto as the historical capital of the Californias. Other objects, such as a wooden boat and nineteenth-century sugar mill brought over from San José de Comondú, demonstrate how the early settlers got along in the region.

Parque Nacional Bahía de Loreto

The city's greatest asset is the giant body of protected waters along its eastern shore. **Parque Nacional Bahía de Loreto** was established in 1996 to protect over 2000 sq km of the Sea of Cortez from overfishing and other activities detrimental to the marine life and the sea's ecology as a whole. The park takes in Isla Coronados in the northwest, the large Isla Carmen directly east of Loreto and the smallish Islas Danzante, Monserrat and Santa Catalina, as well as half a dozen tiny ones. Plenty of sport fishing still takes place in the park (see p.211), but when and what type is regulated by SEMARNAP.

Outdoor activities around Loreto

For the outdoor enthusiast, there is no better place on the peninsula to make a base than Loreto: the opportunities for superb **diving**, **snorkelling**, **kayaking**, **hiking** and **cycling** are near limitless. The inviting waters of Parque Nacional Bahía de Loreto are so picturesque and rich in marine life that nearly everyone will be drawn to try their hand at either snorkelling or sea kayaking. The latter option is as good a way as any to explore the bays, snorkel the ledges around the many islands and, for the more ambitious, to make your way down the coast. Gear rental is reasonable, with half-day tours starting at around M$450 and full-day tours at about M$800, while some US-based companies offer week-long all-inclusive kayak "safaris" between Loreto and Mulegé or La Paz that can creep up towards US$1000. Many of the same companies offer hiking and biking excursions into the Sierra de La Giganta mountains to the west of town or between Loreto and Mulegé or La Paz. You can either book trips by the day once you've arrived or you plan your entire trip around a multi-day excursion through a local or US-based outfit; companies catering to both approaches are listed below.

Book in Loreto

C & C Tours Nopoló ⓣ613/133-0151. Walking tours of Loreto and guided tours of San Javier, Primer Agua and Parque Nacional Bahía de Loreto.

Desert and Sea Expeditions Av Hidalgo s/n, at C Pino Suarez ⓣ613/135-1979, ⓦdesertandsea.com. See the cave paintings and history around San Javier (see p.212) and San Borjitas (see p.199), as well as take trips to and hikes around Isla Coronados.

Dolphin Dive Center Av Juárez, between C Mateos and C Davis ⓣ613/135-1914, ⓦdolphindivebaja.com. Day-long package dive trips to Isla Coronados, Isla Danzante and other islands includes tanks, all gear, snacks, guide, boat and park fees for M$950. They'll rent gear if you want to go out on your own and offer dive certification if you're a newbie (multi-day training runs US$400).

Las Parras Tours C Madero 16 ⓣ613/135-1010, ⓦlasparrastours.com. This established operator can set you up with gear for diving, kayaking and snorkelling. A two-tank dive will run you M$800; a full eight-hour day of kayaking M$280. They also do tours to see cave paintings at San Borjitas and La Trinidad for M$1500.

Velas de Loreto C Madero, at Benito Juárez ⓣ613/135-1247, ⓦvelasdeloreto.com. Half- and full-day yacht excursions into Parque Nacional Bahía de Loreto. Food and drink are included, as is the snorkelling equipment.

Book before arrival

Baja Outpost on the malecón ⓣ613/125-1134, ⓦbajaoutpost.com. Dive, snorkel and kayak trips, as well as package deals that include B&B-style rooms.

Outdoor Odysseys USⓣ206/361-0717, ⓦwww.san-1.net/kayak-baja. Six to ten-day camping tours of Parque Nacional Bahía de Loreto by kayak.

Sea Quest Expeditions USⓣ360/378-5767, ⓦsea-quest-kayak.com. Eight-day camping and kayaking trips in Parque Nacional Bahía de Loreto as well as the Pacific side of the peninsula.

Tour Baja USⓣ1-800/398-6200, ⓦtourbaja.com. Guided mule-pack and mountain biking trips into the Sierra de La Giganta, as well as guided kayak trips around the marine park. Tour Baja is based in the US, but Las Parras Tours manages the Loreto portion of the trip while Tour Baja handles travel logistics.

△ Fishermen and their panga

To set foot on any of the islands you need permission from SEMARNAP, Mateos at Atamisio Carrilla (☎613/135-1429, ✉loreto@conanp.gob.mx) and must pay M$20 per day unless you're with a tour. Isla Carmen is the largest of the islands and is popular with divers and fishermen, but Isla Coronados is the real treat. The west-facing half-moon bay has a white-sand beach and small reef popular with snorkellers. Any of the tour companies along Hidalgo can arrange a day-trip to the island and typically include lunch in the package.

South along the coast

The borders of Loreto continue to expand past the airport and **southward along the coast**, effectively taking in Nopoló and the marina at Puerto Escondido. Between the airport and Nopoló there's a sign pointing to **Primer Agua**, 7km off Mex 1 Loreto–Ciudad Insurgentes. The spot is little more than a stand of palm trees, but it's notable as the first spot Spaniards found water in California. There are hiking trails branching off from the tree stand that lead up into the hills. They're not well-marked though, so if you're doing more than just stretching your legs you should go with a guide from Loreto.

Nopoló

A FONATUR planned community on Loreto's south side that never panned out, **NOPOLÓ** has been subsumed into the growing Villages at Loreto Bay residential community (see p.202). The *Whales Inn* and *Inn at Loreto Bay* are both situated along the beach (see box, p.210), but it's possible to go swimming there without staying at either. For years it's been most notable for **Campo de Golf Loreto**, Paseo Misión de San Ignacio s/n, Nopoló (☎613/133-0554, ✉golfloreto@prodigy.net .mx; M$550 includes cart) an 18-hole, par 72 course that's the only place to play between Ensenada and Los Cabos. Next door, the **Centro Tenístico de Loreto**, also known as the John McEnroe Tennis Center (☎613/133-0129; M$85), has a pool and eight illuminated tennis courts and one with tiered seats if you're in the mood for showing off.

The new, new Nopoló

Of the five sites designated as tourist development zones by FONATUR – Cabo San Lucas, Ixtapa, Cancún and Huatulco being the other four – **Nopoló** has mostly just been a three-decade long series of failures rather than ecological and sociological conflict zones the other sites have become. In 1970 FONATUR built a series of roads and set up a utility grid on the south side of Loreto. They also created a John McEnroe Tennis Center and an 18-hole golf course in anticipation of the development boom. No one, including McEnroe, showed up. In 2002, FONATUR allowed a US-based developer to create a new master plan for the site that resulted in a shift of emphasis from hotels to private residences.

The new Nopoló, now called the **Villages at Loreto Bay**, has been selling second homes to US and Canadian residents that, when the owners aren't using them, will be rented out by the night or week to guests. The project will eventually result in six thousand homes in the area laid out in walkable clusters according to New Urbanism principles. In theory, the development will abide by sustainable principles, but there are growing concerns about whether natural resources, most notably water, can keep up with Loreto's rapid growth.

Puerto Escondido

Puerto Escondido is set on a large bay 25km south of Loreto. Like Nopoló, it was once part of a grand plan to transform the central coast into a tourism centre. An extensive road and lighting grid were laid out and a hotel stands half-built, but it has yet to create any feeling of permanence along the shores. The Mexican government along with FONATUR are now positioning Puerto Escondido as the first step in their grand *Escalera Nautica* plan to transform both coasts of Baja California into a boater's paradise – the marina is packed with more yachts and fishing vessels than you'll see anywhere else north of La Paz. To that end, the development work of the 1970s has been joined by recent upgrades to the area, such as a Pemex station and an additional hotel, which both sit unfinished at the time of publication. In the meantime, the port is only notable as the starting point for some of Loreto's fishing trips and an RV park that lies south of the marina's opening to the sea.

The **beaches** south of Puerto Escondido are largely untouched, and you'll likely have them to yourself. There are two eco-resorts near Mex 1's turn inland from the coast, both of which have a handful of solar-powered palapa-covered huts along the seashore. *Danzante Adventure Resort*, Km 32 Mex 1 Loreto–Ciudad Insurgentes (US☎408/354-0042, Ⓦdanzante.com; ❽), is set on ten acres along the coast, directly across from its island namesake. It isn't for the budget traveller, but all meals, drinks and snorkelling and kayaking equipment are included in the price, allowing for a complete escape. All rooms have sea views and hammocks on their patios. A second resort at Km 86 Mex 1 Loreto–Ciudad Insurgentes, *El Santuario* (☎613/104-4254Ⓦel-santuario.com; cash only ❺) is more hippy than *haute*, but the sea views are the same and they also include three meals a day and use of kayaks.

Eating and drinking

The availability of fresh fish along with renewed tourist interest in the city have spawned some of the region's better **restaurants**, but the irregular flow of visitors has meant that the life spans are more erratic than is typical for the industry. Prices are overall quite moderate and decrease the further you move away from the Plaza.

Loreto sport fishing

The marine park status granted to Loreto's bay means that large-scale fishing here is illegal, which leaves plenty of fish for the **sport fishing** aficionados, who flock here for conditions that are as optimal as those found around La Paz but with far fewer crowds. Snapper swims around the bay year round, while billfish like marlin are only populous in late spring and summer. Catch-and-release is increasing in popularity among local outfitters, so if you want to mount a marlin above your fireplace, you'll have to get a boat in Los Cabos.

Of the operators listed below, some are retail operations and others are local guides who are consistently recommended by hotels and locals. Everyone aboard a fishing boat must have a Mexican fishing license – which you should request from the operator when booking – whether angling or not. Baja Big Fish's website offers the most detailed info about the local scene and current conditions. Full-day trips run around M$2000 and half-day ones about M$1200, depending on the size of the boat and the equipment used.

Arturo's Sportfishing on the malecón at Zaragoza ☏613/135-0766, ⊛arturosport .com.

Baja Big Fish Company ☏613/135-1603 and 104-0781, ⊛bajabigfish.com.

Chema Murillo Navarro ☏613/135-1173.

El Fuerte Puerto Escondido ☏613/133-0789, ⊛elfuerte.com.

Jose Torres Fishing Charters Puerto Escondido ☏613/104-4030, ⊛loreto.com/josetorres/index.htm.

Ricardo's Sportfishing, at the *La Pinta Hotel*, ☏613/135-0025 and 135-0126, ⓔricardosport@hotmail.com.

Café Olé Av Madero s/n, at Av Hidalgo ☏613/135-0496. Popular for its good-value breakfasts – try the cinnamon rolls – and *antojitos* like *ceviche* and *avadaco* and *queso* salad in the afternoon.

El Canipole C Pino Suarez s/n, between Av Salvatierra and Av Juárez ☏613/135-1886. The outdoor seating in the courtyard and tableside preparation of guacamole and salsa give *Canipole* the feeling of eating at a friend's home. And when the owner insists you go home with her recipe for *mole* you'll realize you have.

🏃 Coco Loco C de la Playa and Constituyentes, above *Chile Willie*. This beachside restaurant serves a mix of Mexican and continental seafood dishes from breakfast through dinner, while upstairs bands and DJs play until at least 4am on weekend nights.

Macaws C de la Playa s/n, between C Jordan and Av Hidalgo. A gringo favourite for both the 5–7pm half-price happy hour and its satellite TV football and baseball games from the US. There's both a covered area and an open courtyard. The kitchen churns out large platters of tacos, burritos and other Mexican basics.

Mike's Bar Av Hidalgo s/n, at C Collegio ☏615/135-1126. A mix of locals and visitors fill this second-storey dance floor on weekends and happy-hour crowds come all week long.

Playa Blanca and McLulu's Av Hidalgo, at Salvatierra. Glorified food stands that are wonderful for cheap eats and local seafood, and the latter has some of Loreto's better fish tacos.

El Rey del Taco Av Juárez at C Misioneros. Serves cheap tacos for breakfast and lunch. Closed Mon & Tues.

El Taste Av Juárez s/n, at Pino Suárez ☏615/135-1489. The warm, low lights and strolling musicians make this romantic by steakhouse standards. It attracts both tourist and wealthy with garlic-braised catch of the day (M$120), Pacific lobster (M$240) and a giant rib-eye steak (M$260).

La Terraza Av Madero s/n, above *Café Olé* ☏613/135-0496. This outdoor restaurant cooks up inexpensive seafood and steaks, and, as you may have guessed, has a terrace, which is perfectly pleasant.

Tiffany's Pizza Parlour Av Hidalgo s/n, near Av Independencia ☏613/135-0004. Excellent, if pricey, thin-crust pizza, though they are not always open in the off-season.

Tío Lupe's Av Hidalgo s/n, at C Colegio ☏613/135-1882. There's a standard Mexican menu, but also has local seafood and a few continental dishes.

Into the Sierra de La Giganta

When Mex 1 was built, the new Transpeninsular Highway was relatively successful in connecting all of Baja California's major points of interest, both revitalizing those that had faded with the years, like San Ignacio, and creating new settlements like San Quintín. Towns that didn't make the cut, however, tend to get by much as they always have. Among those are the settlements of the **Sierra de la Giganta** range, including the historic towns of **San Javier**, **San José de Comondú**, **San Miguel de Comondú** and **La Purísima**. An existing paved highway north from Ciudad Insurgentes to La Purísma may one day be extended all the way to San Ignacio and provide an alternative route to the central coast highway. Until then these towns will remain outside most visitors' itineraries, which is a shame, really: an **exquisite mission**, **stunning cave paintings** and **palm-packed canyons** are just some of the area's highlights.

San Javier

Misión San Javier de Vigge, located in the village of **SAN JAVIER**, was founded in 1699 during Loreto's first wave of expansion. It stands alone among the Baja missions as being wholly worth an out-of-the-way trip; even though it's in the middle of nowhere it's been better preserved than any other mission on the peninsula. Like San Ignacio to the north, San Javier is tucked in a forest of palm trees, the size of which are put in greater perspective by the dramatic cliff that rises behind them. In addition to the church, a complex of stone buildings and crumbled gardens and fountains

△ Misión San Javier de Vigge

surrounds the property, giving visitors a clear sense of how missions operated in their prime. The chapel itself looks as if it was relocated to the peninsula from Moorish Spain, with a carved stone exterior of whimsical columns and symbols attributable to a variety of religious orders. A set of large wooden doors framed by a stack of columns twenty metres high gives way to a large chapel. Inside, the cupola rises dramatically over the centre and the altarpiece is adorned with eight oil paintings and a statue of San Javier.

The town of San Javier, reached by exiting Mex 1 Loreto–Ciudad Insurgentes westbound at Km 118 and following the dirt road 32km to the town, is a collection of dusty roads surrounded by orchards fed by the mission's old irrigation system. The otherwise low-key enclave comes alive every December 3 for the Feast of San Javier. The *Casa de Ana* in San Javier (☎613/135-0211, ⓦcasadeanaloreto.com; ❸) is the place to sleep in town, but still the owners aren't lax about upkeep of the rustic cabins. They are quite basic, hot showers and private bathrooms are the frills, and electricity goes off at 10:30pm.

San José de Comondú and San Miguel de Comondú

During the nineteenth century, the little-visited valley villages of **SAN JOSÉ DE COMONDÚ** and **SAN MIGUEL DE COMONDÚ** in the Sierra de La Giganta were agricultural centres fuelled by spring-fed orchards and fields and a smart cultivation project devised by the missionaries. In the latter, Padre Juan de Ugarte filled in the Aranjuez canyon with 160,000 mule loads of earth so that they could plant sugar cane and vineyards. The land in both churned out vegetables and fruit, and the nearby farms were thick with cattle. Despite their prime location, the villages faltered in the mid-1800s, and all dwindled to almost nothing until a group of mestizo Indians from the mainland resettled it and began planting again. Besides the unique foliage, all that's left of the glory days are a mission in San José and an elementary school notable for being constructed out of a former mission in San Miguel. The topography is the main draw, made dramatic by the foliage and remnants of the volcanic activity that shaped the region.

Both Comondús are reached via the same exit from Mex 1 as San Javier, but you turn right 7km before San Javier at the junction near Rancho Viejo. It's an additional 43km dirt and rock road drive from here. If you're coming from the south, you may save time by driving up BCS 53 from Ciudad Insurgentes, exiting northeast at Francisco Villa and driving an additional 41km along dirt roads.

La Purísima

LA PURÍSIMA is the largest town on the Pacific side of Sierra de La Giganta, and it's best to think of it as Guerrero Negro with beautiful scenery. Located in a large canyon fed by the Ojo de Agua spring, the town is an agricultural power that's known mostly for **El Pilón**, a 400-metre-high peak that rises from a field of palms. Its other, quite dubious, claim to fame is as being the site of a demolished mission that in seven decades wiped out a native population of two thousand Cochimí. Besides farming, there's little to see here, but it will become a more important town if a branch of the Transpeninsular Highway is built through here as planned. For now, you can access it three ways: over a 65km long bumpy, dirt road heading west at Km 57 Mex 1 Santa Rosalía–Loreto; the 30km dirt road from Comondú; or the partially paved, 80km road leading north along BCS 53 from Ciudad Insurgentes.

Travel details

Buses

Buses to and from Santa Rosalía and Mulegé run along Mex 1 in each direction twice a day, although the schedule often changes without notice and neither town has a bus station from which to purchase tickets. A more dependable option is to take a southbound bus to Loreto where long-haul buses that don't stop in smaller towns are available, and there is an office that can sells tickets in advance.
Loreto to: northbound cities from Mulegé to Tijuana (5-6 daily; 2 to 15 hours), southbound cities from La Paz to San José del Cabo (5 daily; 31/2 to 51/2 hours)
Mulegé to: northbound cities from Santa Rosalía to Tijuana (2 daily; 1 to 13 hours), southbound cities from Loreto to La Paz (2 daily; 2 to 5 hours)

Santa Rosalía to: northbound cities from San Ignacio to Tijuana (2 daily; from 45 min to 12 hours), southbound cities from Mulegé to La Paz (2 daily; 1 to 6 hours)

Ferries

Santa Rosalía to: Guaymas (7hr) Mon, Thurs & Sat 8pm; reservations ☎ 622/222-0204, US☎ 1-800/505-5018, ✉ ventas@ferrysantarosalia.com; M$550 per person, M$2500 per car, shared cabin M$200 extra per person.

Flights

Loreto to: Hermosillo (daily; 1 hour), Los Angeles (2 weekly; 2 ½ hours), Los Cabos (4 weekly; 45 mins)

6

La Paz and the
Magdalena Plain

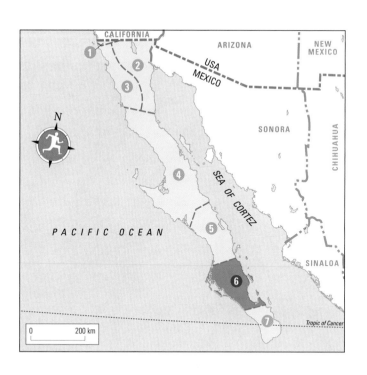

CHAPTER 6

Highlights

* **Bahía Magdalena** Take a *panga* out on the sheltered waters of the southernmost birthing and mating lagoon for the California gray whale. See p.220

* **Malecón jog** Join the locals for a morning run down La Paz's waterfront. See p.230

* **Tax-free shopping** La Paz's commercial district offers some of the best discount shopping on the peninsula. See p.230

* **Dive with sea lions** Los Islotes is one of the few places in the world where sea lions and scuba divers frolic together. See p.233

* **Baja Camp** This posh tent resort is the only way you can spend the night on Isla Espíritu Santo. See p.234

△ La Paz malecón

6

La Paz and the Magdalena Plain

S et in the heart of the fertile **Magdalena Plain**, the farming towns of **Ciudad Insurgentes** and **Ciudad Constitución** are marvels of modern agriculture but downright snoozes for anyone not involved in matters of the earth. They are, however, efficient gateways to inland locations to the north and the west along the Pacific, with a paved road leading north to La Purísima and other paved roads heading to the ports of **Puerto San Carlos** and **Puerto Adolfo López Mateos**. These last two are the primary staging points for catching a *panga* into **Bahía Magdalena**, the southernmost lagoon in the world for the winter's gray whale migration and the subsequent mating and birthing rituals. It's a bit far south for the humans who make their own yearly migration to Laguna San Ignacio or Liebre de Ojo, but it's a more than manageable distance for the La Paz or Los Cabos traveller who wants in on the gray whale phenomenon.

The Magdalena Plain stretches southeast almost to crescent-shaped **La Paz** on the Sea of Cortez. To southbound travellers the vibrant city is the first large commercial settlement since Ensenada; a place where the inhabitants aren't scraping by on cave painting and sport fishing tours or the pull of a crumbling mission. Coming from the luxury resorts of the south it appears as the first sensible city, one where a visitor isn't certain to get fleeced by a coterie of taxi drivers, waiters and hotel clerks. Therein lies much of its considerable charm, but its real appeal lies in the ways you can spend your days here: a morning of **kayaking** can be paired with an evening at the movies; an afternoon of **shopping** can end with a stroll on a malecón that's perfectly integrated into the life of the city.

The marshy **El Mogote** peninsula and the brackish waters that collect in the southwest portion of the **Bahía de La Paz** mar the view of the Sea of Cortez from the malecón throughout much of downtown, which is partly why locals are so fond of the **beaches** farther north near **Pichilingue** and the **ferry terminal**, where the vistas are especially stunning. Just beyond the city, the area's waters and the islands dotted throughout churn with sea life

The **Mex 1 kilometre markings** are reset at Ciudad Insurgentes, northbound travellers start at zero, southbound traffic towards La Paz begins at 220.

217

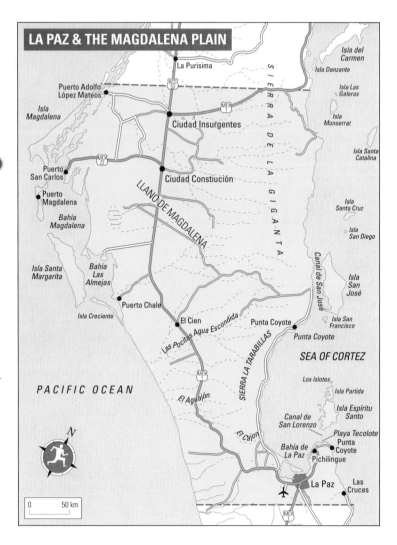

LA PAZ & THE MAGDALENA PLAIN

Isla del Carmen

La Purisima

Isla Danzante

Isla Las Galeras

Puerto Adolfo López Mateos

BCS 53

MEX

Isla Magdalena

Ciudad Insurgentes

Isla Monserrat

Isla Santa Catalina

Puerto San Carlos

MEX 22

Ciudad Constiución

Puerto Magdalena

LLANO DE MAGDALENA

Isla Santa Cruz

Bahía Magdalena

Isla San Diego

Isla Santa Margarita

Bahía Las Almejas

Canal de San José

Isla San José

Puerto Chale

Isla Creciente

El Cien

Agua Escondida

Punta Coyote

Isla San Francisco

Punta Coyote

Las Pocitas

SIERRA LA TARABILLAS

MEX

SEA OF CORTEZ

Los Islotes

PACIFIC OCEAN

El Aguajón

Isla Partida

Isla Espíritu Santo

Canal de San Lorenzo

Playa Tecolote

El Cajon

Punta Coyote

Bahía de La Paz

Pichilingue

N

La Paz

Las Cruces

0   50 km

MEX

that's unmatched around North America. **Isla Espíritu Santo** in particular is something of a Galapagos of the north, with over eight hundred species of fish thriving around its shores. Jacques Cousteau, who made frequent expeditions here, described the sea around La Paz as "the aquarium of the world".

The Magdalena Plain

One of the peninsula's principal agricultural centres, Baja California Sur's **Llano de Magdalena**, or **Magdalena Plain**, is a flat, sandy area lying between the **Bahía Magdalena** and Sierra de La Giganta and covering some 300 km. Though its rich soil is well suited for a number of crops, the water used for irrigation is being pumped out faster than it is being replaced, and saltwater seeping in from the nearby coastline may eventually take its toll on the region's productivity. In the meantime, farming – not whale watching – remains the area's life force and the twin cities of **Ciudad Insurgentes** and **Ciudad Constitución** are nothing if not secure in their regional importance.

Ciudad Insurgentes and Ciudad Constitución

Ciudad Insurgentes and Ciudad Constitución are linked by shared names, geography and spirit; unfortunately for visitors, the spirit of Los Ciudades is centred on cotton fields and irrigation systems. The flat Magdalena Plain signals the end to the dramatic Sierra de La Giganta range, giving the topography a feeling akin to the US Midwest – a change of pace, true, but there's nothing to either city that necessitates lingering longer than having lunch and filling up on fuel before continuing on Mex 1 or turning west to Bahía Magdalena.

Ciudad Insurgentes and Ciudad Constitución directly to the south are connected by a 25km, four-lane length of Mex 1; one of the few segments of the Transpeninsular Highway that has more than two lanes and no threat of crossing cows. **CIUDAD INSURGENTES**, the younger of the two, was developed in the 1950s when the state government turned a dusty village into a centrally planned agricultural community. It grew quickly, and the distance between it and Ciudad Constitución was soon filled with crops. The town has a few scattered cafés leading up to the northernmost road towards Puerto Adolfo López Mateos and the bay, but has nothing else to detain travellers.

Though you can't tell from its cultural offerings, **CIUDAD CONSTITUCIÓN** is Baja California Sur's second largest city after La Paz. One of the peninsula's principal farming centres, the city is proud of the region's agricultural prowess, and bronze statues of farmers and their families stand on many of its corners, but there's not much in the way of diversions. Within the city limits, Mex 1 becomes Boulevard Agustín Olachea, the city's main strip; drive with caution along this route, as there doesn't seem to be a great deal of correlation between right of way and the signal system.

Locals **shop** for clothes and housewares at the sidewalk sales and stores that line Olachea and on the intersecting blocks to the east; there's also a popular indoor **market** between calles Hidalgo and Brako. The activity in this direction peters out at Boulevard 20 de Noviembre, a four-lane dirt road with a shuttered movie theatre, a filthy city park, dying trees and statues of faded heroes. Were it not for the heat, you'd think you were in a former Soviet republic.

Practicalities

For all it lacks in charm, Ciudad Constitución does at least make a convenient pit stop. The **Pemex** stations are on Mex 1 between here and Ciudad Insurgentes; no matter what direction you're headed be sure to fill up in the area as it's a couple hundred of kilometres in any direction before you'll have another chance. Bancomer and Santander have **bank branches** and **ATMs** on Olachea, at Pino Suarez and Galeana, respectively. They both cash traveller's cheques until 1pm and stay open from 9am–5pm during the week. Compu Solutions on Hidalgo, just east of Olachea (Mon–Sat 10am–8pm; M$15/hr), has four **Internet** terminals.

Accommodation in Ciudad Constitución is geared toward travelling businessmen, so expect mid-priced chain-style offerings with local TV stations, a/c and private baths. *Hotel Conchita*, Blvd Olachea 180 (T613/132-0266; ❸), the city's largest and most comfortable, is a four-storey structure on the north side of the plaza that has a restaurant off the lobby that serves breakfast through dinner. If *Conchita* is booked, there are two other decent options on streets at right angles to Olachea: *Hotel Oasis*, Vicente Guerrero 284 (T613/132-4458, ❸hoasis01@prodigy.net.mx; ❸) and *Hotel El Conquistador*, Nicolás Bravo 161, at Olachea (T613/132-1555; ❸).

There are numerous **dining** options up and down Olachea. While you're not going to have the best meal of your trip here, you can fill up on fat *tortas* for less than M$20, particularly at a handful of open-air fast food counters on the east side of Olachea. The outdoor patio and brick arches give *Asadero Tribi*, Blvd Olachea and Pino Suarez, some atmosphere to go with its popular lunches and dinners. The palapa-covered *Mariscos El Pescador*, Olachea at Nicolás Bravo serves seafood caught in nearby Bahía Magdalena. There's also an outpost of the chain *La Cochinita Japanese Food Factory*, Olachea at De la Saro Domínguez (Wwww.lacochinita.com.mx) right at the southern entrance to town. A number of storefront shops sell frozen fruit snacks and *Thrifty Ice Cream*, just south of Hidalgo, sells US-style *helados* for M$10 a scoop. *Coffee Star*, just across Olachea from *Hotel Cochinita* on the north end of town is one of the few places you can get a cappuccino between Ensenada and Los Cabos.

Bahía Magdalena

Each year from December to March some of the migrating gray whales bypass the Peninsula de Vizcaíno lagoons for the secluded **Bahía Magdalena**. Four large islands, among them Santa Magdalena and Santa Margarita, protect the massive bay and an expansive network of canals and estuaries feeding into and branching off of it. This is the southernmost whale spawning grounds and its size rivals Laguna Ojo de Liebre and Laguna San Ignacio to the north. Though there is a fair amount of commercial activity around its two ports, **Puerto Adolfo López Mateos** to the north and **Puerto San Carlos** in the south, the bay is comparatively less crowded with *panga* boats. It's also quite popular with sport fishermen and kayakers in the whales' off-season.

Just like Ojo de Liebre and San Ignacio, the best way to enjoy the bay's sights is on a **tour**. While there are a few hotels in the area, the most enjoyable and location-appropriate lodgings are to be found in the temporary, modern campsites erected by tour groups each winter. In addition to the organizations listed in Basics (see p.23), there are Loreto and Ciudad Constitución-based options that may have week or longer trips to the area. It is possible to take a day-trip

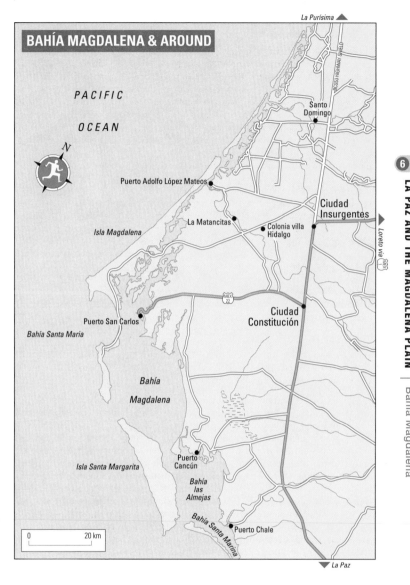

BAHÍA MAGDALENA & AROUND

PACIFIC

OCEAN

N

La Purísima

Santo
Domingo

Puerto Adolfo López Mateos

Ciudad
Insurgentes

La Matancitas

Isla Magdalena

Colonia villa
Hidalgo

Loreto via MEX

Puerto San Carlos

MEX
22

Ciudad
Constitución

Bahía Santa Maria

Bahía

Magdalena

Puerto
Cancún

Isla Santa Margarita

*Bahía
las
Almejas*

Bahía Santa Marina

Puerto Chale

0   20 km

La Paz

6

to Puerto San Carlos and watch the whales without getting in a *panga* boat; the city has built a pier specifically for the watch that cuts into the bay from a road across from the Pemex station.

Some history

With its strategic location along the coast and protected channel for entry, Bahía Magdalena has long been attractive to naval powers and ambitious expansionists. The first Spaniard to enter the bay was one of Cortez's pilots,

△ Whale watching in Bahía Magdalena

Francisco de Ulloa, who in 1539 called it Bahía San Abad, but he didn't stay around long enough to make the name stick. While he and his men were out looking for fresh water they were attacked by the local Guaycura, who wounded Ulloa and, unknowingly, walked away from one of the few encounters with Cortez's men that didn't end in genocide or enslavement. In 1602 the Spanish explorer and ambassador to Japan Sebastián Vizcaíno visited the bay and gave it the name that stuck.

The bay remained almost entirely unused by the new arrivals, even during the Jesuit expansion of the first half of the eighteenth century. Whalers made it popular in the mid-1800s until over-killing made the journey here no longer profitable. Despite the shortage of water, **La Matancita**, a ranch southeast of Puerto Mateos, received a large land grant in 1822, only the second post-independence one made by the Mexican government. A larger grant to a mix of Mexican and US businessmen led to grand plans to develop the valley. In 1870 three ships packed with eager US farmers landed in Puerto Mateos and set about farming the Valle Santo Domingo. They gave up before the year was up, but battles over the land concession lasted until the 1960s.

There is a healthy farming culture in the area, thanks to a complex irrigation system, but the bay's future is predicated on how well they manage the needs of the gray whales and the enviable port. In 1934 the Mexican navy put an end to century of incursions by US and Japanese naval vessels by establishing a permanent naval base between Bahías Magdalena and Almejas on the north side of Isla Santa Margarita. This was followed by modern shipping facilities at Puerto San Carlos – mainly to distribute the valley's agricultural output – that were completed in 1969. The **gray whales** drive the tourism industry, but their needs aren't always considered, as the potentially disruptive power plant on the north side of San Carlos makes clear. Unlike San Ignacio, the waters here are not protected by any environmental accords.

The birth of California gray whales

California gray whales (*Eschrichtius robustus*) migrate south every year from the Arctic waters of the Bering and Chukchi seas to give birth and mate. Baja California's Pacific coast has the right combination of the warm waters and shallow lagoons that are necessary to help newborn calves coordinate their swimming and breathing. Female grays only **give birth** to one calf each season and wait two or three years between pregnancies. A whale calf weighs almost a ton (their parents weigh thirty to forty tons at maturity) upon birth and measures five metres long. Unlike their barnacle-covered parents, the calves are born tender and dark black.

Bay practicalities

To **access** Puerto Mateos and the northern parts of the bay, drive north at the bend in Mex 1 at Km 0 in Ciudad Insurgentes. After two and a half kilometres, turn left and drive west for 32km to reach the port. Besides seeing the whales in season, there are great places to fish and kayak, but only if you bring everything you need with you – there's nothing here for visitors, or locals for that matter. If you're not with a whale-watching group, it's possible to hire a *panga* boat at the embarcadero on the south side of town, or simply walk out along the whale watching dock south of the fish cannery; expect to pay about M$350 per person. This is also a good place to launch your **kayak** or **small boat**. There's no fuel, banking or lodging in Mateos, but there are a few restaurants along the embarcadero. Although you'll likely see campers in tents near the embarcadero, you may be hassled for a camping fee from more than one person if you set up there. It's best to proceed south to Puerto San Carlos for an established campsite.

San Carlos is more than double the size of Mateos, but actually offers less in the way of non-whale activities; kayakers and fishermen will find the ship traffic bothersome. If you want to stay the night, you can camp at the small *Hideout RV Park* (☎613/136-0195, ⓦwww.hideoutrv.com; ❶) with hot water and flush toilets or try the very simple and worn rooms of *Hotel Brennan*, Calle Acapulco s/n, between Pichiligue and Loreto (☎613/136-0288; ❸), or *Hotel Palmar*, at Morelos and Vallarta (☎613/136-0035; ❷) with a/c and television.

La Paz and around

With just over 200,000 inhabitants and an idyllic setting, cosmopolitan **LA PAZ** is something of an anomaly on the peninsula. Aside from Ensenada, it's the only city on Baja California where there's a rich enough mix of culture and industry to seem as if it could get by just fine without all the tourists. It's also about the only place on the peninsula where the majority of visitors arrive by plane or ferry from mainland Mexico – not the US west coast – largely due to the affordability and low-key nature of its hotels and restaurants that lures Mexicans for whom a week in Puerto Vallarta or Los Cabos is too expensive or garish a prospect.

By any standards – even those that apply to Baja California – La Paz is very young and, whether by intent or neglect, it has made few connections with its pre-nineteenth-century history. The site of Cortez's first incursion (see below) is thought to be near Pichilingue, but there's nothing marking the spot; and nobody is quite sure where the Jesuit mission building was located, even though it was built in the mid 1700s. It's a pleasant surprise, then, that La Paz has largely retained its early post-capital layout, with a number of old government buildings, private homes and shops that occupy the urban landscape much the same way they did a little over a century ago. Buildings of historic note, even if they're not too impressive, are fronted by Spanish and English-language placards outlining their history.

Visitors inevitably gravitate down towards the picturesque malecón, drawn either by the serenity of the bay or, in stark contrast, the activity along Avenida Obregón. Across the water, the sandy Península El Mogote reaches into the Bahía de La Paz from the southwest like a giant arm, protecting the city from the Sea of Cortez's autumn hurricane season and making it quite easy to drop anchor without worry; it also adds a degree of serenity to the otherwise bustling capital. A few nice **beaches** line the shores northeast of La Paz, particularly past **Pichilingue**, from where the ferries to mainland Mexico depart and arrive.

The best time to visit is from November to May, as the heat comes on strong in summer and **hurricanes** do the same in September. During the last week in February La Paz holds its **carnival**, with colourful parades and cultural events transforming the town; book ahead if you plan to come during this time.

Some history

Twice **Hernan Cortez** tried unsuccessfully to colonize the peninsula from Pichilingue, just north of La Paz; his first attempt in 1533 ended in the killing of his pilot Fortún Ximénez, while his second in 1535 resulted in his being chased off the shore – both slights courtesy of the **Pericú** tribe. The Pericú lived in settlements along the shore and on **Isla Espíritu Santu**, and subsisted mainly on seafood and small game. They showed a fondness for the pearls in the bay that would eventually become the city's namesake, and their practice of diving nude for oysters persisted long after their demise – carried out by Spanish descendents and Yaqui from the Mexican mainland – and up to the invention of the diving suit in 1874.

After they dispatched Cortez and his cronies, the Pericú allowed **Sebastián Vizcaíno** to settle in 1596 on the same site. He, too, pushed his luck and was kicked out within the year. The Pericú did allow some pearling expeditions in the bay and eventually allowed Spaniards to settle in small numbers. Bahía de La Paz was also attractive to pirates looking for a place to hide before and after attacking galleons shuttling between Mexico and the Philippines. Over time, intermingling between the tribes of the south and the international contingent of pirates created a mixed race population that was nothing if not hostile to any attempts Spanish missionaries or settlers would make to occupy the southern part of the peninsula.

That's one reason, of course, why the Jesuits picked Loreto and its population of peaceful Cochimí as their base for expansion and first converts, rather than La Paz. The order eventually came down to the bay in the early 1720s and set up one of four missions on the southern cape. The Pericú, along with other Indians in the region, wiped out all four missions in 1735, sending the Jesuits running. Although Jesuits were chased out, their European diseases lingered, and in just over two decades La Paz was practically abandoned.

Fishermen, farmers and other settlers began to trickle back in by the first decade of the nineteenth century, and the outpost experienced a small population boom after the War of Independence. La Paz got its biggest break when a hurricane flattened Loreto and the **territorial capital** was moved to the bay in 1829. Its elevated status did not go unnoticed by US troops who occupied the city in

Baja California's ancestors

There's a growing body of knowledge that asserts Baja California's, and all of western North America's, **original inhabitants** were southern Asians and Pacific Islanders who arrived in North America by boat over fifteen thousand years ago. Remains found in the La Paz area, when put in context with similar remains found in the US state of Washington and in Chile, point to a wide dispersion of early settlers who have more in common with Australian aborigines than Aztecs or Apaches. This throws a spanner in the theory that all the ancestors of modern Amerindians arrived from Siberia over the Bering Strait land bridge; something which pleases neither entrenched archeologists nor contemporary American Indians, who like to think their ancestors came first.

One of the primary archeological links is the similarity of the southern Asian skull type to these paleoamerican remains. The remains of La Paz's Pericú tribe, which died out along with the others by the mid-1700s, share commonalities, adding to the argument that two distinct native cultures existed side by side in Baja California for at least some of their history, aided by the region's isolation from other tribal groups and settlements on the mainland. Unfortunately, the research undertaken around La Paz can't be seen in any of its museums, though there is some information about the work at Loreto's mission museum (see p.207)

1847–48 during the Mexican War; though they left after convincing Washington that Baja California wasn't worth fighting for. The US freebooter William Walker invaded the city again in autumn 1853, thinking it would make a good capital for his own kingdom. He changed his mind and left by ship for the Ensenada area in the spring, but not without taking the former and current governors as hostages, as well as the town's archives.

The pearl trade pretty much dried up in the 1940s, often falsely attributed to Japanese fishermen who supposedly poisoned the beds, but most likely due to disease amongst the oysters. But since the 1960s La Paz has prospered; first because of the ferry service to the mainland, and then because of fly-in US fishermen attempting to emulate John Wayne and Bing Crosby, who dropped their own hooks in the sea from here. It's now fed by every sector of the peninsula's tourism: visitors from mainland Mexico, drivers on a Mex 1 road trip, outdoor enthusiasts who kayak to the islands and Los Cabos tourists on day-trips.

Arrival and information

Car and bus traffic from northbound **Mex 1** comes into the city via Calzada Forjadores; southbound Mex 1 enters along Abasolo which turns into the waterfront Obregón. If you're travelling between major cities in Baja California Sur, the bus is finally a viable option – especially from San José del Cabo. Service is frequent, buses stick to a schedule and the station is central. Buses from there and everywhere else arrive at the modern **Central Camionera** along the busy malecón at Calle Independencia. The station serves ABC, Águila, Ejecutivo and EcoBaja lines, can help arrange tours, and even has Internet terminals available for a nominal cost (M$20/hr).

Getting a **taxi** is never difficult, especially if you use one of the many stands along the waterfront or on Plaza Jardín Velasco; there are stands on the malecón in front of *Hotel Perla* and *Seven Crowns* and on both sides of the cathedral on the plaza. They are metered, so make sure these get used.

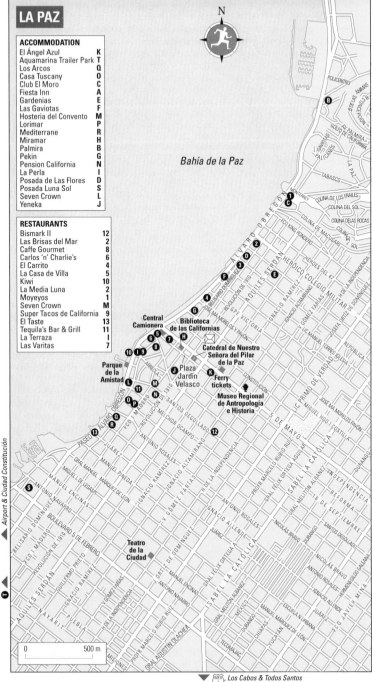

Ferry, Pichilingue, Beaches via ⑪MEX & ▲ Ⓐ

N

LA PAZ

ACCOMMODATION
El Ángel Azul	K
Aquamarina Trailer Park	T
Los Arcos	Q
Casa Tuscany	O
Club El Moro	C
Fiesta Inn	A
Gardenias	E
Las Gaviotas	F
Hosteria del Convento	M
Lorimar	P
Mediterrane	R
Miramar	H
Palmira	B
Pekin	G
Pension California	N
La Perla	I
Posada de Las Flores	D
Posada Luna Sol	S
Seven Crown	L
Yeneka	J

RESTAURANTS
Bismark II	12
Las Brisas del Mar	2
Caffe Gourmet	8
Carlos 'n' Charlie's	6
El Carrito	4
La Casa de Villa	5
Kiwi	10
La Media Luna	2
Moyeyos	1
Seven Crown	M
Super Tacos de California	9
El Taste	13
Tequila's Bar & Grill	11
La Terraza	I
Las Varitas	7

Bahía de la Paz

Central Camionera

Biblioteca de las Californias

Catedral de Nuestro Señora del Pilar de la Paz

Parque de la Amistad

Plaza Jardin Velasco

Ferry tickets

Museo Regional de Antropología e Historia

Teatro de la Ciudad

0   500 m

▼ ⑪MEX Los Cabos & Todos Santos

Ferry passengers arriving at Pichilingue (see box, p.236) are met by buses which drop off riders at the Central Camionera. Individual taxis run about M$95 to the city centre, while shared taxis cost M$30; negotiate the price ahead of time. La Paz has two main **marinas** that account for two-thirds of the private boat traffic: Palmira, Km 2.5 Carretera a Pichilingue (℡612/121-6159, ⓦwww .marinapalmira.com) on the northeast end of the malecón, and La Paz, Topete 3040 (℡612/125-2112), to the southwest. The slips tend to operate near capacity, so make arrangements in advance of your arrival.

Manuel Márquez de León International Airport, Km 10 Mex 1 Ciudad Insurgentes–La Paz (℡612/122-2959), is 12km southwest of the city just off Mex 1 Ciudad Insurgentes–La Paz. Hertz, Avis and Dollar **rental car** companies have desks in the airport's only terminal. Taxis to hotels on the malecón cost M$250, while shared rides start around M$80 a person; buy your ticket for either service at a small kiosk near the terminal's eastern exit. You can also rent cars downtown at one of the international chain agencies clustered around Pineda and Obregón.

The most useful **tourist office** (daily 9am–8pm; ℡612/122-5939) is on the waterfront at Obregón and 16 de Septiembre, though there is another with the same hours and information on Mex 1 5.5km north of town.

Accommodation

La Paz has the best collection of hotels in Baja California – ranging from dependable **budget** choices to unique **luxury** properties – and it's one of the few places where lower end options can claim water views. Since everywhere you'll want to go is within a few blocks of the malecón or the city centre, there's no reason to look outside of these two areas. Light sleepers should request non-water views; the malecón is noisy with pedestrian and automobile cruising on weekend nights. There's a slightly run-down area west of the plaza; if you're staying here, use caution during the evening.

On the malecón

Aquamarina Trailer Park C Nayarit 10 ℡612/122-3761, ℻612/125-6228. Primarily used by small caravans, but with spaces for tent camping along the bay. There are hot showers, a swimming pool and laundry facilities. ❶

Los Arcos Paseo Obregón 498 ℡612/122-2744, ⓦwww.losarcos.com. Along with *La Perla*, this hotel has been serving the sport fishing community since the 1950s. *Arcos* has steadily grown and has expanded beyond an older wing to now offer standard rooms with balconies as well as a collection of deluxe cabanas around the courtyard and pool. The cabanas and old rooms have more character, but the standard ones are cheaper. ❻

🏃 **Club El Moro** Km 2 Carretera a Pichilingue ℡612/122-4084, ⓦwww .clubelmoro.com. This two-storey whitewashed hotel is set around a large central courtyard with a pool, hot tub and bar. Rooms range from inexpensive doubles with satellite TV and private bath to multi-room suites with kitchenettes and patios.

Breakfast is included in some packages, and there's free wireless access around the pool. ❺

Fiesta Inn Km 7.5 Carretera a Pichilingue ℡612/123-6000, ⓦwww.fiestainn.com. With its bright red stucco and carefully orchestrated views, this four-star compound, finished in 2005, looks like it was relocated from the Los Cabos corridor. The modern rooms – all with balconies, TVs, a/c, full baths and minibars – are situated around a new marina and waterfront complex with restaurants, pools and even a Pemex station. It's a thirty-minute walk into town or a five-minute cab ride. ❻

Palmira Km 5 Carretera a Pichilingue ℡612/121-6200, ⓦwww.araizahoteles.com. Conventioneer-friendly hotel and meeting space just across the road from the bay. It's not too posh, but the contemporary rooms have the full suite of businessman-style amenities. ❻

Pekin Paseo Obregón 875 ℡612/125-0995. Budget hotel above the Chinese-Mexican restaurant of the same name. The beds are creaky and the rooms are pretty dated, but almost all have sea views, and the location is perfect for malecón cruising. ❸

La Perla Paseo Obregón 1570, at C La Paz ☎612/122-0777, ⓦwww.hotelperlabaja.com. Once the most popular place in town, this Spanish colonial gem is still a good deal. Tiled throughout, Western-style rooms have a/c, TVs and some bay views. There's also a playground for children, a pool and a gringo-packed restaurant. ❹

Posada de Las Flores Paseo Obregón 440 ☎612/125-5871, ⓦposadadelasflores.com. Well-designed rooms with Mexican-Colonial chic decor

and plush bath products and a mini-bar; you'll pay more here for the posh boutique hotel experience than it's worth, but the location on the malécon and the view from the attached second-storey restaurant are superb. ❽

Seven Crowns Paseo Obregón 1710, at C Degollado ☎612/128-7787, ⓦwww.sevencrownhotels .com. This glass, steel and aluminium hotel sits on a sliver of the malecón, right next to a *Burger King*. Rooms are modern, if a bit scuffed, and guests have use of a Jacuzzi on the roof and PC in the lobby. ❺

Around the plaza and city centre

El Ángel Azul C Independencia 518 ☎612/125-5130, ⓦelangelazul.com. A tastefully restored 150-year-old courthouse, with sparsely furnished rooms around a garden courtyard. The nine rooms and two suites have a/c and free wireless Internet access, while the front of the inn has an art gallery and a small café for breakfast, lunch and evening cocktails. ❻

Casa Tuscany C Nicolás Bravo 110 ☎612/128-8103, ⓦtuscanybaja.com. The distinctive decorations that adorn the four bedrooms in this B&B come from Guatemala and Italy and all rooms have access to the rooftop terrace. There's also a shared library of books and videos. ❹

Gardenias C Aquiles Serdán 520 ☎612/122-3088, ⓦwww.hotelgardenias.com.mx. This fifty-six room, two-storey hotel sits about ten blocks east of the plaza. Even though it's not huge, the pink stucco exterior and large parking lot make it difficult to miss. The rooms, with a/c and local TV, are all quite large, if a little dark, and face the courtyard's pool. ❸

Las Gaviotas C Salvatierra 100 ☎612/123-5298, ⓔlasgaviotasresort@yahoo.com.mx. Bay-facing balconies make you feel like you're right on the water, even though you're a block away from the malecón. Rooms are standard stucco and tile affairs with TV and a/c, and some with kitchenettes. There's also a courtyard pool and an outdoor eating area. ❺

Hosteria del Convento C Madero 85 Sur ☎612/122-3508. The first of La Paz's two *casa de huéspedes* is in a blue and yellow building on the site of a former convent and has features similar to the *California* (below), but is smaller and, if you ask for a room away from the road and lobby, quieter. ❷

Lorimar C Nicolás Bravo 110 ☎612/125-3822. This small hotel two blocks from the malecón is La Paz's best budget option, especially when you factor in the helpful desk staff. No TV in the rooms but each has a private bath and is immaculate. ❸

Mediterrané C Allende 36 ☎612/125-1195, ⓦwww.hotelmed.com. Each room has its own Hellenic name at this Greek-themed B&B a block off the malecón. Rooms have a/c, cable TV, wireless Internet and white tile floors; some have domed ceilings and refrigerators. The only part of the hotel that's not dripping with Greekness is the restaurant, which is Swiss-Italian. ❺

Miramar Av 5 de Mayo s/n, at C Domínguez ☎612/122-0672, ⓦhotelmiramarmexico.com. The view of the sea is the fanciest feature at this twenty-five room hotel halfway between the plaza and malecón. Rooms have a/c, mini-bars, cable TV and décor that's been cleaned, but not updated, since the 1970s. ❹

Pension California Av Degollado 209 ☎612/122-2896, ⓔpensioncalifornia@prodigy.net.mx. The aged but wonderful *Pension California* is in an old building with a courtyard. The spare rooms all have bath and fan and public areas include a communal kitchen, laundry and free high-speed Internet access. ❷

🏃 **Posada Luna Sol** C Topete 564, between Av 5 de Febrero and C Navarro ☎612/123-0559, ⓦwww.kayakbaja.com. The location, along a residential block west of the marina, is a bit removed from the action, but the rooms – with artisan-tiled private baths, flat screen TVs and a/c – break from the cookie-cutter hotel norm and the knowledgeable staff are excellent local resources. There's also secure, on-site parking. ❺

Yeneka C Madero 1520 ☎612/125-4688, ⓔynkmacias@prodigy.net.mx. The funkiest hotel on the peninsula also bills itself as *Museo Posada Antiquario*. Folk art fills the two-storey courtyard and eccentric furniture decorates the comfortable, clean rooms, some of which come with a/c and TV. The helpful staff actually encourage you to negotiate your room rate (a/c will always be about M$70 more). ❸

The Town

The city's two centres of activity are the malecón and, just a few blocks to the south, Plaza Jardín Velasco and the streets that branch off of it; everything within this area is best reached on foot. A tertiary area, the chain stores and movie theatres near where Mex 1 La Paz–San José del Cabo enters the city limits, is really only useful to tourists bypassing the city along Mex 1 or the traveller looking for a cinematic respite from the summer heat.

Museo Regional de Antropología

The small, Baja Sur-centric **Museo Regional de Antropología y Historia**, 5 de Mayo and Altamirano (Mon–Fri 8am–6pm, Sat 9am–2pm; free; ☎612/122-0162), ten blocks from the waterfront, is a fitting place from which to start exploring the city. It isn't as comprehensive as Tijuana's CECUT or as quirky as Loreto's Museo de las Misiones but it provides enough background for the average visitor. The museum's four rooms house over a thousand historic objects, among these a rather high number of reproductions. Mannequins posing in native garb illustrate the region's now-extinct pre-Hispanic inhabitants – who are also remembered with a replica of a burial site – and photos and facsimiles of cave art demonstrate the early work of their unknown predecessors. The museum has an adjacent small botanical garden that showcases the region's plants, and serves as a space for cultural events, as does the **Biblioteca de las Californias**, opposite the cathedral on the plaza (Mon–Fri 9am–4pm; free), where Spanish speakers can go for more detailed historical records about La Paz and the peninsula.

Catedral de Nuestra Señora del Pilar de la Paz

Walking north on 5 de Mayo brings you up along the east side of the plaza and the **Catedral de Nuestra Señora del Pilar de la Paz**. Keeping with the

△ Catedral de Nuestra Señora del Pilar de la Paz

region's lacklustre approach to holy edifices, the cathedral is rather modest in all respects – a three-storey brick chapel flanked by two towers – though it does at least have a nice symmetry with the library across the plaza. The cathedral's aesthetic shortcomings are a direct result of the town's economic situation at the time it was built in 1861–65, and the Catholic church's not too distant removal from the halls of the Mexican power structure. The towers at the front two corners were added one at a time; the first in 1910, the second in 1920. Its interior is only worth a look for the miniature replica of St Peter's in Rome.

Plaza Jardín Velasco

Much like the malecón, **Plaza Jardín Velasco**, named for Colonel Máximo Velasco who laid it out in 1876, is where La Paz's denizens come to congregate, albeit on a smaller scale. A giant gazebo at the centre typically plays a central role in any city festival or holiday event and passes as an outdoor exhibition space during Christmas and Easter celebrations, while a replica of the **Hongo de Balandra**, a mushroom-shaped rock formation in the nearby bay of the same name, sits at the centre of a fountain on the plaza's south side. The plaza comes alive at dusk, when residents begin to trickle onto the square for a stroll, game of checkers or to get their shoes shined. By nightfall, it's a bustling centre of social interaction that's often accompanied musically by buskers or the speakers from a parked car. It's best enjoyed with a cup of coffee from the nearby *5th Ave Café* or a cone of *helado* from the *Thrifty Ice Cream* shop on the plaza's east side.

The commercial district and around

West of the plaza, La Paz's main **commercial district** is a warren of one-way streets that slope down to the waterfront. There are a few tourist-oriented shops here, and most cater to La Paz's residents. Prices are lower here than anywhere else in Baja, both because of the city's duty-free status and the fact that the goods are directed at Mexicans. Even if you're not into shopping, it's a pleasant place to wander: the sidewalks are shaded by trees and tin awnings and you can pop into any one of a number of cafés and bars. Among these streets is the sporadically open **Teatro Juárez** on Calle Belisario Dominguez s/n, at Calle 16 de Septiembre. Built in 1906, it hosts cultural activities from time to time, but is largely in an ongoing state of rehabilitation (when events do take place, they will be listed at El Teatro de la Ciudad).

Outside of the plaza and commercial district, there are a few sites worth trekking to. Evening performances at **El Teatro de la Ciudad**, Av Navarro 700 (☎612/125-0004), feature regional arts groups and seasonal visits by major Mexican acts like the Orquestra de Baja California. A small gallery with rotating exhibits by local artists is open daily even when there aren't performances. This is a block from the **Museo Comunitario de la Ballena**, Calles Navarro and Altamirano (Mon–Sat 11am–1pm; free; ☎612/125-0207), which is more of a whale-centric neighbourhood art gallery than a museum. The odd collection of whale portraits, sculptures and casts of bones is housed in a one-room, equally peculiar, ersatz geodesic dome.

The malecón

The city centre's main streets slope down to the coast and empty out on Avenida Obregón – the **malecón** – for twenty blocks; the most heavily trafficked ones lie between the *Los Arcos* and the *El Moro* hotels. One side of the avenue is lined with restaurants, cafes and shops, the other side is a wide sidewalk that snakes along the shoreline. Like the rest of the city streets, the malecón is quiet at midday, when work and the heat keep people indoors. But in the morning and from dusk until after midnight, it hums with urban life that's completely absent from the rest of the peninsula. Soon after the sun rises, people of every age come out for morning exercise. The scene is repeated during the evening, when teens, young couples and families stroll and talk. Everyone pauses, if only for a short while, at the **Parque de la Amistad** to walk out along the small fishing pier sticking out of its west side, or walk up the flight of steps to the two-storey-high pavilion that rises out of the middle of the park. The city **beach**, which runs about half the length of the malecón, is dirtier than the beaches to the north and is mainly used for sunbathing or resting beneath the permanent palapa umbrellas that line its length. A second beach, **Playa El Coromel**, where Obregón turns into the Pichilingue road, is nicer, especially since the city extended the malecón sidewalk this far and added some exercise stations too.

Almost as if it was trying to be hidden, the **Museo Acuario de Las Californias**, Km 5 Carretera a Pichilingue (Mon–Fri 10am–2pm; free), is at the northeast end of the waterfront in the old state governor's mansion. A series of enclosed freshwater pools with the odd sea creature swimming about just metres away from a body of water referred to as "the aquarium of the world" is a relatively unnecessary exercise. There are a few exhibits featuring shells and snails as well.

Eating and drinking

The **food** in La Paz isn't as inventive as Tijuana or Ensenada and doesn't begin to approach the flashiness – or, thankfully, the cost – of Los Cabos. Instead, restaurants opt for a cross-section of Baja California cooking; locally caught fish dominates, and there is a wide selection of raw-bar quality shellfish. The cows you've seen wandering onto Mex 1 may in one form or another very well end up on your plate here, too. Prices are very reasonable, casual dress is standard – that doesn't include tank tops, though – and cash is preferred in most places. In addition to the places listed below you can typically get excellent tacos from street vendors in the commercial district. As always, only buy from places where there's a queue.

La Paz is not a nightlife hot spot, and is surprisingly sedate for such a large city. **Drinking** is largely confined to the malecón's combo restaurant/bars, which mainly serve only libations after 10pm from Thurs through Sun.

Bismark II Av Altamirano and C Degollado ☎612/122-4854. Excellent seafood – order the fresh catch grilled ($M75–110) – without having to pay inflated waterfront prices. Also runs a *taquería* of the same name towards the southern end of Obregón, with some of the best tacos in town.

Las Brisas del Mar Paseo Obregón at C Colegio Militar ☎612/123-5055, ℮ lasbrisasdelmbcs @hotmail.com. When locals want to have a fancy night out, they come here for seafood and steaks. Prices are higher than other malecón spots – dinner for two with drinks will run M$500 – but it's one of the few places with atmosphere and a wine list.

Caffe Gourmet C Esquerro 1520 ☎612/122-6037. This glassy corner shop in the commercial district serves coffee, tea and dessert throughout the day in a manner more befitting a patisserie in France than a coffee shop in La Paz.

Carlos 'n' Charlies Paseo Obregón and C 16 de Septiembre ☎612/122-9290. As everyone walks by during early evening and late night, it's more about the social scene here – and the drinks, too – than the food, a pan-Mexican hodge-podge of a menu. Two levels of outdoor space along Obregón give it the edge over other malecón pub crawl stops.

El Carrito Paseo Obregón at C Morelos ☎612/125-6658. An unpretentious restaurant that's popular with locals who come for the *ceviche* and other great seafood, all reasonably priced.

La Casa de Villa Paseo Obregón and C 16 de Septiembre ☏612/128-5742. The evening begins at happy hour at this multi-level dance club and pool hall with a split personality; sink the stripes indoors or head up to the roof deck for dancing amongst a mix of locals and visitors.

Kiwi Paseo Obregón at Blvd 5 de Mayo. ☏612/123-3282. Local and regional cuisine for decent prices, with tables set right in the sand on the beach. Try the stuffed fish fillet (M$130), a house speciality. Oldies bands play weekend evenings.

La Media Luna Paseo Obregón 755. You'll pay a bit more for sunset drinks or a dinner at this lightly upscale restaurant and bar, but the ever-changing seafood selection and the view of the bay make it worthwhile.

🏃 **Moyeyos** Paseo Obregón s/n, next to *Club El Moro*. The plastic chairs aren't comfy and you're liable to get sand in your thongs, but it's entirely possible to stuff yourself full of *ceviche*, clams, *cockteles mariscos* and even a large margarita for less than M$100 – with bay views to boot. Lunch only.

Seven Crowns Paseo Obregón 1710, at C Degollado ☏612/128-7787. This glass and steel hotel has a stylish roof bar and restaurant open to non-guests. The water views are wonderful, and there are several small terraces for those seeking private sunset inebriation.

Super Tacos de California C Esquerro, at C Arreola. Seafood tacos and help-yourself salad stand; a lobster taco goes for M$260.

El Taste Paseo Obregón at Juárez ☏612/122-8121. This sister establishment to a Loreto restaurant of the same name has local seafood and the best rib eye (M$180) in town.

Tequila's Bar & Grill C Ocampo 310 ☏612/121-5217. Equally enjoyed by tourists and locals, *Tequila's* is one of the few places you can play pool while the kitchen cooks up what you've caught in the bay (M$40 per fish). There's a full seafood-centric menu for those who haven't been fishing, too.

La Terraza Paseo Obregón 1570, at C La Paz. As the unofficial starting point for a malecón cruise, this café-restaurant under the *Hotel Perla* is a popular spot to people watch in early evenings – not least because of the shade and breeze. Food, though, can be lacklustre and pricey for what you get, a combination of Mexican basics and warmed-over Continental standards – stick to *cerveza* and *antojitos*.

Las Varitas C Independencia 111 ☏612/125-2025. The city's premier live music club tends to be crowded even when there isn't a show. A second-storey covered balcony overlooks the street below and provides a temporary escape if the music starts going downhill. Cover M$40.

Listings

Airlines and flights Aerocalifornia ☏612/125-1023, 🌐www.aerocalifornia.com.mx; and Aeroméxico ☏612/122-0091 or 0092, 🌐www.aeromexico.com; for comprehensive flight details, contact the Viajes Perla travel agency, on the corner of 5 de Mayo and Domínguez (Mon–Sat 8.30am–7.30pm & Sun 9am–2pm; ☏612/122-8666).

American Express Esquerro 1679, behind the *Hotel Perla* (Mon–Fri 9am–2pm & 4–6pm, Sat 9am–2pm; ☏612/122-8300).

Banks Branches with ATMs line Mex 1 La Paz–San Jose del Cabo as it comes into town; there are also a number of outposts west of the plaza.

Bookstore Libros Libros, Constitución 195 (☏612/122-1410), sells many English-language newspapers and books.

Car rental Most car rental agents have offices at the airport or on the malecón, including: Alamo ☏612/122-6262; Avis ☏612/122-2651;

Budget ☏612/122-7655 or 123-1919); Dollar (☏612/122-6060; Hertz ☏612/122-5300; National ☏612/125-6585; and Thrifty ☏612/125-9696.

Hospital Nicolás Bravo 1010 (☏612/122-1497).

Internet access Several Internet joints line the malecón. *Café Callejón*, just in from the water on Callejón, has a restaurant and outdoor café (daily 8.30am–10pm, M$15/hr); *La Paz Net*, as you head away from the malecón on Ocampo, on the right just past Revolución (closed Sun, M$20/hr). On the plaza, *5th Avenue Café* has both wireless access and a desktop terminal (daily 8am–10pm; M$20/hr)

Laundry La Paz Lava, Mutualismo 260 ☏612/122-3112 (daily 8am–midnight; US$2/load).

Post office Corner of Revolución and Constitución.

Spanish courses Se Habla La Paz, Madero 540 ☏612/122-7763, 🌐www.sehablalapaz.com.

Around La Paz

It's easy enough to visit La Paz without setting foot on the nearby **beaches** or **islands**, but you'll leave without seeing the sights that lured Cortez, generations of pirates and pearl divers, John Steinbeck, Jacques Cousteau and fleets of kayakers (as well as Engelbert Humperdinck, who bought a hotel). As enjoyable as the city's malecón is, it doesn't frame the sea well; for this you'll need to take the bus or drive north of the city towards the Pichilingue ferry terminal along the Carretera a Pichilingue, and on to the beaches at Punta Coyote.

The beaches

The first few kilometres from the city centre to the Pemex refinery are being rapidly developed into resort areas and residential neighbourhoods, the largest of these being Marina Cosat Baja, a marina and condos complex that also includes the *Fiesta Inn* (see p.227). It is a lovely setting, but the Pemex refinery disturbs the views and scents from its perch on Punta Prieta. Past this eyesore there are two sets of beaches before and after **Terminal Pichilingue**.

The first area consists of two basic beaches that are well suited for simple daytrips, either via taxi or bus, from the city centre. **Playa el Tesoro**, the southernmost one, is down a slope from Mex 1. The white sand beach stretches north from a palapa-covered pavilion where you can rent kayaks, eat lunch and down Modelo beer. **Playa Pichilingue**, just a short drive up the coast from Tesoro, also has an outdoor restaurant and bar, but you'll have to bring your own kayak or content yourself with swimming in the bay's blue-green waters. Buses from La Paz traverse this coastal route often in order to pick up harbour traffic and the lucky students at the beachfront branch of the Universidad Autónomo de Baja California Sur. The last bus back is at 5pm; camping isn't allowed on either beach.

The road beyond the harbour eventually ends seven kilometres later at the northern tip of **Punta Coyote**, but not before it takes in two of the region's best beaches. **Puerto Balandra**, five kilometres past the harbour, is home to the mushroom-shaped rock formation that's the unofficial symbol of La Paz and, more importantly, several beaches around a saltwater lagoon. The lagoon has eight shallow bays, most of which are no more than waist-deep and perfect for families. **Playa Tecolote** is the larger of the two, with rustic campsites for tents and RVs and a restaurant (☎612/122-8885) that rents kayaks, snorkel gear and beach equipment and can arrange trips to Los Islotes. Both are perfect day-long escapes from the city and far surpass the quality of Los Cabos' beaches. While it's possible to take a taxi to, you can't be assured you're going to get a ride back. It's best, then, to take your own car or stick to the beaches on the other side of the harbour.

Isla Espíritu Santo and Los Islotes

Most of the credit for La Paz's reputation as a biologically diverse maritime wonderland belongs to **ISLA ESPÍRITU SANTO**, a ninety-square kilometre island 8km northwest of Punta Coyote, and smaller **LOS ISLOTES** immediately to the north. Steinbeck and his marine biologist partner Edward Ricketts compared its marvels to the Galapagos Islands and, despite decades of attention and growing numbers of visitors, it has managed to maintain a vibrant mix of life, even though it's much diminished from Steinbeck's day. For snorkellers, scuba divers and kayakers there are very few places in the world that can compete with the overall richness – including vibrantly coloured schools of fish and seal colonies – of the waters surrounding the islands.

△ Pelican on Isla Espíritu Santo

Isla Espíritu Santo had a few hundred Pericú Indians living on it when Cortez arrived in the sixteenth century. Surprisingly, they survived his visit and even weathered being assigned to a mission in La Paz, which the tribe mostly ignored. They lived on what they fished and hunted and traded frequently with settlers and other tribes in La Paz. Like their mainland comrades, they got caught up in the rebellion in the 1730s, only to succumb to disease after the missionaries were dispatched. The island's only other inhabitant was a Frenchman who set up a pearling operation that opened and closed within a few short years of the Mexican Revolution. The island is now protected from development, although it is possible to camp if you're with an organized, licensed group or if you're one of the lucky who can afford a first-class tent at *Baja Camp* (below).

Island practicalities

There are only a handful of ways to get to the island and each requires some planning. Pre-booking boating and kayaking trips is the easiest option. Tour operators based in the US organize multi-day kayak trips that circumnavigate the island and even travel farther afield, both up and down the coastline (see Getting there, p.23). You can also arrange a trips at *Los Arcos*, *La Perla* and any number of operators along the malecón (see box, opposite), depending on what you'd like to do around the island. Day-trips for all water activities typically begin with an early morning drive from the city to Playa Tecolote, where *panga* boats are loaded with the day's supplies before motoring across the water to Espíritu Santo or Los Islotes.

Divers primarily head to two sites: **Los Islotes** to swim with playful sea lions, and the *Salvatierra* shipwreck south of Espíritu Santo. The seal colony at Los Islotes is famous for teasing divers and swimmers; if you're uncomfortable getting bumped by friendly sea mammals, it's best to stay out of the water. The only **accommodation** on the island is the simple yet elegant *Baja Camp*

Dive services

Each of the operators below offers specialized **dive services**, from all-inclusive day packages to à la carte assistance for the diver who knows what he or she wants. All organize trips to the waters around Espíritu Santo, and some also go to Isla Cerralvo.

Baja Diving and Service 1665 Obregón ☎612/122-1826, ⓦclubcantamar.com. Full-service outfit offering equipment rental, live-aboard boats, courses for newbies and vets, and multi-day packages. A basic day-trip with equipment runs M$1000. They also have the region's only decompression chamber.

Beach Club El Tecolote Smaller operation on the beach opposite Espíritu Santo is well positioned for spur-of-the-moment diving and snorkelling excursions, including basic equipment like tanks and snorkelling gear. Cash only.

Centro de Buceo Carey Marqués de León and Topete ☎612/123-2333, ⓦbuceocareycom. Trips to Espíritu Santo for diving (M$1100) or snorkelling (M$700), as well as fishing trips and land tours. Air compressor on premises.

Cortez Club Km 5 Carretera a Pichilingue ☎612/121-6120, ⓦwww.cortezclub.com. Cortez runs beginners' courses through to divemaster for PADI dive certification.

Tour operators

The **operators** below run similar trips to Espíritu Santo and other areas outside of La Paz but do not have the dive expertise, focusing instead on kayaking, snorkelling and some land-water combinations.

Baja Coast SeaFaris ☎612/125-9765, ⓦbajaseafaris.com. *SeaFaris* has two boats that accommodate small groups, on which they host custom trips for bird watching, kayaking, fishing, island hikes and other activities.

Baja Expeditions de México Sonora 585 ☎612/125-3828, ⓔbemst@prodigy.net .mx. Half-day M$380–620, full-day M$680–780. Includes boat transportation, kayaks, lunch and guide.

Baja Outdoor Activities Km 2 Carretera a Pichilingue (up the hill) ☎612/125-5636, ⓦwww.kayactivities.com. Kayak rental and snorkelling outings to nearby volcanic islands, or to the sea-lion colony at Los Islotes.

Funbaja Km 2.5 Carretera a Pichilingue ☎612/121-5884, ⓦfunbaja.com. Large operator with a suite of aquatic outings for many different skill levels, such as a 45m dive at La Reina and overnight dives at San Francisquito.

Katun Tours Benito Juárez 1445 ☎612/348-5609, ⓦwww.katun-tours.com. Bicycle tours originating in La Paz, including single-day trips and overnight journeys with a mix of camping and hotel stays.

(ⓦwww.bajacamp.com; four-day minimum, all-inclusive; ⓭), owner-chef Andrea Tamagnini's safari-like outpost on the west side of the island. The four tents have private showers from which you can survey the sea.

Moving on from La Paz

To travel north from La Paz **by car**, take Obregón southwest; it eventually joins Mex 1 Ciudad Insurgentes–La Paz on the west side of town. For Los Cabos, you can follow the same route and then cut south at the Libramento Sur bypass road, or take city streets to Calzada Forjadores southbound, which

If you're planning to take the **ferry** from **Terminal Pichilingue** across the Sea of Cortez to **Mazatlán** or **Topolobampo** (the port for Los Mochis), you should buy tickets as far ahead of time as possible. You should also scour the Internet for updates to routes and schedules, as they change often and routes can close unexpectedly for months at a time. You may also find information about infrequent service to other cities. In mid-2005, the state-run SEMATUR company ceded control of the long **La Paz–Mazatlán** route to **Baja Ferries**, which already ran the Topolobampo service, and **TMC**, a smaller, cargo-focused line. For all ferry services, arrive at least three hours in advance of the departure time.

La Paz–Mazatlán

Baja Ferries leaves La Paz at 5pm on Tuesday, Thursday and Saturday and arrives in Mazatlán the next morning around 9am. *Tourista* class seats start at M$250, for *cabina* it's M$650; *cabina* and *salon* is M$950. **TMC** leaves La Paz every day at 5pm and arrives in Mazatlán at 8:30am the next day. The cheapest tickets start at M$570.

La Paz–Topolobampo

Baja Ferries makes the journey to Topolobampo Monday through Friday at 4pm (arriving at 9pm) and Saturday at 11pm (arriving at 6am). *Salón* class seats are M$650; for *cabina* it is M$1410. Cars are an additional M$970.

Tickets

On Baja Ferries' La Paz-Mazatlán route there four classes of service: *salón* class, which is a reclining seat, and three types of cabins – *turista* (four bunks, shared bath), *cabina* (two bunks, private bath) or *especial* (suite with private bath, sitting area and TV). There's rarely any problem going *salón* class (entitling you to a reclining seat), for which tickets are only available a day in advance. The La–Paz-Topolobampo route has two classes: *salon* (a reclining seat), and *cabina* (four bunks with a private bath).

Baja Ferries has a ticket office downtown at Morelos 720 (☎612/125-7443, ⊛www .bajaferries.com). Ferry schedules change frequently and it's always best to call ahead to check the schedule (toll free in Mexico ☎01-800/696-9600, US☎1-800/884-3107). Tickets can be paid for with major credit cards. **Bicycles** go free. Tickets for the **TMC** ferry must be purchased in cash or with Visa and MasterCard at its counter at Terminal Pichilingue (☎01-800/744-5050, 612/123-9226, ⊛ferrytmc.com).

Before buying tickets, car drivers should ensure they have a **permit to drive** on the mainland. This should have been obtained when crossing the border into Mexico, but if not you may have some joy by taking your vehicle and all relevant papers along to the customs office at the ferry terminal a couple of days before you sail. If for some reason you've managed to get this far without having your **tourist card** stamped, you should also attend to that before sailing – there's an immigration office at Obregón 2140, between Juárez and Allende.

To **get to Terminal Pichilingue** catch a bus from the Central Camionera (hourly 8am–5pm; M$13), or take a taxi from town (M$200). According to signs at the terminal, it is illegal to take your own **food** on board, but since the catering is so poor, everyone does and nobody seems to mind. Try one of the *loncheros* by the docks for quesadillas, burritos and drinks to take along.

eventually turns into Mex 1 La Paz–San José del Cabo. Once you're 25 minutes outside of the city you'll have the choice of Mex 1 or Mex 19 south. The latter is faster by about two hours and has the added benefit of taking you through Todos Santos. If you want to visit San Antonio, Los Barriles and other southeastern cape settlements, Mex 1 is the road to take.

To get to the beaches and settlements on the Bahía la Ventana, follow Forjadores to BCS 286 Carretera a San Juan de los Planes, which heads east at the Nueva Plaza Comercial complex on the south side of town. **Fuel** is readily available at the start of each of these roads so take the opportunity to fill the tank before leaving town completely.

Ten regular daily service **buses** head north, three going as far as Tijuana, 22 hours away (at 8am, 10am, and 10pm), another to Mexicali (1pm). Buses leave from the Central Camionera roughly hourly (6.30am–6.30pm) for Cabo San Lucas and San José del Cabo; some are routed via Todos Santos, others take the eastern route direct to San José. The western route is quicker and more scenic as it follows the coast for quite a way below Todos Santos. Since this is one of the few dependable routes on the peninsula it also means it's crowded; it's highly advisable to book your tickets at least a day in advance or, better yet, when you arrive in La Paz. The same advice goes for catching a Topolobampo or Mazatlán-bound **ferry** (see box, opposite). The **ferry ticket office** is at Morelos 720 (see box, opposite) and at the terminal itself.

Travel details

Ferries

La Paz to: Topolobampo (6hr) Mon–Fri 4pm and Sat 11pm; Mazatlán via Baja Ferries (18hr) Tues, Thurs & Sat 5pm; Mazatlán via TMC (18hr) daily 5pm.

The Cape

CHAPTER 7

Highlights

✱ **Café Santa Fe** The pinnacle of dining on the western cape, Todos Santos' courtyard Italian restaurant is worth a visit no matter where you're staying on the Cape. **See p.248**

✱ **Off-road on the eastern cape** Technically, there's a road here, but you'll need a day and a 4WD to appreciate – and survive – the wonders of the scenic coastal route from Cabo Pulmo to San José del Cabo. **See p.250**

✱ **Marina Cabo San Lucas** The Cape's unofficial town square teems with life from morning to late night. **See p.256**

✱ **Whale Watcher's Bar** The margaritas are decent at the highest point in Los Cabos, but the real draw is the extraordinary views across the Pacific Ocean. **See p.260**

✱ **Bahía Chileno** Los Cabos' most accessible and family-friendly beach. **See p.265**

△ Marina Cabo San Lucas

The Cape

The peninsula narrows to just a few dozen kilometres across at the **Isthmus of La Paz**, the informal northern border of the **Cape** – the land's end where the **Pacific Ocean** and **Sea of Cortez** come together in spectacular fashion. This isthmus is the only visual cue that separates the geography of the Cape region from the rest of the peninsula, though they were two distinct geological masses prior to colliding with one another a few million years ago. In many ways, the Cape is still a land unto itself, driven largely by international investment into **Los Cabos**, the series of **bays** and **beaches** at the southernmost tip of the peninsula, and partially by the promise of more dollars to come along the eastern and western shores. Though the immense hype would suggest otherwise, the Cape doesn't eclipse the rest of the peninsula scenically. That said, there are lovely, much-photographed natural landmarks like **El Arco** and lush vegetation around the **Tropic of Cancer**.

After running parallel for over 1500 kilometres, the ocean and sea meet dramatically at the sister towns of **Cabo San Lucas** and **San José del Cabo** – collectively known as Los Cabos – easily the most exclusive parcel of land in Baja California. Undeniably beautiful and home to the lion's share of the peninsula's lavish resorts, golf courses and oft-photographed beaches, the area places a hefty price tag on it exclusivity. For decades its remoteness was its main selling point, but as more and more hotels popped up along its edges and more international flights began landing here, it now banks on a level of luxury unmatched on the rest of the peninsula. Los Cabos in particular is one of the fastest-developing areas in Mexico – heavily promoted by the authorities and a boom for the big hotel chains and resort builders.

But Los Cabos is just a tiny part of the Cape and its most remarkable areas still require a great deal of time and preparation to access. North of Los Cabos, the region is largely defined by **three main roads**: the fast new Mex 19 road runs straight up the Pacific coast from Cabo San Lucas and through increasingly posh **Todos Santos**; the older **Transpeninsular Highway** route trails north from San José del Cabo through the **Sierra La Laguna**, emerging for only one brief moment at the Sea of Cortez on its long journey to La Paz; and the third, most exhausting route along the eastern Cape. At the moment, these coastal towns between La Paz and San José are reached only via a dirt and sand road, despite years of highway planning to the contrary. The **eastern cape** is still a few hundred kilometres of untouched beaches and small fishing villages, for better or for worse. And remote from everyone without a donkey, guide and time on their hands are the tropical highlands of the Sierra La Laguna where the southern state receives the majority of its rain and **Picacho de La Laguna** rises to a height of 2090m.

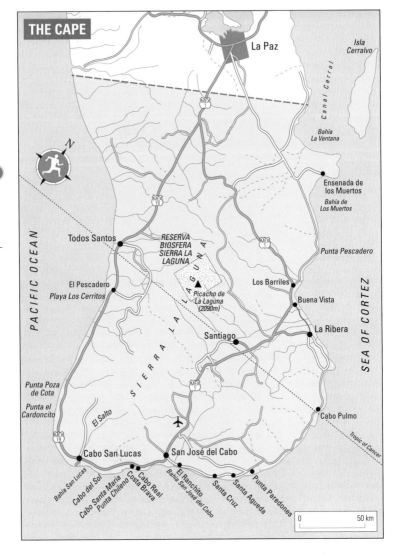

THE CAPE

RESERVA BIOSFERA SIERRA LA LAGUNA

Picacho de La Laguna (2090m)

La Paz

Isla Cerralvo

Canal Cerral

Bahía La Ventana

Ensenada de los Muertos

Bahía de Los Muertos

PACIFIC OCEAN

Todos Santos

El Pescadero
Playa Los Cerritos

Punta Pescadero

Los Barriles

Buena Vista

La Ribera

Santiago

SEA OF CORTEZ

SIERRA LA LAGUNA

Punta Poza de Cota

Punta el Cardoncito

El Salto

Cabo Pulmo

Tropic of Cancer

Cabo San Lucas

San José del Cabo

Bahía San Lucas
Cabo del Sol
Cabo Santa María
Punta Chileno
Costa Brava
Cabo Real
El Ranchito
Bahía San José del Cabo
Santa Cruz
Santa Agueda
Punta Paredones

0   50 km

The western and eastern capes

Largely defined by vast, sometime forbidding coastlines, remote towns at the end of dirt roads and the central **Sierra La Laguna** range, the **western and eastern**

capes have a feel more akin to the rest of the peninsula than with Los Cabos just to the south. Unlike the single-road access to many of the towns and cities of Baja California, there are two divergent routes leading down either coast. The **Pacific route** of Mex 19 bumps up frequently against the **western cape** and the foothills of the Sierra La Laguna. Mex 1 spends most of its time on the opposite side of the peninsula in the Laguna's other foothills, passing through shuttered mining towns, kissing the **eastern cape** at **Los Barriles** and connecting with the Sea of Cortez through long, arduous dirt roads branching off to the east. The landscape of cacti and rock doesn't change as strikingly along the highways as it does further inland, where the effect of crossing the **Tropic of Cancer** produces some lush, hidden oases fed by gurgling streams and run-off from the mountains.

Todos Santos and the Pacific coast

During the 1990s, **Todos Santos** experienced an influx of full- and part-time residents from the US who were lured by word-of-mouth reports that it was a **surfers'** and **artists'** paradise. It's easy to see where the enthusiasm came from: the Pacific laps up against **beaches** reached by dirt roads cut through mangrove and palm stands. You can stroll in and out of the many downtown **galleries** without passing a McDonald's or being harried by a pack of feral dogs. The mild climate, cooled by Pacific breezes, is only slightly uncomfortable during the rainy fall months. Laidback and upscale, Todos Santos accommodates yuppie and hippy tastes in equal measure. The art scene and gallery business are thriving, creating a craft-based industry that complements the leatherwork and other, older artisan works that you'll find in many Baja California towns. There's also some great **whale watching** to be had from the shore: sit on any of the beaches in the winter months and you are bound to see several of the creatures.

Beyond Todos Santos, there is little else to see along the **Pacific coast** unless you're surfing, visiting friends in one of the nascent coastal developments or taking part in an organized tour of the southern parts of **Sierra La Laguna** organized out of Los Cabos. Access to the ocean is limited to unmarked dirt and packed sand roads running both from Mex 19 and parallel to the coast. Surfers drive north of the Tropic of Cancer to catch unspoiled waves at Playa Las Pocitas or La Pastora.

Some history

Padre Jaime Bravo, a Jesuit out of La Paz, settled Todos Santos in 1723 as a farm and base to visit nearby missions. The diocese elevated it to mission status in 1734, the same year the Pericú Indian rebellion began dislodging missionary interests throughout the Cape. By 1736 Todos Santos was rubble, and the thousand Indians who re-established the town over the next few years were wiped out shortly thereafter in the early 1740s by an epidemic that swept the Cape. Subsequent eighteenth-century mission attempts out of La Paz and Loreto fared little better – they too suffered at the whims of disease. It wasn't until the mid-nineteenth century that mestizos were able to gain a foothold in the area and began producing the sugar cane that generated the town's early fortunes. Agriculture has remained a constant since then, fed by water flowing from the Sierra La Laguna although frequent hurricanes – the most recent was Juliette in 2001 – necessitate a rebuilding effort every generation.

In the 1970s the creation of the Transpeninsular Highway funnelled throngs of surfers south in search of giant waves, but to get to Todos Santos they still had to traverse a difficult dirt road from either Cabo San Lucas or the Mex 1

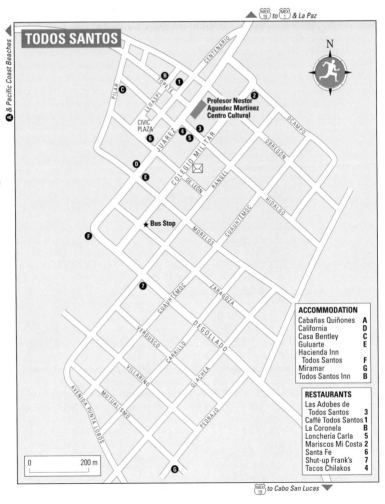

TODOS SANTOS

N

ACCOMMODATION

Cabañas Quiñones	A
California	D
Casa Bentley	C
Guluarte	E
Hacienda Inn Todos Santos	F
Miramar	G
Todos Santos Inn	B

RESTAURANTS

Las Adobes de Todos Santos	3
Caffé Todos Santos	1
La Coronela	B
Lonchería Carla	5
Mariscos Mi Costa	2
Santa Fe	6
Shut-up Frank's	7
Tacos Chilakos	4

0   200 m

turnoff near La Paz. This held off all but those most determined to experience the south's best surfing until 1986, when the paved Mex 19 was completed, connecting Todos Santos with La Paz and Cabo San Lucas and providing a shorter route than Mex 1 across the mountains.

Arrival and information

Mex 19 enters the city from the southeast along Avenida Degollado, meeting the highway's Los Cabos-bound traffic in the centre of town at a right angle with Boulevard Benito Juárez, the town's primary commercial artery. Here, and on parallel Calle Colegio Militar, are the **bank**, shops, **post office** and telephones. Calles Olachea and Topete intersect with Degollado and Juárez, respectively, and twist and turn on their way to the shore.

Buses drop passengers off at the corner of Colegio Militar and Calle Zaragoza, directly across from the town park. Although it's small, the town stretches west towards the ocean along numerous dirt roads. **Parking** on the street is perfectly safe and easy to do, even in high season. There is **no information office**, but the bookstore El Tecolote on Calle Hidalgo at Juárez takes up the slack by providing a monthly magazine with events; it also has a great selection of new and used **books**. You can also check the local monthly publication *El Calendario* (W todossantos-baja.com/elcalendariotodossantos.htm) for details about events such as the occasionally offered historic house tours, mini film festivals and gallery open houses. The print version is available at galleries and restaurants downtown.

Todos Santos has **no airport**, and transfers from either La Paz's or Los Cabos' airports require taxis to their respective bus stations, followed by a wait and then up to an hour and a half-long ride. La Paz is about thirty minutes closer, but Los Cabos serves more destinations. The most cost-effective way to get from either airport to Todos Santos is to **rent a car**, especially since you may want to use it to get between the town and the beaches as well as for day-trips throughout the Cape.

Accommodation

For its size, Todos Santos has a large number of small **inns** and **B&Bs**, most of which are situated in the town centre and along the dirt streets that wind their way to the estuary and Pacific coast. Those travelling in groups will find it easy to rent a shared space, often with kitchen facilities, for about M$300 per person a night. There are usually enough beds for everyone but it's a good idea to book ahead if you have your heart set on a particular place. The town's official website, W todossantos.cc, has extensive links to one- and two-room operations in and around town.

Cabañas Quiñones C Las Playitas 3km from the plaza; follow signs from Juárez and Topete ☎612/126-5113, ✆ 612/145-0219. Six palapa-covered cottages with tiny kitchens, large bedrooms, private bath and ocean-view patios. Also has limited laundry facilties. ❷

California C Morelos, at Blvd Juárez ☎612/145-0525, ✉hotelcaliforniareservations@hotmail .com. An evening's stay at this downtown gem might make it worth parting with some of those pesos you've been setting aside for a rainy day. The owners completed a beautiful restoration of the hotel in 2004, and the rooms are multicultural mestizos of Mexican and Moorish decor. There's a pool and restaurant, as well as ocean views from the top floor. ❼

Casa Bentley C del Pilar 38 W casabentley .com. The *Bentley*'s shared kitchen, bougainvil-lea-covered walls and avocado and mango orchards gives visitors the impression they're taking a break at a friend's country house. The rooms are decorated in a Southwest style, with ceiling fans, tiled floors and couches. There's also a pool in the courtyard. ❼

Guluarte Blvd Juárez, at C Morelos ☎612/825-0006. One of the cheapest places in town, the most basic of *Guluarte*'s fifteen rooms have a fridge and a fan; some have a/c and TV. Also has

a small pool and car park, and sits next to a nice little market. ❷

Hacienda Inn Todos Santos signposted along a dirt road northwest of town ☎612/145-0073, W haciendatodossantos.com. The lavish gardens, pool and Moorish domes are impressive, if out of place, at this near-luxury hotel with TV, a/c, fireplaces and a few rooms with kitchens; some of the twelve rooms have ocean views. There's also a restaurant and laundry services. Without your own transport, it's a bit far from town. ❺

Miramar C Pedrajo and C Mutualismo ☎612/825-0321. Basic rooms, some with views of the Pacific, a short walk from the beach but a little longer to the centre of town. The hotel has a laundry and pool. ❸

Misión del Pilar C Colegio Militar, at C Hidalgo ☎612/145-0114. Moroccan-themed inn with large rooms, private baths and a café that serves some of the town's best coffee. ❸

Playa San Pedrito Playa San Pedrito ☎612/145-0170. This campground off a surfing beach has no amenities other than hot water showers and pit toilets, but the location can't be beat. ❶

Posada la Poza drive southwest on C Olachea and follow signs toward the coast ☎612/145-0400, W lapoza.com. Surrounded by a landscaped desert garden and separated from the Pacific by an estuary, *Posada* enjoys one of the more peaceful settings in town. Rooms have tile floors and pastel-hued adobe walls, a/c, CD players, binoculars and terraces or balconies. **➐**

Teampaty Surf Camp Playa los Cerritos ⓦtodossantos.cc/ecosurfcamp.html. Rustic, bohemian campers and open sand for pitching a camp have made *Teampaty* the epitome of Todos Santos beach camping. Always book ahead, as guests have a habit of staying for a while. Tent camping **➊**, trailers **➋**

Todos Santos Inn C Legaspi 33, between C Topete and C Obregón ☎612/145-0040, ⓦmexonline .com/todossantosinn.htm. This US expat-run inn is surrounded by many of the town's art galleries. The historic structure houses four elegantly decorated rooms and a garden patio. **➐**

The Town

If you're not content with sunning yourself or surfing at one of the **beaches** 3km to the west, you won't find much to do in town; its charm lies in simple pursuits like perusing its hallmark **galleries** or the many arts and craft shops along Juárez and Colegio Militar. It has a pleasant, leisurely pace, though the midday sun can be draining in the summer.

Professor Néstor Agúndez Martínez Centro Cultural

The hub of the town's cultural activities, the two-storey, red-brick **Professor Néstor Agúndez Martínez Centro Cultural**, Juárez s/n, between Obregón and Hidalgo, is worth a visit if for no other reason than to check out the murals adorning the interior breezeways. The five-metre-high walls gave the Diego Rivera-influenced painters room to celebrate farming, industrialization, sport and other solidarity-boosting subjects of the 1930s. The courtyard plays host to musical events and classes such as tai chi and yoga. If you feel like trying your own hand at being creative, you can join any of the **workshops** on offer, including writing, painting water colours, pottery, and even improvisational theatre; postings for the workshops and local events are listed on a bulletin board and advertised on flyers.

The Civic Plaza

The **Civic Plaza**, a bland collection of concrete, brick and a few flowering plants, is one block northwest of Juárez at the corner of De León and Centenario. City hall and the police station anchor the northeast corner, while opposite the pink stucco **Nuestra Señora del Pilar de Todos Santos** adds nothing to the field of religious architecture and little else in the way of history – the church has been repeatedly reduced to rubble by hurricanes. Until the mid-nineties, the **Teatro Cine Manuel Márquez de León** on the northwest corner of the square was the only working theatre in the southern state. Its programme is a mix of cultural events aimed at the Spanish-speaking population with occasional English-language performances of plays such as *The Vagina Monologues* as well as a film series curated by the Centro Cultural (where you'll find the theatre's schedule posted).

The galleries

As the town's reputation as a cultural haven has grown, more merchants and artists have arrived to open **galleries**. The quality of the work has diversified accordingly. Since the town is so small and what's on display can change monthly, the best way to experience what's available is to amble in and out of the galleries; Ezra Katz Gallery, Charles Stewart Gallery and Eli Alexander Fine Art are three of the more standout venues. The majority of the galleries are between Obregón and Morelos on the blocks northwest of Colegio Militar. It's best to visit in the post-siesta afternoon, when the gallery-hopping has a more convivial air about it than the morning, largely because the Cabo bus crowds have already departed to make their glass-bottomed booze cruises by sunset.

△ Crafts store, Todos Santos

The beaches

Several tranquil **beaches** lie within close proximity to Todos Santos. You can access the **southern beaches** from town or directly off Mex 19. Several blocks west from the centre is a dirt road, marked with a sign that reads "Aviso oficial", which brings you to the south edge of **Punta Lobos**. Lobos isn't safe for swimming; you can, though, purchase the day's fresh catch from one of the fishermen who line the shore in the evenings. From here, the rest of the beaches spread south for 10km. **San Pedro** (also known as **Las Palmas**) is the first beach south of Punta Lobos and is excellent for swimming. To get there, look for a sandy road next to a palm grove at Km 57 Mex 19. **Los Cerritos**, Km 64 Mex 19, is good for both surfing and swimming. **Puente del Pescadero** receives some of Todos' overflow at its surf camp at Km 84. Note that due to riptides, steeply shelving beaches and rogue waves, only San Pedro and Los Cerritos are **safe for swimming**.

The **northern beaches** of La Pastora and Las Pocitas are more difficult to get to, but regulars swear they're better for surfing than points south and you'll never feel crowded on shore or in the water. They can be reached first by taking Calle Topete northwest out of town, and then by following the sand and dirt road that is parallel to the shoreline. If you don't have a car, you can **rent a horse** at Todos Santos Outfitters, almost 2km from town in this direction (M$200 per hour). About 5km away from town, and just north of the Tropic of Cancer – unfortunately, unmarked – you'll find a collection of pitched tents north at **Playa la Pastora**. It's not an official campsite but people nonetheless settle on the sand ridge above the shore for days at a time. Access to the rest of the coast along this northern route is limited by farms and residential enclaves that have fenced off the area between the dirt road and waterfront.

Avoid disappointment and hunger by bringing everything you need with you to the beach. **Teampaty Surf Camp** at Los Cerritos (lessons and rentals M$220) is an exception to the rule, hawking everything surfing-related, from day-long board rentals to five-day women-only surf workshops.

Eating and drinking

Places to eat are mainly on Colegio Militar: you'll find street stalls around the bus stop and a couple of decent restaurants at the traffic lights a block away. You'll find more casual, open-air joints throughout town than in Los Cabos, but prices are almost as high.

Los Adobes C Hidalgo, between Blvd Juárez and C Colegio Militar ☎612/145-0203. *Adobes'* peaceful desert garden dining room and adjacent café and WiFi hangout are its greatest assets – not the high priced, over-done gourmet dishes. The café is open 9am–5pm; the restaurant for lunch and dinner.

Café Santa Fe C Márquez de León s/n, on the plaza ☎612/145-0340. One of the Cape's best restaurants and hands-down Todos Santos' top spot, *Santa Fe's* Northern Italian menu showcases locally grown ingredients and a stellar wine list that combines bottles from Valle de Guadalupe and foreign appellations. Dinner runs about M$700 a person, with wine, and tables are set inside an old hacienda or outside on the courtyard patio. Closed Tues.

Caffé Todos Santos C Centenario 33, at C Topete ☎612/145-0340. Decorated by local artists, this expat-run café does fine breakfasts, coffees, teas, muffins and bagels. Lunch and dinner are a few steps above deli fare.

La Copa Wine Bar C Legaspi 33, at *Todos Santos Inn* ☎612/145-0040. Good by-the-glass selections as well as the town's most satisfying margaritas. Intimate and cosy, it's one of the few romantic hideaways in town.

La Coronela C Morelos, at Blvd Juárez, at *Hotel California*. Good, slightly highbrow Mexican cuisine – such as seared tuna – with a country slant, and tapas on a separate menu.

Lonchería Carla C Hidalgo s/n, between Blvd Juárez and C Colegio Militar. An open-air café with flavourful quesadillas and burritos for M$10 apiece.

Mariscos Mi Costa C Colegio Militar s/n, at C Ocampo. Excellent seafood place with a relaxed atmosphere. Try the *sopa de mariscos* or shrimp *ceviche*; also serves decent tacos.

Miguel's C Rango s/n, at Av Delgado. Open-air fish taco joint does a solid job with the same dishes – mainly *ceviche* and soups – *Mi Costa* handles so well, all for around M$100 a person.

Pilar's Fish Tacos Not much more than a stand, *Pilar's* is still one of the town's landmarks. The fish tacos (M$10) here are the best you'll find south of La Paz.

Shut-up Frank's Av Degollado s/n, between C Rangel and C Cuauhtémoc. The town's only sports bar, replete with great burgers and some traditional Mexican food.

Tacos Chilakos Blvd Juárez and C Hidalgo. Cheap, easy and open-air, *Chilakos* is regarded as one of the best places for tacos on the peninsula.

The eastern cape

The **eastern cape** is mostly known for the stunningly beautiful and largely undeveloped expanse of **coastline** between Bahía de los Muertos and San José's estuary. Within these few hundred kilometres there are only a handful of coastal towns of note and a few near-abandoned **mining towns** inland. Ever since the Transpeninsular Highway's paving, developers have longed to transform this area into a resort area to rival Los Cabos in the south. So far, all they've done is clutter the unpaved roads – the only coastal roads here – with one billboard after another promising exclusive luxury enclaves and beautiful views of the sea.

Unless you plan to camp on a deserted beach with no services, it's essential to book **accommodation** in advance. There are very few options available in any class and the less expensive ones are booked in advance by groups of fishermen.

The mining towns

Although the Transpeninsular Highway from La Paz to San José del Cabo is a shorter distance than the Pacific Mex 19, the route spends so much time curving and climbing through the **Sierra La Laguna** that the journey is a good hour longer than the trip through Todos Santos. Along the way it runs through a number of old mining towns, such as El Triunfo and San Antonio, that likely would have been forgotten if the highway wasn't here – as happened to similar shrunken towns scattered throughout the rest of the mountain range. **EL TRIUNFO**'s fortunes have dipped drastically from the days when it served briefly as the capital of Baja California Sur territory. Like Santa Rosalía in the north, Triunfo grew rapidly after precious metals were discovered here, in this case silver rather than copper. In the 1870s, El Triunfo's population of over ten thousand people outnumbered La Paz or any other southern city. After six decades of production, a hurricane hit the area and flooded the already depleted mines. A few attempts to resume operations faltered and all but a handful of people left town by 1926. **SAN ANTONIO**, also a former silver mining town, has fared slightly better. When Gaspar Pisón founded it in 1756, it was the first town on the peninsula that wasn't initially settled as a mission by the Jesuits as well as one of the first non-native settlements in California. San Antonio peaked in the late 1800s; today it's a small settlement of adobe buildings and cobblestone streets with Mex 1 running along its western border.

Los Barriles and the coastal road south

After descending from the Sierra La Laguna, the highway briefly skirts along the coast at the eastern cape's largest and most accessible town, **LOS BARRILES**. A **fishing** and **windsurfing** centre, the town is known for the near-constant strong breeze blowing through **Bahía Palmas**. The wind, best in winter, is brilliant for experienced windsurfers (less so for beginners) and makes the waters offshore a regular venue for international competitions. Oddly, neither fishing nor windsurfing is easily arranged on the spot; book ahead with Vela Windsurf Resorts (US☎1-800/223-5443, ⓦvelawindsurf.com; two-person beginners lesson M$600). Angling is also quite popular 20km to Los Barriles' north at **Punta pescadero**, a one-hotel town that draws sport-fishermen after a big catch and little else.

From Los Barriles and its nearly identical next-door neighbour **BUENA VISTA**, the rough coastal road is almost entirely dirt, rock or packed sand; the trip to San José will take four and a half hours unless you've have 4WD but the views are remarkable. The coastline along this stretch is a mix of sand, clear water and sea life that's been virtually untouched by large-scale development, no matter what the billboards announcing vacation homes say. There are no services along this segment, only fish camps interspersed with large family compounds replete with generators and satellite communications. It is possible to camp along secluded stretches between the large portions that are closed off from the road with thin wire fences; the gaps where campers usually set up are gullies that, while dry most of the year, can fill with rushing water quickly after a rain.

Practicalities

Punta Pescadero, (☎612/141-0101, US☎1-800/426-2252, ⓦpunta-pescadero .com; ❽), the name of the hotel and town are wholly apt, as this twenty-room establishment is a haven for fishermen. The rooms, all with balconies, overlook the sea from the top of a cliff. All meals are included with the price, but they will cook whatever you catch. Los Barriles and nearby Buena Vista have more **accommodation** options than any other town on the eastern cape. Windsurfers book package trips at the twenty-six-room *Playa del Sol* on the beach in Los Barriles (US☎1-800/368-4334, ⓦbajaresorts.com; ❻). At *Martin Verdugo's Beach Resort*, in Los Barriles, turn left at *Hotel Palmas de Cortez* and drive for 1km (☎624/141-0054, ⓦverdugosbeachresort.com; tent camping ❶, rooms ❹); the motel rooms have a/c and the campsites are near the water at this long-time budget favourite. There's a rooftop bar and restaurant as well as a pool that can be used by any guest. The cape's largest resort is the landmark *Palmas de Cortez* resort, follow signage from Mex 1 (T624/141-0050, UST1-800/368-4334, Wpalmasdecortez.com; ❼), which caters primarily to old-school fishermen and windsurfers, and is able to arrange scuba and fishing trips and tours by horseback. Rooms vary; some have a/c, some are suites and there are some with palapa roofs.

In Buena Vista, *Rancho Leonero* (UST1-800/646-2252, Wrancholeonero.com; ❼) is 350 acres of low-key, secluded bliss in an all-inclusive resort. Palapa-covered bungalows and rooms have tile floors, a/c and views of the beach and sea. The staff are experts at local fishing, kayaking and anything else you want to do in the water. There are more traditional resort activities at *Buena Vista Beach Resort*, Km 105 Mex 1 (T624/141-0033, UST1-800/752-3555, Whotelbuenavista.com; ❻), where the grounds are crowded with tennis courts, a pool and hot tub.

Los Barriles, along with Cabo Pulmo to the south, has the largest number of **dining** options along the eastern cape, but that's not saying much. If you're staying at one of the one-resort towns, a meal at the in-house restaurant is likely your only choice – and one that is always made better if you're eating something you caught earlier in the day. The tacos served from Los Barriles' main street staple *Tacos de Silvia* are cheap (on average M$90 each), delicious, and filled with grilled chicken, *carne asada*, chorizo or battered fish. Grilled fish at *Calafia* in the *Buena Vista Beach Resort* is kept simple with butter and garlic sauce (about M$150 per person); in season you can get Pacific lobster. For about M$150 a person, you can stop for a bite at *Tío Pablo's* (T624/141-0334), a US expat-run restaurant with a mammoth menu of delicious burgers, fish and salads, just a block away from *Palmas de Cortez* resort in Los Barriles.

Cabo Pulmo south to San José del Cabo

Like Todos Santos, **Cabo Pulmo** straddles the Tropic of Cancer, giving the area a lush, tropical atmosphere. But unlike its cross-cape tropical double, Cabo Pulmo has yet to become a popular destination for outsiders; the fault of which

△ Parque Marino Nacional Cabo Pulmo

can be directly blamed on the terrible roads that link it to La Paz and San José del Cabo. This remoteness has afforded the town a level of protection for its most beautiful and delicate resources: wide, tranquil beaches and a giant coral reef just offshore in the Sea of Cortez.

Though the smallest national park on the peninsula, **Parque Marino Nacional Cabo Pulmo** contains the largest living coral reef on the west coast of North America and the only one in the Sea of Cortez. Over two thousand species of marine organisms live in the reef, as do 236 kinds of fish. After the Mexican government made it a protected area in 1995, a small cadre of merchants in Cabo Pulmo set up shop along the beaches to support a growing yet still small community of eco-tourists; the most established of the bunch, and the only one with a phone, is Pepe's Dive Center (T 624/141-0001). If you have your own gear, you can just head into the water from the shore and reach a few of the fourteen dive sites. The beaches are also home to five species of sea turtles, two of which lay their eggs in the sand. The park provides protection for the eggs, but they're under constant threat from increased foot and vehicular traffic and the growing popularity in Mexico City of turtle eggs as a perceived sexual stimulant.

Practicalities

Not a resort in the traditional sense, *Cabo Pulmo Beach Resort*'s (T 624/141-0244, W cabopulmo.com; ⑥) twelve-room collection of solar-powered beach cottages is nonetheless a comfortable **place to stay**. The cottages have private baths and killer views, and there's also a two-bedroom house available (M$2200 per night). *Nancy's* (F 624/130-0203; ④), a combination restaurant and two-room B&B, caters to visitors from Los Cabos who come for the menu but stay because the drive back after dinner is such a pain. It's at least a two-hour drive down the coast towards San José before reaching *Villa del Faro*, a third of the way between Vinorama and Los Frailes (W villadelfaro.net; ⑦), a luxe private home turned bed-and-breakfast with suites for over US$300 a night as well as a secluded stone cottage on the beach that fits the budget better. Back in Cabo Pulmo, the candlelit *Nancy's Restaurant* is also run by a US ex-pat, but serves up locally caught seafood like shrimp (M$170) and other dishes based on regionally-sourced ingredients.

Los Cabos

The belief that Baja California was an island, not a peninsula, persisted for generations after the first explorations by the Spanish. Modern **Los Cabos** – consisting of **Cabo San Lucas** (frequently referred to as just "Cabo"), **San José del Cabo**, and the 32km **corridor** between them – might as well be such an island. Its wealth and geographic seclusion at the tip of the peninsula set it apart from the rest of Baja California to such an extent that people will state with authority that they've been to Cabo but haven't been to Baja. The two cities that make up Los Cabos have traditionally been presented as polar opposites – party in Cabo, arty in San José – but they're much more like two sides of the same coin. Development over the past decade has brought the

Most visitors to Los Cabos arrive by air; if you plan to arrive in Cabo San Lucas by car or by bus, see p.255; for San José del Cabo see p.266.

Arriving by air

Los Cabos International Airport, Km 42 Mex 1 La Paz–Cabo San Lucas (☎624/146-5097), serves several Mexican and US West Coast cities, and a few East Coast cities. It lies 10km north of downtown San José del Cabo and a further 32km from Cabo San Lucas. If you're staying at a resort, find out ahead of time if they run **resort shuttles**. Although few places provide free rides, the M$100 or so that many Cabo hotels charge is cheaper than a taxi or shared-ride van.

Beyond a resort shuttle, the cheapest options are the **shared-ride van shuttles** that run on a four-zone system and do not depart until full. If you're staying in San José (M$120) you'll get off the shuttle first; those going to Cabo (M$140) are dropped off last. If you're in a group of five people or more, you can **book the entire van** at M$700 for San José and M$930 to Cabo. For either option you'll do the booking inside the arrivals terminal. **Taxis** are the most expensive option into Los Cabos, costing at least M$550 San José, M$820 to Cabo and between M$600–660 for Corridor resorts.

Car rental agencies have kiosks in the arrivals section of each terminal but these only point you to the shuttle buses that run between the airport and the off-site pick-up. The fastest way from the airport to any other location is along a 19km toll road (M$26) that connects with Mex 1 at Paseo de Los Cabos, right where San José begins to give way to the Corridor. This four-lane highway zips through grazing pastures, taking about a third of the time the free Mex 1 takes to cover the same distance.

towns close together in mentality: San José struggles to maintain an aura of small-town charm in the midst of rapidly developing its waterfront while Cabo tries to class up its margarita and jet-ski image.

Some history

In 1730, the Jesuit father Nicolas Tamaral from Loreto established a mission at San José. Four years later, a Pericú revolt led to their ouster and the abandonment of the Cape by the Spanish. Not that the area didn't continue to thrive, though. Before the Jesuits had shown up, indigenous tribes and an international coterie of freebooters had used San José's estuary to launch raiding parties on galleons returning from the Philippines. The short-lived Jesuit intrusion resulted in a brief pause in the fun, but the thrills returned soon after and continued until pirate commerce waned and the Pericú died from a mix of smallpox and venereal diseases shared by the pirates.

Of the two towns, San José was always the more active and bustling and it established regular commercial links with Mazatlán. When the US navy wanted to blockade Mazatlán during the Mexican-American war, they did so from San José, starting in 1847. Skirmishes in San José and Cabo continued throughout the war, and a casualty of one of these minor battles – José Antonio Mijares – gave his name to San José's main commercial street. Postwar Los Cabos, along with the rest of the south, became a backwater, a collection of worn fishing boats and makeshift housing centred around a canning factory in Cabo San Lucas. In the 1940s it gained some notoriety as a sport-fishing destination, but most visitors in the south stuck to La Paz. It would likely have remained small if FONATUR hadn't picked it as one of the government's five master-planned tourist regions in 1972

Avoid changing money at the airport, as the rates given here are among the worst in Mexico; you're much better off at the banks or ATMs at the airport or in town and the cost of your transportation and tips from the airport can be covered easily in US dollars.

Getting around

Getting between the two towns and to any destination along the Corridor is too far – and hot – for walking. Avoid the insane taxi fares by taking the Suburcabos **bus**; for M$16 you can ride between both towns or to your Corridor hotel. There are stops along the main roads in both towns: the Cabo station is at Niños Héroes and Morelos and in San José at Valerio Gonzáles, just east of Mex 1 with a smaller station at Boulevards Miljares and Juárez. If you're staying on the Corridor, buses will drop off and pick up at the resort entrance (or directly across from it) along Mex 1. These buses run from 5.30am until around 9.30pm (seasonal information ☏ 624/146-0773). Regional Águila buses that do not stop along the Corridor leave from the stations about every hour and cost M$280.

Taxi between Cabo and San José or between hotels on the Corridor and either city will cost you between M$200 and M$450, depending on the time of day and how desperate you look; always agree upon a rate before departing.

If you plan to do forays into the rest of the Cape from Los Cabos or anticipate travelling frequently between the towns and the Corridor, hiring a **rental car** is a good option. Speeding along the Corridor is commonplace, but there are more highway patrols along this stretch of road than the Transpeninsular's other 1700km. Be alert for scams from employees at all Pemex stations: make sure the meter is at zero and count pesos out loud before handing them over.

– a decision that gave Los Cabos an airport at the same time the Transpeninsular was completed. Cabo, San José and the corridor have grown in spurts since then, with successive waves of hotel construction separated by short lulls in activity.

Cabo San Lucas

"Many people had come to Cape San Lucas, and many had described it. We had read a number of the accounts, and of course agreed with none of them. To a man straight off a yacht, it is a miserable little flea-bitten place, poor and smelly. But to one who puts in hungry, in a storm-beaten boat, it must be a place of great comfort and warmth."

John Steinbeck, *The Log from the Sea of Cortez*

When John Steinbeck pulled into the **CABO SAN LUCAS** marina one evening in the 1930s, his boat had to drop anchor in the bay and wait until morning to enter: the lampkeeper only worked the day shift. Cabo and its marina would now be unrecognizable to him, as well as anyone who came before the real estate boom of the 1990s. This one-time base for pirate vessels waiting to pounce on Spanish treasure ships is now home to merchants eager to separate visitors from their money, typically with more panache than the skull and crossbones crowd.

Before its recent explosive growth, Cabo was little more than a fishing and canning village occasionally visited by adventurous sports fishermen with the means to sail or fly to town. It quickly earned a reputation for the marlin that

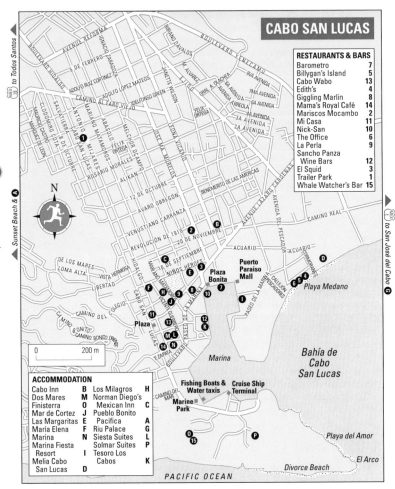

CABO SAN LUCAS

RESTAURANTS & BARS

Barometro	7
Billygan's Island	5
Cabo Wabo	13
Edith's	4
Giggling Marlin	8
Mama's Royal Café	14
Mariscos Mocambo	2
Mi Casa	11
Nick-San	10
The Office	6
La Perla	9
Sancho Panza	
Wine Bars	12
El Squid	3
Trailer Park	1
Whale Watcher's Bar	15

ACCOMMODATION

Cabo Inn	B	Los Milagros	H
Dos Mares	M	Norman Diego's	
Finisterra	O	Mexican Inn	C
Mar de Cortez	J	Pueblo Bonito	
Las Margaritas	E	Pacifica	A
María Elena	F	Riu Palace	G
Marina	N	Siesta Suites	L
Marina Fiesta		Solmar Suites	P
Resort	I	Tesoro Los	
Melia Cabo		Cabos	K
San Lucas	D		

to Todos Santos

THE CAPE | Cabo San Lucas

Sunset Beach &

to San José del Cabo

N

Puerto Paraíso Mall

Plaza Bonita

Playa Medano

0   200 m

Plaza

Marina

Bahía de Cabo San Lucas

Fishing Boats & Water taxis

Cruise Ship Terminal

Marine Park

Playa del Amor

El Arco

Divorce Beach

PACIFIC OCEAN

could be caught here, and the bay is now full of sleek, radar-equipped fishing yachts. Since the completion of the Transpeninsular Highway and the expansion of the Los Cabos airport, the once quiet town has rapidly become the focal point of Los Cabos: million-dollar condos have sprung up, palms have been transplanted, water has been piped in from San José and everything has a high polished sheen. There were less than 3500 rooms for rent in 1998 – today there are over eight thousand in Cabo alone, firmly placing the town on a par with long-established Mexican resorts such as Mazatlán, Acapulco and Cancún. Even a mammoth Wal-Mart has opened here, alongside **Puerto Paraíso**, an enormous mall on the marina comprising a convention centre, a theatre complex, a bowling alley, a huge parking outlet and condos. More like an enclave of the US than part of Mexico, preserving almost nothing that is not geared to tourism, it can be fun for a day or two; if you plan to **fish** or **dive** the allure will last for much longer.

Though prices are higher than in neighbouring San José (see p.266), there's much more of a party atmosphere in Cabo, thanks largely to the younger crowd.

As big as it has become, Cabo is still a small town and you'll be able to walk most anywhere you'll want to go. The downtown area consists of the cluster of streets north of the marina area. The horseshoe-shaped marina has room for a few hundred boats in the centre and a cluster of hotels, shops and the Puerto Paraíso mall. To the east and west of the marina, more resorts spread out in lines along the waterfront.

Arrival and information

From Todos Santos, Mex 19 ends northwest of Cabo San Lucas at Avenida Reforma before entering into a confusing warren of city streets. It's easier to take the less direct yet easier bypass road Boulevard Constituyentes (on some signs it is marked Calle Hidalgo) around Cabo's eastern edge and then double back into town via a right on Mex 1. **Buses** into Cabo arrive at the station at Niños Héroes and Morelos (☎624/143-5020).

Surprisingly, Cabo has **no official tourist office**, just dozens of places dishing out maps and drink coupons, and usually throwing in some timeshare patter while they're at it.

Accommodation

Most of the resorts occupy the prime real estate immediately around the marina, while downtown has a healthy selection of budget **accommodation**. They're not posh, but they have spirit and service common to bed-and-breakfasts, and they're all less than a ten-minute walk from the action. Hotels on the marina will be noisier than downtown, but they're well-suited for night owls. The resorts to the east of the marina empty out onto the active Playa Médano, while those to the west have the unswimmable yet beautiful Playa Solmar and the recently developed Sunset Beach at their doors.

Camping on nearby Playa Médano is not encouraged by the beachfront restaurateurs, nor is it particularly restful or safe – you're more likely to get hit by an errant jet ski than you are to be robbed.

Downtown

Cabo Inn 20 de Noviembre and C Leona Vicario ☎624/143-0819, ⓦcaboinnhotel.com. Small, quiet rooms with a proper local feel just two blocks from the marina. A former brothel, it now has a slightly bohemian travellers' atmosphere. All rooms have a/c, plus there's a small pool, a sun deck and free coffee for guests. ⓺

Dos Mares C Emiliano Zapata s/n, between C Hidalgo and C Vicente Guerrero ☎624/143-0330, ⓔhoteldosmares@cabotel.com.mx. A good location right by the marina and close to the action, rooms here have TV, plus there's a tiny pool, as well as some studios with kitchens. ⓸

Mar de Cortez Blvd Lázaro Cárdenas, between C Guerrero and C Matamoros ☎624/143-0032, ⓦmardecortez.com. Colonial-style decor in a lovely planted setting with a mix of older and modern, larger rooms around a pool; some

have terraces and all have a/c. Also has a good restaurant. ⓸

Las Margaritas Plaza Aramburo 7 ☎624/143-6770, ⓔmargaritas@real-turismo.com. Smack in the middle of Cabo and stumbling distance from *El Squid Roe* (see p.260), the spacious rooms all have a/c, TV and kitchens, but no charm. ⓺

María Elena Matamoros near Cárdenas and Niños Héroes ☎624/143-3296, ⓕ624/143-3289. A basic motel in the less touristy area between the bus station and town. Nothing special, but fairly clean rooms and just next to a laundromat. ⓷

Los Milagros C Matamoros 116 ☎624/143-4566, ⓦlosmilagros.com.mx. Tasteful, studio-like rooms with high-speed Internet connections, a small pool and a sun deck make this a real find, just a few blocks from the action. Reservations recommended. ⓹

Norman Diego's Mexican Inn Av 16 de Septiembre and Abasolo ℡ 624/143-4987, ⓦ themexicaninn.com. The dirt road just outside the doors gives a false impression of the comfort at this small B&B. Coffee and *postres* are served around the courtyard's fountain every morning and Mexican tile work, queen-size beds, a/c, TVs and DVD players adorn the rooms. ❺

Siesta Suites C Zapata s/n, between C Hidalgo and C Guerrero ℡ 624/143-2773, ⓦ cabosiestasuites.com. This expat-run establishment offers clean, studio rooms with TV, a/c, free local calls and close proximity to the marina, as well as a pool and restaurant. Weekly and monthly rates available. ❺

The marina and waterfront

Finisterra Blvd Marina s/n, at Playa Solmar ℡ 624/143-3333, ⓦ finisterra.com. This hotel on a towering hill isn't at Land's End as its name suggests, though it does have dramatic views of the Pacific Ocean. There are various room configurations available – it's part of many time-share programs – but all rooms have water views, TV, a/c and use of the pools and hot tubs. With the exception of the steep slope, it's an easy walk to the marina. ❻

Marina Fiesta Resort Marina Cabo, east side ℡ 624/145-6020, ⓦ marinafiestaresort.com. Just next to Puerto Paraíso Mall and a five-minute walk to Playa Médano, *Fiesta* still tries to keep guests on site with two pools and three restaurants. Standard rooms have TV, a/c, balconies and kitchenettes. ❽

Melia Cabo San Lucas Playa el Médano s/n, off Paseo el Pescador ℡ 624/145-7800, US℡ 1-800/745-2226, ⓦ www.meliacabosanlucas.com. More South Beach, Miami than Mexico, this style-heavy, substance-light resort has two pools and an outdoor bar scene that will disturb light sleepers. Many rooms have views of the water; inside they're outfitted with TV, a/c and WiFi. ❻

Pueblo Bonito Pacifica Cabo Sunset Beach, off Via de Lerry ℡ 624/142-9696, US℡ 1-866/585-1752, ⓦ pueblobonito.com. The scents of aromatherapy, multiple trickling water features and Pacific breezes create a sense of calm that can be matched only by a few of the hotels on the

Corridor. *Pacífica* is a haul from downtown – across Pedregal and down a curvy road – but the free shuttles to and from sister properties on Playa Médano make getting back and forth easy. Rooms are modern, with wood panelling, high-thread count sheets and private balconies. ❾

Riu Palace Km 4.5 Mex 1 ℡ 624/146-7160, ⓦ riu.com. For now, this all-inclusive behemoth is Playa Médano's newest resort. Each of the over 650 suites has a glimpse of the sea that can only be obscured by the effects of indulging in the in-room tequila, rum, vodka and brandy dispenser; you'll also find a TV, a/c and patios. ❽

Solmar Suites Blvd Marina s/n, at Playa Solmar ℡ 624/143-3535, US℡ 1-800/344-3349, ⓦ solmar.com. Old-school Cabo oceanfront resort with two heated swimming pools with swim-up bars, lap pool, 15-person Jacuzzi and the best sport-fishing fleet in Los Cabos. Rooms vary from predictable resort fare to fancy, but almost all have stunning ocean views. ❻

Tesoro Los Cabos Marina Cabo, west side ℡ 624/143-1220, ⓦ tesororesorts.com. This sprawling marina hotel was formerly called *Plaza Las Glorias* and briefly known as *Costa Real Cabo* before receiving a facelift in 2005 and a rebranding in 2006. The lobby and shopping arcade can be overwhelming, but the rooftop pool, redecorated rooms and view-packed balconies ease the tension. ❼

The marina and waterfront

In the last twenty years, Cabo's **marina** has evolved from a modest collection of fishing boats and small yachts to a high-tech operation that plays host to sophisticated sport-fishing operators and some of North and South America's largest mega-yachts. On land the marina is anchored by the open-air **Puerto Paraíso** mall. Although it's only half-occupied – which seems standard for any mall in Mexico – locals and visitors cruise its walkways, lounge on its steps and take coffee by fountains.

West of the marina are some of the older resorts – *Solmar* and *Finisterra* – and to its east is **Playa Médano**, Cabo's swimming-safe beach. Médano and the sidewalks around the marina are busy with hawkers who constantly tout trips in glass-bottomed boats, fishing, water-skiing, paragliding or bungee jumping, and will rent anything from horses to off-road quad bikes to jet skis and underwater gear. Competition is fierce, prices fluctuate daily and places come and go, so

△ El Squid Roe

shop around. **Scuba diving** and **snorkelling** are perhaps the most rewarding of these activities, though the best sites (out towards Finisterra) can only be reached by boat. For gear rental, snorkelling trips and scuba courses, check out the many companies along Bulevar Marina, especially in the plazas. Or simply rent a snorkel and fins at the marina (M$120), take a water taxi to Playa del Amor, and swim back to **Pelican Rock** (see opposite).

El Arco and Playa del Amor

If it wasn't for the forbidding rocks and dangerous cliffs, you could easily walk from the marina southwest to **Playa del Amor** and the tip of the peninsula.

Hiring a boat

If you plan to set foot on the marina's walkways, count on multiple offers of cruises, fishing trips, water taxis and a few services best not mentioned in polite company. While the marina is always a good place to **hire a water** taxi to Playa Médano, Playa del Amor or elsewhere, you should arrive well informed before plunking down cash for a trip on a **fishing** or **tour boat**.

Fishing

The better fishing deals can be **booked online** as a package before you arrive in Los Cabos. There are particularly good deals for groups of four or more and they generally include airport transfers, lodging, fishing license and whatever length of time you're planning to spend on the boat. *Solmar Suites* (see p.256) is the oldest operator in town and, although not the cheapest, is one of the most reliable and offers the widest range of services; they arrange trips for both advance of travel and day of excursion. Other hotels that arrange trips include *Cabo San Lucas* (℡624/143-3457), *Finisterra* (see p.256) and *Hacienda* (℡624/143-0663).

If you arrive in Los Cabos without the intent to fish and then get taken in by the promise of a big catch, stick with a business that has a storefront on the marina or, failing that, a booth near the cruise ship terminal. Always confirm that the operators have a fishing license. For questions about the process or your operator, the Secretary of Fishing has an answer line at ℡624/143-0564. The cost of a trip – which typically includes bait, licenses and a meal – is based on the size of the boat; a four-person *panga* will run about M$2200 for a seven- or eight-hour tour, a larger boat with better amenities (like toilets) runs up to M$7000. Three trusted companies are *San Lucas Yachts* (℡624/147-5679), *Picante Bluewater Sportsfishing* ℡624/143-2474, and *Pisces Sportfishing Fleet* (℡624/143-1288, ⊛piscessportfishing.com).

For a more relaxed angling trip, drive, or take a taxi (about M$100 from San José) to La Playita. The fishing boats here are four-person *pangas*, and the guides are pros.

Boat tours

Boat tours – some of them glass-bottomed – to Land's End and around take place throughout the day and evenings and, in season, are often combined with whale watching (though not as intimate as you'll get in the lagoons to the north). You can purchase these at multiple tour agencies along the marina, but it's quite likely your hotel will have a pre-arranged discount with one operator. You can also find coupons at the tourist-centric restaurants around Puerto Paraíso Mall. The two- to three-hour trips typically involve unlimited beer and margarita servings and, for about M$100 extra, a buffet of Mexican basics.

Pricing depends on the season, your ability to haggle and the coupons you're holding. Expect to pay M$35 per person for taxis from the marina to Playa Médano and about M$80 for return trips to Playa del Amor and El Arco. Glass-bottomed booze cruises run M$400 per person.

The shore of "Lovers' Beach" has shrunk (see Beaches, p.264) and severely diminished both its beauty and the amount of space free for swimming. Del Amor does have a second beach on the Pacific side, that's for looking only – the riptide will finish off any swimmers. From the safe side of Del Amor it's possible to swim in the direction of the marina to **Pelican Rock**, where the underwater shelf is home to schools of tropical fish. Experienced divers shouldn't miss the rim of a marine canyon, also off Playa del Amor, where unusual conditions at 30m create a "**sandfall**" with streams of sand starting their 2000-metre fall to the canyon bottom. The marine life in such a habitat is unique to beachfront areas. The peninsula comes to its conclusion just over another pile of rocks from Del Amor. **El Arco**, the huge **rock arch** at Finisterra – Land's End, where the Sea of Cortez meets the Pacific – is an extraordinary place, with a clear division between the shallow turquoise seawater on the east and the profound blue of the ocean out to the west; a colony of sea lions lives on the surrounding rocks. It is possible for the skilled climber to walk over to El Arco from Playa Solmar and then Del Amor. Most people, though, opt for trips via water taxi or tour boat. The water taxi will cost a negotiable M$150.

Eating and drinking

Trying to find a non-touristy **restaurant** or **bar** in Cabo is a waste of time, so focus instead on getting a good meal, which is possible throughout town. If you're after inexpensive food, head for Morelos and the streets away from the marina and waterfront. Some words of warning: the marina is surrounded by US chain restaurants and large pan-Mexican dining halls where the size of the giant plates is only matched by the size of the margaritas, with none of them tasting that good. These places compete for partying patrons by offering **happy hours** (often 6–8pm) and novel cocktails.

Restaurants

Barómetro Puerto Paraíso Mall, west side ☏624/143-1466. There's a lounge scene at this sleek outdoor tapas and cocktail joint that straddles the marina's sidewalk; one side hangs cantilevered over the water. The menu includes a mix of appetizers and wood-fired thin crust pizzas.

Billygan's Island Playa el Médano s/n, at Paseo del Pescador ☏624/143-4830. One of the three beach bar-restaurants that caters to beach party-goers from 8am–11pm. Breakfast, lunch and dinner is served right on the sand, and tropical drinks poured and consumed fairly nonstop.

Edith's Playa el Médano s/n, at Camino a Playa ☏624/143-0801. Tin lanterns hanging from the palapa roof at *Edith's* add some genuine ambiance to a stretch of Médano that's more raucous than romantic. The outdoor mesquite grill is used for freshly caught fish, filet mignon, lamb and shellfish. Dinner for two runs about M$800.

Mama's Royal Café/Felix's Fine Mexican & Seafood Hidalgo, at Zapata ☏624/143-4290, ⓦfelixcabosanlucas.com. Breakfast, lunch and brunch are served under the *Mama's* moniker, dinner and drinks go by *Felix*; either way, this

restaurant is cheaper (about M$150 per person) and better than most of what Cabo has to offer. Both menus are large, with two-dozen *huevos* choices in the morning and a dozen shrimp variations in the evening. The centrepiece is a three dozen-strong salsa bar that sounds much hokier than it tastes.

Mariscos Mocambo Av Leona Vicario and 20 de Noviembre ☏624/143-6070. A palapa roof covers this unpretentious seafood restaurant popular with Mexicans and the fisherman crowd. *Mocambo* is known for its regional specialities, especially its grilled red snapper, and competent takes on *ceviche* and *cockteles*.

Mi Casa Av Cabo San Lucas, at Lázaro Cárdenas ☏624/143-1933. This old Cabo joint has new Cabo prices in its otherwise low-key open-air restaurant decorated with handmade lanterns. The pan-Mexican menu – Yucatan-style baked fish, chicken in *mole*, Puerto Nuevo-style lobster – runs close to M$200 per entrée. Lunchtime provides some decent deals.

Nick-San Blvd Marina s/n, Plaza de la Danza ☏624/143-4484. Plenty of restaurants in Baja will sell you raw fish without knowing what they're doing with it – *Nik-San* is the exception. In addition to the extensive selection of locally caught sushi and sashimi – try the tuna – the Indonesian-inspired lobster soup is especially tasty. Dinner for two M$900.

The Office Playa el Médano s/n, at Camino a Playa ☎ 624/143-3464. The beach-side *Office* is at its calmest during breakfast, when diners chow down on so-so *huevos con chorizo* (M$95) and tasty Bloody Marys and morning margaritas. It gets rowdier as the day goes on – especially during happy hour – and often climaxes in a classic rock-driven beach party in the evening.

La Perla Lázaro Cárdenas, between Matamoros and Abasolo. Very inexpensive and surprisingly untouristy place right in the tourist zone; tortas, tacos and burgers for less than M$40.

Trailer Park Matamoros and Mijares ☎ 624/143-1927. Large platters of surf and turf for M$260 include some of the best budget shellfish and steak in the region.

Bars and clubs

Cabo Wabo Calle Vicente Guerrero, at Lázaro Cárdenas ☎ 624/143-1188. Rocker Sammy Hagar owns this boisterous club, which makes a popular tequila of the same name. Loud and lively, often with a heavy charge, but still a good place to hear live music – and if you're going here around a holiday, perhaps you can catch Sammy himself on stage.

Giggling Marlin Blvd Marina s/n, at Matamoros ☎ 624/143-1182. A Cabo institution, drawing an older set than other places on the strip. Mostly a place to drink and dance to Latin standards: chances of getting out without hearing *La Bamba* are slim.

Sancho Panza Wine Bar and Bistro Blvd Marina, inside Costa Real ☎ 624/143-3212. The cover charge (around M$110) will set you back, but the live jazz, blues and bossa nova beat strolling mariachis any day. There's a full menu and no cover earlier in the evening.

El Squid Roe Blvd Lázaro Cárdenas s/n, at Zaragoza ☎ 624/143-0655. If you just want to go nuts, this Cabo classic should be your first stop; a wild party atmosphere where table dancing is allowed, if not encouraged. There's a full dinner menu of Tex-Mex dishes alongside cocktails such as the yard-long margarita. Open late.

Whale Watcher's Bar Blvd Marina s/n, at Finisterra ☎ 624/143-3333. They serve food here, but everyone comes for the stunning views of the Pacific Ocean. The bar is on the hotel's top floor – the highest point in Cabo – and lines up tables along its outdoor balcony and flush against sliding glass doors.

Listings

Airlines Aero Calafia ☎ 624/143-4255 and 143-4302; Aeroméxico ☎ 624/142-0397; Alaska ☎ 624/149-5800; Continental ☎ 624/142-3890; Mexicana ☎ 624/143-5352; and United ☎ 624/142-2880.

Airport For enquiries call ☎ 624/142-0341.

Banks and exchange There's an ATM, and the best exchange rates, at Bancomer (cheques cashed 8.30am–noon) on Lázaro Cárdenas at Hidalgo; after hours, several casas de cambio (one by *Giggling Marlin*; see above) offer decent rates until 11pm.

Bookstore Libros Libros at Blvd Marina 20.

Buses Áquila ☎ 624/143-7878 or 7880 in Cabo.

Car rental Cabo San Lucas: Avis ☎ 624/143-4606 or 146-0201; Budget ☎ 624/143-4190 or 1522; Hertz ☎ 624/146-5088 or 142-0375; National ☎ 624/143-1414; and Thrifty ☎ 624/146-5030 or 143-1666.

Consulates Canada ☎ 624/142-4333, US: Blvd Marina Local C-4, Plaza Nautica, ☎ 624/143-3566

Emergencies ☎ 060 for police and fire department and ☎ 065 for Red Cross.

Hospital Hospital General, Km 2.5 Mex 19, Cabo ☎ 624/143-1444.

Internet access and phones A number of coffee shops near the marina offer free WiFi with the purchase of a cup of coffee. *Caboclipper* in Puerto Paraiso Mall is M$65 an hour and also has Internet phone service. *Cabomix*, on Matamoros at Niños Héroes, has the best rates in town and also has phones (including Internet phone services); there are also several small Internet places near the old bus station at Zaragoza and 16 de Septiembre, as well as a number of good but expensive Internet providers along the strip, including *Internet Services* on Plaza Náutica.

Post office Lázaro Cárdenas, east of the marina (Mon–Fri 9am–6pm).

The Corridor

The distinction between Cabo San Lucas and San José del Cabo blurs further each year as new resorts are erected along **the Corridor** separating the two towns. Even with the construction, the corridor is not packed with glass, steel and stucco eyesores but is a series of rolling and rocky hills, wide beaches, manicured golf courses and rather tame resorts hidden behind bougainvillea-covered gates. Many of the prime coastal spots have been occupied for decades, but new destinations are constantly being created while long timers keep pace with multi-million dollar makeovers. Each resort aims to be an end unto itself, with enough dining, drinking, relaxing and entertainment options to keep you from venturing out too often. Unlike downtown Cabo, Corridor resorts don't typically offer package meal plans, and a few days of carefree dining can result in staggering bills.

With few exceptions, all the development takes place on the south side of Mex 1 near both rocky shores and swimming-safe beaches. It's not possible to swim at all beachside resorts, and at the ones where it is, it's not always possible year-round. Resorts typically make concessions for this – offering shuttles to good ones, for example – but if diving into the surf yards from your room is important to you, be sure to check about a resort's shores before making reservations.

Golfing in Los Cabos

Arid, desert-like climates aren't the best places for growing thousands of acres of grass, but Los Cabos has managed to become a hotbed for **golfing**. Every course has at least partial views of the Sea of Cortez, if not a few holes right on the water. Green fees typically start at US$160 and can go above US$300 in high season.

The distances for the courses below are measured east from Cabo San Lucas towards San José del Cabo, 33km away.

Cabo del Sol Km 10 ☎624/145-8200, US☎1-800/386-2465, ⓦcabodelsol.com. There are two courses here, a Tom Weiskopf-designed course with an island-like green rising from the sea, and the Ocean course from Jack Nicklaus.

Cabo Real Km 19.5 ☎624/144-0040, US☎1-877/795-8727, ⓦcaboreal.com. The course begins in the mountains and rolls down to the sea at this Robert Trent Jones II championship course.

El Dorado Km 19.5 ☎624/144-5450, US☎1-800/393-0400. The second, newer course at Cabo Real was designed by Jack Nicklaus and is only open to members and their guests.

Mayan Palace Km 29.5 ☎624/142-0905, US☎1-866/465-7316, ⓦmayanresorts .com.mx. This former municipal course is the cheapest place to play in Los Cabos, doesn't take reservations and doesn't have any sea frontage.

Palmilla Km 27.5 ☎624/144-5250, ☎US1-800/637-2226. Jack Nicklaus' first Latin American creation, a 27-hole, cactus-packed course, is open only to guests at One & Only Palmilla.

Querencia Km 27 ☎624/145-6600, US☎1-888/236-2229, ⓦloscabosquerencia .com. Only members of the club and guests at Las Ventanas can tee up at this coveted 18-hole course designed by Tom Fazio.

Raven Via de Carlos Lote 601 ☎624/143-4653, ⓦ1-888/328-8501. Like Playa del Amor, Raven got clobbered by Hurricane Juliette in 2001. It took five years to reopen, and is now one of the cheaper places to play in the area, mainly because it can't claim any holes along the shore.

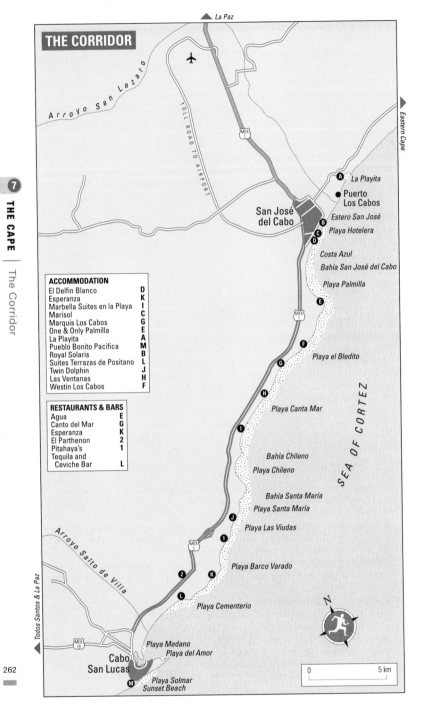

THE CORRIDOR

▲ La Paz

Eastern Cape ▶

ⒶLa Playita

● Puerto
Los Cabos

San José
del Cabo

Estero San José

Ⓑ

Ⓒ Playa Hotelera

Ⓓ

Costa Azul

Bahía San José del Cabo

Playa Palmilla

Ⓔ

Ⓕ

Playa el Bledito

Ⓖ

Ⓗ

Playa Canta Mar

Ⓘ

Bahía Chileno
Playa Chileno

Bahía Santa María
Playa Santa María

Ⓙ

Playa Las Viudas

❶

Playa Barco Varado

❷

Ⓚ

Ⓛ

Playa Cementerio

S E A   O F   C O R T E Z

ACCOMMODATION

El Delfin Blanco	D
Esperanza	K
Marbella Suites en la Playa	I
Marisol	C
Marquis Los Cabos	G
One & Only Palmilla	E
La Playita	A
Pueblo Bonito Pacifica	M
Royal Solaris	B
Suites Terrazas de Positano	L
Twin Dolphin	J
Las Ventanas	H
Westin Los Cabos	F

RESTAURANTS & BARS

Agua	E
Canto del Mar	G
Esperanza	K
El Parthenon	2
Pitahaya's	1
Tequila and	
Ceviche Bar	L

◀ Todos Santos & La Paz

Arroyo Salto de Villa

Ⓜ

Cabo
San Lucas

Playa Medano
Playa del Amor

Playa Solmar
Sunset Beach

N

0   5 km

Outside of the resorts, the beaches, and the golf courses, there's little to see and do along the Corridor. Any activities in the area – be it golfing or horseback riding – are arranged at the resorts themselves or in Cabo and San José.

Accommodation

There are practically no budget options in the Corridor; the only way to get a bed under M$2500 a night here is by booking a package trip ahead of time through an airline or consolidator. For all that cash, Corridor **resorts** typically deliver stunning views of the Sea of Cortez, at least one infinity pool, excellent customer service, maybe a swimming beach, a full service spa, golf course access (at another M$1500 or so) and a celebrity sighting or two.

Esperanza Km 7 Mex 1 ☎624/145-6400, US☎1-866/311-2226, ⊛esperanzaresort.com. Even the bathrooms have a view of the sea at this fifty-six suite resort where the terraces come with hammocks and the smallest room is 80 sq m. Swimming isn't possible at the beach, but it's not too far from the inviting Bahía Santa Maria. ❾

Marquis Los Cabos Km 21.5 Mex 1 ☎624/144-0906, US☎1-877/238-9399, ⊛marquisloscabos.com. Wedged into a tiny spot between Mex 1 and the sea, *Marquis* still manages to have a very wide and deep white-sand beach. The included breakfast is delivered to your room every morning and placed, alongside a summary of the world news, inside a butler's cubby-hole. Bulgari bath products, 300-thread count sheet and private balconies complete the pampering. ❽

 One & Only Palmilla Km 27.5 Mex 1 ☎624/146-7000, US☎1-800/637-2226, ⊛oneandonlyresorts.com. A US$75 million renovation of the 1950s *Palmilla* has turned the property into one of the continent's best resorts. There isn't a bargain to be had within its gates, but you'll get service unparalleled on the peninsula and rooms that, even at their most basic, are first-class – plasma TVs, climate control system, nightly snacks and even a personal butler. In addition to the two pools (one for adults only), there's a swimmable beach at the eastern end of the resort and a spa open only to guests. ❾

Marbella Suites en la Playa Km 17 Mex 1 ☎624/144-1060 ⊛marbellasuites.com. It's a short walk from the Corridor's second-cheapest option to Bahía Chileno, and while the junior suites don't have sea views, they do have kitchenettes, a/c and a living room. ❺

Suites Terrazas de Positano Km 4 Mex 1 ☎624/143-9383, ⊛hotelpositano.net. This small

△ Golfing along the Corridor

Playa del Amor near Land's End exemplifies the dual nature of the area's **beaches**. The marina side of the beach can be lovely for a swim, while the Pacific side, just across a football field's worth of sand, has undertows and crashing waves that kill – which is why this half is called Divorce Beach. As a general rule, Sea of Cortez beaches may be swimmable and Pacific beaches never are, but before you swim or surf anywhere in Los Cabos, ask a local and read any posted signs. Obey any signs warning you off wet sand and know that beaches which are safe one season may not be safe year-round – summer especially can be hazardous.

The good news is that every beach is free and open to the public, though getting to and from them can be a hassle without your own car. With the exception of Playas Médano and Cementario in Cabos and Palmilla in San José, you can't comfortably reach any of the beaches **by foot** unless you're staying at one of the adjacent resorts. If you've got **your own transportation** you can turn off Mex 1 at any of the beaches and park in the sand; stick to beaches that are adjacent to hotels to ensure that you can get a ride back if you're taking the **bus**. When **renting equipment** at any of the beaches, be sure to verify the price in advance and agree upon the state of the equipment to prevent post-use gouging by operators who insist you "damaged" their property. There are no bathrooms or lifeguards at the beaches and if you want shade, food or drink, bring your own.

Apart from Sunset, Solmar, Del Amor and La Playita, all **distances** are measured east from Cabo San Lucas towards San José del Cabo, 33km away.

Sunset 4km west of Cabo. The giant white-sand beach at the latest Pueblo Bonito resort area is big enough for multiple soccer and volleyball games (and probably even an airfield), but the signs and guards along the tide warn bathers from the deadly shore.

Solmar 1km west of Cabo. Surf fishing and strolls are the only activity that's safe at this Pacific-side beach; the strong undertow makes swimming deadly. Whale watching is possible from Jan–April.

Del Amor southeast of the Cabo marina. Los Cabos' most-photographed site was torn up by Hurricane Juliette in 2001 and the safe side of the beach is still awaiting the return of most of its sand. For now it's not worth the water taxi fare unless you want to snorkel.

Playa el Médano Km 1. More a mall than a beach, you'll be harassed by vendors, menaced by jet skis and squeezed for space by everyone else. The sands in front

---

hotel on the second floor of a shopping plaza is the cheapest option on the Corridor. All eight suites look out onto the sea and have kitchenettes, TV and a/c, and the owners gladly prepare custom Italian dinners. ⑤

🏃 **Twin Dolphin** Km 12 Mex 1 ☎624/145-8191, US☎800/421-8925, ⓦtwindolphin .com. Though it's one of the oldest hotels along the coast the *Dolphin* is by no means rough around the edges; the low-slung stone and wood resort has a mid-century modern feel that's fancy without being garish. The forty-four rooms are decorated in shades of white, have views of the water and include luxury bath products; there are no TVs or phones. ❽

Las Ventanas al Paraíso Km 19.5 Mex 1 ☎624/144-2800, US ☎888/767-3966,

ⓦrosewoodhotels.com. If a resort can be both luxurious and minimalist at the same time, *Ventanas* is such a place. Suites – some with roof decks and private Jacuzzis – skip the Mexican craft style for John Pawson-like aesthetics. While privacy is encouraged by the layout of plantings and sidewalks, you're likely to run into a boldface tabloid name at either the *ceviche* bar or swim-up cantina. ❾

Westin Los Cabos Km 22.5 ☎624/142-9000, ⓦwestinloscabos.com. Architect Pepe de Iturbe's now iconic facade – notable for a multi-storey hole that frames the sea – conceals 243 rooms, all of which have flat-screen TVs, a/c, balconies, plush beds and high-speed Internet access and water views. There are seven pools, five restaurants, four bars and organized activities like pool volleyball. ❾

of the now-shuttered *Hacienda Cabo San Lucas* near the marina and the *Pueblo Bonito Rosé* at the other end are less crowded, though not nearly as calm as the out-of-town beaches.

Cementerio Km 4. Beautiful white-sand swimming beach. Access on foot from Playa el Médano.

Barco Varado, Km 9. The remains of a Japanese trawler that sank in 1966 lay offshore making diving the main focus of this beach, though it's also a popular surfing spot, too. To reach the beach, take the marked dirt access road off the highway, but mind the rocks on your way down.

Las Viudas Km 12.5. Secluded beach with tidal pools and just next to the *Twin Dolphin*. Swimming is sometimes possible but almost never during summer.

Bahía Santa María, Km 13. You can scuba and snorkel on rock reefs at both ends and go swimming at the protected beach in the middle. There's a secure parking lot a ten-minute walk from the beach.

Bahía Chileno, Km 14.5. There's a bus stop along Mex 1, a bathroom and a dive shop that rents water-sports equipment (nothing with a motor, though), making Chileno one of the easiest beaches to get to and enjoy. Excellent for swimming, diving and snorkelling, or just relaxing along the well-packed sand.

Canta Mar, Km 16. Appropriately dubbed "surfing beach," with occasional point breaks.

Punta Palmilla, Km 27. Good, safe 1.5km-long beach used by San José hotel residents needing escape from the strong riptide closer to home. Point and reef breaks when surf's up. Access the beach by following signs to *One&Only Palmilla* and taking the only dirt-road cut off to the left, about 2km from Mex 1.

Costa Azul, Km 28. The region's best surfing beach is known for the Zippers and La Roca breaks during the summer (look out for rocks at low tide). Swimming is possible during the late winter and early spring, but ask at *Zippers* beach restaurant before you dip in.

Playa Hotelera, San José town beach. San José's resorts line this wide, flat beach; the drop-off and current make it unsafe for swimming.

La Playita, 2.5km east of San José via a dirt road. Excellent for fishing; swimming is also possible, but look out for the plentiful surfers. Ongoing development around the San José estuary and new marina complex may change the beach significantly.

Eating and drinking

The region's best high-end **restaurants** are in the resorts along the Corridor; inventive chefs experiment with locally sourced food and produce some thrilling takes on pan-Latin and Asian dishes. The dust and noise that pervades Cabo and San José is replaced by cool breezes, candle-lit tables and the sound of crashing waves. But like the resorts they're located within, price tags at the restaurants, **bars** and **clubs** are exorbitant, and you'll still need to shell out extra cash for a taxi or bus if you're not staying on site.

Agua Km 27.5 Mex 1, at *One & Only Palmilla*. Though the prices at *Agua* are half what they are at *C* (the hotel's marquee restaurant run by Chicago and Las Vegas celeb-chef Charlie Trotter), they still aren't low – but if you're going to splash out at one restaurant in Los Cabos, this is it. Skip the wine and let the chef pair a tasting menu of

Mediterranean-tinged Mexican dishes with flights of small-batch tequila. Expect to pay about M$700 per person.

Canto del Mar Km 21.5 Mex 1, at *Marquis Los Cabos* ℡ 624/144-2000. Smoked duck with truffles and carrot and saffron pie expose the haute cuisine ambitions of the French chef behind the *Marquis*' smaller, more intimate restaurant.

Esperanza Km 7 Mex 1 ☏624/145-6400. The expansive restaurant practically spills down towards the shore in a series of terraces. The seafood-centric menu uses local fish like Robalo, Lenguado and Cabrilla in non-local ways: honey baked, dusted with sage or on top of mushroom lasagna. Dinner for two M$1200.

El Parthenon Km 4.5 Mex 1 ☏624/144-4475. This dance club's facade looks like a Looney Tunes version of a Greek temple, with pastel colours and faux broken Doric columns. The inside is all twentieth-century techno, with flashing lights and booming sound systems, as well as a predominantly local crowd.

Pitahaya's Km 10 Mex 1, *Sheraton Hacienda del Mar* ☏624/145-6126, ⓦpitahayas.com. The global menu takes in crab cakes and potstickers (dumplings), blackened catch of the day and salsa of mango and papaya. Dinner for two M$1500.

Tequila and Ceviche Bar Km 19.5 Mex 1, at *Las Ventanas al Paraíso* ☏624/144-2800. With over one hundred tequilas on the menu, there's little doubt how to proceed. The *ceviche* bar changes menu daily, depending on the catch and the season.

San José del Cabo

SAN JOSÉ DEL CABO, 33km east of Cabo San Lucas, is the older and altogether more sedate of the two towns. Founded as a mission in 1730 by Jesuits, it was abandoned after the Pericú revolt in 1734. A mix of ex-pirates, lapsed missionaries and drop-out miners began to repopulate the town in the early nineteenth century and turned the area into an agricultural centre and small port. Although frequently referred to as colonial, modern San José, like Cabo, is a product of late-nineteenth-century construction and planning. No traces remain of its first settlement, and none of the more historic buildings dates further back than the late 1880s.

Arrival and information

Mex 1 from La Paz enters San José from the north and becomes Boulevard Mauricio Castro before heading out of the city southwest along the Corridor towards Cabo San Lucas. **Bus** traffic from the north arrives at the station, Valerio Gonzáles s/n at Mex 1 (☏624/142-1100), a fifteen-minute walk from the centre.

The Los Cabos **tourism office** is on Avenida Mauricio Castro at Plaza San José (Mon–Fri 8am–3pm; ☏624/142-3310, ⓦvisitcabo.com). Although it's quite far out on the highway, they do offer helpful **information** on the area.

Accommodation

The **San José** beach hotels – the *zona hotelera* – are slightly cheaper than those found along the Corridor but they're stuffed into less space and front an enormous, dangerous beach. **La Playita**, a neighbourhood east of downtown, is the only area that has low prices and safe beaches for swimming. Like Cabo, downtown San José has a handful of decent budget **hotels**, the cheapest of which are located around the plaza alongside more expensive boutique hotels.

The waterfront

El Delfin Blanco Calle Delfines s/n, Pueblo la Playa ☏624/142-1212, ⓦeldelfinblanco.net. Rustic but well-maintained cabañas (with shared bath) and casitas (private baths) just off the beach. All rooms have ceiling fans and refrigerators and there's use of bicycles and a lending library. Shared bath ➌; private bath ➍

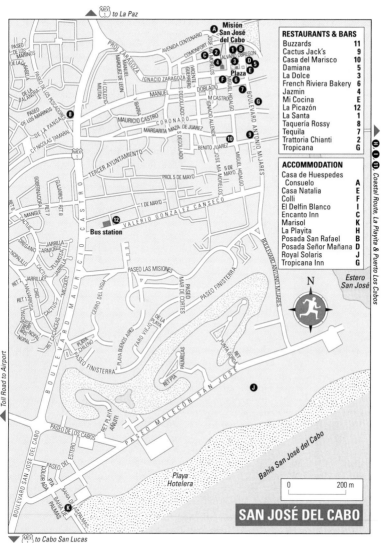

Image labels:

RESTAURANTS & BARS

Buzzards	11
Cactus Jack's	9
Casa del Marisco	10
Damiana	5
La Dolce	3
French Riviera Bakery	6
Jazmin	4
Mi Cocina	E
La Picazón	12
La Santa	1
Taquería Rossy	8
Tequila	7
Trattoria Chianti	2
Tropicana	G

ACCOMMODATION

Casa de Huespedes Consuelo	A
Casa Natalia	E
Colli	F
El Delfin Blanco	I
Encanto Inn	C
Marisol	K
La Playita	H
Posada San Rafael	B
Posada Señor Mañana	D
Royal Solaris	J
Tropicana Inn	G

SAN JOSÉ DEL CABO

Marisol Plaza Garuffi, Zona Hotelera San José ☎624/142-2040, ⓦmarisol.com.mx. Each of the eight rooms in this inn atop a shopping plaza has a balcony and views, as well as satellite TV, a/c and a cooler you can take to the beach. ⑤
La Playita Pueblo la Playa ☎624/142-4166, ⓦlaplayitahotel.com. A pleasant waterside alternative that's removed from the crowds, a three-storey hotel and restaurant with comfortable, spare rooms overlooking a small pool and an outdoor dining

area. The hotel can arrange fishing trips for you and the restaurant will cook your catch. ⑦
Royal Solaris Zona Hotelera San José ☎624/145-6800, ⓦclubsolaris.com. Numerous pools, activities and some in-house childcare facilities make this a good spot for families – as does the all-inclusive deal. All rooms have balconies and at least partial views of the Sea of Cortez, which makes up for the dated decor. ⑨

267

Casa de Huéspedes Consuelo C Morelos s/n, at Colonia 10 de Mayo ☎624/142-0643. Shared showers and stiff beds are the rule at San José's only guesthouse and cheapest non-camping option. ❷

Casa Natalia Blvd Mijares 4 ☎624/142-5100, US☎1-888/277-3814, ⓦcasanatalia.com. A rather striking architectural mix of European and Mexican styles, housing a classy, award-winning hotel and restaurant; each room is individually decked out with Mexican artwork and each has glass doors leading to a private balcony. Amenities include an in-room spa service, comfy bathrobes and daily paper delivery. ❾

Colli C Hidalgo, between C Zaragoza and C Doblado ☎624/142-0725. Comfortable, three-storey, family-run place, though the plain rooms only have fan ventilation. ❸

El Encanto Inn C Morelos 133 ☎624/142-0388, ⓦelencantoinn.com. Lovely colonial Spanish hotel with several types of rooms – including some suites – around a quaint, tree-lined courtyard. Rates can be as much as 50 percent less in the low season. ❺

Posada San Rafael C Obregón s/n, north of the plaza ☎624/142-3878. A lot better than it looks from the outside, this is the best bet in its price class. Very clean rooms and operated by a friendly staff. ❷

Posada Señor Mañana C Obregón 1, at the plaza ☎624/142-0462, ⓦwww.srmanana.net. Run by a hospitable Swedish woman, offering spacious, palm-lined surroundings and charming, clean rooms with or without a/c. There's also a pool and large communal kitchen. ❹

Tropicana Blvd Mijares 30 ☎624/142-2311, ⓦtropicanacabo.com. This two-storey inn has tidy, luxury-style rooms and an attractive pool with a swim-up bar at the centre of a courtyard; price includes breakfast. ❻

The town and beaches

Though increasingly hemmed in by shopping centres along Mex 1 to the west, resorts on the coast to the south, and the new Puerto Los Cabos to the east, the old **plaza** and the **Paseo Mijares** are still more or less intact as they were originally built. The **Plaza Antonio Mijares** teems with life in the evenings as children on scooters and balloon sellers mix with their parents and tourists. The town's activity branches out from the park, along Boulevard Mijares and the intersecting side streets. Numerous shops and restaurants line these streets and shady courtyards are interesting enough, the latter offering a good variety of cuisine, though prices are high.

To get to the **beaches** it's a 2km walk down Mijares to Paseo Malecón San José and the **zona hotelera**. If you haven't already seen enough cacti in their natural environment, you can stop along the way at the botanical garden and museum **Cacti Mundo**, Blvd Mijares just north of the Mayan Palace golf course (☎624/146-9191; M$10, students and seniors get a 50 percent discount). The park exhibits eleven thousand examples of the plant from all over Mexico, arranged into shapes – Mickey Mouse's silhouette, for example – that aren't exactly indigenous. From here it's an additional challenge to wind your way through construction sites and other man-made barriers to find some empty sand: the beaches stretch for miles so keep walking until you find a quiet spot. Bikes, scooters, kayaks and other sporting goods are available for rent at Tio Sports Ocean & Desert, across from the *InterContinental Presidente*. There's also a taxi stand adjacent to Tio.

La Playita

One of the lesser-known alternatives to Cabo and San José's beaches lies just 2km to the east of the plaza. **Pueblo La Playa** (**La Playita**) is a hundred-year-old fishing village that offers numerous options for swimming and sport fishing, but will soon be altered to an unknown extent by encroaching development. The waters at the seamount of Gordo Banks here house the highest concentrations of gamefish in the waters of Los Cabos (guides at Gordo Banks Pangas;

T624/142-1147, Wgordobanks.com). The **estuary** between La Playita and San José is home to hundreds of birds and makes for an interesting hour or two; it can be reached by kayak or on foot. The peacefulness of La Playita and the estuary will end soon, as the massive **Puerto Los Cabos** development project – a new marina, golf course, hotel and condo complex – nears completion. The estuary will ostensibly be protected, but with all the building it's doubtful that the avian population will maintain their current numbers.

Eating and drinking

With a few exceptions, San José's **waterfront** isn't much of a dining or drinking destination, but there's a huge variety of upmarket **restaurants** downtown along Mijares. To find places with local prices move west from the square towards Mex 1.

Buzzards East Cape Road, 20min drive from San José T624/148-2415. If you're spending a day surfing on the eastern cape, this is one of the few places you can get a beer, margarita and a bite to eat. It closes by 9pm, but what surfer stays up that late?

Cactus Jack's Blvd Mijares, at C Benito Juárez T624/142-5601. Serves inexpensive Mexican breakfasts and seafood dishes off a large international menu, but the karaoke and big-screen TV here are the main draw for the locals.

Casa del Marisco C Benito Juárez, at C Miguel Hidalgo T624/142-6350. Typical Mexican takes on seafood are augmented by pan-Asian takes like coconut shrimp in mango (M$180).

Damiana Blvd Mijares 8 T624/142-0499. The candlelit, bougainvillea-covered courtyard helps take the sting out of pricy takes on Mexican basics like *chiles rellenos* and *enchiladas suizas* (around M$350 per person). Dinner only.

La Dolce Blvd Mijares, at C Miguel Hidalgo T624/142-6621. Standard Italian cuisine, including wood-fired pizzas and pastas for relatively good prices (under M$100). Popular among tourists.

French Riviera Bakery C Manuel Doblado, at C Miguel Hidalgo T624/142-3350. Its popularity has spawned fancier Corridor and Cabo outposts, but people keep coming to this original location just off the square for coffee, French pastries, cakes and both savoury and sweet crepes (M$60).

Jazmín C Morelos, between Zaragoza and Obregón T624/142-1760. The best-value traditional Mexican food in town. Also has excellent breakfasts – perhaps the best *chilaquiles* on the Cape.

Mi Cocina Blvd Mijares 4, inside *Casa Natalia* T624/142-5100. The torch-lit atmosphere is captivating, and Chef Loïc Tenoux's French-influenced Mexican dishes are inspired. Charred *poblano chiles* stuffed with lamb share the menu with crayfish over couscous and a grilled Romaine Caesar salad. Dinner for two runs M$1200.

La Picazón C Valerio Gonzalez s/n, next to the bus station T624/119-1859. All sorts of great inexpensive Mexican seafood specialities and *antojitos* served outside in a colourful, tropical atmosphere. Try the *tacos del pulpo al mojo de ajo* – soft tacos with octopus cooked in garlic. Closed Sunday.

La Santa C Obregón 1732 T624/142-6767, Wlasanta.com.mx. Wine bar and tapas joint that attracts a large contingent of locals in the hospitality industry and one of the few places in San José that's open past midnight. Closed Sunday.

Taquería Rossy Mex 1 at C Manuel Doblado T624/142-6755. This storefront on the west side of Mex 1 just before downtown San José is the lunchspot of choice for budget travellers and big spenders after fish tacos. Battered pieces of fillets, marlin, Dorado and *carne asada* tacos go for less than M$10 each and cold Pacifico beer is M$25 a bottle.

Tequila C Manuel Doblado 1011, between Blvd Mijares and C Hidalgo T624/142-1155. The top choice in town, with a quaint garden atmosphere and attentive (overly attentive) waiting staff; overpriced wines and cigars.

Trattoria Chianti C Obregón at C Morelos. Serves excellent Italian food in a romantic courtyard setting; the pasta dishes and wood-fired pizza oven here make it a local gringo favourite.

Tropicana Blvd Mijares 38 T624/142-1580. A colonial-style restaurant with an attractive tiled, palapa-covered sitting area that's a popular choice. Serves excellent seafood, often with Cuban dancers providing entertainment.

Listings

Airlines Aero Calafia ℗ 624/143-4255 and 143-4302; Aeroméxico ℗ 624/142-0397; Alaska ℗ 624/149-5800; Continental ℗ 624/142-3890; Mexicana ℗ 624/143-5352; and United ℗ 624/142-2880.

Airport For enquiries call ℗ 624/142-0341.

Banks and exchange You'll find two ATMs and the town's best rates at Bancomer, on Zaragoza and Morelos (Mon–Fri 8.30am–4pm, Sat 10am–4pm), and Banamex, Mijares and Coronado (Mon–Fri 9am–4pm, Sat 10am–2pm).

Bookstore Libros Libros at Mijares 41.

Buses Áquila ℗ 624/142-1100. Buses begin in San José del Cabo and move through Cabo San Lucas on the way to Tijuana and the border (hourly departures; 24hr; M$900) via La Paz (3hr; M$200), and Loreto (6hr; M$330).

Car rental Avis ℗ 624/142-1180 or 146-0201; Hertz ℗ 624/142-0375. National ℗ 624/142-2424; Quick ℗ 624/142-4600, ℗ www.quickrentacar .com; Thrifty ℗ 624/142-1671.

Emergencies ℗ 060 for police and fire department, ℗ 065 for Red Cross.

Hospital Hospital General, Av Hidalgo and Calle Coronado, ℗ 624/142-0180.

Internet access and phones Espacio Internet, on Doblado five blocks west of the plaza, across from the Coppola department store, has cheap rates (daily 10am–9pm, US$3/hr). Trazzo Digital Internet, off the plaza, is more expensive, but has a much faster connection and reasonably priced international phone service (Mon–Fri 8am–9pm, Sat 9am–7pm, US$4/hr).

Post office Mijares, on the way to the *zona hotelera* from the beach (Mon–Fri 9am–6pm).

Travel details

Buses

Buses begin in San José del Cabo and move through Cabo San Lucas on the way to Tijuana and the border (hourly departures; 24hr; M$900) via La Paz (3hr; M$200), Loreto (6hr; M$330).

Contexts

Contexts

History

"The difficulties of joining different historical periods of the peninsula in space and time were enormous. This was also true when it came to relating events in Mexico's national scene with local and international happenings."

Pablo L. Martinez, *A History of Lower California*

Much like its geographical remoteness, Baja California's history is quite separate from the rest of Mexico; the revolutions and reforms that dramatically shaped the mainland had minimal impact on societies here. The men and women who impacted both its pre- and post-colonial history were the sort who don't typically star in history books and most left behind scant traces of who they really were; from the painters who covered the cave and mountain walls of the sierras with massive murals to the mestizo pirates who raided Manila galleons from secluded bays on the southern cape. The peninsula's history up to now mainly consists of archeological studies that have learned much from very little and the observations and transcriptions of generations of members of the religious orders that were the first long-term colonial interlopers.

The **prehistory** set out below is based on archeological theories that are generally, but by no means universally, accepted. There are still significant riddles – especially concerning the origins of the peninsula's tribes and the extent and nature of the contact between these groups and other aboriginal groups on the Mexican mainland – which, should they be solved, may overturn many existing notions.

Before the Europeans

Of the estimated fifty thousand **Amerindians** that populated Baja California at the time of the first intrusion by Europeans, only one thousand remain. Their languages are largely lost as are clues to their origin. Recent studies, however, have created compelling and sometimes controversial theories as to how they first arrived, as archaeological studies in Baja California and the west coast of South America challenge one of the once-firm theories of how the western hemisphere was populated. The well-established timeline of migration into North America typically begins around 10,000 BC, when tribes crossed from northeast Asia via Siberia and the Bering Strait and onto the continent first through Alaska and then southward, eventually reaching South America. Recent findings suggest, though, that the first arrivals skipped the northerly route and arrived in Baja California by boat from Australia and Southeast Asia about 1,500 years earlier.

Skulls from near La Paz, along with ones found in Chile and Brazil, are quite different from those of other Amerindians. Whereas Amerindians are ethnically similar to Mongolians, Siberians and some Chinese, the La Paz skulls and the Chilean and Brazilian findings create a direct link with Australia's aboriginals. What's unique about the La Paz skulls is that they are only a few centuries old, suggesting that the isolation of the peninsula allowed the descendants of the Southeast Asian arrivals to remain ethnically separate for at least twelve thousand years, during which their ethnic ancestors in other parts of Central and South America were killed off or assimilated by the Bering Strait arrivals.

The La Paz remains belonged to the **Pericú**, one of the three dominant Amer-indian groups that existed on the peninsula at the time of the first European land-fall. The Pericú inhabited the extreme south, from present-day Cabo San Lucas and San José del Cabo – known to them as Yenecamú and Añuití, respectively – to Todos Santos on the west and Bahía de la Paz on the east. To their immedi-ate north lived the **Guaycura**, who may also have had Southeast Asian roots as well, and who probably shared similar linguistic patterns with the Pericú. The Guaycura populated both coasts from Bahía Magdalena and La Paz northwards to just south of Loreto. The **Cochimí**, who are directly related to the Yuma tribes of Sonora and Arizona, dominated everything from Loreto (Conchó) to Tijuana ('Ipa'c'aa). Unlike the southern groups, the Cochimí still have living descendants, about one thousand people split between the Cucapá tribe near Mexicali and the Kumai tribe around the Guadalupe and Santo Tomás valleys.

What is known about the Pericú and Guaycura is limited and based primarily upon small archaeological studies and reports of early Spaniards and Jesuit mis-sionaries. The language of the Pericú and Guaycura has only survived in written notation by the first Jesuits. The Cochimí legacy has fared slightly better; not only because a few descendants survived but due to their cordial relationship with the Jesuits who landed at Loreto – an alliance solidified by the city's his-torical name, Loreto Conchó.

One generalization that can be made about the three groups is that their sys-tems of government were not as complex as that of their mainland counterparts. Although settlements have been found and examined – the most notable being a site at Comondú only open to archeologists – substantial public works projects and centralized power did not exist. The groups largely existed as small tribes that focused on hunting deer, rabbit and elk or fishing in the Sea of Cortez. Remnants of their societies consist of simple tools and human and animal remains, and their one lasting contribution is the most difficult to understand. Rock art sites throughout the peninsula – the most impressive and complex are on the mountainsides and in the caves of the Sierra de San Francisco – speak to a clear understanding of the environment, a hierarchy among food sources, and the movement of heavenly bodies. Who exactly executed them, whether Pericú, Guaycura or Cochimí, is an ongoing source of debate among archaeologists. Carbon dating on wooden pegs found near some of the sites suggests that the Cochimí did at least a little touch-up on them in the fifteenth century, but dating on other parts places their creation between 5000 and 7500 years ago.

Cortés and the European explorers

Hernán Cortés subjugated the Aztecs and took Tenochtitlán in 1521, just over two years after he and his 550 men landed on the coast near modern-day Veracruz in April of 1519. For the next eleven years Cortés and his fel-low conquerors expanded their control throughout present-day Mexico and areas further south, fuelled by discoveries of vast amounts of gold and other precious metals. Like other European explorers, they were partially driven by legends of cities made entirely of gold – the seven rich cities of Cibola – and the elusive all-female land of the Amazons, known as Calafia. In 1532, con-vinced that Calafia lay just across the Mar de Bermeja, as the Sea of Cortez was then known, Cortés sent two ships across the sea. They never made it;

the men left the boats along Mexico's Pacific coast where they fell into the hands of Cortés' rival Nuño Beltrán de Guzmán.

Cortés attempted another visit the next year, but it could only be called a success in comparison to the previous year's journey. On this excursion, one captain discovered the Archipiélago de Revillagigedo southwest of Cabo San Lucas, then jumped ship for Acapulco. The other, a relative of Cortés, was betrayed by his pilot and killed in his sleep by his men. The pilot, Fortún Jiménez, took charge of the ships and sailed into present-day Bahía De La Paz. The pearls the Spaniards found on the shores encouraged the legend of a wealthy land, but Jimenéz and his men angered the resident Guaycura, first by scooping up quantities of pearls from the coast and then by attacking the women. The Guaycura responded in kind, killing at least twenty of the invaders and forcing Jiménez' men back across the sea. Jiménez died in the initial Guaycura attack or across the sea at the hands of Guzman's men who sacked and looted the ship after its crossing. Either way, relaying the promise of vast wealth on the new island was up to the few scraggly survivors who finally made it back to Cortés.

Urged on by the promise of pearls and other riches, Cortés set out leading a 300-man expedition himself in 1535 and became the first European to successfully get all his ships from one side of the sea to the other. The Guaycura greeted Cortés' arrival in La Paz' bay – which he named Santa Cruz – with hostility, refusing to dive on command for pearls and keeping the newcomers out of the bay. Cortés was instead forced to establish his small colony on the northeast tip of the bay. The men he left behind here fared poorly, forced to subsist on supplies brought from the mainland and to gather exposed pearls from the coast because they were too frightened to dive down towards the pearl beds themselves. The settlement was abandoned in 1536, after less than a year. Cortés' efforts to explore the new land resulted in incredible financial loss, wasted years of planning, near-death experiences at sea and on land, and almost no financial gain – the exception being a few exceptional pearls.

Despite his own failure, Cortés attempted additional expeditions to the peninsula between 1539 and 1542, spurred on by another tale of riches beyond the Río Colorado. The first of these was led by **Francisco de Ulloa** who followed the Pacific coast of Mexico up past Guaymas and into the mouth of the Río Colorado near present-day Mexicali. The journey resulted in the discovery that California was not an island – although the idea persisted for at least another century – and the claiming of much of northern Mexico, California and Arizona for the Spanish crown. Ulloa then sailed back into the sea and around Cabo San Lucas to the Pacific. Along the way he travelled into Bahía Magdalena and at least as far north as Isla Cedros off the Península de Vizcaíno. From Isla Cedros, Ulloa sent word back to Cortés of his discoveries and then sailed north, never to be heard from again. Over the next ten years, rival explorations were mounted and Cortés returned to Spain to complain about this interference on his territory as conqueror and ended up staying there the remainder of his life.

One of those competing explorations was led by the Portuguese navigator and former Cortés partisan **Juan Rodríguez Cabrillo**. The nearly year-long expedition sailed from the port at Navidad on June 27, 1542. Cabrillo reached San José del Cabo five days later and proceeded around the coast to Bahía Magdalena. The journey continued north past Ensenada (which Cabrillo named San Mateo) to San Diego (San Miguel, originally). Cabrillo perished on the return.

Throughout these early explorations, perceptions of the peninsula's geographical nature and the names used to describe it changed regularly. Ulloa determined that it was a peninsula, and this was backed up by Cabrillo's later journeys, but the myth of it as an island persisted for years. Its name too, caused confusion and, centuries later, its origins are still debated. Cortés called the land Santa Cruz in every communication. The first use of the name California by an explorer was one made by Ulloa most likely referring to a portion of the Bahía de la Paz. The most likely scenario for the peninsula's naming comes from a best-selling 1510 Spanish novel called *The Adventures of Esplandian*. The fictional explorer describes a land called California that's similar to the legend that lured Cortés to begin with, one ruled by women of incredible strength and covered in gold.

Pirate days and the second wave of explorers

The myth of a gold- and pearl-packed land began to wane under the considerable evidence that Baja California was rather harsh and unforgiving and was disregarded entirely once the Spanish began focusing on the riches possible across the Pacific. The crown instituted a Manila-Acapulco route in 1565 and the southern cape of the peninsula began to gain significance, not as a source of wealth but as a place for sailors to recover after their trans-oceanic journey. Unfortunately for the Spaniards, **pirates** thought the region – with its multiple coves, small islands and bays – made a nice spot for attacks and began using it, as well as Bahía de la Paz, to launch assaults on treasure-laden galleons arriving from the Far East. Both Francis Drake and **Thomas Cavendish** plundered Acapulco-bound ships in the 1580s, infuriating the Spanish and delighting the English.

During one of Cavendish's raids, he abandoned a boatload of Spaniards in San José and set their ship afire. One of the men left behind, **Sebastian Vizcaíno**, rallied his fellow stranded men and women and rescued the burning ship, eventually repairing it enough to enable a journey back across the sea. Vizcaíno was rewarded with command of a fleet of ships to further explore the peninsula. His first stop was inhospitable La Paz, where a handful of priests created good relations with the Guaycura that was quickly undone by the sexual escapades of the troops, forcing them to flee after two months. Leaving the sea, Vizcaíno's fleet entered the Pacific and sailed northward, stopping to give his name to the peninsula east of Isla Cedros and eventually exploring Monterey Bay and renaming San Diego in Alta California. He was called off the exploration of California by the Spanish viceroy as the crown's interest was directed further east to Japan. Vizcaíno and his galleons were dispatched to Asia where they made a disastrous mess out of Spain's relationship with the Japanese. Shortly after Vizcaíno's departures, Japan closed its borders to the West for two and a half centuries.

The English pirates were followed by the Dutch, who raided the galleons with equal glee for four decades beginning around 1600. During the seventeenth century the Spanish crown instituted a series of *cédulas*, or royal decrees, demanding that the peninsula be further explored and, if possible, settled. The men who carried out the orders, among them Alonzo Gonzalez (who travelled extensively around Cabo San Lucas) and Bernardo Bernal de Piñadero (who promised his minders fertile fields and docile natives) did little to provide concrete evidence of the now-outlandish claims of riches and natural resources. Isidro de Atondo y Antillón, the last of the early European explorers, took with him the Jesuit padre **Francisco Kino** on his 1683–85 journey. Atondo quickly proved to be a poor diplomat and not terribly bright when he responded to one of the first extended displays of hospitality by the Guaycura of La Paz by executing ten of them at a banquet. After fleeing the growing hostility at La Paz, he led his ships north where the men eventually disembarked and began the most extensive explorations to date of the central part of the peninsula. Their journeys took them across California to the Pacific Ocean and the areas around what is now La Purísima. Most of the excursions, and all the contacts with the tribes the Spaniards met, were led by Padre Kino, who displayed a knack for diplomacy that would later enable the Jesuits to succeed in California where others had failed. Atondo's exploratory force returned to New Spain in May of 1685. In December of the same year a Spanish decree prohibited further exploration of the peninsula.

The Jesuits

Into this gap rushed the order of the **Jesuits** who, with seventy years and private funding from around the world, were finally able to create a European presence on the peninsula. Unlike the explorers, they behaved well enough and built relationships among the three major Amerindian groups. But by the time they were expelled by order of the crown in 1767, their fourteen missions had gone from being outposts in a supposedly heathen land to centres of smallpox, venereal disease and starvation. The Cochimí tribes in the north survived, though their numbers were thinned drastically, while the Guaycura and Pericú populations were all but exterminated.

It didn't start that way. **Padre Kino**, who had been part of the last exploration of California in the 1680s, spent the next decade petitioning New Spain officials for the right to spread Catholicism to the peninsula's tribes. He was

The Society of Jesus

In 1534, soldier-turned-fervent believer Iñigo López de Loyola created the **Society of Jesus** religious order along with six students. They dedicated themselves to the spread of Catholicism and the will of the Pope and, after receiving his blessing three years later, became priests. The order received a papal bull in 1543 that expanded its rights, and quickly set about founding schools that created missionaries to both spread their gospel as well as stem the tide of encroaching Protestantism.

As Catholic missionaries, they were incredibly effective at both converting new followers and providing a buffer between colonizing forces and indigenous populations. They were, though, intent on spreading their religious beliefs and ran rough-shod over established belief systems and angered displaced religious leaders. To expand their reach, Jesuits became devout scholars of languages and foreign cultures, and within the first few decades in existence travelled to India, China, Tibet and most of Latin America. Their openness and dedication to learning was ironic considering that the Jesuits expanded considerable effort suppressing the openness of the Protestant Reformation.

Pope Clement XIV, responded to pressure exerted by European colonial powers, banned the order in 1773. Over the previous half-century, the Society's efforts had drawn the ire of local powers in far-flung colonies who resented the order's refusal to submit to their authority and the padres' liberal attitude towards the rights of indigenous people. Controversy continued to dog the Society, even after its restoration in 1814; conservative Catholics blame it for the Vatican II reforms and anti-Catholics accuse it of proto-Fascist tendencies.

joined in his lobbying efforts by **Padre Juan María de Salvatierra**, a fellow Jesuit who went about raising funds from the newly wealthy overlords of New Spain; essential work, as the crown refused to pay for the Jesuits' activities. When they finally received approval in February of 1697, Kino and Salvatierra arranged a force that would sail from Hiaqui on the Sonoran coast. Because of Amerindian unrest, Kino was prevented from departing along with Salvatierra's crew on May 10; Salvatierra sailed into Bahía Concepción one day later. The expedition stopped sailing six days later at Conchó, the Amerindian settlement that eventually became Loreto.

Throughout its lifespan, the Jesuits' hold was tenuous – partly because of Amerindian resistance, partly because of lack of funds. Within the first eighteen months, Salvatierra's men fought off at least two assaults by various Amerindians – including the Monqui, a Guaycura tribe – and struggled to feed themselves. The newcomers eventually won over a segment of the local population, impressing them with sailing trips to the Sonoran coast and non-indigenous animals like pigs, but there were regular incidents as religions clashed. On one occasion, a Guaycura *guama* – a member of the priestly order – was dragged to the mission in chains and whipped within an inch of his life in public; his offence had been to advise fellow tribesmen to remember their own religious rituals. Still, after he had gained a modicum of trust, Salvatierra set about building the mission complex at Loreto and began excursions to areas that Kino had visited a decade and a half earlier, starting with the construction of Misión San Francisco Javier in nearby Santo Tomás.

The Central Coast region was at the northern extreme of Guaycura territory and the southern extreme of the Cochimí; mission records recount regular conflict between the two. The Cochimí always fare better in these reports, praised for their willingness to accept Catholic sacraments as well as to guide the missionaries into the bush. The Amerindian population was still very large by later comparison – in the rural areas more populous than it is now – and it was uncommon to travel for a day and not see villages, camps, *rancherías* and other rich signs of life. Tribes often helped the Spanish build their missions, inclined as everyone was to the two deciding factors that the Jesuits used to pick a site: clean water and soil that was good for farming.

The Jesuit padres exercised ultimate authority in California. Soldiers and any visitors were entirely under their command and settlements at Loreto and elsewhere were focused entirely on conversion. This arrangement created a great deal of resentment among troops who were used to taking advantage of their position to create great wealth for themselves. It was also an immense financial burden on the Society, required as they were to have and pay troops for their protection. Back in New Spain, the viceroy pushed for the Jesuits to use their power to harvest pearls in Bahía de La Paz, but Salvatierra rejected out of hand this deviation from his purpose.

The Jesuits steadily branched out from Loreto, reaching Mulegé in 1704 and Comondú in 1708. A smallpox outbreak in 1710 would have been a boon for the *guamas* and anti-Jesuit forces if so many Amerindians hadn't succumbed to the disease. In 1716, Salvatierra tried to expand his mini religious empire into La Paz with the typical disasters that befell any European effort in this region: Upon arrival, the padre and his men instigated a scuffle between La Paz Guaycura and tribesmen that had followed him from Loreto. When the Jesuits withdrew there were a number of local women who had been beaten to death with stones.

Although not the best thing ever to happen to him, Salvatierra's death in 1717 had great positive consequences for the settlement. The padre's assistant Jaime Bravo petitioned the viceroy in New Spain and convinced him to fulfill financial obligations that had been made to the mission. Bravo also successfully pushed for new rights and responsibilities of the Society, ones that at the mission's origin would have been far outside their religious intentions. In order to finance upwards of fifty soldiers from royal coffers, Bravo proposed that these men aid in securing the southern cape against continued pirate activity. He also got approval to mine salt from Isla Carmen in Bahía Loreto, was given a new ship for supplies and funds for a seminary aimed at Amerindian youth. The changes invigorated the rather defeated mission colony. In November of 1720, Padre Ugarte, one of Salvatierra's most trusted lieutenants, finally succeeded in creating a semi-permanent settlement in La Paz. San José del Cabo was founded ten years later, to be followed in 1733 by Todos Santos, then called Santa Rosa.

The Pericú revolt

In three decades, the Jesuits created a mission circuit that looped from Mulegé on the central coast all the way south to the tip of the Cape and touching the Sea of Cortez and Pacific Ocean. As the missionaries grew in strength, they became relentless in trying to convert the Amerindians and preached against long-established customs (such as taking more than one wife). This, of course, did not sit well with many of the Guaycura and Pericú, or any of their tribes. Beginning in early 1734, the **Pericú** began destroying missions in the south – killing a handful of soldiers and padres and burning their buildings. By 1735, a coalition of Pericú and Guaycura controlled La Paz and all points south, and the remaining missionaries and soldiers based in Loreto formed a small army of sympathetic Amerindians to prevent any further encroachmen.

There remained a stalemate of sorts until late in 1736 when the Governor of Sinaloa **Manuel Huidobro** was dispatched by Mexico City to root out the insurrection. Huidobro attempted to lure the rebels with gifts and promises of clemency, but ultimately resorted to open battle to quash the movement, which he finally did in 1737. Huidobro made his disapproval of the Jesuits readily apparent in his refusal to treat the rebels harshly and by this act, set a tone of antagonism between New Spain and the Jesuits that would pervade their relationship until the Jesuits were expelled. Although there was relative peace between the Jesuits and the tribes, between 1742 and 1748 five out of every six Guaycura and Pericú died – killed off by measles, smallpox and venereal diseases that may have come via the Manila galleons. La Paz was completely abandoned and, with the exception of a few Pericú that were evacuated to Todos Santos from Isla Espíritu Santo, their entire race was eliminated.

Franciscans, Dominicans and expansion

Even among the destruction and death, the Jesuits continued to establish missions in California, pushing past the 28th parallel into what's now the northern state of Baja California. Their campaign officially came to its end on June 24, 1767, when orders from Madrid arrived in Mexico City to expel all Jesuits from Spanish colonies. At the time there were sixteen on the peninsula, but it took until February of the following year to relay the message and arrange a boat that would take them to Veracruz for their expulsion to the European papal states.

The Jesuits' departure was followed shortly thereafter by the arrival of the **Franciscans**, fourteen of whom arrived in Loreto – on the same boat the Jesuits used to depart – on April 1, 1768. The Franciscans were disappointed to discover that they would not be in charge of the farms and ranches that the Jesuits had established. They also weren't happy when José de Galvez, an inspector-general sent by Spain's King Charles III, arrived and began issuing decrees that were grudgingly heard and half-heartedly carried out. Among his handful of ill-conceived notions was an order which forced Cochimí crowded into northern missions to relocate to the depopulated south, where the Pericú had been destroyed. Galvez got his way, and less than a year later the newcomers fell victim to the same diseases.

The purpose of Galvez' visit was twofold: to see if there were any precious metals that the Jesuits had been holding back and to expand Spain's reach deeper into California in order to ward off Russian ambitions in Alta California. On the former point, Galvez failed to find anything out of the ordinary. Where the second was concerned, he sent expeditions northward by land and sea, one of which was led by the Franciscan padre **Junípero Serra**. Because of Galvez' meddling, the Franciscans found it difficult to operate in California. Serra, though, deftly used his San Diego exploration to plan a frog-leap over the barren California and shift his order's focus to Alta California, which held more promise both financially and politically. He used the years immediately following his return to Loreto to pass along responsibility for the Jesuits' hand-me-down missions to the **Dominicans** who were eager to move into California, apparently unaware that the real game was in the north. When the Dominicans arrived in 1774, the order took over fourteen former Jesuit missions. In the following years, they established nine more, all of them along a line headed north to Alta California that the Franciscans had laid out in the late 1760s.

Both the old Jesuit missions and the ones the Dominicans founded quickly began to wane due to of lack of funds and, most importantly, the extermination of most of the people they were originally designed to serve. Even Loreto, the birthplace of the missions, declined to barely a settlement following a devastating hurricane in 1829. The capital was moved later that year, first to San Antonio and then to La Paz which, now free of defensive Amerindians, was a growing fishing and shipping port. In September of 1830, the governor of California secularized the missions between San Borjas and San José del Cabo and three years later did the same for every mission in the California territory. By 1849, every mission on the Peninsula had been sold off or given away.

Mexican Independence and the war with the United States

The story of **Mexican Independence** from Spain is largely a mainland affair, as California was too sparsely populated and of too little strategic importance to matter to the Spanish crown or its myriad rivals. As the most remote of the colony's territories, battles here were afterthoughts, some actually taking place after treaties had ended the wars they fought for. A brief history of the war for independence is necessary, if only to illustrate the general sense of confusion that permeated the future nation and its western peninsula, especially as these events relate to the following battle with the United States over the Pacific territories.

By the beginning of the nineteenth century Spain's status as a world power was in severe decline. In 1796 British sea power had forced the Spanish to open their colonial ports to free trade, and in 1808 Spain itself was invaded by Napoleon, who placed his brother Joseph on the throne. At the same time new political ideas were transforming the world outside, with the French Revolution and the American War of Independence still fresh in the memory. Although the works of such political philosophers as Rousseau, Voltaire and Paine were banned in Mexico, the opening of the ports made it inevitable that their ideas would spread – especially as it was traders from the new United States who most took advantage of the opportunities. Literary societies set up to discuss these books quickly became centres of political dissent.

The spark, though, was provided by the French invasion of Spain, as colonies throughout Latin America refused to recognize the Bonaparte regime (and the campaigns of Bolívar and others in South America began). In Mexico, the "gachupine" rulers proclaimed their loyalty to Ferdinand VII (the deposed king) and hoped to carry on much as before, but creole discontent was not to be so easily assuaged. The literary societies continued to meet, and from one, in Querétaro, emerged the first leaders of the Independence movement: Father Miguel Hidalgo y Costilla, a creole priest, and Ignacio Allende, a disaffected junior army officer.

The royalists discovered Hidalgo and Allende's plans for a coup, forcing them into premature action. At first, this didn't hurt them: Hidalgo's army of Indians and mestizos swiftly took the major towns of San Miguel, Guanajuato and others to the north of the capital, but their behaviour – seizing land and property, slaughtering the Spanish – horrified the wealthy creoles who had initially supported the movement. In spring 1811, the rebel army moved on the capital, but instead of trying to overpower the royalist army, retreated. His forces broke up as quickly and within months, Hidalgo, Allende and the other ringleaders had been captured and executed. Hidalgo's efforts were continued by the priest and radical José María Morelos, who instituted a highly successful series of guerrilla campaigns. By 1813 he controlled virtually the entire country (with the exception of the capital and the route from there to Veracruz), but the royalists quickly won back the country and executed Morelos in 1815.

Ironically, it was the introduction of liberal reforms in Spain, of just the type feared by the Mexican ruling classes, which finally brought about Mexican independence. Worried that such reforms might spread across the Atlantic, many creoles pre-empted a true revolution by assuming a "revolutionary" guise themselves. In 1820 Agustín de Iturbide, a royalist general but himself a mestizo, threw in his lot with Vicente Guerrero, who had inherited the loyalty of Morelos' men. In 1821 Iturbide proposed the Iguala Plan to the Spanish authorities, who were hardly in a position to fight, and Mexico was granted independence.

Independence brought no real social change and it left the new nation with virtually no chance of successful government: the power of the Church and of the army was far greater than that of the supposed rulers. There was no basis on which to create a viable internal economy, and if the state hadn't already been bankrupted by the Independence struggle, it was to be cleaned out time and again by the demands of war and internal disruption. There were no fewer than fifty-six governments in the next forty years. In what approaches farce, the name of **General Santa Ana** stands out as the most bizarre figure of all: becoming president or dictator on eleven separate occasions and masterminding the loss of more than half of Mexico's territory. Santa Ana and Mexico's first defeat came when Texas, a Mexican territory but largely inhabited by migrants from the US, declared its independence in 1836. In the short war that followed, Santa Ana was defeated and captured at the battle of San Jacinto, and rather than face execution he signed a paper accepting Texan independence. Meanwhile, in 1838, the French chose to invade Veracruz, demanding compensation for alleged damages to French property and citizens – a small war that lasted about four months.

In 1845 the United States annexed the recently independent Texas. The US's redefinition of the territory to include most of Arizona, New Mexico and California made yet another war inevitable, and in 1846 clashes between Mexican troops and US cavalry in these disputed western zones led to the declaration of the **Mexican–American War**. California played no real role in the war, but the actions of US naval forces spoke to their ambitions for the region. US Naval Commodore Robert Stockton claimed all of California for the US. During a blockade of Mazatlán in 1846, naval commanders quickly secured a promise of neutrality from the governor in La Paz, but soon left (it was hurricane season). Ships under the command of John Montgomery returned to La Paz the next spring, raised the US flag and gave the town's population the rights of US citizens before departing once again. During a third visit that July, US naval forces were again greeted warmly. Beginning in the autumn of 1847, Mexican loyalists working with Dominicans eventually put up a show of force, first in Mulegé, and then throughout the Cape. On February 2, 1848, Mexico and the US signed the Treaty of Guadalupe Hidalgo.

The two Californias

For $15 million, Mexico gave up most of Texas, New Mexico, Arizona and California, along with parts of Colorado and Utah; in 1854 the present borders were established when Santa Ana sold a further strip down to the Río Grande for $10 million under the Gadsden Purchase. It was a surprise to both the US forces in California and the Mexicans who had supported them that the treaty returned the lower half of the territory to Mexico – especially since many of its inhabitants had considered themselves US citizens for the last two years. US Secretary of State James Buchanan made the decision to give it up, instructing his negotiators at the end of the war to abandon their designs on the peninsula if it would ensure the acquisition of New Mexico and Alta California. The entire affair appeared haphazard from the outside; the first border halving California in two was drawn straight west from the mouth of the Río Colorado but revised when Mexico argued that cut off access to the peninsula by land. After their protests, the border was moved north and granted Mexico the lands that became Tijuana, Tecate and Mexicali. The US called its new territory **California** and, by default, Mexican California became **Baja California**.

While the south grew weak following a series of hurricanes, disease outbreaks and friction with mainland Mexico, the northwest part of the peninsula began to grow in importance. Even prior to Mexico's loss of power through independence and wartime blundering, interest in the peninsula had moved from the Sea of Cortez to the Pacific Coast. German, English, American and Japanese merchants and fishermen regularly plied the coastal waters from Monterey in central Alta California all the way south to Bahía Magdalena.

Beginning in 1849, thousands of Americans and Mexicans migrated to California with the dream of striking a rich vein of gold. Thinking that it was just

More than just Baja

After the Treaty of Guadalupe Hidalgo separated what was then Alta California (presently the US state of California) from California (now the two "Baja" Mexican states) in 1848, the US territory dropped the "Alta" and adopted the name of its Mexican half. The few people living at that time in Mexican California weren't too happy that their name was co-opted by their conquerors, and their heirs aren't too pleased that they're permanently saddled with a name that means "lower." You won't make any Mexican friends on the peninsula if you refer to their territory as "Baja," but that doesn't stop most English-speaking visitors and guidebook authors from bandying about the truncated description at every opportunity. Stick with "Baja California" every chance you get, or even drop the "Baja" and you may just get a free round of drinks from a true Californiano.

as likely to be found in Baja California, miners began prospecting in the northwest. Small claims were made in 1850 and 1851, but a significant find in June of that year at Rancho San Isidro sparked an influx of men from both sides of the border. The La Margarita mining company was set up to exploit San Isidro and other gold, silver and quartz mines in the region and soon began shipping their precious metals from Ensenada to San Francisco. The claims of the 1850s turned out to be so modest that by the end of the decade many of the miners had moved elsewhere. They returned in larger groups in 1870 when veins were found on Ensenada's southeast side. Mexico wanted its share of the foreigners' findings, so it set up a customs house in what would become Tijuana and began extracting duties from miners. A third discovery in 1889 turned into a fiasco for its participants. In five weeks, five thousand men rushed to Santa Clara near Ensenada. They found only US$200,000 worth of gold there; not bad, but the cost of getting to the claim and financing the dig cost the miners a collective US$250,000.

Throughout the region, this influx of foreigners and Mexicans from other parts of the country began to create problems, not just in terms of violent crime and rival claims on property (which weren't helped when Santa Ana reversed his predecessor's grants) but with public health, especially water, which would be a recurring problem. Outside of these boomtown and borderland growing pains were the near constant attempts throughout the 1850s and '60s by a cast of freebooters and would-be revolutionaries to annex the peninsula on behalf of the US or to declare it an independent republic of its own. Men such as the American William Walker and the angry *caudillos* Antonio Melendrez and Santiago Álvarez instigated the territorial authorities or entered into months-long campaigns to take control completely. They failed, but their activities always threatened to provoke the US and Mexico into a repeat of their recent war. Understandably, it was a difficult time for *Californios* on both sides of the border: until just a few years earlier they were all part of a territory that spanned from San José del Cabo to San Francisco. Even the Catholic Church had trouble; in 1853 the peninsula was placed under the jurisdiction of the Archbishop of Mexico, but his counterpart in San Francisco continued to send padres to the abandoned missions of the northwest.

Then again, most of Mexico was struggling with its meaning and purpose in the latter half of the nineteenth century. Porfirio Díaz assumed the presidency in 1877, and was to rule as dictator for the next 34 years. What began as a radical administration – including full implementation of the Reform Laws and a decree of no re-election to any political office – soon turned into a long, brutal policy of modernization. During his dictatorship some 16,000km of railway were built, industry boomed, telephones and telegraph were installed, and major towns, reached at last by reasonable roads, entered the modern era. In the countryside, Díaz established a police force – the notorious *rurales* – which stamped out much of the banditry. The costs were high: rapid development was largely achieved by handing over the country and its labour to foreign investors, who owned the vast majority of the oil, mining rights, railways and natural resources. At the same time there was a policy of massive land expropriation, in which formerly communal village holdings were handed over to foreign exploitation or simply grabbed by corrupt officials.

One massive development project – this one led partially by John Spreckels and Harrison Gray Otis, two US railroad, real estate and newspaper magnates – was the irrigation of the Imperial Valley in 1902. Shortly after Spreckels finished the San Diego-Arizona railroad, he reassigned the largely Chinese labour force to build a series of dams and canals alongside the Colorado River. Mexicali was affected the most by these moves, turning into a centre for cotton almost overnight and swelling with a new population of Chinese workers and central Mexican farmers.

The Mexican Revolution

The years surrounding the **Mexican Revolution** coincided with rapid growth in Tijuana as successive leaders and businessmen from both sides of the border took advantage of the discord to create a gaming fiefdom that rapidly became a playground for wealthy Americans and Mexicans. In 1910 Francisco Madero stood against Porfirio Díaz in the presidential election. The old dictator responded by imprisoning his opponent and declaring himself victor at the polls by a vast majority. Madero, however, escaped to Texas where he proclaimed himself president, and called on the nation to rise in his support. Several small bands immediately took up arms in northern states such as Chihuahua – where Pancho Villa and Pascual Orozco won several minor battles. In May 1911 Orozco captured the major border town of Ciudad Juárez, and his success was rapidly followed by a string of Revolutionary victories. By the end of the month, hoping to preserve the system if not his role in it, Porfirio Díaz had fled into exile. On October 2, 1911, Madero was elected president.

Madero could hardly conceive the forces he had unleashed. He freed the press, encouraged the formation of unions and introduced genuine democracy, but failed to do anything about the condition of the peasantry or the redistribution of land. Emiliano Zapata and his peasant Indian movement in the southwest did not put down their arms, neither did Villa, who had shifted from banditry to revolutionary with the ease of an actor playing a part. In Mexico City, Madero struggled with US interests and holdovers from the Díaz regime, including the general Victoriano Huerta. Madero was shot and killed in 1913 and Huerta took power. Villa and Zapata immediately took up arms against Huerta, along with Alvaro Obregón, governor of Sonora, and Venustiano Carranza, governor of Coahuila, forming a loose coalition of Constitutionalists.

In 1914, the Constitutionalists began to move south, and in April of that year US troops occupied Veracruz in their support (though neither side was exactly happy about the foreign presence). Huerta fled the country in July, and in August Obregón occupied the capital, proclaiming Carranza president. Of course, more fighting broke out, with the previous coalition fracturing into the president and his backer and the rest of the revolutionary leaders on the other side. The three years of fighting that followed were the most bitter and chaotic yet, with petty chiefs in every part of the country proclaiming provisional governments, joining each other in factions and then splitting again, and the entire country in a state of anarchy. Each army issued its own money, and each forced any able-bodied men it came across into joining. By 1920 it was reckoned that about one-eighth of the population had been killed.

Gradually, however, Obregón and Carranza gained ground – Obregón defeated Villa several times in 1915, and Villa withdrew to carry out border raids into the United States, hoping to provoke an invasion (which he nearly did: US troops pursued him across the border but were never able to catch up, and withdrew following defeat in a skirmish with Carranza's troops). Zapata, meanwhile, had some conspicuous successes – and occupied Mexico City for

Naming Baja's streets

Well-marked streets aren't Baja California's forte, but shared **street names** do manage to lend some semblance of stability to the peninsula. The men whose names appear regularly are a cast of military leaders, presidents, reformers, teachers and explorers who shaped modern Mexico.

Estéban Cantú Both as governor and military leader, Cantú pulled most of the levers in northern Baja California in the 1910s. He's most closely associated with encouraging and profiting from the vice industries in Mexicali and Tijuana. President Huerta sacked Cantú in 1920 after the upstart governor claimed autonomous control over Baja California.

Lázaro Cárdenas This radical reformer is remembered not too fondly for shutting down the nation's casinos in 1934 – just when they were turning northern Baja California into North America's Monte Carlo; he also nationalized the oil industry.

Venustiano Carranza In addition to being part of the below-mentioned quartet, Carranza was a Madero supporter and president from 1917–21. He became paranoid after failing to appoint his lackey as successor and fled Mexico City on a train packed with gold. His paranoia was warranted: he was betrayed and murdered during a stopover on his way to Veracruz.

Porfirio Díaz This one-time partisan of Benito Juárez turned on his friend after failing to beat him in two presidential races. Diaz' legacy has been as enduring as his former friend's: he went on to rule Mexico for 35 years and inspire two generations of revolutionaries seeking to overthrow his increasingly corrupt regime.

Benito Juárez Mexico's Abraham Lincoln typically gets to be the main boulevard, and for good reason. This Oaxaca-born, Zapotec Indian lawyer was the central figure of the mid-19th century, shaping Mexico's future as a soldier, rebel leader, supreme court justice and president. Of all his achievements, he's perhaps most revered for dismantling the special privileges of the clergy that had long allowed them to dominate public life, which is a bit ironic considering how many streets named after him intersect with those named after priests.

Francisco Madero After losing an election to Díaz, Madero fled Mexico. He then fomented rebellion from the US and in 1911 overthrew Díaz. Madero lasted only two years before a subsequent rebellion, led by one-time ally Victoriano Huerta, overthrew and then killed him.

Alvaro Obregón Along with Pancho Villa, Emiliano Zapata and Venustiano Carranza, Obregón helped overthrow Victoriano Huerta in 1914. Like Juárez, Obregón could seemingly do anything – farm, fight, lead, adjudicate – and do it well. Factionalism drove the quartet apart, and Obregón later lost his arm while leading a rout of Villa's troops. Even with his injury, he outlasted his contemporaries and served two terms as president, the last one ended by a fanatical Catholic assassin.

much of 1915 – but his irregular troops tended to disappear back to their villages after each victory. In 1919 he was tricked into a meeting with one of Carranza's generals and assassinated; Villa retired to a hacienda in his home state, and was murdered in 1923.

Carranza set up a constitutional congress in 1917 to ratify his position. The document they produced – the present constitution – included most of the revolutionary demands, among them workers' rights, a mandatory eight-hour day, national ownership of all mineral rights and the distribution of large landholdings and formerly communal properties to the peasantry. Carranza was formally elected in May 1917 and proceeded to make no attempt to carry out any of its stipulations, certainly not with regard to land rights. In 1920 Carranza was forced to step down by Obregón, and was shot while attempting to escape the country with most of the contents of the treasury.

Obregón, at least, was well intentioned – but his efforts at real land reform were again stymied by fear of US reaction: in return for American support, he agreed not to expropriate land. In 1924 Plutarco Elias Calles succeeded him, and real progress towards some of the ideals of the revolutionary constitution began to be made. Work on large public works schemes began – roads, irrigation systems, village schools – and about eight million acres of land were given back to the villages as communal holdings. At the same time Calles instituted a policy of virulent anticlericalism, closing churches and monasteries, and forcing priests to flee the country or go underground.

These moves provoked the last throes of a backlash, as the Catholic Cristero movement took up arms in defence of the Church. From 1927 until about 1935 isolated incidents of vicious banditry and occasional full-scale warfare continued, eventually burning themselves out as the stability of the new regime became obvious, and religious controls were relaxed. In 1928 Obregón was re-elected, but assassinated three weeks later in protest at the breach of the "no reelección" clause of the constitution. He was followed by Portes Gil, Ortiz Rubio and then Abelardo Rodríguez, who were controlled behind the scenes by Calles and his political allies, who steered national politics to the right in the bleak years of the 1930s Depression.

Lázaro Cárdenas and World War II

With the election of **Lázaro Cárdenas** in 1934, such doubts were finally laid to rest. Cárdenas established the single broad-based party that was to rule for the next 71 years, the PRI (Party of the Institutionalized Revolution). He also set about an unprecedented programme of reform, redistributing land on a huge scale (170,000 square kilometres during his six-year term), creating peasant and worker organizations to represent their interests at national level, and incorporating them into the governing party. He also relaxed controls on the Church to appease internal and international opposition.

In 1938 he nationalized the oil companies, an act which has proved one of the most significant in shaping modern Mexico and bringing about its industrial transformation. For a time it seemed as if yet more foreign intervention might follow, but a boycott of Mexican oil by major consumers crumbled with the onset of **World War II**, and was followed by a massive influx of money and a huge boost for Mexican industry after Mexico joined the Allies in 1942 following a brief flirtation with the Japanese and Germans. Despite his successes, he's still spoken of poorly in northwest Mexico, where his reform of gambling laws in 1935 changed Tijuana from a glamorous destination town south of San Diego to a city that thrived on an underground culture of sex and narcotics.

By the time he stood down in 1940, Cárdenas could claim to be the first president in modern Mexican history to have served his full six-year term in peace, and handed over to his successor without trouble. Over the next thirty years or so, massive oil incomes continued to stimulate industry, and the PRI maintained a masterly control of all aspects of public life. Of course it is an accepted fact of life that governments will line their own pockets first, but the unrelenting populism of the PRI, its massive powers of patronage, and above all its highly visible and undoubted achievement of progress, maintained it in power with amazingly little dissent.

The Transpeninsular Highway

Moving from one place in Baja California to another was an arduous affair for most of the twentieth century; in some parts of the southern territory the paths were the same ones the Jesuits has laid out over two centuries earlier. Mining companies and ranchers had been building their own system of regional, unpaved roads since the early 1900s, and the territorial government in the north had packed dirt roads to connect towns such as Mexicali and San Felipe. Still, to get any place easily, one had to have a boat or plane at their disposal, and then a good mule once they arrived.

After World War II, every Mexican presidential candidate promised to link Tijuana with San José del Cabo along a highway, yet in the early 1960s the only good paved road was a significantly shorter Mexicali–Tijuana–Ensenada circuit. By the end of the decade a paved road linking La Paz with Santa Rosalía (it was built on top of the mining company's route) opened and, as there were a good 900km left to cover in asphalt, the chances for a complete road stopped seeming like just another campaign promise.

Surprisingly enough, President Luis Echevarría kept his word – one that he had initially made along a transpeninsular campaign journey behind a road grader. Between his election in 1970 and December 1, 1973 workers paved the **Transpeninsular Highway** – a two-lane road that links Tijuana with the Cape. The only complaints came from towns that were bypassed on this new express route, settlements like La Purisíma and the two Comondús that watched as their cross-sierra rivals Mulegé and Loreto linked up with the highway. The feeling of isolation was exacerbated by Loreto's subsequent selection by FONATUR, the state tourism development company, as one of the nation's premier locations for development.

Land reform and foreign influence

As always in Baja California real estate and development deals, what's said will happen and what actually transpires are as distant from one another as Cabo and Tijuana. The PRI began to lose its grip on power beginning in 1988 when its candidate Carlos Salinas came up against stiff competition, following wins by the right-wing opposition PAN in Baja California and Baja California Sur. Into the contest between PRI and PAN, a number of tiny splinter groups emerged, one led by Cuauhtémoc Cárdenas, son of the legendary and much loved Lázaro Cárdenas. He united the Mexican left under the banner of the National Democratic Front, or FDN, who immediately had spectacular success: Cárdenas officially won 32 percent of a presidential vote in which PRI ballot rigging, voter intimidation and vote buying reached new heights. Opposition parties won seats in the Senate for almost the first time since the PRI came to power.

Despite the threats, Salinas moved forward with a series of **reforms** that began to reshape Baja California, especially in the north. As president, Salinas' policies encouraged economic and social polarization; by 1993 forty million Mexicans were living below the official poverty line (about half the population), while 24 Mexicans were listed in the Forbes list of the 500 richest men in the world. Salinas encouraged **foreign companies** to invest by holding down wage levels, and he created the *maquiladora* that's set the tone for cross-border economic relations along the entire border, but most notably in Tijuana. He also pushed through the North American Free Trade Agreement (NAFTA; TLC in Spanish) that created a free market between Canada, the US and Mexico. (see box, p.73)

Land reform had been enshrined in the original article of the constitution, and land redistributed after the Revolution was parcelled out in communal holdings, known as *ejidos*, which could not be sold as they belonged to everyone. At a local level the land was held in common, divided up by the communities themselves, following the pre-Hispanic and colonial tradition. Salinas changed all that by allowing the sale of *ejido* lands. Many peasants and indigenous communities feared that their landholdings were now vulnerable to speculators, especially as many poor communities exist in a state of almost permanent debt, and believed that their land would be seized to cover outstanding loans, worsening their economic plight still further. Developers have snatched up some land, but wise stewardship by the communal owners, along with the complexity of Mexican title claims, has for the most part protected all but the most dysfunctional *ejido* lands.

Even Cárdenas and the PAN opposition had to concede that economic progress had been made, and that Salinas would leave the presidency in a much better state than he found it, giving the PRI a new lease of life and a virtual lock on the presidential election scheduled for 1994. But on March 23, Luis Donaldo Colosio, the presidential candidate for the PRI, was shot dead on the campaign trail in Tijuana. Considering the geography of the assassination, it is widely thought that the drug cartels were involved. Whatever the truth, for many the act – along with the previous high-profile killing of an archbishop and the later assassination of a PRI reformer – represented the strength and arrogance of the drug cartels and their increased power in border areas and national government and law enforcement. In Colosio's absence, the political hack Ernesto Zedillo Ponce de León became the candidate and immediately became enmeshed in the revolt in the state of Chiapas.

Into the 21st century

On July 2, 2000, **Vicente Fox Quesada**, the PAN candidate, was voted in as president and inaugurated in December that year. It was a landmark event. Not only was he the first opposition candidate ever to have been democratically placed in power, it was also the first peaceful transition between opposing governments since Independence. In the years since, Fox's ambitions for constitutional and structural reforms have been partly hampered by the fractured nature of PAN, with major differences existing between members, and partly by the PRI, which controls Congress, more than half the state governorships and most of the bureaucracy.

PAN was dealt a setback in Baja California, its stronghold, when **Jorge Hank Rhon**, the multi-millionaire son of a lifelong PRI bureaucrat, wrested control of Tijuana's mayoral seat in 2004 from PAN. He's exactly the type that PAN should be able to take advantage of: he runs a massive ring of off-track betting parlours, spends the city's money lavishly and is linked both to the narco traffickers who've made the city so dangerous and the assassination of a prominent newspaper editor.

Rhon, like his rivals, knows that the future of Baja California is intricately linked with that of the southwestern US. Even as immigration has become more tightly controlled in the urban areas of Tijuana, Tecate and Mexicali, cross-border familial and commercial ties have grown stronger; just as Americans flock to Tijuana for cheap goods, tens of thousands of Tijuana residents flock to San Diego shopping centres for quality goods. One side effect of the US real estate boom of the early 2000s was a second-home buying spree by southern California and Arizona residents priced out of one American dream and into another. Massive cross-border industrial projects will link the two further. Despite environmental concerns, construction has already begun on an offshore liquid natural gas terminal near Playas Tijuana and Ensenada that would service both US and Mexican customers. To the south of Ensenada, a proposed and fast-tracked international port project at Punta Colonet, if built, would turn the *ejido* village into a boomtown rivalling the rapid growth of Rosarito. The volume of containers being offloaded here will eventually surpass that of Los Angeles and Newport Beach combined.

In Baja California Sur, recent growth has all been tourism-based, both in the Los Cabos area and in Loreto. In the former, the San José estuary has been converted into both a marina and a golf resort, radically changing San José del Cabo's image as a sleepy alternative to Cabo San Lucas. To the north in Loreto, the massive infusion of US and Canadian dollars for homes in the FONATUR-backed Loreto Bay project will eventually transform the central coast as drastically as Padre Salvatierra's first mission did back in 1697.

△ Pelican along the Sea of Cortez

Flora and fauna

Baja California's exceptional coastline provides sanctuaries for a wide variety of marine mammals, including the major wildlife attraction of the area, the migratory gray whale. The lagoons where the whales gather can also offer superb views of other great whales, including blue, humpback, fin, minke, sperm and orca (killer whales). Dolphins and sea lions and a variety of sea birds, including pelicans, ospreys and numerous waders such as plovers and sanderlings also inhabit the lagoons – in all, millions of birds come through the peninsula's lagoons every year. The sparse vegetation provides roosting sites for both jaegers and peregrines and even the occasional coyote may be seen wandering over the sandy shores.

Offshore, there are several small islands whose protected status has encouraged colonization by highly diverse animal communities. At the mouth of

Champions of the sea

The Sea of Cortez and Baja California's Pacific coast have long had devoted followers and inspired caretakers in equal measure. Before Jacques Cousteau dipped his toes into the sea, the biggest name to swing through the region – besides Hernan Cortés, Desi Arnez and John Wayne – was **John Steinbeck**. Steinbeck sailed to the Sea of Cortez with his friend, marine biologist **Edwin Ricketts**, on a six-week research trip in 1940, which he retold in his little-known gem *Log from the Sea of Cortez*. Amazed by the diversity of life in the sea, the two named thirty-five previously unnamed species during their voyage.

Much as many of the peninsula's visitors time their arrival with that of migrating whales, so too did **Jacques Cousteau** when he filmed an episode of his groundbreaking "Undersea World of Jacques Cousteau" in the Pacific lagoons. Cousteau and the crew of the *Calypso* tracked the whales 8000 kilometres south from the Bering Sea and lingered longer to explore the waters around Isla Espíritu Santo. Subsequent forays into the Sea of Cortez led him to famously call it "the aquarium of the world".

Gray whale migration and breeding

It is the **gray whales** and their well-documented migrations off the west coast of the peninsula that remain the outstanding spectacle of the region and continue to attract an estimated 250,000 visitors each year. Times have not always been so peaceful for these graceful leviathans; less than 150 years ago, the secret breeding grounds of the whales were discovered by **Charles Melville Scammon**. The Laguna Ojo de Liebre (renamed in recent times after the infamous whaler) was rapidly denuded of almost all of these magnificent beasts, and it wasn't until the establishment of **Scammon's Bay** as the world's first whale sanctuary in 1972 that their numbers began to recover. The population in the area is currently estimated at about 20,000 – a dramatic recovery within the time span.

The whale's **migratory route** runs the length of the American Pacific seaboard, from Baja to the Bering Sea and back; this is a round-trip of some 20,000km, which remains the longest recorded migration undertaken by any living mammal. They remain in the north for several months, feeding on the abundant krill in the high Arctic summer, and building up body reserves for the long journey south to the breeding lagoons. The migration begins as the days begin to shorten and the pack ice starts to thicken, sometime before the end of January.

Nowadays the human interest in the whales is purely voyeuristic, **whale watching** being a million-dollar industry, and in 1988 the Mexican government extended the range of the protected area to include the nearby **San Ignacio Lagoon**, forming an all-embracing national park, the **Biósfera El Vizcaíno**. The San Ignacio Lagoon offers a daunting entrance of pounding surf and treacherous shoals, but once inside, its calmer waters flatten and spread inland for 15km towards the distant volcanic peaks of the Santa Clara mountains. Accessible points for land-based observation lie further north in the **Parque Natural de Ballena Gris** ("Gray Whale Natural Park"), 32km south of Guerrero Negro.

Bahía Ensenada is **Isla Todos Santos** where sandy beaches, festooned with the remnants of shellfish, are used as occasional sunning spots by the resident harbour seals. The atmosphere is ripe with an uncommon blend of guano, kelp and Californian sagebrush. The Pacific swell frequently disturbs the resting cormorants, which bask in the hot sunshine, and the skies are filled with wheeling western gulls (similar to the European lesser blackback gull) from the thriving colony on the island.

Farther south lies the island of **San Benito**, which is just to the northwest of the much larger **Isla Cedros**. The former provides ideal nesting grounds for migrating ospreys, which travel south from the United States. The hillsides are covered by the tall agave (century plants) whose brief, once-in-a-lifetime blooms add an attractive splash of colour to the surrounding slopes. These towering succulents produce a broad rosette of golden florets, which provide a welcome supply of nectar for resident hummingbirds, while ravens wheel above, searching for carrion. The island, along with Isla Cedros (home of the protected Cedros deer) and the distant **Isla Guadalupe** (now a biological reserve), also provides a winter home to thousands of elephant seals, now happily recovering after years of overhunting. The large adult males arrive in December and the pebbly coves are soon crammed with the noisy and chaotic colony of mothers, calves and bachelor bulls, ruled by one dominant bull (or beach master) which can weigh up to two tonnes. The males make a terrifying spectacle as, with necks raised and heads thrown back, they echo their noisy threats to any would-be rival who challenges the mating rights within their harem.

The interior of the peninsula has several areas of wildlife interest, many of which now have the protected status of nature reserve. Most significant of all are the national parks of the **Sierra San Pedro Mártir** and the **Desierto Central**. Here the chapparal-covered hills cede to forests of Jeffrey pine and meadow tables, interspersed with granite *picachos* (peaks) and volcanic mesas. Bighorn sheep roam from San Felipe down the east side of the peninsula to La Paz. Herds of Pronghorn antelope are now limited to parts of the Desierto Vizcaíno, but they used to run throughout the peninsula. Mountain lions slink through **Sierra la Laguna** in search of cattle or wild goats to pick off.

The **Parque Nacional de Constitución de 1857** is another green oasis amongst the arid lowlands, where the coniferous woodlands form a picturesque border to the central **Laguna Hanson**. These sierras are renowned for the numerous palm-filled canyons that cut deep into the eastern escarpment; they make spectacular hiking areas with their miniature waterfalls, ancient petro-glyphs, caves, hot springs and groves of fan palms.

Books

F or the average reader, the contents of many **books** about Baja California will resemble the peninsula's geography: dry, dusty and often lifeless. Even John Steinbeck becomes tedious during large portions of *Log from the Sea of Cortez* when he describes the land, and lesser writers – especially naturalists trying to follow in his wake – manage to siphon off all the peninsula's grandeur. Writing about Baja California is difficult because short judgments and short stories tell the tale best in a place where the blue sky is endless, the water teems with sea life and the vast empty plains and sierras are timeless.

There are few English-language history books devoted to Baja California and many of the ones that do exist are out of print and difficult to track down. There is, however, a rich selection of specialized texts, dealing with geography, marine life or similar, nature-centric subjects. As for novels, there are an unfortunate number of titles that fall into the "I went on a binge in Tijuana" variety and little else, whether in English or in translation. The ones that are worth reading are listed below, along with some general Mexico titles that provide insight into current events and illuminate historical ones. In Mexico, the best and most complete series of guides are those published by Guías Panorama – they have small books on all the main archeological sites, as well as more general titles ranging from *Wild Flowers of Mexico* to *Pancho Villa – Truth and Legend*.

The abbreviation o/p means a book is out of print, but may still be found in libraries, secondhand bookstores or on the Internet. Books with a ⚡ symbol are highly recommended.

History and natural history

Johann Jakob Baegert *Observations in Lower California* (University of California Press, o/p). After this Jesuit padre was kicked out of the peninsula and forced to return to Germany he channelled all his anger, bitterness and racism into this often bizarre, yet illuminating text.

⚡ **Harry W. Crosby** *The Cave Paintings of Baja California* (Sunbelt Publications). After being teased by some minor cave paintings in the north, Crosby was led to more dramatic sights in the Sierra de San Francisco in the 1960s and began cataloguing and photographing hundreds of sites. This reissue is richly photographed and filled with details on finding sites.

Pablo L. Martinez *History of Lower California* (Editorial de Baja California, o/p). Hilariously opinionated (but not on purpose), meticulously researched reference text by a San José del Cabo historian. The most detailed of any history books, if a little dry and dense.

Dick Russell *Eye of the Whale* (Shearwater Books). A history of the Pacific lagoons, including some nice words about killer turned naturalist Charles Scammon and the most comprehensive explanation of the battle over Laguna San Ignacio and the expansion of the Mexican-Japanese salt consortium in the 1990s.

Edward W. Vernon *The Spanish Missions of Baja California* (University of New Mexico Press). Lushly photographed coffee-table book devoted to the peninsula's weary remnants of religious expansion, where the quality of photography outshines the architecture of its subject.

Travelogues and literature

Marc Bojanowski *The Dog Fighter* (William Morrow). First-person narrative set in a 1940s fictional Baja California town where young men fight dogs and landowners dream of creating a beachside tourist resort.

Erle Stanley Gardner *The Hidden Heart of Baja, The Land of Shorter Shadows, Hovering Over Baja, Hunting the Desert Whale, Mexico's Magic Square, Off the Beaten Track in Baja* (all o/p). Gardner explored the peninsula by burro, truck, helicopter, blimp and ATV, producing six titles in the process and spurring on a resurgence of US interest in the area. His writing is breezy, yet detailed – indicative of a writer who made his fortune creating Perry Mason and churning out pulp detective novels and radio plays (and who typically kept two secretaries in tow during his trips).

Graham Mackintosh *Into a Desert Place* (WW Norton). Mackintosh has written a trio of books about walking through the peninsula – once with his dog, another time with a burro – but his first journey was a 4800km trip around the coast he executed entirely on foot.

Kem Nunn *Tijuana Straits: A Novel* (Scribner). Drugs, surfing, border-jumping and environmental activism add up for a very American version of Tijuana's grittier side.

John Steinbeck *The Pearl* (Penguin). After becoming familiar with La Paz during his trip with Ricketts, Steinbeck returned to the sea – this time in novella form – for this tragic tale of wealth and discontents in the pearl fishing community.

John Steinbeck and Edwin Ricketts *Log from the Sea of Cortez* (Penguin). The division of labour on *Log* has always been a subject of debate, but it's well understood that the theories of biological interdependence and attention to detail were Ricketts', with Steinbeck sexing up the otherwise academic-leaning text.

Luis Alberto Urrea *By the Lake of Sleeping Children* (Anchor), *Across the Wire* (Anchor). Urrea, a university professor who was raised in Tijuana, addresses the complexities of the border region with more wisdom and sympathy than any other writer in English. Both titles here deal with border issues in reportage-style profiles, and his fiction touches on northern Baja California from time to time.

Society, politics and culture

Michael Dear, ed. *Postborder City* (Routledge). Since it's a collection of academic essays about border issues, annoying terms like "bajalta California" are to be expected. But much of its essays' jargon-free insight into the region's ongoing transformation is often surprising.

Strange New World: Art and Design from Tijuana (Museum of Contemporary Art, San Diego). This bi-lingual catalogue to a touring museum exhibit about Tijuana's emerging art and music scene successfully straddles academia and pop culture.

Other guidebooks

Mike and Terri Church *Traveler's Guide to Camping Mexico's Baja* (Rolling Homes Press). A second camp-centric title from a husband and wife team, the Churchs' slimmer volume is nonetheless packed with more info and less opinion than *Magnificent*. You can download updates at the publisher's website.

Howard Gulick and Walt Wheelock *Baja California Handbook* (o/p). The original guide to the peninsula was first published in 1956 and was updated until 1978, shortly after the completion of the Transpeninsular and the change in the way people travelled. The old editions are helpful in figuring out what now-abandoned towns once were.

Walt Peterson *The Baja Adventure Book* (Wilderness Press). You can trust Peterson when he tells you where to dive, kayak or do anything else in the peninsula, because he's been doing it since the 1960s. It's currently on its third edition and, although the photos need updating, it's still the best resource for outdoor enthusiasts.

Jack Williams *Magnificent Peninsula* (HJ Williams Publications). If you want to get into the mind of a San Felipe RVer, just pick up this vanity-press title written by a husband and wife team. They'll tell you where to park your rig, fix your flat and buy those US products you left behind on the other side of the border.

Language

Language

Mexican Spanish

O nce you get into it, **Spanish** is actually a straightforward language – and in Mexico people are desperately eager to understand and to help the most faltering attempt. **English** is widely spoken, especially in the tourist areas, but you'll get a far better reception if you at least try to communicate with people in their own tongue. You'll be further helped by the fact that Mexicans speak relatively slowly (at least compared with Spaniards) and that there's none of the awkward lisping pronunciation.

Rules of pronunciation

Relative to English, the rules of **pronunciation** are clear-cut and strictly observed. Unless there's an accent, words ending in d, l, r and z are stressed on the last syllable, all others on the second last. All vowels are pure and short.

A is between the A sound of "back" and that of "father"

E as in "get"

I as in "police"

O as in "hot"

U as in "rule"

C is spoken like S before E and I, hard otherwise: cerca is pronounced "serka".

G is a guttural H sound (like the ch in "loch"); before E or I, a hard G elsewhere: gigante becomes "higante".

H is always silent.

J the same sound as a guttural G: jamón is pronounced "hamon".

LL sounds like an English Y: tortilla is pronounced "torteeya".

N as in English.

Ñ with the tilde (accent), spoken nasally: mañana sounds like "manyana".

QU is pronounced like an English K.

R is rolled, RR doubly so.

V sounds more like B, vino becoming "beano".

X has an S sound before consonants; between vowels in place names, it has an H sound, like México ("meh-hee-ko").

Z is the same as a soft C, so cerveza becomes "servesa".

Useful words and phrases

Although we've listed a few essential words and phrases here, if you're travelling for any length of time some kind of **dictionary** or **phrasebook** is obviously a worthwhile investment: the *Rough Guide to Mexican Spanish* is the best practical guide, correct and colloquial, and will have you speaking the language faster than any other phrasebook. One of the best small Latin American Spanish dictionaries is the University of Chicago version (Pocket Books), which is widely available in Mexico. If you're using an older dictionary, bear in mind that CH, LL and Ñ are traditionally counted as separate letters and are listed after the Cs, Ls and Ns respectively; most current dictionaries, however, follow more familiar alphabetizing procedures, though Ñ retains its own section.

Basics

Sí, No	Yes, No	Aquí/Acá, Allí/Allá	Here, There
Abierto/a, Cerrado/a	Open, Closed	Gran(de), Pequeño/a	Big, Small
Por favor, Gracias	Please, Thank you	Éste, Eso	This, That
Empujar, Tirar	Push, Pull	Más, Menos	More, Less
¿Dónde?, ¿Cuándo?	Where?, When?	Hoy, Mañana	Today, Tomorrow
Con, Sin	With, Without	Barato/a, Caro/a	Cheap, Expensive
¿Qué?, ¿Cuánto?	What?, How much?	Ayer	Yesterday
Buen(o)/a, Mal(o)/a	Good, Bad	Ahora, Más tarde	Now, Later

Greetings and responses

¡Hola!, Adiós	Hello, Goodbye	(No) Hablo español	I (don't) speak Spanish
Buenos días	Good morning	Mande?	What (did you say)?
Buenas tardes/noches	Good afternoon/night	Me llamo...	My name is...
¿Qué tal?	How do you do?	¿Como se llama	
Hasta luego	See you later	usted?	What's your name?
Lo siento/discúlpeme	Sorry	Soy inglés(a)	I am English
Con permiso/perdón	Excuse me	americano(a)	...American*
¿Cómo está (usted)?	How are you?	australiano(a)	...Australian
De nada/por nada	Not at all, you're welcome	canadiense	...Canadian
		irlandés(a)	...Irish
(No) Entiendo	I (don't) understand	escosés(a)	...Scottish
¿Habla (usted)	Do you speak	galés(a)	...Welsh
inglés?	English?	neozelandés(a)	...New Zealander

*Mexicans are from the Americas too, so describing yourself as American can occasionally cause offence. Better to opt for "estadounidense" (from "Los Estados Unidos", Spanish for the United States) if you are a US American.

Hotels, transport and directions

Quiero...	I want...	(una semana)	(one week)
Quisiera... por favor	I'd like...	¿Está bien,	It's fine, how
¿Sabe...?	Do you know...?	cuánto es?	much is it?
No sé	I don't know	Es demasiado caro	It's too expensive
(¿)Hay...(?)	There is... (Is there...?)	¿No tiene algo	Don't you have
Dame...	Give me...	más barato?	anything cheaper?
(uno así)	(one like that)	¿Se puede...?	Can one...?
¿Tiene...?	Do you have...?	¿...acampar	...camp (near) here?
...la hora	...the time	aquí (cerca)?	
...un cuarto	...a room	¿Hay un hotel	Is there a hotel
...con dos camas/	...with two beds/	aquí cerca?	nearby?
cama matrimonial	double bed	¿Por dónde	How do I get to...?
Es para una persona	It's for one person	se va a...?	
(dos personas)	(two people)	Izquierda, derecha,	Left, right,
...para una noche	...for one night	derecho	straight on
		Por acá, por allá	This way, that way

¿Dónde está...?	Where is...?		¿De dónde sale el bus para . . .?	Where does the bus to . . . leave from?
...la camionera central	...the bus station		Quisiera un boleto (de ida y vuelta) para . . .	I'd like a (return) ticket to . . .
...la estación de ferrocarriles	...the railway station		¿A qué hora sale (llega en...)?	What time does it leave (arrive in...)?
...el banco más cercano	...the nearest bank		¿Qué hay para comer?	What is there to eat?
...el cajero automático	...the ATM		¿Qué es eso?	What's that?
...el correo (la oficina de correos)	...the post office		¿Cómo se llama éste en español?	What's this called in Spanish?
...el baño/sanitario	...the toilet			

Numbers and days

un/uno/una	1		ochenta	80
dos	2		noventa	90
tres	3		cien(to)	100
cuatro	4		ciento uno	101
cinco	5		doscientos	200
seis	6		quinientos	500
siete	7		setecientos	700
ocho	8		mil	1000
nueve	9		dos mil	2000
diez	10			
once	11		primero/a	first
doce	12		segundo/a	second
trece	13		tercero/a	third
catorce	14		quinto/a	fifth
quince	15		décimo/a	tenth
dieciséis	16			
diecisiete	17		lunes	Monday
veinte	20		martes	Tuesday
veintiuno	21		miércoles	Wednesday
treinta	30		jueves	Thursday
cuarenta	40		viernes	Friday
cincuenta	50		sábado	Saturday
sesenta	60		domingo	Sunday
setenta	70			

Glossaries

Terms and acronyms

Ahorita diminutive of *ahora* (now) meaning "right now" – but seldom applied as literally as a visitor might expect.

Alto stop; also means "high".

Ayuntamiento town hall/government.

Barrio area within a town or city; suburb.

Basura garbage.

Biznaga barrel cactus.

Boojum large, twisting tree species found in the central deserts, *cirio* in Spanish.

Camino blanco unpaved rural road, so called because it is paved with limestone gravel

Cantina bar, usually men-only.

Casita cottage.

Ceiba large tropical silk-cotton tree.

Cinturón de seguridad seat belt.

Comal large, round, flat plate made of clay or metal used for cooking tortillas.

Comedor cheap restaurant, literally dining room; also called a *cocina económica*.

Convento either convent or monastery.

CTM central union organization.

Descompuesto out of order.

Don/Doña courtesy titles (sir/madam), mostly used in letters or for professional people or the boss.

Ejido communal farmland.

EPR Ejército Popular Revolucionario, the Popular Revolutionary Army. Guerrilla group, not allied to the Zapatistas; their first appearance was in Guerrero in 1996.

EZLN Ejército Zapatista de Liberación Nacional, the Zapatista Army of National Liberation. Guerrilla group in Chiapas.

Feria fair (market).

FONART government agency to promote crafts.

FONATUR government tourism agency.

Fray Spanish word for friar.

Frontera Spanish word for border, yet also refers to the Tijuana-San Diego region as a whole.

Ganado Livestock; usually seen on road signs warning "Precaución Zona de Ganado."

Gringo not necessarily insulting, though it does imply North American – said to come from invading US troops, either because they wore green coats or because they sang "Green grow the rushes oh!..."

Guayabera embroidered Cuban-style shirt, usually for men.

Güera/o blonde; a very frequently used description of Westerners, especially shouted after women in the street. Not intended as an insult.

Hacienda plantation estate or the big house on it.

Hacendado plantation owner.

I.V.A. 15 percent value-added tax (VAT).

Ladino applied to people, means Spanish-influenced as opposed to Indian; determined entirely by clothing (and culture) rather than physical race.

Librería bookstore.

Licensio A common title, literally meaning "graduate" or "licensed"; abbreviated Lic.

Llantera Tire repair shop.

Malecón seafront promenade.

Mariachi quintessentially Mexican music, with lots of brass and sentimental lyrics; derives from northern Mexico.

Mestizo mixed race, of Indian and Spanish descent.

Metate flat stone for grinding corn; used with a *mano, a* grinding stone.

Milpa a small subsistence farm plot, tended with slash-and-burn agricultural practices.

Mirador lookout point.

Muelle jetty or dock.

NAFTA the North American Free Trade Agreement that includes Mexico, the USA and Canada; see also TLC below.

Ola wave.

Palacio mansion, but not necessarily royal.

Palacio de Gobierno headquarters of state/ federal authorities.

Palacio Municipal headquarters of local government.

PAN Partido de Acción Nacional (National Action Party), conservative party that took power when Vicente Fox became president in 2000.

Panga Small, fiberglass boat used for fishing or whale watching.

Paseo a broad avenue, but also the ritual evening walk around the plaza.

Peligrosa/o Dangerous; seen on road signs as "Curva Peligrosa."

PEMEX the Mexican national oil company.

Planta baja ground floor – abbreviated PB in lifts.

PRD Partido Revolucionario Democrático (Party of the Democratic Revolution), the left-wing opposition formed and led by Cuauhtémoc Cárdenas; has the second largest number of seats in Congress.

PRI Partido Revolucionario Institucional (Party of the Institutional Revolution), the ruling party for eighty years, until the surprise PAN upset in the 1999 elections.

PT Partido del Trabajo (Workers Party), small party but with opposition seats in Congress.

PVEM Partido Verde Ecologista de México (Green Party), small opposition party.

Quetzalcoatl the plumed serpent – most powerful, enigmatic and widespread of all ancient Mexican gods.

Stele freestanding carved monument; plural stelae.

TLC Tratado de Libre Comercio, the Spanish name for NAFTA.

Tope speed-bump or other barrier on rural roads for slowing traffic.

Vaca cow.

Vado dip in the road, or ford on river.

Velocidad Speed; typically used on road signs in combination with "disminuya su …", "Slow down."

Art and architectural terms

Alfiz decorative rectangular moulding over a doorway.

Arabesque elaborate geometric pattern of Islamic origin.

Artesonado intricate ceiling design, usually of jointed, inlaid wood.

Atrium enclosed forecourt of churchyard or monastery; *atrio* in Spanish.

Azulejo decorative glazed tile, usually blue and white.

Churrigueresque highly elaborate, decorative form of Baroque architecture (usually in churches), named after the seventeenth-century Spanish architect.

Camarín room in a church used for storing and dressing sacred statues.

Convento monastery residence that includes the cloister.

Dado ornamental border on the lower part of an interior wall.

Escudo shield-shaped decoration.

Espadaña belfry, usually on top of the front wall of a church.

Fluting vertical grooves in a column.

Fresco technique of painting on wet or dry plaster.

Garita ornamental pinnacle or battlement which looks like a sentry box.

Grotesque ornamental style depicting fantastic birds, beasts and foliage.

Herrerian imperial style named after sixteenth-century Spanish architect Juan de Herrera.

Lunette crescent-shaped space above a doorway or beneath a vault.

Merlón decorative pyramidal battlement.

Mudéjar Spanish architectural style strongly influenced by Moorish forms.

Ogee curved, pointed arch.

Palapa palm thatch. Used to describe any thatched/palm-roofed hut.

Pila font or water basin; also commonly found in domestic buildings.

Pilaster flattened column used as decorative element.

Pinjante glove-shaped decorative pendant, popular in eighteenth-century architecture.

Plateresque elaborately decorative Renaissance architectural style.

Portales arcades.

Portería entry portico to a monastery.

Predella base panel of an altarpiece.

Purista severe Renaissance architectural style, originating in sixteenth-century Spain.

Retablo carved, painted wooden altarpiece.

Zapata wooden roof beam, often decoratively carved.

Food and drink terms

On the table

Azúcar	Sugar	Pimienta	Pepper
Cuchara	Spoon	Queso	Cheese
Cuchillo	Knife	Sal	Salt
Cuenta	Check (bill)	Salsa	Sauce
Mantequilla	Butter	Servilleta	Napkin
Pan	Bread	Tenedor	Fork

Cooking terms

Asadero	Barbecue or grill	Con mole	In mole sauce, based on a rich spice paste – mole poblano (with bitter chocolate) is the most common
Asado/a	Broiled		
Al horno/horneado	Baked		
A la tampiqueña	Meat in thin strips served with guacamole and enchiladas		
		A la parilla	Grilled over charcoal
A la veracruzana	Usually fish, cooked with tomatoes, onions and green olives	A la plancha	Grilled on a hot plate
		Empanizado/a	Breaded
En mojo de ajo	Fried with slow-cooked garlic	Frito	Fried
		Poco hecho/a punto/ bien cocido	Rare/medium/ well-done
Barbacoa/pibil	Wrapped in leaves and herbs and steamed/cooked in a pit		

Breakfast

Chilaquiles	Tortilla strips with shredded chicken and tomato sauce		cheese, tomato sauce, peas and fried sweet plantains
Huevos…	Eggs…	…rancheros	…fried, served on a tortilla and smothered in a hot, red chile sauce
…a la Mexicana	…scrambled with tomato, onion and chile		
…con jamón	…with ham	…revueltos	…scrambled
…con tocino	…with bacon	…tibios	…lightly boiled
…motuleños	…fried, served on a tortilla with beans, ham,	Pan dulce	Pastries

Soups (sopas) and starters

Antojitos	Smaller hot snacks – like tacos or flautas – served with fast-food style or with drinks		stew that is said to cure hangovers
		Sopa…	Soup…
		…de frijoles	…creamy black-bean soup
Caldo	Broth (with bits in)	…de lima	…chicken soup with tortilla strips and lime
Entremeses	Hors d'oeuvres		
Menudo	Tripe and chile	…de verduras	…vegetable soup

Tortilla and corn dishes (antojitos)

Chiles rellenos	Stuffed peppers	Quesadillas	Toasted or fried tortillas topped with cheese
Enchiladas	Rolled-up tacos, covered in chile sauce and baked	Queso fundido	Melted cheese, served with tortillas and salsa
Enchiladas suizas	As above, with green chile and cheese	Salbutes	Crisp-fried tortillas topped with shredded turkey, lettuce, avocado and pickled onions
Flautas	Small rolled tortillas filled with red meat or chicken and then fried		
Molletes	Split roll covered in beans and melted cheese, often with ham and avocado too	Tacos	Soft corn tortillas with filling
		Tacos árabes/al pastor	Tacos filled with spicy pork, sometimes served with a slice of pineapple
Panuchos	Like salbutes, but with black beans as well		

UK & Ireland
Britain
Devon & Cornwall
Dublin **D**
Edinburgh **D**
England
Ireland
The Lake District
London
London **D**
London Mini Guide
Scotland
Scottish Highlands & Islands
Wales

Europe
Algarve **D**
Amsterdam
Amsterdam **D**
Andalucía
Athens **D**
Austria
The Baltic States
Barcelona
Barcelona **D**
Belgium & Luxembourg
Berlin
Brittany & Normandy
Bruges **D**
Brussels
Budapest
Bulgaria
Copenhagen
Corfu
Corsica
Costa Brava **D**
Crete
Croatia
Cyprus
Czech & Slovak Republics
Dodecanese & East Aegean
Dordogne & The Lot
Europe
Florence & Siena
Florence **D**
France
Germany
Gran Canaria **D**
Greece
Greek Islands
Hungary

Ibiza & Formentera **D**
Iceland
Ionian Islands
Italy
The Italian Lakes
Languedoc & Roussillon
Lanzarote **D**
Lisbon **D**
The Loire
Madeira **D**
Madrid **D**
Mallorca **D**
Mallorca & Menorca
Malta & Gozo **D**
Menorca
Moscow
The Netherlands
Norway
Paris
Paris **D**
Paris Mini Guide
Poland
Portugal
Prague
Prague **D**
Provence & the Côte D'Azur
Pyrenees
Romania
Rome
Rome **D**
Sardinia
Scandinavia
Sicily
Slovenia
Spain
St Petersburg
Sweden
Switzerland
Tenerife & La Gomera **D**
Turkey
Tuscany & Umbria
Venice & The Veneto
Venice **D**
Vienna

Asia
Bali & Lombok
Bangkok
Beijing
Cambodia
China
Goa

Hong Kong & Macau
India
Indonesia
Japan
Laos
Malaysia, Singapore & Brunei
Nepal
The Philippines
Singapore
South India
Southeast Asia
Sri Lanka
Thailand
Thailand's Beaches & Islands
Tokyo
Vietnam

Australasia
Australia
Melbourne
New Zealand
Sydney

North America
Alaska
Baja California
Boston
California
Canada
Chicago
Colorado
Florida
The Grand Canyon
Hawaii
Las Vegas **D**
Los Angeles
Maui **D**
Miami & South Florida
Montréal
New England
New Orleans **D**
New York City
New York City **D**
New York City Mini Guide
Orlando & Walt Disney World® **D**
Pacific Northwest
San Francisco
San Francisco **D**
Seattle
Southwest USA

Toronto
USA
Vancouver
Washington DC
Washington DC **D**
Yosemite

Caribbean & Latin America
Antigua & Barbuda **D**
Argentina
Bahamas
Barbados **D**
Belize
Bolivia
Brazil
Cancùn & Cozumel **D**
Caribbean
Central America
Chile
Costa Rica
Cuba
Dominican Republic
Dominican Republic **D**
Ecuador
Guatemala
Jamaica
Mexico
Peru
St Lucia **D**
South America
Trinidad & Tobago
Yúcatan

Africa & Middle East
Cape Town & the Garden Route
Egypt
The Gambia
Jordan
Kenya
Marrakesh **D**
Morocco
South Africa, Lesotho & Swaziland
Syria
Tanzania
Tunisia
West Africa
Zanzibar

D: Rough Guide
DIRECTIONS for
short breaks

Available from all good bookstores

Travel Specials
First-Time Around the World
First-Time Asia
First-Time Europe
First-Time Latin America
Travel Online
Travel Health
Travel Survival
Walks in London & SE England
Women Travel

Maps
Algarve
Amsterdam
Andalucia & Costa del Sol
Argentina
Athens
Australia
Barcelona
Berlin
Boston
Brittany
Brussels
California
Chicago
Corsica
Costa Rica & Panama
Crete
Croatia
Cuba
Cyprus
Czech Republic
Dominican Republic
Dubai & UAE
Dublin
Egypt
Florence & Siena
Florida
France
Frankfurt
Germany
Greece
Guatemala & Belize
Hong Kong
Iceland
Ireland
Kenya & Northern Tanzania
Lisbon
London

Los Angeles
Madrid
Mallorca
Malaysia
Marrakesh
Mexico
Miami & Key West
Morocco
New England
New York City
New Zealand
Northern Spain
Paris
Peru
Portugal
Prague
The Pyrenees
Rome
San Francisco
Sicily
South Africa
South India
Spain & Portugal
Sri Lanka
Tenerife
Thailand
Toronto
Trinidad & Tobago
Tuscany
Venice
Vietnam, Laos & Cambodia
Washington DC
Yucatán Peninsula

Dictionary Phrasebooks
Croatian
Czech
Dutch
Egyptian Arabic
French
German
Greek
Hindi & Urdu
Italian
Japanese
Latin American Spanish
Mandarin Chinese
Mexican Spanish
Polish
Portuguese
Russian
Spanish

Swahili
Thai
Turkish
Vietnamese

Computers
Blogging
iPods, iTunes & music online
The Internet
Macs & OS X
PCs and Windows
PlayStation Portable
Website Directory

Film & TV
American Independent Film
British Cult Comedy
Chick Flicks
Comedy Movies
Cult Movies
Gangster Movies
Horror Movies
Kids' Movies
Sci-Fi Movies
Westerns

Lifestyle
Babies
eBay
Ethical Shopping
Pregnancy & Birth

Music Guides
The Beatles
Bob Dylan
Classical Music
Elvis
Frank Sinatra
Heavy Metal
Hip-Hop
Jazz
Book of Playlists
Opera
Pink Floyd
Punk
Reggae
Rock
The Rolling Stones
Soul and R&B
World Music (2 vols)

Popular Culture
Books for Teenagers
Children's Books, 5-11
Conspiracy Theories
Cult Fiction
The Da Vinci Code
Lord of the Rings
Shakespeare
Superheroes
Unexplained Phenomena

Sport
Arsenal 11s
Celtic 11s
Chelsea 11s
Liverpool 11s
Man United 11s
Newcastle 11s
Rangers 11s
Tottenham 11s
Poker

Science
Climate Change
The Universe
Weather

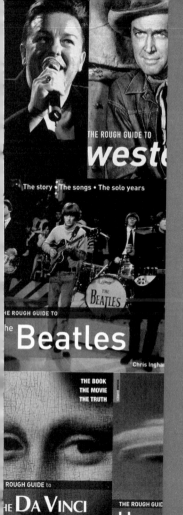

Index

Map entries are in colour.

INDEX

Map symbols

maps are listed in the full index using coloured text

▬ ▬ ▬ ▬	International border	★	Bus stop
▬ ▬ ▬	Chapter boundary	⛺	Campsite
▬▬ ▬ ▬	State border	♥	Museum
	Motorway	🍇	Vineyard
▬▬▬▬	Major road	🗼	Lighthouse
▬▬▬▬	Minor road	♦	Point of interest
▬▬▬▬	Pedestrianised road	🔭	Viewpoint
▬▬▬▬	Unpaved road	◲	Observatory
- - - - - -	Path	ⓘ	Tourist office
━━━━	Railway	◉	Accommodation
▬▬▬▬	River	👮	Immigration post/border
- - - - -	Seasonal river	⌣	Bridge
〰️	Mountain range	✈	Airport
▲	Mountain peak	⊠	Post office
/ᐱ\	Volcano	✝	Church (regional maps)
🏔	Butte	⬭	Stadium
◠	Cave	▬	Building
🌊	Surf area	⊞	Church (town maps)
⟆	Dune	▦	Park
ᙁ	Spring	▦	Beach/desert
🎋	Waterfall	⬭	Saltpan

MAP SYMBOLS

335